NOTES FROM THE
VALLEY OF SLAUGHTER

STUDIES IN ANTISEMITISM

Alvin H. Rosenfeld, editor

NOTES FROM THE VALLEY OF SLAUGHTER

A Memoir from the Ghetto of Šiauliai, Lithuania

—⚍—

DR. AHARON PICK

TRANSLATED BY

GABRIEL LAUFER AND ANDREW CASSEL

INDIANA UNIVERSITY PRESS

This book is a publication of

Indiana University Press
Office of Scholarly Publishing
Herman B Wells Library 350
1320 East 10th Street
Bloomington, Indiana 47405 USA

iupress.org

Manufactured in the United States of America

First printing 2023

Cataloging information is available from the Library of Congress.

ISBN 978-0-253-06557-5 (hdbk.)
ISBN 978-0-253-06558-2 (pbk.)
ISBN 978-0-253-06559-9 (web PDF)

CONTENTS

ACKNOWLEDGMENTS

WE WERE BROUGHT TOGETHER BY chance after we had separately approached the US Holocaust Memorial Museum about translating Pick's diary,
and it proved both a productive and rewarding partnership. Thanks for invaluable assistance and encouragement to Beth S. Wenger, professor of history, University of Pennsylvania; Ellen Cassedy, author and speaker on the Holocaust
in Lithuania and translator of Yiddish literature; Mark Alsher, Yiddish and
Hebrew teacher and scholar; the late Zvi Halevy of Tel Aviv; Devorah Shatz
of Tzur Yigal, Israel, granddaughter of Dr. Aharon Pick, who provided us with
invaluable insights about the family, its survival, and its life in Israel after the
Holocaust; Aryeh Shcherbakov of the Association of the Lithuanian Jews in
Israel, for valuable comments on the manuscript and for making the association's material available for this work; and Suzy Snyder and Ron Coleman of
the United States Holocaust Memorial Museum for introducing us to this diary
and to each other.

RETRIEVING A VOICE
FROM THE GHETTO

ANDREW CASSEL

INTRODUCTION

Late in the winter of 1943, in a Nazi-created ghetto in northern Lithuania, a Jewish doctor put a Jewish infant girl to death.

It wasn't just another abortion, although the makeshift ghetto hospital, set up in a building once used ritually to clean corpses for Jewish burial, had seen many of those. The mother had violated a German order prohibiting Jewish births. Although the ghetto's Jewish council[1] had encouraged and even forced pregnant women to abort, a few had managed to carry their babies to term. Previous efforts to euthanize such newborns with high doses of morphine and other toxins had not proved effective, moreover. One baby had lived for a week after being injected. That would not do: German agents were nearby, and if they learned of a live birth in the ghetto, the mother, her family, and others would likely be killed as punishment. "It became necessary to kill the girl, and to do this terrible thing soon," the doctor wrote. "So, we decided . . . to drown her!!! We took a bucket of cold water and put the girl's head in and held her there until there were death convulsions—a total of six minutes, twice the time required to kill an adult by strangling. We removed the girl, her little mouth open, her nostrils filled with foam, and covered her with a blanket."[2]

The doctor, Aharon Pick, wrote that this horrifying incident became still more shocking when the medical staff attempted to bury the infant after falsely reporting the birth as a miscarriage to the ghetto authorities. "To our astonishment," Pick wrote, "when the baby was about to be lowered into her grave, she was found to be still alive! It was beyond belief! Day-old infants wondrously defy medical theory, surviving procedures fatal to adults!"

Pick recounted the incident in a journal he kept from 1942 until shortly before his death in 1944—the years 5702, 5703 and 5704 in the Hebrew calendar. A remarkable document on several levels, it depicts an individual and a community responding to intense physical and psychological stress. When Pick began it, he was already among the minority of Lithuanian Jews not yet murdered by the Nazis and their local collaborators. Stripped of rights, possessions, and nearly all hope, he was confined to the ghetto of Šiauliai, the midsized Lithuanian city where he had spent most of his adult life. He recorded his experiences, observations, and concerns in cursive Hebrew in three notebooks, which he titled "Notes from the Valley of Slaughter" [*Reshimot m'gei ha-haregah*]. (The Hebrew term describing the "valley of slaughter" was borrowed from Jeremiah 7:32: "Assuredly, a time is coming—declares the LORD—when man shall no longer speak of Topheth or the Valley of Ben-Hinnom, but of the valley of slaughter; and they shall bury in Topheth until no room is left.")

After the war, Pick's son Tedik took the notebooks to Israel, where they remained largely unknown for nearly fifty years. A Hebrew transcription was published there privately in 1997. In 2018, the US Holocaust Memorial Museum, which had purchased the original notebooks in 2000, set in motion a translation project, the result of which is this volume. Admittedly, no translation can fully convey the nuance and flavor of an original. This one is especially vulnerable, both because of Pick's unusual literary style and because the English version is the work of interested volunteers rather than trained scholars or linguists. Gabriel Laufer, who undertook the initial translation, is an Israeli-born emeritus professor of engineering who has studied and written about his own family's Holocaust experience. Andrew Cassel, who edited the English text, is a retired journalist with a family connection to the diary's author.

DISCOVERING AHARON PICK

Aharon Pick was born in the early 1870s (sources vary between 1872 and 1875) in an ethnically mixed community of some five thousand souls, about half of them Jews. It was called Keidany by its Russian officials and Keidan by the Yiddish-speaking Jews who made up the bulk of its traders, artisans, and merchants. Today it bears the Lithuanian name Kėdainiai, remaining a town with a proud, aristocratic past. It was owned from the sixteenth to nineteenth century by the Radizwiłł family, important members of the Polish-Lithuanian nobility. In the early seventeenth century, Krzysztof Radizwiłł, a Calvinist, invited tradesmen and artisans "of good character" to settle there, attracting communities of Germans and Scots as well as Jews. By the nineteenth century, Keidan was home to Protestant Reformed, Lutheran, Russian Orthodox, and Catholic churches as well as a half dozen Jewish synagogues and study houses.[3]

Pick, like many in his generation, was making a transition from tradition to modernity, mainly through three channels: urbanization, revolution, and Jewish nationalism. The first led to movement to Russia's growing cities and/or emigration to the West; the second to the underground tumult of leftist politics; and the third, in most cases, to Zionism. The three paths were not mutually exclusive: individual trajectories and hybrid movements often combined them in different measures. Pick himself provides a vivid illustration. Sent by his parents to study at the famous Orthodox yeshivas of Slabodka, near Kaunas, he wrote later that he was "already a completely devoted *maskil*" (an adherent of the "enlightenment" spreading through the Jewish world of eastern Europe): "I had already studied, with the help of my first teachers, my brother and brother-in-law, Russian grammar and arithmetic, including problem solving. I had already read 'external' books in Hebrew and easy Russian. My 'enlightenment' reached such a high level that one of my friends and I dared to purchase a copy of Malinin's Algebra and studied it secretly in the *beit midrash* [study house], keeping the book under the stand, without an instructor."

As his worldview broadened, Pick added to his Talmud tractates the study of modern languages, science, music, and art. He also was drawn increasingly to the growing Jewish national movement, both its political form—Zionism—and its cultural expressions. In the late 1890s, he and his friend Boruch Chaim Cassel (grandfather of the author of these lines(, responded to a call for "intellectuals with ties to the masses" to collect Jewish folksongs. The 140 lyrics contributed by Pick and Cassel comprise nearly 40 percent of what became known as the "Ginzburg-Marek collection," published in 1901 in St. Petersburg.

Pick eventually managed to obtain a baccalaureate—essentially a high school–equivalency degree—from a *gymnasium* in the provincial city Šiauliai, sixty miles northwest of Keidan. Russia's strict quota system for Jews frustrated his efforts to gain admission to a university, so he worked as a teacher in Šiauliai's government schools and gave private lessons until he had saved enough to pay his way to Paris, where his sister Raine was living. He hoped she would support him while he continued his studies but found her gravely ill on his arrival. So he scraped by, tutoring to finance his studies, finally receiving a medical degree just as World War I was breaking out. He spent the war years working as a doctor in southern France and then returned to his native country.

It was not the same country he had left. The city known as Shavli when it was part of the Russian empire was now Šiauliai in the newly independent nation of Lithuania. Ethnic Lithuanians, who for centuries had lived as peasants, working the estates owned by Polish or Russian-speaking magnates (often overseen by Jewish managers), were now politically dominant, rapidly urbanizing, and determined to assert their national identity politically, culturally, and economically.

In its first half decade, the young Republic of Lithuania made significant efforts to incorporate and ally with its Jewish minority, the country's second-largest group at 7.6 percent of the population.[4] Jews served in the Lithuanian army, held seats in the Seimas (parliament), and enjoyed a level of communal autonomy under an official Ministry of Jewish Affairs.[5] That status soon came under pressure, as Lithuanian national ambitions tapped into centuries-old wells of anti-semitism. The Catholic Church, the Lithuanian press, and populist politicians all portrayed Jews as exploitative outsiders, hostile to the new state's interests. The Jewish Affairs Ministry was abolished by 1924, and by the early 1930s, Jews had been almost entirely excluded from national and local government. Lithuanian trade associations and cooperatives also moved aggressively to reduce what they saw as Jews' outsized presence in commerce and industry. Whereas Jews had owned 83 percent and Lithuanians 13 percent of the country's commercial and retail enterprises in 1923, by 1936 nearly half were Lithuanian-owned.[6]

The makeup of elite professions was somewhat slower to change. Even in 1937, more than 40 percent of Lithuania's doctors were Jews.[7] In Šiauliai, with a population around twenty-five thousand, both Jewish and Christian doctors maintained practices, and many thrived. Yet Aharon Pick was the only Jewish physician employed in the municipal hospital, where he oversaw the internal and infectious disease wards, and through the late 1930s, ethnic tensions grew sharper and more personal. As he recalled in his journal: "Divisions grew between my colleagues and me regarding Lithuanians and Jews, and particularly about policies that infringed our rights, rights that had been ensured in Lithuania's constitution. A theme emerged during these conversations, summarized in the slogan 'Lithuania for the Lithuanians.' It is true that this was not said aloud at first, but only hinted at; shortly, however, the insinuations were replaced by open, loudly expressed opinions."

The interpersonal landscape became far muddier and rockier after the Soviet takeover—an event that, if not for what followed it, would rank among the most traumatic and disruptive chapters of European Jewish history. Pick, whose Zionist activities made him highly suspect under the Soviet regime, was unsparing in his criticism of the cruelty and incompetence of those he called Bolsheviks. Yet his attitude was tempered by both an underlying sympathy with socialism's egalitarian ideals and a clear understanding that the Soviet occupation had protected Lithuania's Jews from something far worse: "It is undeniable that the Bolshevik regime was founded on the principles of law and justice. Yet it is also impossible to deny that in general, and in our city in particular, its actions were characterized by injustice, wickedness, stupidity, madness and folly.... Although the Bolshevik regime destroyed the economic well-being of merchants and entrepreneurs, who made up the majority of Lithuanian Jews, at the same time it saved us all from the hands of those who sought to kill us."

THE HOLOCAUST IN ŠIAULIAI

By the time Pick began his journal, the Nazi Einsatzgruppen and their Lithuanian accomplices had wiped out more than 160,000 Lithuanian Jews, nearly 80 percent of those who came under German occupation.[8] In Šiauliai, which had had a prewar Jewish population between 6,500 and 8,000, only 4,000 to 5,000 Jews remained, confined in two adjacent ghetto areas. These Jews were spared because the Germans needed their labor. Many worked in what had been Šiauliai's largest industry, a leather goods factory that the Germans appropriated for military production. Others worked for Christians in the city, filling jobs in workshops and stores and even as domestics in the homes of people who had been their friends or acquaintances before the war. Still others were forced into labor gangs and dispatched to work on roads, airfields, peat mines, or lime quarries.

Thanks to the intervention of a prominent local Lithuanian doctor named Domas Jasaitis, who had somehow managed to retain his standing under both the Soviet and Nazi regimes, Pick was among a half dozen Jewish physicians given jobs as lab technicians outside the ghetto. Such jobs paid little to nothing but were still prized for the opportunities they gave Jews to barter for food, obtain information, and occasionally escape to the countryside.

Šiauliai's was the third largest of the principal Nazi ghettos set up in Lithuania. It was far smaller than those in Kaunas and Vilnius (which themselves were perhaps one-twentieth of the size of the Warsaw ghetto), which may help explain why Šiauliai has received less attention. But the suffering there was no less acute, and the stories no less dramatic, than those more widely known and studied.

PHYSICIAN AND DIARIST

As they did elsewhere, the Germans ordered Šiauliai's Jewish community leaders to administer the ghetto's internal affairs themselves. Within weeks, and despite continued violence, the Jüdenrat (as it was called in German) had set up an extensive structure, including police, courts, health clinics, and food-distribution services. Its leaders also considered their legacy. In late November 1941, they invited both Pick and two others to take on roles as record keepers. Pick declined to do so officially but said he would continue to keep notes and work on his own journal. Eliezer Yerushalmi, a former teacher, became the council's semiofficial (although covert) secretary and archivist.[9]

Pick organized his text methodically, dividing it into four large sections (labeled with the Hebrew equivalents of "A" through "D"), with subsections and further divisions in the first three. The last section is in diary form, with dated entries beginning in May 1942 and continuing until June 7, 1944. The narrative covers the final days of Lithuania's independence, when antisemitism was growing sharply, and the first Soviet occupation, when Lithuania was first incorporated into the USSR. There follows an almost minute-by-minute account of the days before, during, and after the Soviets fled and the Germans took over. Pick's account takes a personal turn when he describes how he himself was arrested and briefly jailed in September 1941—a critical period in which Lithuanian and German police were still rounding up large numbers of Jews and murdering them in nearby forests. Shortly after his release (for which he credits the dogged pleading and lobbying of his wife, Devorah), the couple moved into the ghetto.

In subsequent sections Pick placed himself in the role of journalist, recording survivors' and witnesses' accounts of the extermination in the ancient towns of northern and western Lithuania. His descriptions of life focus in turn on the Šiauliai ghetto's appearance, its inhabitants' physical and mental health, and the economic, cultural, and spiritual conditions under which Jews were forced to live. The descriptive passages are punctuated with anecdotes and observations, with Pick detailing his personal experiences, impressions, and fears: "Walking on the sidewalks is banned for Jews. . . . Naturally, the question arose of how to manage this in winter, when snow piles up on the edges of the streets. Moreover, it appears heaven is against us: This year winter came early. In November, the cold intensified, and with it came plenty of snow. We experienced the pleasure of stumbling into the snow piles as we struggled over ice and slippery roads; like the righteous, we fell and rose seven times. But no problem! If they leave us alive, we will endure this too."

In others he acts as the ghetto chronicler, evaluating the Jewish council's efforts to organize the hospital, food supplies, and other functions: "The Jewish council established two stores in the ghetto to provide for our needs. At first, those with ration cards could purchase bread, potatoes, turnips, cabbages, and groats, but nothing else. . . . Meat, fish, milk, butter, cheese, eggs, and so on were nowhere to be seen. These shortages began to have an effect: Significant and visible weight loss affected nearly all ghetto dwellers. People often meet and cannot recognize each other's thin faces, although much of that is also caused by unceasing emotional torment."

Elsewhere he writes as an analytic reporter, reading motives and goals in the actions of the German and Lithuanian overlords and the news from the battle-front: "30 July [1942]—The Germans boast endlessly of their victories. I am reminded of how they vowed last year to finish off the Russian army. Although they are advancing and winning battles, their victories are not decisive. If they cannot end Russian resistance in the next four or five weeks, fall will arrive and then winter, and there will be no resolution until spring. If we do not die, maybe we will be blessed to see salvation and consolation. For now it is bitter, bitter."

THE MEANING OF A LITERARY STYLE

Pick trained his medical and scientific eye on the people around him, noting their physical and mental conditions as hunger, stress, and fear took their toll. At the same time, Pick himself was acutely aware of how his own constraints related to his goal of recording and witnessing his community's destruction for future generations. Right at the start of his journal, he says: "My family's experience in recent years reflects the awful and bitter recent fate of the entire Jewish population in Lithuania. Thus I will merge the memories of my personal misfortunes with descriptions of the general persecutions, because in this re-spect *there exists in the general only what exists in the particular.*[10]

That last, italicized, phrase comes from the Talmud, the massive collection of rabbinic writing from the first millennium that constitutes the curriculum at yeshivas like the ones Pick attended. His diary shows it: Talmudic learning infuses his prose from start to finish. Pick wrote in what has been called "Has-kalah style" Hebrew, a richly evocative literary form common among writers of the nineteenth century.

Readers of Pick's diary in Hebrew describe it as eloquent, resonant in its frequent use of biblical allusion, references to rabbinic writing, and liturgical imagery. Yet Pick's decision to compose in this style both challenges translators and raises questions regarding his meaning and intentions. To take the most salient example: Throughout his notebooks, Pick refers to Germany as *Ashke-naz*, the term used by first-millennium rabbinic writers to describe the lands of central Europe. Pick's choice seems both deliberate and puzzling, since by the 1940s Hebrew writers were already referring to Germany as *Germaniya* and its inhabitants as *Germanim*. Moreover Pick's term for the invaders, *Ashkenazim*, is now almost universally used to describe European Jews and their descendants, as distinguished from those with roots in Iberia (*Sephardim*) or the Middle East (*Mizrachim*). Here and elsewhere, Pick employs terms so archaic that, in the Hebrew transcription published in 1997, the editors thought it necessary to insert contemporary equivalents [in brackets] to enable Israeli readers to follow the text.[11]

WINDOW AND MIRROR

Pick's Zionist-modernist outlook is an important consideration not only for those attempting to understand his writing but also for showing the place of his diary in the literature of the Holocaust. That enormous and growing historiography is itself an active subject of study, as both window and mirror. How societies have recounted and interpreted the disaster that swept across the world in the 1940s can tell us something about their, and our own, ideals and self-conceptions.

Holocaust research in the first decades after the war concentrated on documenting the atrocities and connecting them to specific policies and decisions by the perpetrators. Exemplified by the work of Raul Hilberg and others, this approach placed German actors in the foreground, inadvertently fostering the notion of Jews and others as helpless victims, stereotypical "sheep led to slaughter." Politics also colored the historical narrative: Scholars based in the Soviet Union, Israel or the United States tended to interpret events along teleological lines that supported socialist, Zionist, or Western democratic narratives, respectively.[12]

Over time, scholarly attention has shifted to the response of individuals and communities to catastrophe. The question became: "Is it a story . . . that tells how the Germans and their collaborators murdered the Jews, or is it a Jewish story—one telling how Jews lived and acted under the Nazi regime?"[13] This was accelerated by the gradual emergence of diaries and journals written as the experience was unfolding.

From France to Lithuania, scores of diaries, journals, and testimonies were written, typically in secret, and the paths these documents took from creation to discovery and wide dissemination was haphazard. Some, such as Emanuel Ringelblum's Warsaw ghetto archive, had to be literally dug up and reassembled over several decades.[14] Herman Kruk's Vilna journal, although obtained by the Yiddish Scientific Institute (YIVO) in New York in 1947, was not published in its original Yiddish until 1961 and not in English translation until 2002.[15] The journal of Avraham Tory, secretary to the Kovno (Kaunas) Jewish ghetto council, was unknown until Tory brought it from Israel to Tampa, Florida, to be used as evidence in the 1982 deportation trial of a former Lithuanian official. It was published in Hebrew in 1988 and in English in 1990.

The Pick diary's postwar path was no less circuitous. Its author succumbed to what he describes only as an "intestinal ailment" only weeks before the Germans moved to liquidate the Šiauliai ghetto in July 1944. When it became clear that its residents were to be transported and probably killed (the majority, including Pick's wife, Devorah, were gassed at the Stutthof camp near Danzig), Tedik Pick used his position on the Jewish police force to escape the ghetto.[16] Before leaving, he managed to seal up and bury his father's notebooks. After the Red Army retook Šiauliai, Tedik returned and recovered the Hebrew journal, taking it with him to Israel in 1948.[17] (A second Pick diary, written in Yiddish, remained in Lithuania and today is held by a Jewish museum in Vilnius.) With other survivors of the Nazi ghettos and camps, Tedik Pick helped found a kibbutz, Netzer Sereni, where he lived until his death in 1975. According to his daughter, he seldom spoke of his wartime experiences, or of the diary, even with his family.[18] In the late 1990s, with the Israeli kibbutz movement's economic crisis negatively affecting her family's financial situation, Tedik's widow, Chaya Pick, was persuaded to share the document with a group of Šiauliai survivors, who published a transcription. The resulting volume, annotated with an introduction, was released in paperback by the Association of Lithuanian Jews in Israel in 1997.[19]

It joins a varied but colorful canon of sources, most in Yiddish or Hebrew, that have gradually illuminated the story of the Šiauliai Jewish community's tragic end. Some first-person accounts were collected by organizations such as Israel's Yad Vashem; others appeared as personal testimony or memoir, occasionally published privately or (beginning in the mid-1990s) posted on various personal or purpose-built internet sites.

Probably the most comprehensive documentation of Šiauliai's ghetto years was compiled by Eliezer Yerushalmi, who took notes at council meetings and collected testimony from witnesses, in addition to recording his own observations. Yet this full archive has apparently never been reassembled, although an English version of Yerushalmi's own summation of his diary appears on a website devoted to Šiauliai's Jewish community: https://kehilalinks.jewishgen. org/shavli/YerushalmiUmkum.pdf. A 1949 memoir, published in Yiddish, by survivor Levi Shalit, adds details about the Šiauliai ghetto underground and its abortive efforts at resistance.

Over the decades, other accounts (some varying in details) from Šiauliai emerged in other formats.[20] Author and Yiddish translator Ellen Cassedy combined archival research with interviews and accounts of a relative who served on the Šiauliai ghetto's Jewish police force.[21] A 2011 book by Keith Morgan, a Canadian journalist, dramatized the experience of a survivor who narrowly escaped the children's aktion in November 1943 (described in a moving passage by Pick).[22] Other testimonies have been collected and made available for study by archives in Israel, Lithuania, and the United States, including the US Holocaust Memorial Museum, which in 2000 added the Pick diary to its collection.[23]

A quite different, but far from irrelevant, body of literature includes testimonies and memoirs written by non-Jewish Lithuanians after the war, only some of which has been translated into English. Notably, a major contributor was the same Domas Jasaitis whom Pick identifies as his Šiauliai patron and prewar colleague.[24] Jasaitis, who like Pick had studied medicine in France, fled to Germany when the Soviet army returned to Lithuania in 1944; he moved to the United States in 1950. Over the next quarter century, he became a leading figure in the Lithuanian exile community and collected numerous letters and other documents, attesting to Lithuanian efforts to protect and rescue Jews during the Nazi period. Before he died in 1977, Jasaitis also promoted the concept of Lithuania's "double genocide" at the hands of both Soviets and Nazis, with blame apportioned more or less equally—a notion that continues to inflame Jewish-Lithuanian discourse to the present.[25]

This translation, imperfect as it may be, offers the prospect of wider access and hopefully a more open discourse about this aspect of the Holocaust. It is our hope that it will attract the attention of Western scholars, including those inside Lithuania, who have begun exploring and challenging accepted narratives about that country's twentieth-century experience.

In that sense, our project aims to retrieve this voice from the ghetto.

NOTES ON THE TEXT

AHARON PICK COMPILED HIS JOURNAL from notes he began keeping early in the period (at least from the late 1930s). His Hebrew manuscript fills three notebooks, one of which appears to have been a rough draft or notes, as its content is repeated in the other two. The notebooks were buried in the ghetto after his death and retrieved after the Soviets reoccupied the town.

Pick's literary style—a product of his traditional yeshiva education—makes extensive use of phrases and expressions drawn from biblical, Talmudic, and other rabbinic writing. Wherever possible, these sources are noted, along with references to Russian or other modern literature. We place the notes wherever the references occur in the text, deviating from standard style placing notes at the end of sentences. Where necessary, we have also noted incorrect or questionable dates.

Any document from this part of the world must deal with the multiple languages in use there, and transliteration further complicates the choices that must be made regarding the spelling of names. Pick's own name is a good example. Its Hebrew- and Russian-character spelling is clear, its Latin orthography less so. Some sources render the name as Pik, while those in Lithuanian archives use Pikas. Postwar documents suggest the family spelled it Pieck. Most previously published works use Pick; to maintain archival consistency, we retain that spelling here. The names of other individuals are rendered in the form they would most likely use themselves—that is, Lithuanians with Lithuanian spelling conventions and Jews with transliterations of Yiddish. In many cases the manuscript mentions people only by surname or by initials. Wherever these could be identified, the notes provide full names and other relevant information. Where confirming phonetic or Latin-alphabet sources could not be located, the spellings reflect conventions in use in that region (Abramovich, for example, rather than Abramowitz and Günter rather than Ginter).

For places, we use their contemporary Lithuanian names (Šiauliai or Kaunas, for example), in some cases adding their Yiddish or Russian equivalents (Shavli or Kovno, in the same example). Where round parentheses occur they are from the original manuscript; square brackets denote words inserted by the editors for clarity. In most cases, quotation marks in the text match those in the original manuscript.

Pick wrote the first three parts of his journal in the spring of 1942, during a period of relative calm after the pogroms and mass murders of Jews had subsided. He used that period to organize his notes about life in the ghetto thematically, as well as to recount the events leading up to the ghetto's creation. He divided his text into outline-style sections, using a combination of Hebrew letters and Arabic numerals for division and subdivision headings. His schema is reflected in the table of contents. (The table also mirrors one used by Golan.)[1]

PART A

ONE

—ᴍᴍ—

BEFORE THE BOLSHEVIKS'
ARRIVAL (A PREFACE)

IT WAS NOT SO LONG ago that Lithuanians, whether rural peasants or urbanites, whether clerks or intellectuals (many themselves the descendants of peasants), showed deference[1] to Jewish physicians and lawyers, holding them in high regard. But those times are over and gone.[2] These days, very few of those who once benefited from the help of Jewish physicians and lawyers show any respect for them or sympathy for their recent misfortune. The majority of the Lithuanian people, even the educated, are now hostile toward all Jews, regardless of their previous social status. Under the malicious influence of the modern Haman,[3] they blame the Jews for all global disasters and so justify laws against us. They think that scorn and annihilation are due us[4] for our apparent connection to the Bolsheviks. Thus, the Lithuanians became willing servants and appeasers of the modern-day Amalek.[5] The slightest hint was sufficient to trigger a predatory attack on the Lithuanian Jews, with a cruelty that has not been seen in over two thousand years of Jewish history. Innocent people were slaughtered, old and young,[6] even pregnant women and infants. Indeed! A horrible cruelty without precedent, carried out coldly, indifferently, as one kills flies, something not seen since the age of the Pharaohs, even worse than the pogroms.

Those who blame us for the misdeeds of the Bolsheviks make no distinctions; as far as they are concerned, there is no difference between an everyday Jew and me. No gratitude is shown for my service as a physician in private practice and at the municipal hospital, bringing relief and healing[7] to thousands of Lithuanians. My family's experience in recent years reflects the awful and bitter recent fate of the entire Jewish population in Lithuania. Thus, I will merge the memories of my personal misfortunes with descriptions of the

3

general persecutions, because in this respect "there exists in the general only what exists in the particular."[8]

In this preface to my description of the bitter fate of the Jews in Šiauliai—which for centuries has been a home to Israel in Lithuania—I think it suitable to emphasize my personal situation in the old days, before the horror came into our lives. This was a time when social status, class, and education mattered; we were not all lumped together like a herd of leprous lambs, as the housepainter who commands the German army would have it.

During the sixteen and a half years I managed the internal and infectious disease wards at the Šiauliai municipal hospital, I was the only Jewish physician, and I had many Christian colleagues. As such I had the opportunity to see the changes in how Lithuanians, particularly the upper classes, treated the Jews. Physicians hold respectable positions near the top of Lithuanian society, whose doctors and priests are its "fine flour and oil."[9]

The "eternal hatred of the eternal people"[10] was long present in Lithuania as well, of course, but the nature of Lithuanian antisemitism, as recently as sixteen years ago, when I first assumed my position at the hospital, was completely different. Now, thanks to the malicious propaganda flowing constantly like poison from the West, we are viewed as loathsome lepers, as filth and refuse.[11] Sixteen years ago I could discuss Jewish-Christian relations—a frequent topic—with the hospital administrator, who later took a key position in the Lithuanian government. He would complain that Jews were reluctant to assimilate, citing mixed marriages he knew of as "very successful" with offspring who "rose beautifully" in Lithuanian society.

Once when I responded that a nation of higher culture should hardly be expected to assimilate into a nation of lower culture, he was offended. This man, the son of rude villagers, who treated people much as his parents had, grunted: "What is Jewish culture? Lice and bedbugs?" I gave him a lesson about the Bible, the Talmud, and secular Hebrew literature, pointing out the great gulf in quality and quantity separating Judah Halevi from Kudirka,[12] their national poet who composed the Lithuanian national anthem, etc. Apparently, I won the argument: he made no further claims, and peace was restored.

My position in the hospital was secure, and my salary was the same as those of my Christian colleagues. They were more than polite to me; yet outside the hospital we seldom interacted, perhaps because they knew I was a card-carrying Zionist and a longtime Jewish nationalist. In fact I made no efforts to befriend them and always felt there was a barrier between us. Still, inside the institute we were equal in every respect. Even among the lower-level hospital personnel, no one opened a mouth to peep[13] about my being a

Jew, at least openly. There was one time when a nurse, bandaging a little child who wouldn't stop crying, attempted to silence him with a popular peasant threat: "Be quiet! A Jew is coming!" I happened to enter the room as she said this, and as I laughed, she turned as red as dyed wool[14] with embarrassment. Indeed, my friends and hospital colleagues treated me with as much respect as could be expected.

Over time antisemitism increased in Lithuania, both in the streets and in official policy. More Jewish signs were covered with tar, even as the Seimas eliminated the Ministry of Jewish Affairs,[15] the last miserable remnant of our autonomy. Among the historical reasons for this growth in antisemitism, a primary one was the ambition of Lithuania's peasants. Previously serfs who gained freedom with their country's political independence, they wished to become fully equal urban citizens, filling all important positions in a proud, independent state without foreign interference. They saw themselves ready to take over key sectors of industry and commerce and so began to restrict "foreign competitors"—Jews—every way they could.

Divisions grew between my colleagues and me regarding Lithuanians and Jews and particularly about policies that infringed our rights, rights that had been ensured in Lithuania's constitution. A theme emerged during these conversations, summarized in the slogan "Lithuania for the Lithuanians." It is true that this was not said aloud at first, but only hinted at. Shortly however, the insinuations were replaced by open, loudly expressed opinions. I remember that one of my friends, a well-known intellectual with a good mind, tried to put me in a corner by asking if the land of our ancestors,[16] which we are busy building right now, would welcome non-Jews as clerks or in other positions. I answered that it is not the same for many reasons. Lithuania is not being built from its foundations currently; it is developing and modernizing, and it needs the help of experts and professionals who are in short supply among the Lithuanians. This is very different from hesitating to provide employment [in Palestine] to foreigners such as the Arabs, who harass and fight us, and who could undermine the country we are building. We have just begun building a new country. This can't be compared with the ambition of some people to destroy the status achieved by [Jewish] professionals, traders, and artisans, who have disproportionately helped Lithuania's development and who are loyal citizens who could bring it tangible benefits. Finally, I explained the laws of the Torah regarding foreigners, and the equity that has existed since biblical times between strangers[17] and citizens of Jewish communities.

And then the government started to bombard the Jews with rules and restrictions in the fields of commerce, arts, and education. There were too many to recount here, so I will limit myself to those in education, medicine, and law, with which I am more familiar.

First, the school of medicine all but shut its doors to Jewish high school graduates. Enrolling became as difficult as parting the Red Sea, with only a privileged few, who had recommendations from high-ranking, influential people, allowed to enter the "orchard"[18] of medicine. The situation in Lithuania became far worse than [it had been] in tsarist Russia. There at least there was a quota: 5 to 10 percent of those admitted to high schools and universities were Jews. But in Lithuania no attention was paid to percentages, and Jews were rejected wholesale. Of course they invoked their holy constitution as a pretense and made all sorts of excuses. First a committee was set up to review the health of medical school applicants, chaired by a well-known sadist, the anatomy professor Žulinskis—a son of the Lithuanian soil like most scholars from that period, one whose scholarship carried the smell of sweat, and to whom a Kaunas city councilor once said during an argument in the city council, where Žulinskis was also a member: "Mr. Professor, this is not the university. Here we need to use our heads." Of course, all the Jews they wanted to reject were found to be in unsatisfactory health. There was a story about a young man whom the committee rejected as too feeble in body. The young man cried out, "The Lithuanian army found my body strong enough to serve, but I am too feeble to study medicine? Bafflement upon bafflement."[19] The committee was embarrassed. This young man, who had various privileges, would not be put off with a straw.[20] So the committee considered his appeal.

Their other trick to get rid of pesky Jews was to demand they pass a proficiency test in the Lithuanian language. The literature and orthography of this ancient tongue, which was recently revived, still produces many arguments and disagreements among Lithuanian linguists, and errors are common even among well-known writers. So when people are tested and evaluated by examiners "scrupulous to a hairsbreadth"[21] the number of failures will not be small. This was as intended, even though some Jewish students had mastered the Lithuanian language superbly.

Another ruse aimed to eliminate Jewish specialists from such fields as surgery, obstetrics, ophthalmology, etc. The government declared that any doctor who wanted to become a specialist had to work as an aide in his chosen field in a relevant hospital department for a certain number of years—three years for eyes, four for surgery, etc. This demand was essentially proper and logical. But even as the requirement was announced, an order was issued quietly to hospital managers to stop hiring Jewish aides in the hospitals' specialty departments. Since work in these departments was a necessary precondition, the possibility of Jewish doctors becoming specialists was foreclosed, and the medical profession was destined eventually to be rid of Jewish doctors.

For Jewish lawyers things were even worse. Here they did not deal with specialization but simply barred Jews from receiving the title of lawyer. Obtaining that title required working as a "candidate" in a court for a certain period, and one bright morning, admissions of such candidates stopped altogether.

Other restrictions were imposed on Jews at the same time. Artists, professionals, and those with government or municipal jobs were pushed out gradually, so as not to make too great a fuss. With new jobs impossible for Jews to obtain, restrictions on university admissions, the lack of medical specialization options, and the foreclosing of legal or official positions, the appeal of higher education faded for intelligent young Jews. Rather than aspiring to study in the halls of learning, as had been so common among Jewish adults, the young now wished to leave the land of Lithuania, which had been like a stepmother to them, and emigrate to our ancestors' land or sail across the oceans to those refuges where Jews could still do creative and productive work.

In the hospital as well, the atmosphere turned difficult. While in the past there had been no distinction between me and the Christian doctors regarding such matters as salary, that now began to change for the worse. Over time all our salaries had been cut back, but surgeons and obstetricians received bonuses for the procedures they performed. Thus at the end of the month, their pay was still respectable while my pay remained meager, without any supplement. But as antisemitic propaganda spread throughout the country, I fell into insecurity and doubt and dared not ask for a raise, even though I filled the roles of several doctors. I was asked to manage the departments of internal medicine and infectious diseases and consulted with the departments of surgery and obstetrics-gynecology. Also, the Jewish vice-mayor, Petuchauskas,[22] a person "preeminent among ten thousand"[23] who was later killed by the villains in Vilnius and who was responsible for [Šiauliai] city finances, sensed the worsening antisemitism and cautioned me that it was "not the right time in city council to bring up the issue of a raise for a Jewish doctor in the hospital."

So my Christian friends saw a nice monthly salary for their work, while I was forced to be satisfied with my insultingly low compensation. Notably, my friends did not see anything abnormal in this discrimination, as over time they came to accept the notion that merely tolerating a Jewish doctor in the hospital was burden enough. I should point out that the city hospital is located in a building that before the world war[24] belonged to the Šiauliai kehilla.[25] When the city took over the building from the Germans,[26] to appease its true owners, it agreed to pay the kehilla a small sum as rent and also agreed to appoint a

Jewish doctor at the hospital—an appointment that was given to me. "Lovely indeed was my estate."[27]

The new chief doctor of the hospital, Dr. Y.K., a Pole who despised Lithuanians, nonetheless shared their hatred of Jews. In fact, he had no real fixed principles and considered things carelessly, "half serious, half in jest," as the Russians say. But he too adjusted to the current climate of opinion and became a complete antisemite. My other colleagues followed after him: the obstetrician D.S., despite his wife's Jewish origin, and the surgeon T.K., a descendant of the Tatars, whose ancestors presumably arrived during the days of Vytautas the Great[28] and assimilated over time among the Lithuanian and Polish population. Although our dealings in the hospital remained polite and friendly, the chief began to employ the term "Aryan" to mean the opposite of "Jewish," although his tone remained half in jest.

Then there was the case of a young Jewish doctor, who was completing the one-year term required for a medical diploma and asked to be appointed assistant doctor on the night shift because this is a well-paying position. After some thought, the chief doctor said the "higher-ups" were pushing him to give this job to an "Aryan" doctor. Of course he was acting on his own; there were no higher-ups constraining him. He seemed to joke, but his refusal to provide a salary to a needy Jew was part of the antisemitism spreading through Lithuanian society.

My Christian colleagues, not satisfied with the mere slogan "Lithuania for the Lithuanians," not satisfied with a defensive war against their unwanted competitors, increasingly took the offensive, barely hiding their hatred. Jews, they believed, dominated those branches of commerce and industry that were most needed to nurture Lithuania's culture, and were uninterested in aiding the country's development. Doctor T.K. was particularly fierce in his hatred. Since his facial features and his last name indicated that he was not ethnically Lithuanian, he made an effort to demonstrate his commitment and loyalty to the "pure" Lithuanian nation by trying to conceal his origins as best he could. The behavior of this Tatar toward me was remarkable: inside the hospital, despite our arguments, we were like loyal friends. Outside, when he found me in the company of Christians, such as at a party or a meeting, he ignored me and refrained from all conversation with me. A Franco-Lithuanian club existed in Šiauliai before the Bolsheviks came, and he had been one of its pillars. I once gave a lecture in French there, which was very well received.[29] Yet even at this club's receptions, he was reluctant to talk to me or to show any sign of friendship. He would only nod his head subtly, as though coerced by a demon, so as not to be suspected of befriending a Jew in this new era.

In short, the hospital's atmosphere worsened as well, and my previously secure status there was undermined by the new conditions, which made even breathing difficult. The popular and political antisemitism had a reciprocal effect on each other, making it hard to discern which was the driving force. The Lithuanian press ceaselessly published shameful propaganda against the Jews; even the official paper printed articles from time to time, mocking Jews and exposing their malicious plots: "They cheat and rob the people; they suck Lithuania's essence like leeches; they bring their female servants to sin, they take advantage of innocent peasant girls," and on and on. (As a doctor who treated female conditions, I can attest that perhaps one in a thousand of those peasant women were "innocent." By the time they arrived in the city there was nothing left to spoil... I'll say no more.)

The extent of hatred and incitement in the Lithuanian press can be seen in the following example, which would be funny if it were not so sad. In summer, when the bathing season at Palanga[30] was in full swing, the editor of the local official paper devoted an entire article to Jews, claiming they contaminated the sea at Palanga. As evidence, he told of a Jew who could not control himself while bathing and was caught red-handed, doing something "Semites" allow themselves to do all the time....

Along with the slanderous articles, the press began to publish proposals for legislation to influence the Seimas. The purpose of these proposals was to undermine and eradicate Jewish autonomy in Lithuania, "the beauty and the glory"[31] of our country. Thus, it was proposed that all Jewish businesses and in-stitutions must observe Christian holidays and that all schoolbooks and official ledgers be in the Lithuanian language. It was also suggested to bar Jews from employing Christian women as domestics. A proposal that drew much atten-tion was to allocate a segregated beach for the Jews at Palanga. Jews reacted by threatening to boycott Palanga entirely, prompting resort owners there to lobby against the plan out of fear for their financial losses. Lastly, to illustrate how Lithuania's antisemites constantly stirred up hatred for the Jews, we should add this: along with the restrictions and discrimination in commerce, industry, and academia, the government mandated that Jewish craftsmen and artisans pass theoretical and practical examinations. If this had been enforced, it would have put them out of business entirely. Tens of thousands would have lost liveli-hoods, condemning them to starvation. These were simple, everyday people, working as tailors, cobblers, and carpenters, who, outside of cheder[32] or yeshiva, had never been exposed to formal study or examinations; their lives had been entirely spent simply making a living. You can imagine them having to prepare for exams in arithmetic, drawing and so on, all in the Lithuanian language....

Besides these active attempts to restrict and harass Jews, the government showed its malice through passive measures as well. After Germany annexed the city of Klaipėda,[33] many Jews who had owned factories and laboratories there returned to Lithuania. They came with experience and respectable sums of money and offered to restart their businesses in Lithuania. The government turned them down, refusing to issue the needed licenses. Queen Elizaveta Petrovna's[34] declaration—"From the enemies of Christ I want no profit"—was repeated, albeit quietly (to avoid offending the constitution) and made into a guideline for the government's treatment of Jews.

The antisemitic propaganda, the evil writs[35] and decrees, the hostile attitude toward Jews even among the upper classes, took root throughout Lithuanian society, spreading its poison weed and wormwood[36] among the masses as well. The charged atmosphere needed only a spark to explode and cause damage. The environment was being primed for a pogrom, and indeed such a thing was being enthusiastically prepared. Knowledgeable people asserted that the "Maistas" meatpacking plant was storing up axes, knives, steel bars and such, to be used when the day came to murder Jews. Of course there was no short-age of volunteers for this butchery. Leading the mob were to be the "Maistas" plant's workers, experts in beheading pigs, cattle, sheep, and goats. They would be assisted by other Šiauliai factory workers, many of them employed by Jews, who supported them and their families. Over time, attacks against Jews on the streets became more frequent, particularly at night, leaving Jews afraid to go out in the evenings. Community representatives complained to city officials about the street violence but their complaints went unheeded.

The secret police, as usual, blamed the "insolent, cheeky kikes" for every-thing. In one case, a supposedly intelligent Lithuanian man, who was probably under the influence of drink, insulted one of the *chalutzim*[37] on the main street. Friends of the offended one pushed the hooligan into a side alley and beat him up. It turned out that he belonged to a Lithuanian patriotic group whose members later gathered and, late at night, broke into the *chalutzim* clubhouse, armed with sticks and other weapons, wounding nearly all the young men and women inside. The municipal physician and other city officials downplayed it as an insignificant schoolboy brawl which they claimed the Jews had started. But when it was learned that a score of people had been injured, several seriously, the administration could no longer ignore it and punished the rioters with a fine. Their fine was paid by the famous antisemitic city councilors Stankus[38] and Schutz, raven-black haters of Israel, whom the Bolsheviks later arrested and deported into the USSR.

A date for the pogroms was finally set. Jews were to be attacked in a mass uprising scheduled for June 15, 1940—a date that would be long remembered. It was to be a festive day, a Sunday, when workers would be free to participate in the looting and murder.

"Do not rely on miracles,"[39] we are told. Yet as scattered sheep[40] among the world's wild beasts, the Jewish people can only have survived due to miracles and wonders. It is still hard to believe what actually took place—how on the very day chosen for our destruction, the villains' plans were thwarted; the haters of Israel were prevented from carrying out their evil deeds. As in times of old, a great miracle happened then.[41] On June 15, an event occurred whose importance will be engraved in the historical record and the memories of generations to come.

Even before dawn on that day, the rumble of engines and wheels could be heard, moving slowly up the Tilsit road. At first, fear spread through the city. But soon the tumult became a joyful noise, pleasing to the ears of almost all Šiauliai Jews, a wonderful harmony, a heavenly music! It was the roar of Russian tanks and artillery, coming on like a storm, their arrival miraculously timed to save the Jews of Šiauliai and all Lithuanian Jews from the doom and destruction they had expected. In huge numbers the Russians arrived, streaming in endless columns as far as Joniškis, near the [Latvian] border.[42] All our enemies and haters became silent. And the workers who had been planning to take part in pogroms turned overnight into Bolsheviks, loyal to the proletarian dictatorship and the equality of workers of all nations without distinction! And the Jews found relief and deliverance forever![43]

Oh, but that salvation came at a very dear price, one that we could not foresee and which we are still paying! Our lives hang by a thread, and we are oppressed under the Germans' spiked boots and the fists of their Amalekite partners who blame us for the crimes of the Bolsheviks.

THE BOLSHEVIKS IN LITHUANIA

AND SO THE BOLSHEVIK REGIME took control on June 15, 1940, bringing many benefits as well as faults. It is hard to be critical now, since it was replaced by the damned Hitler regime, which took us from the heights to the depths, from a paradise of light and joy to a terrible hell, where the terror of death[1] afflicts us constantly. Although the Bolshevik regime destroyed the economic well-being of merchants and entrepreneurs who made up the majority of Lithuanian Jews, at the same time it saved us all from the hands of those who sought to kill us. Now in our poverty and anguish, when we remember the treatment of Jews by the Bolshevik regime, the high places we occupied according to our abilities, our spirits fail within us.[2] Indeed, there is no way to describe succinctly the many enormous changes brought to our country and our lives by the Bolshevik regime, because the pace of events was so rapid that it caused our heads to spin and strained our nerves so that many events simply did not register in our minds. Thus a fair recounting and proper appraisal of all the events in chronological order is very difficult. I will try as best I can, though, to set down in detail the changes brought to our lives and our city during the Bolshevik period, dispassionately and without bias,[3] suppressing my own yearning for that regime and my sorrow for its replacement by the cruel German fist.

It is undeniable that the Bolshevik regime was founded on the principles of law and justice. Yet it is also impossible to deny that in general, and in our city in particular, its actions were characterized by injustice, wickedness, stupidity, madness, and folly.[4] On the one hand, it aimed to liberate workers from capitalist exploitation, improve their material and moral conditions, and create a "dictatorship of the proletariat" (the need for which was questionable even in Russia, with its underdeveloped economy, but whose goals and aspirations were understandable). On the other hand, it falsely portrayed every bourgeois as a villain, to be shunned[5] and eradicated from under heaven[6] and believed that taking systematic revenge on individuals and their descendants for the sins of an entire class was a necessary step in society's development. On the one hand, the regime set out to eliminate those enterprises that benefit only individuals, to remove owners and managers from stores and factories and to sack old clerks who, while perhaps knowledgeable and experienced at their jobs, might be antagonistic and prepared to sabotage the new order. On the other hand, the administration placed capricious, unprepared amateurs in serious jobs requiring maturity, education, and experience, and appointed officers from among the thugs and bullies, those who turned themselves overnight into faithful Bolsheviks and just as quickly transformed themselves back into nationalist partisans and pogromists.

What we witnessed was the Bolshevik revolutionary strategy, which aspires to uproot the capitalistic order at one stroke, in such haste that it unleashes pandemonium and disorder. The USSR's new rulers believed that repairing human society through the proletarian revolution could not wait; therefore, there was no time to train skilled people to carry out Marxism's ambitious program. As has been noted, it takes a long time to change human nature. Two thousand years after the founder of Christianity preached a gospel of love, his followers still turn easily into bloodthirsty beasts. Of course the Marxist response, which is to some extent justified, is that as long as the rule of Sodom persists—where "mine is mine and yours is yours" can easily deteriorate into the wicked quality of "mine is mine and yours is mine"—as long as there is exploitation of one by another, as long as private property is dominant and all-encompassing, not just among individuals but also among nations, no real ideal can materialize. Thus, the first step toward repairing human society is to eliminate private property. There is certainly much truth in this. Yet even assuming it is all true and firm,[7] and that eliminating individual ownership will lead to a perfect world, here is a question: without trained, honest experts in every profession, who will implement the new order? Can ex-political prisoners fill these roles? During their short reign, the Bolsheviks promoted leaders who had learned their skills in prison, where they became "experts" in all matters of economy and state administration. Could such people bring salvation—people like Slavich, the Šiauliai governor who took over right after being released from prison, and immediately fell victim to megalomania? On the one hand, these people believed that "I am and there is none but me";[8] on the other, they believed the world can only be repaired by cruelly persecuting all classes other than the proletariat and by exterminating individuals for the sins of entire generations. As for the daily, necessary work of governing, that would take care of itself.

So immediately after entering Šiauliai, they began to establish and strengthen their rule here, eliminating the capitalist order and the influence of the bourgeoisie. First they disbanded the police, arresting the entire secret police administration and its agents. Then they shuttered all public institutions that had existed in Šiauliai, demanding that those wishing to remain in operation submit requests to that effect. They closed the only newspaper published in Šiauliai. They appointed commissars to oversee the factories and dismissed all managers deemed suspect. Also they started arresting the leaders of right-wing parties and bourgeois organizations along with anyone who "deviated from the road"[9] that the Bolsheviks dictated. Hebrew culture suffered quite a lot, unnecessarily because its secular adherents were by and large modern thinkers who could easily adjust, up to a point, to the new conditions and requirements. Thus for example they dismantled the Jewish public library, seizing the Yiddish books to establish a new library for "proletarians" and archiving the Hebrew books. It is worth noting that one of the teachers in the Hebrew gymnasium[10] who quickly became a Bolshevik activist and a servant of the GPU[11] recommended that the Hebrew books be burned. (The new regime caused such destruction of a Jewish soul more than once.) In addition to the library, the Hebrew gymnasium, which had been the pride of the Šiauliai Jewish community for the quality of its instruction, the wealth of its library, and its elegant building, was also closed. Also the Hebrew elementary school was closed and replaced by Yiddish schools. They also imprisoned the gymnasium's principal, a sophisticated man, loyal and dedicated to the depth of his soul to Hebrew culture and to socialism. At the same time they searched the homes of the Zionist organization's leadership. But these were only a prelude to what came later: the nationalization of the factories and stores, the confiscation of their merchandise and cash, and the seizure of the largest and most elegant private homes. Then the searches began, mostly of the homes of merchants suspected of hiding goods for speculation. Many, mostly Jews, were tried and given the severest punishment for even minor offenses; they were sentenced to many years' imprisonment, and their property was confiscated. The regime also harassed the bourgeoisie, treating them vengefully even when the courts found them innocent.

The searches and imprisonments threw fear into the Jewish community. One [of those arrested] was a Zionist official; another was a merchant; a third was a relative of a merchant suspected of speculation; a fourth hoarded too much flour or sugar. A fifth buried a few gold coins and feared his treasure might be discovered. A sixth owned foreign currency, and so on. In short, with the exception of laborers and those with ties to the party who had been political prisoners under the past regime, everyone lived in fear. They began to dread every little sound at night, worrying it meant NKVD agents were on their way. Few in the Jewish community were able to sleep, and their nerves were so strained that it became impossible to engage in serious intellectual work.

I myself expected to be arrested as well. I was the vice-chair of the General Union of Zionists in Šiauliai, the chair of the *"Tarbut"*[12] branch, a member of the Jewish public library board, a member of the parents' committee of the Hebrew gymnasium and, at least by appearance, also its first director. (The gymnasium's license was issued in my name because the director had to possess an advanced degree, and our first director had not yet received his when we began.) In short I was a well-known member of a bourgeois Zionist party, active and close to its leadership, and also known as a proponent of Hebrew who occasionally wrote in that language. My positions were known to the [Lithuanian] secret police and thus, naturally, to the NKVD. What else was needed to have me arrested?

And what I dreaded came upon me,[13] although I was neither handcuffed nor chained: my bourgeois sins merited a different sort of punishment. One bright morning I was summoned to the city hall. Our noble mayor, Mr. Linkevičius,[14] greeted me with a grave face and, looking almost sad, addressed me with these words like sword-thrusts:[15] "I invited you to deliver unpleasant news, for which I am of course not responsible, because it does not originate with me. It has been decided to fire you from the hospital." Even though I had braced myself for some sort of personal affront, his announcement still affected me deeply. I had labored by the sweat of my brow[16] in the hospital for sixteen years, devoting all my energies to it, and, as mentioned, I filled the roles of several physicians. Although in recent years I had received some help from young residents, whom the university placed with us for a year of practical training before they received their diplomas, I had worked at the hospital for a dozen years without aides or deputies. And now I was to be kicked out like an old dog without any compensation, as was customary under the new regime.

It became clear over time that my firing had been precipitated by lapdogs in the Šiauliai [Communist] party, who, to demonstrate their loyalty, had invented tales about me spying and informing. This was quite common at that time. They said my appointment sixteen years earlier as the Jewish doctor in the municipal hospital on the recommendation of the kehilla, had occurred only because I belonged to the Zionist group. Our new leaders thus concluded that as part of the drive to eradicate all "rebels against the light"[17] and bourgeois elements from society, it was only right that a Jewish doctor harboring Zionist sympathies should be replaced by one of their own, that is, a Communist. And if such doctor were not available now, then at least he should be replaced by a leftist doctor, a party supporter—and such a doctor was found in Šiauliai. The new candidate of course lacked the scientific knowledge and experience of the previous doctor, but who cared? These shortcomings would be remedied over time, and ideology covered all sins. Here is the place to mention that when the municipality had decided to appoint a Jewish doctor to the hospital as compensation to the kehilla for using its building, the kehilla chose me because I had cared for the Lithuanian refugees who returned from Russia. I also served as the resident doctor of the orphanage without compensation, I founded the Šiauliai branch of "OZE,"[18] I was an active member of the kehilla's board, and I was among the founders of the Jewish public library. Moreover, I was more learned in Hebrew than the other Jewish doctors so that the title of "Jewish doctor" fit me better than Dr. L.N., my main competitor (an assimilated Jew and a crude man, given to rude remarks). My Zionism had not even been taken into consideration back then, especially since not all the members of the kehilla council were Zionists.

Among the aforementioned lapdogs was Dr. L., who certainly had a hand in my firing. I think it is appropriate to mention here some details about this man's character and qualities, to show what sorts the new regime, which lacked cadres, lifted up and made pillars of the party in our city and across Lithuania.

Under the old regime, Dr. L. had befriended the Šiauliai tax inspector, Mr. Nuseida, the head of the Lithuanian nationalists in our city and a total black-souled antisemite. When the "Fund for the Liberation of Vilnius"[19] was announced, Dr. L. volunteered to be among the fundraisers, and his partner was that antisemite Inspector Nuseida. They pressured Jews for large donations—larger by far than Christians—with threats from the tax inspector, that insatiable leech, against Jewish merchants. During the "brother-in-law government" of President Smetona and Prime Minister Tūbelis,[20] when the latter visited Šiauliai, Nuseida was among the most active organizers of a banquet in his honor. To satisfy the constitution's mandate for equal rights in Lithuania he invited two or three Jews to participate, among them his "pet Jew," Dr. L., who bragged for a long time about the great honor. At the same time, Dr. L. was very active in the Lithuanian Riflemen's Union,[21] providing free medical care, lectures on first aid and so on. In short, Dr. L. had by the Bolsheviks' standards a long list of transgressions, but this man had a talent for blowing with the prevailing winds. He was also a gifted talker and knew how to seize the moment.

As luck would have it, he had once allowed his home to be used to hide forbidden literature intended for the old regime's political prisoners. This great operation (!)—a reflection not of his principles (because he was not a socialist) but rather his desire to be liked by all sides—helped demonstrate his leftist political leanings when the time came and gave him an opening to approach the Bolsheviks in Šiauliai. With his smooth tongue, he fooled them into believing that all his deeds under the old regime had been intended to mask his leftist positions. In addition to the hidden forbidden books, he managed to highlight several other credits: he had paid dues to the "MOPR";[22] he was a Yiddishist[23] and far from Zionism (though not an opponent, because he lacked any principles). These traits helped him ingratiate himself with leaders of the local administration and become one of their most loyal supporters. His timing, moreover, was excellent. The person in control of health, an important issue for the Bolsheviks, was XXX.[24] The Bolsheviks badly needed an adviser who understood health and medicine better than that cretin; therefore they accepted Dr. L. with "open arms," and he became the authority on all things medical in our city. Everything hung on his say-so, and Dr. L. was given the responsible position of director at our municipal hospital. The city health department still needed a director, but no one dared step into this job. It was decided to give the position to a Christian doctor so the gentiles wouldn't say, "How come Jews win all the important positions?"—an argument that certainly had to be considered. That position was given to Dr. Jasaitis.[25] He was known as the "best non-Jewish doctor," had a good reputation and could speak and write well in Lithuanian. He was not an open antisemite: on the contrary, he would sometimes show signs of affection to his Jewish friends. Although not really a serious man, and something of a hypocrite, no one else among the Christian doctors was better fit for the position of health department director. (Dr. Jasaitis will also be remembered positively for his role during German rule: he kept his position like some other Lithuanians who rose under the Bolsheviks but were forgiven, and he interceded with the Germans to keep six Jewish doctors on as lab technicians in various medical institutes. I was among them.)

As I learned discreetly later, Dr. L. had undermined me by saying, "I doubt Dr. Pick deserves to direct internal and infectious medicine at the municipal hospital. After all, he is a Zionist." He flattered and deceived party leaders to demonstrate his political loyalty and, as mentioned, pretended to be a leftist Yiddishist and anti-Zionist. Who needs more? His smooth tongue, his compliments, and his lies did the trick. (Another aid to his rise was the fact that Dr. Cohen, the first minister of health, was "of his own flesh,"[26] the son of his mother-in-law's brother and a villain worse than Dr. L., cruel, arrogant, and corrupt, concerned only with his own pocketbook and career. He was soon removed from this high position, however.)

But back to our business! As a matter of fact I was not overly concerned with fixing blame for my firing. My entire attention was consumed with the end of my sixteen-year career as a doctor in the Šiauliai municipal hospital and my uncertain future. I was a known sinner—a Zionist, a criminal, a "rebel against the light," a "hater of the people"—a title bestowed on us by one of the leading Bolshevik orators. In short, after a long, active life, I was suddenly a has-been, a person of no standing, one of the legion of ghostly souls without a present and possibly without a future, part of the former establishment that the new regime had overturned.

A clear example of how the Bolsheviks targeted and brought low members of the bourgeoisie was my brother-in-law Zilberman. A man of talent and initiative, he managed (with the help of some investor partners) in just a few years to establish a textile factory in Šiauliai. Thanks to his hard work, character and tenacity, the factory flourished and seemed destined to succeed. And then suddenly, disaster: the Bolsheviks arrived and with them the days of punishment and retribution[27] against the bourgeoisie. Of course they targeted my brother-in-law and his partners: they nationalized his business, confiscated his house, and seized his bank deposits. They threw him out of his own factory and left him and his family without a livelihood. Days of trouble and poverty came upon him because he had reinvested all his profits in the factory, expanding and increasing productivity by buying new machines and hiring more workers. Now he lost everything and was left without assets or capital.

It may appear from my brother-in-law's story that my sympathies are with his class, the bourgeoisie. But it is not the case that I supported the capitalist regime in all its aspects. I for one cannot justify in any way the exploitation of workers for the owners' profit. True, they take the initiative, providing capital, machinery, management, and organization, but their profits are often excessive and soaked with the sweat of workers. And to reward themselves for their enterprise they inflate their compensation at the workers' expense. In a word, the capitalist order was certainly erected on a shaky and unjust foundation. But on the other hand, to toss out the founder of an establishment, the one who knows it best, like a piece of scrap paper, is unnecessarily cruel and a mistake. The capitalist class itself is a necessary product of human social development and thus not deserving of such slight anger.[28] Even if we assume that capitalism's time has passed, that its significant historic role has ended, its replacement must necessarily take place gradually and without the terrible cataclysm of revolution. It is also a mistake to remove one who knows all the operating details of a factory or store because he started and built it up over many years, and replace him with someone who has no clue how to operate it and is only there because he belongs to or supports a political party. While it may sometimes be difficult to trust owners because they may damage or sabotage their plants if they agree to continue under new conditions and subject themselves, even under duress, to the new regime; it is preferable to appoint supervisors to oversee them. At any rate, there is no need to take harsh revenge against the capitalists. It is illogical, unnecessary, and unjust.

I have strayed from the account of my dismissal from the hospital longer than I should. But my brother-in-law's story illustrates the plight of the bourgeoisie under the Bolsheviks, and a few more details are worth adding. The nationalization of his factory and the seizure of his real estate did not end his troubles. (I am saving for later the worst part: his and his family's deportation to the USSR during the final days of Bolshevik rule in Lithuania.) More woes awaited us—a collective tragedy that was particularly hurtful to those who had owned their homes. I'm speaking of the housing problem, which the Bolsheviks brought with them. Our new rulers intended to settle among us and put down roots, and therefore they brought their families: wives, children, and often their elderly mothers and mothers-in-law. Along with the Russian army came numerous aviators and administrators, and they all needed apartments or at least decent rooms. Also the party's leaders and dignitaries, past political prisoners, senior workers, "Stakhanovites,"[29] their families and friends. They all needed new apartments, spacious and comfortable places as rewards for years of living in crowded prisons and small, moldy flats. To this end they began to "aggregate" people, moving them from one apartment to another. New occupants were moved in with existing ones; military clerks took civilian apartments. It is hard to describe the agony and discomfort this caused, particularly as the new arrivals regarded themselves as masters and lorded it over the old residents, who often were the real owners. As is written, "he came here as an alien, and already he acts the ruler."[30]

Particularly harsh was the treatment of homeowners whose property was confiscated, leaving them with only narrow corners of their former houses to live in as punishment for their past lives of comfort. That was my brother-in-law's fate: he, his wife, and their two children were allocated only two small rooms on the third floor of his house. Two other rooms were given to Dr. R., whose previous second-floor apartment was now occupied by privileged workers with special rights.

To more vividly illustrate the apartment mess, one should note another detail of the "aggregation" that was so common it was seen as normal: the "war among women." Housewives thrown together in the same apartment were like "cats in a sack." My sister-in-law and Dr. R.'s wife were an example: two grumpy women who could not coexist under one roof. A war developed between them that made the lives of the two families miserable, and continued until the Bolsheviks "evacuated" my brother-in-law's family to the USSR. Such disputes were common because of the crowding caused by the new regime.

(Of course, as much as we complained about the crowding and discomfort then, we didn't dream that a day would come when our crowding would become catastrophic, and we, in sorrow and with broken hearts,[31] would remember the Bolshevik era as incomparably better and happier than we are now in the ghetto. Here we suffocate amid the crowding, filth and parasites that poison our lives. Here we live like herrings in a barrel, despite the efforts of our mortal enemies to increase our space by reducing our numbers, using those former slaves, the Lithuanians, to murder us randomly, like an ox blindly striking out[32] right and left. This cruelty will never be erased; its memory will live in our hearts and our descendants' hearts forever.[33])

We too had apartment trouble. From our six-room flat (excluding the kitchen and bathroom) of which three rooms served us for living and three for my clinic (my office, X-ray room, and waiting room), they took one room and installed an aviator, the battalion commander Tzikin. That was not overly burdensome as the room was vacant—it had belonged to our son, who was a student at Vilnius University—and our new neighbor was a very kind man, polite and well-mannered, and we were pleased with him. (Where is he now? Most probably he met his death long ago because many pilots have since been slain.[34] Too bad for this kind man.)

Our tenant had to leave Šiauliai and move to Latvia even before the start of the war. That was when we were moved from our spacious apartment on the second floor to the lower floor in the same building, where we were allotted only three rooms for us and the clinic combined. There were two additional rooms in that apartment that were given to the G. family. They were a pleasant couple; despite the shared kitchen, we never feuded even once, and we lived in peace until we left for the Trakų ghetto and they were relocated to Kaukazas.[35] I should mention that the director of the apartment police was Furman the sadist, and for the privilege of obtaining a small, crowded, apartment one had to be fully humiliated and beg before this pinhead. He would in his kindness show "generosity"[36] and give an "order" for a new apartment, after making repeated fraudulent promises. He behaved this way not only with the troublesome Jews but also with Christians. His behavior stemmed from his lack of initiative or talent, his sadistic nature, and the pleasure he took in wielding power and causing trouble for those who needed him. Later on, many Lithuanians—the "victimized Cossacks"—remembered his actions and put the blame for them on all Jews, "servants of the cruel Bolsheviks, oppressors of the innocent."

After this digression "as long as the exile"[37] which I intended to paint a picture of Bolshevik rule in our city, I will return to my own activities during those days when we swung from sorrow and despair to hope for the future and back again randomly, as opposed to now, when our world has turned dark without any spark of light, and clouds surround us in all directions.

At the time when the mayor notified me of the administration's decision to remove me from my position in the municipal hospital, a Dr. Mikas was serving as director of the health department in Kaunas. He had formerly served for a long time as the Šiauliai hospital's director before moving to Kaunas, where he built himself a nice house. As Kaunas health director, he had great influence in Lithuania and not just in the medical and pharmaceutical fields. Although the Bolsheviks had named a new national minister of health and eliminated Dr. Mikas' position, he was a man of great drive, initiative, and insight, and he managed to remain in the department by the minister's order, as a medical consultant and executive officer. He remained an important official despite his "regressive" politics and his ownership of a fine, walled estate, where he raised silver foxes and other expensive fur animals, a hobby he had become devoted to along with a zoology professor from Kaunas University, Prof. Ivanauskas.[38]

Based on these facts, I decided to travel to Kaunas the day after receiving the bad news from the mayor and try to speak to Dr. Mikas. Perhaps with his influence he could help me annul the evil decree.[39] As stated, in matters of medicine he still had influence, even among the Bolsheviks. On the second day, after finishing my regular work at the hospital—as I had been ordered to do pending the formal receipt of my dismissal notice and the arrival of my replacement—I went to the mayor to request permission to travel to Kaunas for a few days to plead my case with Dr. Mikas and do several other errands. I also wanted to inquire whether my dismissal had become official, which would mean I was free to go without requesting permission. I was quite surprised when the mayor, after hearing the reason for my visit and the nature of my request, ordered me not go anywhere and continue my work as if nothing had happened. Of course I was anxious to know the reason for this sudden change. But Mayor Linkevičius, a strict, cold-hearted bureaucrat, ignored my question and provided no reason for the sudden change of heart. He simply restated his order to stay put, without indicating whether my position was secure. Perhaps there had been some secret change in plans and, just as he had cared little about my dismissal, he now was indifferent to my staying on. Perhaps he just viewed the matter as being of no great concern to him. Whatever it was, I felt a heavy load being lifted from my heart, although I was not certain for how long, and I dared not leave lest my dismissal reappear some bright morning. But I could worry about all that later. Later I heard a rumor that when the minister visited the mayor in his office, he ordered that all the hospital doctors remain in their positions to prevent medical chaos, at least until all the changes planned for this field were put in place. So the minister's order kept me in the hospital for another four months. And after that I unexpectedly received a promotion rather than the demotion I had dreaded.[40] Still, for those four months I felt constantly worried and insecure, remembering my sins: my Zionism, my nationalism. And concern for what each day would bring[41] never left my mind.

The Bolsheviks placed a high value on public health, and the USSR made many improvements in the fields of health and medicine. Among the many benefits they brought in this area, free healthcare occupied an important place. The ability to consult with different doctors at no cost and universal access to hospitals were among the more important principles of medicine in the USSR. The same arrangement was implemented here, which led to two other decisions: to expand the hospital's internal medicine department, and to create a competent ambulatory clinic, where patients who were not bedridden could be seen and find counsel.[42] The expansion of the internal medicine department and its transfer to a new building created the need for another doctor to serve as my deputy while I remained the department's director. Among the top candidates was Dr. K., a Jew who was despised by his Christian colleagues and who acted as a private dispenser of medicinal drugs. He was also two-faced, narrow-minded, jealous, and nosy, always looking to see what was cooking in other people's pots. This slimy doctor was liked by the mayor, but I knew I could not work with him in peace. For these reasons, I referred another candidate, the young Dr. B.R. whose residency at the municipal hospital I supervised. He was far more honest, always respected me as his teacher, and appreciated my professional knowledge and experience. I tried to have him hired because I knew that as my deputy he would obey me and we could work together without friction. The chief doctor, who knew Dr. K.'s character, supported me. Our efforts bore fruit, and Dr. B.R. received an offer to become deputy to the director of the municipal hospital's internal medicine department.

But Dr. B.R., a young doctor who had managed to attract enough patients for a private practice, lacked hospital experience, and many disputed his appointment, particularly Dr. Jasaitis, the head of the Šiauliai health department. So Dr. B.R. began making personal visits to cultivate his relations with party leaders. He pretended to be an avid supporter of the Bolshevik regime and was clever enough to flatter the right people. That, along with support from me and the chief doctor, helped Dr. B.R. secure his job. He was also helped quite a bit by Dr. L., whom he was acquainted with and who had established himself by that time as the director of the hospital, in spite of many objections.

But even as Dr. B.R. was feeling more secure in his job, he was beginning to disappoint me. He accepted my authority inside the hospital but at the same time, he managed to penetrate the Šiauliai administration and, together with Dr. L., turned himself into something of an expert on local Šiauliai medical affairs. Meanwhile the question of my employment was brought up again. Dr. B.R. agreed that the department should be headed by a better "comrade" than me, someone with clearer leftist tendencies. But he would not agree to my outright dismissal, and so the advisors recommended that I remain at the hospital as a radiologist. This uncertain status lasted for several months, a time of worry, doubt, and dark thoughts about my future.

All this happened to me, as I said, because of my membership in the Zionist organization and my devotion to Hebrew culture. I never displayed a lack of support for the new regime, just the opposite. When I compared the Bolsheviks' treatment of the Jews with that of the Germans, I felt great warmth and gratitude toward the Bolshevik regime, and my behavior matched my feelings. Further aiding my positive views of the Bolsheviks was that after their arrival I could have correspondence with my family members in Moscow, and in particular with my brother, who became a respectable professor of "workplace health maintenance"—that is, a specialist in occupational diseases.[43] My nieces and nephews, moreover, are professionals in the various sciences: chemists, engineers, etc. The fact that Jews in the USSR could attain such high levels in science, as well as politically, at a time when the Lithuanians, with their inferior culture, began to put restrictions on us in science, commerce, and industry—not to mention the pathological cruelty of the Germans toward us—that alone was enough to make me admire and support the Bolshevik regime. But I did not get the chance to publicly demonstrate my positive feelings toward the regime as I would have liked. I once suggested to one of the Bolshevik activists that I give a series of lectures on hygiene, a topic on which I was an experienced speaker. This activist had heard one of my hygiene lectures before the Bolsheviks' arrival, and had been fascinated by it; but now, with the changed conditions, my offer went unanswered. Consequently Šiauliai's party leaders continued to regard me as a right-leaning Zionist, as in the old days, and they treated me with disdain. I was particularly offended by Comrade Furman, that crazy sadist who became the chair of the medical professional association.

The obvious question is, how did that tramp Furman, who was just a dentist with a foreign diploma, come to be elected chair of the medical association, which was made up not only of common medical workers but also of physicians, including some in high favor[44] and advanced in years?[45] Here is the answer: elections in those days were not conducted in the usual manner. Elements of the dictatorship took over and ruled everywhere. Leaders of the various professional organizations were chosen by this principle: party heads first got together to select the chairpersons and committee members and then presented them to the assembly, whose members would not dare to vote against the leaders' selections. That was how this power-mad ignoramus was selected as chair of our association.

As for the respected physicians mentioned previously, none of whom were named to the association's executive committee, their treatment by the chairman and party leaders was beyond despicable. It resembled the manner in which simpleton[46] rulers treated their learned subjects. Exceptions were the Drs. Jasaitis, L., and B.R., whom the party trusted; the other doctors counted for nothing. Most of the Christian doctors were no more than clerks, while the Jewish doctors were not considered part of society and were excluded from social and policy matters. But there were also some doctors who were publicly active and devoted much time to benefit the Šiauliai community. I was counted among the latter, but my community work was seen as tainted by Jewish nationalism and therefore a liability rather than a credit. Consequently I was met with antagonism everywhere I went. Here is an illustration: once, at a meeting, the nasty chairman would not recognize me to speak. When I insisted and he could no longer ignore me, he left the stage to demonstrate his disdain for my views, and when he returned he passed a note demanding that I stop speaking immediately. He often made a point of insulting me during banquets, although in truth I found this more ridiculous than insulting. My deputy, Dr. B.R., used to sit next to me during meetings. Sometimes Dr. L. would honor us with his presence and sit beside us. As was customary, the chairman would invite honored members to sit at the head table during the banquet and always included my younger neighbors, Drs. L. and B.R., leaving me, the senior doctor, alone and unacknowledged. Of course this was meant to show I remained a suspect member of the bourgeois class. For me however, the repeated insult was not especially hurtful and rather caused me to smile at the ridiculous ritual.

On one occasion I was truly insulted by one of our city's leaders. It took place in this way: several days after the mayor notified me of my firing and the abrupt reversal of this decree, I learned that the teachers in the Hebrew elementary school and gymnasium, all of them Zionists, had agreed to switch to teaching in Yiddish and to follow the Bolshevik regime's educational program, and as a result were allowed to remain in the Jewish schools. This made quite an impression since my own situation was not quite clear; the mayor's order to continue working had not fully reassured me about my job security. So drawing my own conclusions, I told myself this: educating a new generation in the Bolshevik spirit, as the party leaders see it, is an important responsibility and a top priority. Yet they allowed educators whose backgrounds were suspect to continue teaching without worrying that their bourgeois Zionist influence would pollute young minds. They were satisfied with the teachers' promises to teach in Yiddish and to submit to the regime's demands. If all that were so, of course a doctor of internal medicine and infectious diseases, who cares only for his patients' bodies and has nothing to do with their political views, should remain in his position and continue doing useful work.

I wanted to confirm this notion with the Šiauliai party leaders and explain to them the injustice of my firing and the resulting potential loss to the institute. Among all the officials of the Šiauliai party, I was specifically acquainted with "Comrade" Grinfeld, a seemingly polite young man who had graduated from the Hebrew gymnasium and spent a considerable time in prison for his association with the Lithuanian Bolshevik underground. I had examined this young man many times when he was a student, twice a year in my capacity as gymnasium doctor, and had often chatted with him. So I decided to approach him with my thoughts about the treatment of the Hebrew teachers and my conclusion regarding the connection between their treatment and me. I respectfully entered the party office and asked the guard to notify Comrade Grinfeld that Dr. Pick would like to talk with him. The guard returned quickly with a curt answer: "Comrade Grinfeld said that for hospital matters, you should see Dr. L.N." From this it was clear that my employment was still in question and that the matter I wished to discuss was obvious to him. He had "tipped his hand" that Dr. L.N. was in charge of hospital matters and therefore would decide my fate. On hearing Grinfeld's answer I did not argue, I merely turned back in frustration.[47] An unpleasant idea troubled my mind. In my whole adult life, no one had refused me an audience: not Russian clerks, nor French officials, nor the Lithuanians. Yet here an official of the new regime had declined to show even the appearance of respect with a face-to-face answer. "New birds, new songs."[48]

Regarding the new rules for free healthcare, one issue remained unresolved: creating a facility for walk-in patients. For some years, there had been a medical office near city hall where indigent patients could be examined for free for several hours a day. This office was managed by a Lithuanian-born German doctor who was terrible at treating patients but excellent at drinking liquor. This position had fallen to him thanks to his friendship with the previous mayor, Weil. When the Bolsheviks arrived this small, sloppy office was closed. In keeping with the Bolsheviks' plan to provide medical care to all those who needed it freely and efficiently, a central polyclinic was opened, with several departments headed by reasonably qualified doctors who knew what they were doing. The polyclinic was established in an appropriate building but without the most important element: a director to manage the clinic and its departments. The party officials and their advisors consulted with the head of the health department but had problems finding a decent candidate. Even the field of medicine lacked a supply of ready "cadres." The previous director of the clinic—the German doctor—was not an option. The other Christian doctors were already filling various administrative posts; plus, they owned houses and estates, making them suspect as anti-Bolsheviks. As for the Jewish doctors, there was me, Dr. L., and Dr. B.R., who already had jobs, and the rest of our colleagues—spineless, unprincipled people with no interest in politics or public affairs.

What united most of the Jewish and Christian doctors was that the job description for the new polyclinic director—a responsibility requiring the right experience, habits, and initiative for work in a public institute—did not fit any of them. They could be useful as medical advisors to the various departments but nothing more. The only exception among those who were available was one Jewish doctor, Dr. D., a talented man, a good speaker, with theoretical medical knowledge (though not practical) and an inclination for scientific research. This doctor deserved a decent job, particularly since he was always considered a leftist and a Yiddishist. Indeed, they had considered this doctor to replace me at the hospital, and all his life he had yearned for this kind of a job, to the point where he resented me because I held such a position. I should mention that this doctor was an honest man, with solid moral principles, who never thought I should be pushed out of my job for his benefit. One can assume that his insistence on treating me fairly helped avert my firing so he could replace me. Dr. Jasaitis offered Dr. D. the polyclinic director's position, but he was reluctant to become an administrator and have to order people around, and finally declined the offer. The party officials and Dr. Jasaitis found themselves in a difficult position: after Dr. D., they had no other decent candidates.

Around that time Dr. Jasaitis called me on the phone and asked if I would become director of the polyclinic. I knew nothing of Dr. D.'s rejection of that job and therefore did not pretend to hesitate or decline, as etiquette would dictate when another doctor had already rejected it. I wholeheartedly[49] said that the position interested me, and if I were not busy at the hospital, I would have accepted. But the offer excited me for several reasons: first, I was thrilled that the Bolsheviks had finally agreed to give me a responsible post in an esteemed public institution, since after all they had to know about this. Second, I hoped this job would allow me to slow down a bit after years of hard work in the hospital. My positive answer was received with satisfaction, and shortly an arrangement was made. Dr. D. and I were both invited to the office of the Šiauliai health department director, Dr. Jasaitis, and in a resolute tone that left no room for doubt, as was typical under the dictatorship, we were notified that I had been appointed director of the central polyclinic, and Dr. D. would succeed me as director of the departments of internal medicine and infectious diseases in the municipal hospital. We were both quite satisfied. Dr. D. finally had the job he had wanted since becoming a physician. He was certain he would be able to perform research there; moreover, he always believed that hospitals were the best possible places for treatment and cures. I, as I said, was satisfied that the party trusted me enough to place me in such a responsible job, managing nearly all the city's ambulatory care, and in particular with the raise in salary I would be receiving. I also thought that the work would surely be easier than managing two hospital departments while consulting with the others.

Later we both realized that we had been muddled in our vision[50] and were to be sorely disappointed. The work of healing is certainly more productive and consistent in a hospital [than elsewhere] because it is possible to examine a patient multiple times, give him the necessary attention, and observe changes in his condition over time. It is also possible to make use of the laboratory research that takes place in any respectable hospital. However, only a young and inexperienced doctor would assume that healing is always better in a hospital. Sometimes being at home surrounded by relatives, receiving their care and attention, is far more beneficial than being in the hospital. Moreover, a gravely ill patient who cannot be cured at home will often be no better off in the hospital. Of course, if the institution is headed by a famous professor "preeminent among ten thousand," or even just by an outstanding physician, the fate of many patients might be changed for the better. But if a young and inexperienced doctor is in charge of the hospital he can look forward to numerous disappointments. The many difficulties and disappointments he will encounter might leave him with feelings of guilt and annoyance that hinder his efforts at scientific research. With the mundane tasks of administration taking all his time and attention, little remained of Dr. D's aspirations for research and he did not publish a single paper in the medical journals.

My own misjudgment was even bitterer. My hope of finding an easier job after sixteen and a half years in the hospital was badly disappointed. I fell into a maelstrom in which I was bounced about like a ball and thrown every which way.

The polyclinic's work had expanded to an extent I could not have predicted. As I mentioned it had departments for nearly every major branch of medicine as well as a sizeable bureaucracy. A large dental clinic was there as well, and two emergency clinics outside the city were attached to it. They all required management and supervision. My responsibilities also included assigning doctors and nurses to the night shift—a difficult and complex task that required me to browbeat those who refused to work at night, even once or twice a month. In addition I chaired a committee that sent patients who belonged to professional associations to sanatoriums and special facilities in Lithuania and the USSR, and another committee that reviewed the health of those seeking drivers' licenses. I also had to examine patients seeking release from work, mental patients about to be institutionalized in Kalvarija,[51] and those called up for military service.

As can be seen from this, the work at the polyclinic was plentiful and diverse. I plunged in and committed my heart and soul to the work, fulfilling my allotted role faithfully and with vigor, and earned praise from all who visited our institution—and there was no shortage of visitors. Representatives of the local party came often to the clinic, as did important guests from Kaunas, Vilnius, and the USSR.

But success had a heavy price. During the first days of January (1941), when it was very cold, I stepped outside while my full body was sweating, both from hard work and from my quarrels with a colleague whose behavior did not bring much glory to our institution (a Russian doctor who courted the nurses with particular fervor). I caught a chill that inflamed the nerves of my left leg and right hand, leaving me on a bed of pain.[52] My agony was so terrible that I was biting my lips and grinding my teeth to keep from screaming. I was so miserable that for weeks sleep deserted me.[53] Every movement intensified my pain. I could neither sit nor lie down properly. This disease kept me in bed for six weeks. For three weeks I tossed and turned on my bed at home, and I spent three more weeks in a Vilnius hospital where I was treated with "short waves"[54] until the critical phase of my disease passed. But remnants of this disease kept bothering me for a long time, though not critically. Even today I have not fully recovered from this disease and occasionally still feel pain and weakness in the affected areas—a reminder of those days, which even with my illness were still so much better than the present! Now death and darkness surround us,[55] while back then we were filled with bright hope.

I should add that besides the bodily pain caused by my disease, I suffered serious mental anguish as well. The rule that "a prisoner cannot free himself, and a doctor cannot cure himself" was confirmed for me. With a bias toward severity, and knowing of the most complex and rare complications of a disease, a doctor can easily make a deformed judgment.[56] There is a neurological disease caused by a defect in the spine, which also includes anemia and low stomach acidity. Called *myelosis funicularis*,[57] it is serious and incurable. A person affected by this would be considered terminal. Two of its symptoms were present in my case: a lack of stomach acid and a low level of hemoglobin. With the newly added neurological symptoms, I concluded that I was afflicted by this deadly disease and that my days were numbered. Furthermore, I was certain that I would remain an invalid and unable to work until my death, which would come "speedily and soon."[58] And this disaster had occurred only two months after I had achieved success, winning a position that could bring me honor, respect, and a good salary. Contemplating this depressed and saddened me no end. Thinking of how my sick wife and my young son would be left without support, I shed many secret tears.

But to my great delight, in Vilnius I learned that my diagnosis was wrong, and my condition began to improve. The Polish professor and his neurology colleague assured me that I had only a simple inflammation of the nerves. Still, the mistake had left my mind deeply scarred, which added to the troubles that beset my and my wife's family during the Bolsheviks' brief rule here. Whenever I speak about our troubles under the Bolsheviks, I cannot avoid saying a hundred and one times that those troubles were less than nothing[59] compared with the mental and physical torture we are suffering under the new Amalek led by the modern-day Haman. Still, it is true that our troubles and woes during the Bolshevik time were enough to make people depressed and crushed in spirit[60] even before the arrival of the far more terrible Germans, who aim to destroy our entire nation without exception, for the sin of merely being who we are.

In his righteousness, the Holy One, blessed be He,[61] saw to it that the Bolsheviks lacked cadres and therefore had to turn to others, even those suspected bourgeois who had not been their supporters from the start. This I witnessed myself: first they fired me from my job at the hospital for the sin of Zionism. In the end, they gave me a far more responsible position, managing all the ambulatory care in Šiauliai. It is certain that Dr. Jasaitis recommended me to the party leaders and that Dr. L.N. had no choice but to agree when no better candidate was found to manage the polyclinic. Moreover my deputy, Dr. B.R., affirmed that my attitude toward the Bolsheviks was somewhat positive, particularly since my brother and other family members are in the USSR. But even if all these factors made up for my past sins, it was the shortage of cadres that first pushed them to consider a candidate like me.

Over time the party representatives in Šiauliai made their peace with me, enough so that when a meeting was held regarding public health in Šiauliai,

I was invited along with Drs. Jasaitis, L.N., and the "jewel" Furman. There I had the opportunity to meet the "big fish" of the Šiauliai party: Solovyov, the first-among-equals, a pleasant and charming man with a strong sense of law and justice in the old style, not the new; Jurgis, a man with a rough face, very unpleasant but also honest and well educated, a political prisoner for many years, and a zealous party member; [and] Slevičius, a product of Šiauliai from a despised family, a young man with talents developed during his seven years as political prisoner. He had schooled himself in the Lithuanian language, yet he inherited the crudeness of his ignorant, insolent father. Among those present were also the new mayor, Ulpis, and his deputy, inconsequential people, and several others whom I no longer remember. My participation on this committee convinced me of the incompetence of the new regime, which did everything in a rush without properly preparing people. While they had not erred in giving me my assignment, which as I said I performed faithfully and diligently, still there were many opportunities for failure. On one occasion there was a serious blunder: a candidate for the Seimas, whom the party trusted, was found to have been a provocateur, a former member of the tsar's secret service. Interestingly, after that first meeting, I encountered Solovyov several other times and he always greeted me warmly, particularly at a music school concert where after the first intermission he invited me to sit with him and the school director near the stage. They both were amazed at my understanding of music.

The party once honored me with a special mission; they ordered me to travel to Joniškis with an inspector from the NKVD, to confiscate the clinic and X-ray lab of Dr. Vitkūnas, who was then in prison and was later sent to Russia as an enemy of the state. (In the army, he had been part of the fascist "Iron Wolf"[62] battalion). This is not the place or time to detail the events of that mission or how the inspector tormented the doctor's wife like a cat with a mouse. That bright period passed all too quickly and we are left now to our lamentations under the spiked boots of the villains.

THREE

—ɯɯ—

MY SON'S ADMISSION TO THE LITHUANIAN UNIVERSITY

THINKING ABOUT OUR CITY'S SUFFERING during the Bolshevik period has actually become a source of solace to me now, as I find a kind of satisfaction in analyzing the details of the troubles they caused us. Emphasizing the dark sides of that period makes the light ones appear brighter, bringing out the positive aspects of the Bolshevik regime. Their defects were numerous, but their benefits were innumerable in comparison with the Germans. Yet the Bolsheviks did have their dirty side.

In addition to the bodily and emotional suffering caused by my neurological disease, with my imaginary and misleading diagnosis and also the business of my dismissal from the hospital, which left deep and lasting scars and depressed me immeasurably,[1] I received another sharp blow during the Bolshevik period. While it did not last long and its painful consequences passed quickly, it so shook my soul that even after the storm had passed it left a mark, an unpleasant memory not easily erased. I am referring to the rejection of my son's application to the university in Vilnius.

Since my son had no interest in pursuing a medical career like his father, he decided he should continue to study what had interested him in high school, that is, history and literature, which he liked very much. Therefore he applied for admission to the Faculty of Humanities of Vilnius University. His intention was to study in the history department, with no plan for a future career. After all he was still young, only eighteen. The antisemitic Smetona government had sharply restricted the admission of Jews to departments of medicine. Requirements that lawyers spend three years working in courts had effectively closed the law school to Jews as well. But other university departments, whose graduates' careers were not likely to be so lucrative and did not provoke such envy

31

among the citizens, were not so restricted. Therefore under the old regime, applicants like my son were not turned down. But now, under a new regime of freedom and equity, justice and law, they saw a young man who was only looking to learn, with no particular career aspirations, and rejected his request for admission to the university.

Why was this?[2] They found out that he was from a bourgeois family. Thus his fate was the same as that of many other young people, children of suspected bourgeois fathers, who were shut out of institutes of higher learning. Once again we ran into the regime's nice way of achieving social equality: visiting the guilt of the parents upon the children.[3] The university stated the principle that doctors were part of the bourgeoisie and therefore rich enough to provide for their children's higher education. When I received the infuriating notice that my son's university application had been rejected, my heart shrank as if afflicted with prickling briars.[4] This was particularly hard because my son had already lost a year since graduating gymnasium and had not had a job. He had used that year to serve the public, although the public never asked him to, and one could assume it had not been necessary. Leaders of Hashomer Hatzair[5] had recruited him to become an organizer, which meant postponing both study and career while he traveled about, setting up new branches and cells in which young people would prepare to rebuild the land of our forefathers. Obviously this work was for naught[6] and my son had wasted his time and talents for an entire year, since if there had been any way for young Jews to emigrate to Eretz Israel at that point, most would have left eagerly[7] with no encouragement required. Indeed, the limitations being placed on Jews then would have been motivation enough to leave. I also must confess that despite my wife's condition and her agitation over my son's decision to postpone his studies, I did not argue against it. I wanted him to experience life and become somewhat independent, and supporting himself for a year seemed worthwhile. I also thought he would grow bored and thus more motivated to resume his studies the following year. And my prediction was borne out: after a while he had had his fill of wandering and idleness and committed himself wholeheartedly to his studies. Our changed living conditions and the impossibility of making *aliyah*[8] after the Bolsheviks' arrival had a lot to do with the decision. Thus at the start of the academic year, my son applied to the university—and then, "O, misery!"[9] His application was rejected! The danger loomed that my son would never study again: If he remained out of school another eighteen months, he would have to report for military service, which would keep him away for another two years after that. More than four years away from learning and science would destroy his motivation to study, an irreversible loss.

My whole desire[10] was for my son to become a professional or, at least, to be educated in whatever field he chose, even if it offered no clear material prospects. If he excelled and mastered a field that he loved, which he surely would do with his talent and dedication, he would be happy and fulfilled as anyone who can rise above the mediocre would be.

That was my thinking in those early days. The university's rejection thus seemed like a catastrophe, a tragedy, and left me completely desperate. And how far are those thoughts now from our bitter reality! How much have world events altered our psychology! History has given us quite a lesson: on the one hand we learned that the independence of a small country is worthless; any slight wind can bring it down. But we also learned that one thing remains solid and never loses its value: a permanent national homeland. Both under the Bolsheviks and now under the rule of the evil regime, people attached to the land were treated with consideration. The larger portion[11] of the Lithuanian people did not leave their homes and were not driven from their land. And how forgiving is their homeland! Even those [Lithuanians] who showed pro-Bolshevik tendencies by taking substantial roles in the [Soviet] government later received forgiveness, pardons, and absolution. The villains accepted their excuses that the Bolsheviks had deceived, misled, or coerced them. That is how those who could claim this as their own native soil, their homeland, were treated. Although the Germans treat us [Jews] differently, even in the land of our forefathers, one can assume that if we truly had a homeland of our own, things would not have come to this; that the Germans would leave us to sit in peace under our own vines and fig trees,[12] because even a conqueror does not wish to see a vanquished land so ruined that it cannot be exploited.

Indeed! Happy is the nation that possesses its own homeland. Better a dry crust[13] and the skills to work our ancestral land than to live as wealthy professionals in exile, to be seen as aliens, unwanted and unneeded, with all our achievements as fragile as spiders' webs that any random breeze can blow away. This simple truth was always obvious, but during our time of trouble and distress it has been driven home to the depth of our souls. Too bad, too bad that our son did not make *aliyah* when that was still possible. Although parting from our only child would have been very difficult, particularly for my sickly wife, we have since had to endure separation from him many times, along with the fear that he might be taken from us violently and permanently, and we have suffered it all in silence.

The rector of the Vilnius university was Michael Biržiška[14] (he still serves in this position); he is known as an honest man, a true Lithuanian patriot, and to a large extent an idealist. Our paths had crossed several times in the past, providing me an opening to approach him. He, like his two brothers, also professors, had studied in the Šiauliai gymnasium, where I too earned my baccalaureate as an extern. His younger brother knew my younger brother, a professor in Moscow. Moreover his father was a doctor in the town of Viekšniai,[15] and more than once had invited me to visit his patients with him on consultations. I had also examined the father once after he fell ill with a terminal disease. Given all these connections, I decided to travel to Vilnius and plead my son's case for admission to the university in person.

I harbored a strong hope that an audience with this gentle, good-natured man would be fruitful, but I could not imagine that getting there would cause me so much anguish. I had to wait four days before I could get a meeting with the rector. And during my long wait, my hopes for success were plagued by doubts and uncertainty, which, combined with my impatience, infuriated and depressed me to the point that I was literally sick.

I treated Rosh Hashanah as if it were a regular day and on the morning of the first day of the holiday, which fell on Friday,[16] I arrived in Vilnius, hoping the rector would see me the next morning, as Saturday was a day on which he received callers. Imagine my surprise when the receptionist told me the rector had gone to Kaunas and would not be back until Monday. I was needed back at the polyclinic, and staying in Vilnius for several days was risky: the national health ministry had recently forbidden doctors from being absent without written permission. Such permissions were issued by Dr. Cohen, a strict and meticulous man; had I run into him in Vilnius then I would have "met my fate" which could have been quite harsh because he was far from a good-hearted or forgiving man. Still, I decided to chance it and tried to avoid thinking about the problems that would await me in the polyclinic while I forced myself to remain in Vilnius until Monday.

My impression of Vilnius, where I had once spent two of my best years, is a topic by itself, and this is not the place to discuss it in detail. In general, I will say that, in outward appearance, the city has seen many positive changes, but its inner life has not evolved similarly. As an aside I should note that during my three-day stay in Vilnius I visited my former students, the Morgenstern brothers, under whose roof I had stayed as their teacher and mentor forty years earlier. How different things were now and how much worse! In place of their former comfortable, spacious living quarters with all its richness and luxury, the entire family was now crowded into two rooms and a tiny kitchen, the part of their grand, gated house that had been allocated to them after it was nationalized. Poverty and decline were in evidence everywhere. The father had died, and the mother, bright and full of life in the past, was now old and sick. My elder

pupil, who lacked initiative and boldness, had remained unmarried with no occupation to provide for himself. His younger brother, who had taken over the
family business when the father died, was now also without work, and carried
the burdens of his complicated family. The decline of this once wealthy family,
particularly after the confiscation of both their house and the lumberyard that
had provided their livelihood, was pitiful to see and it depressed me to my soul,
adding to the pain caused by my son's trouble.

One detail does not really belong here, but my mind forces me to record it.
When I visited the Morgenstern family, I met one of the sisters. In the old days,
nearly forty years ago, I had nearly fallen in love with her and courted her with
the ardor of youth. A maiden, eighteen years old, beautiful, fresh, happy, and
full of joy, she had become a "cow of Bashan"[17] over the years—a fat woman
with few interests. Reflecting back on the long time that passed, I took account
of myself and realized that I too had aged, without achieving even half of my
aspirations, and my heart was faint.[18]

The emotional torment grew even worse when I saw how my son, who
thirsted for knowledge like a parched man for water, was excluded from the
university. We strolled the streets and met several of his friends, who as the sons
of proletarians had been admitted to the university and were already attending
lectures. It was torture to see how attentive my son was to details of one of the
professor's lectures as recounted by one of his friends. I will not soon forget
those painful and infuriating moments.

Monday morning I arrived at the rector's office early. I gave my card to the
receptionist and remained in the corridor to wait for the rector with others
who had arrived even earlier. Hours passed, and no visitors were being received
because the rector was not yet in his office. At noon the receptionist called
the rector's home and was told he had not yet returned from Kaunas because
important matters had delayed him; he would return to Vilnius tomorrow. My
sense of desperation grew: I had already spent three days in Vilnius without
a permit, and my further absence from the polyclinic could lead to a variety
of unpleasant complications. So I decided to return home, at least for a day,
and return to Vilnius Tuesday evening in order to report to the rector's office
Wednesday morning. I left my son in Vilnius to his vocal displeasure, and returned alone to Šiauliai in a depressed mood. There I met Dr. Jasaitis, the head
of the health department, and explained the reasons for my absence. I took care
of the most urgent matters at the polyclinic, and on Tuesday night returned
to Vilnius. I prepared for my conversation with the rector at length and in
detail. I rehearsed the conversation in my mind, collected the certificates and
Lithuanian-language papers that I had published, thinking they might prove

useful, and on Wednesday morning I appeared at the rector's office, armed with everything I had brought and prepared to highlight my virtues and accomplishments for a man I did not know and who held my son's future in his hands, or so I believed then.

The rector received me very cordially, likely because he saw himself as a son of Šiauliai and could see from my card that he was dealing with someone of importance in that town. As a matter of fact, the receptionist had given him my card on Tuesday when he returned from Kaunas; when I failed to appear in the office that day, because as I said, I had returned to Šiauliai, he had asked the receptionist about me. In response to my astonished complaint that my son had not been admitted to the university, the rector said that the university's humanities faculty had received eight hundred applications for three hundred openings, and could accept no more students than that. Given this state of affairs, they had to be scrupulous to a hairsbreadth when evaluating applicants, looking at their backgrounds and giving priority to the sons of true proletarians. The admissions committee also included party officials from Vilnius, who had received detailed information about the applicants from many cities, including Šiauliai. It was worth pointing out, the rector added, that Jews were particularly strict and rigorous when reviewing applicants of their own nationality, much more than they were for others. The rector also felt free to share some details that he said could only be "discussed among friends." Among these, he told me that if he tried to intercede for certain applicants and took up their cause he might put the university at risk. Regarding my son's application, he said it was rejected because, first, party members on the admissions committee had learned of my involvement with a suspect political group (the Šiauliai Zionist organization), and second, they saw on the application that I had graduated from medical school in Paris. They immediately concluded that if I had gone as far as Paris to study, rather than in nearby Germany, which had plenty of medical schools, I must be from a wealthy, bourgeois family, rich enough to let me spend years having fun in that famously expensive city. Hearing these words, I felt obligated to tell the rector my real history, as follows:

I was born into a family with many children—seven in all—the son of a wretchedly poor[19] *melamed* and a baker.[20] I had a traditional Jewish education in the fullest sense, attending cheders and yeshivas. My parents, old-fashioned religious Jews, wanted me to prepare to become a rabbi by studying the Talmud and rabbinic literature. But new ideas were in the air in those days, and the spirit of freedom even penetrated the yeshivas, those fortresses of ancient learning and custom. And so I started to study secular subjects, even though a bit late, and after some time I obtained a certificate to teach elementary school, which made it possible for me to get a job in the Šiauliai Talmud Torah, a government school.[21] I worked for six years in that school, and during that period I studied for my baccalaureate and passed tests at the Šiauliai gymnasium, first in four departments, then in six other departments. Finally I obtained the baccalaureate I had so hoped for. Even while employed at the Talmud Torah, I worked hard to pass these exams. My diligence and hard work can be shown by my mastery of Russian language and literature, which earned me the highest grade, even though I was self-taught and taking a test in a foreign language—and also despite the fact that the Russian language instructor, Archangelski ("Dimitri," said the rector as I was telling my story, as he had been his teacher, too) was not known as a "philosemite," to say the least.

After obtaining the baccalaureate, I left my position at the Talmud Torah and started working as a private instructor, which resulted in a much better income. (Among my pupils, I inserted proudly, was the daughter of Count Zubov from Ginkunai,[22] a close acquaintance of the rector.) I had to remain in Šiauliai giving private lessons for two full years to save enough money to execute my plan, which was to travel abroad and enroll in a school of higher learning, because my efforts to enroll in a university in tsarist Russia had failed.

After two years I managed to save enough to travel to Paris, where one of my married sisters lived, hoping to shelter under her roof. But in Paris I found my sister gravely ill and unable to support me at all, so I lived the life of a poor student with all that implies for two years. When my meager savings ran out I experienced poverty and deprivation like any poor student in a foreign country with no material support. I was forced again to engage in private tutoring: to some I taught Latin, to others, mostly foreign students, I taught the first course required in medical school—the famously difficult and complicated "P.S.N."

My younger brother, who had befriended the rector's younger brother, meanwhile finished his medical studies in Dorpat[23] and settled in Novoalexandrovsk.[24] The world war carried him to the USSR, where he found the right circumstances to finish his studies and become a famous professor in the field of occupational medicine. I, after completing my studies at the Paris medical school, returned to my motherland, Lithuania. Here of course I remain a simple physician, but I try as hard as I can to not be merely a writer of prescriptions. Now and then I take up various scientific issues and publish scientific papers in different journals. A letter I received from Radvilas, the editor of the monthly *Kultūra*, who read my article, "Jews and Medicine" in the journal *Medicina*, can testify to the quality of my papers. In it he wrote that my paper provided a great deal of information that would be of interest even to nonphysicians. Therefore he asked me to write an article for *Kultūra* on a topic I had touched on in the *Medicina* article, namely "Medicine in the Holy Scriptures." Following his request, my article appeared in two issues of *Kultūra*.

As a matter in passing, that article led to my meeting with the education commissar, Venclova,[25] because one of the issues that carried my article "Medicine in the Holy Scriptures" also carried one of his articles. I took advantage of the rector's forbearance and his attention to my somewhat long story and showed him my baccalaureate [certificate], the letter from Korsakas-Radvilas, the *Kultūra* issues, and a collection of my papers that were published in the Lithuanian-language journal *Medicina*. After the rector glanced at the material I had brought, which supported my words with real evidence, I asked his forgiveness for taking advantage of his generous attention and said I was about to end my long talk with a few additional words. I did not want to look like an annoying Jew, but concern for my son's fate had literally made me crazy, driving me to do whatever was necessary. And after all, the rector had put up with me, listening to my story attentively, with apparent interest. I should note that during our long conversation I did think about the other visitors, waiting impatiently outside in the hall. So I continued to tell my story as briefly and simply as possible.

Now I am an old physician, I said, in poor health, without money, unable to build a house on land I have owned in Šiauliai for about ten years. While I receive decent compensation for my work, my wife[26] is seriously ill and requires frequent trips to medical centers abroad, which cost me a fortune. My only hope is that my son will continue our family tradition, concentrating on his studies in history and languages. This has been his preferred field since gymnasium and one in which he excels. I reminded the rector that I had treated his father and that I had once had dinner at their home. I ended our discussion by asking the rector to do what he could for my son for "the sake of the past and the present." He listened attentively and asked me to submit an official request with my name on it. I rushed to respond and traveled back home full of hope, confident that the issue would be resolved favorably. And so it was: after a few days, we received the news to our boundless joy, that our son was admitted to the university. We did not predict nor did we sense the bad and bitter days that followed—that we would become like filth and refuse,[27] the scum of humanity, removed not only from schools of knowledge but from all of human society and its cultural accomplishments.

Both my dismissal from my job and my son's rejection by the university had been reversed. Yet they left deep marks in my mind that would not be quickly erased. Their memory did not fade even after the Germans came. Along with the misery of my own illness and my emotional agony, my cup of poison was full. Thus do most of the few [Šiauliai Jewish] survivors keep going, bent under the weight of troubles that began under the Bolsheviks and that will end who knows how?

The Jews, whose participation in Lithuania's commerce and industry had been significant, suffered under Bolshevik rule along with all Lithuanians. They endured a procession of sorrows: nationalization, confiscation, imprisonments, deportation.[28] They endured being crammed into crowded apartments. Those of us who were nationalists watched in agony as Hebrew culture was suppressed, with Hebrew schools closed, Hebrew books removed from libraries, national party leaders imprisoned, etc. I personally had to hide a long manuscript I had written in Hebrew lest it be found in my home—an unforgivable sin! Hebrew, in the Yevsektsiya's[29] opinion, is saturated with antirevolutionary spirit, religious zeal, and an antidemocratic sense of class hierarchy. Moreover my book portrays the Zionist devotion of one of the Bund's[30] leaders in a positive light, which of course is objectionable. In short we suffered much under the Bolshevik regime, both as Jews and as nationalists. Nevertheless, we tolerated these agonies, endured our plagues, and bore in silence the destruction of our economic status and of Hebrew culture. All could be forgiven because we knew and bore witness[31] that, if not for the Bolsheviks, we would have long ago become the prey[32] of our local beasts and would soon be trampled under our western neighbor's boots, which we now feel all too much.

In the Bolshevik days, despite all the pressures and unpleasantness, at least we were not in the hands of murderers whose brutality has no precedent: cold and indifferent, calculated and gradual. Indeed, many of us were "raised up" to respectable jobs and good salaries. Further, we felt like human beings, respected citizens with equal rights. As long as we were innocent of "bourgeois crimes" such as speculation, schools and academies would be open to our sons, and many even received significant support. Therefore, we preferred living under the Bolsheviks to the Lithuanians and Germans, even though we suffered, as I said, more than the general Lithuanian population—even more than the estate owners and *kulaks*.[33] They at least were allowed to keep thirty hectares[34] of land and any necessary buildings, unlike wealthy Jews, who were relieved of all their assets and set aside like empty vessels.[35] Yet we remained quiet, and many of us considered ourselves fortunate, and rightfully so, since, compared with the distress and chastisement[36] that followed, it was like living in paradise.

FOUR

—꿍—

ON THE EVE OF WAR

ALTHOUGH WE DID NOT KNOW it, the end of the Bolshevik regime was slowly approaching. Some in the leadership understood that war between the USSR and Germany was coming and hinted to their underlings that it was time to prepare for what could happen in the coming days. First, they suggested that to avoid trouble, they should eliminate any risk of a "fifth column"—suspicious people who might aid the enemy "in the event of war."[1] This was a correct and desirable goal, but again they had a shortage of people who understood how to execute it properly and effectively. So what did our 'honored guests' do? How would they accomplish this mission? Overnight on June 14 [1941], active members of the [Communist] Party assembled at party headquarters like robbers in a thieves' den,[2] along with Red Army soldiers, and paired off: one party member, one soldier. And then in a perfect display of provincial Bolshevik cruelty and illogic, in the middle of the night the pairs spread out across the city and broke into the homes of formerly bourgeois Jews and Christians whom they suspected as counterrevolutionaries.

Impoverished former merchants and ex-officials who had earlier been dismissed from their jobs were arrested along with their family members. When the patrols could not find the head of a family they were content to take members of the household, including women and infants. These were locked into railcars designed for horses and oxen, which were waiting in the station. Men and women, youths and maidens, civilized and cultured people, were now confined in these wagons, with only a hole in the floor through which to relieve themselves. What a disgrace! The Bolsheviks allowed the prisoners to take only a few necessities. The rest of their belongings—furniture, household and kitchen items—were inventoried and sealed into the "offenders'" houses until they could be appropriated and taken away for the benefit of the government.

Among those arrested on that night of wrath[3] was the family of my brother-in-law Zilberman. My brother-in-law, who had earlier been thrown out of his own factory, "Šiauliai Fabrics," worked as a simple laborer in Kaunas. My wife's sister Paula stayed in their home. A wealthy and elegant woman, she was "reared in the purple."[4] Her eldest son, a talented young man, had been barred from the university as the son of a bourgeois, and had enrolled in business school, a refuge for all those similarly excluded. Her young son was an excellent student in the Hebrew gymnasium. They all were awoken at 5:00 a.m. Bengis, Slavich's brother-in-law and one of Šiauliai's Bolshevik leaders, entered their home along with a Red soldier and arrested them, saying nothing about either the cause or the consequences. The Zilbermans thought they were being punished for being bourgeois. They took nothing with them, wearing only summer clothes and carrying nothing. Their captors found 3,000 rubles in Paula's pocket, and let her keep 1,000, pocketing the rest: this was not permitted even by the tsarist secret service, yet it was permissible for the Bolshevik functionaries in a little Lithuanian town,[5] hooligans who had managed to change their hides but not their nature, particularly when dealing with members of the bourgeoisie to whom the law gave no protection.

We notified our brother-in-law of this catastrophe that same day. He rushed back from Kaunas and turned himself in to the Bolsheviks, who in their abundant kindness,[6] agreed to lock him in the same wagon as his wife and two sons. The nights had grown cold and the prisoners shivered inside their livestock wagons. The guards treated them like seriously dangerous criminals and did not allow them to bring warm clothes. They were scarcely permitted even bread to eat and water to drink.

That is when my wife, full of initiative and courage, jumped into action and began to shake the cosmos. She ran from one official to another—from Solovyov, the head of the Šiauliai Communist Party, an honest and likeable man, to Itzkovich, the NKVD chief, a cruel and miserable man, to the mayor, Ulpis, a man of large physical dimensions but an intellectual lightweight. She lobbied to be allowed to bring warm clothing, boots, and bedding to protect her sister's family from the cold, and equip them for a long trip, since she had heard a rumor that they were being taken to far-off Siberia.

My wife managed to get the officials' permission but still needed the approval of Vice-Mayor Kopilov, a crude, hard-hearted man, and his secretary, Furman, a small-minded sadist who had been promoted repeatedly. The latter ruled that the Zilberman family "had already lived long enough in luxury," and therefore permitted only one warm coat, one duvet and one blanket for the family of four. My wife's tears and begging did not help; finally, we were forced to clandestinely pass them some of our own belongings through the railcar's opening. This kind of cruelty toward innocent people—among them such dangerous "counterrevolutionaries" as Alexander Lipkin and his sons; Zalmanovich, Shlapobersky, Reznik, Leizerovich, etc., etc., people who were as far removed from politics as East is from West—this unnecessary and illogical cruelty distanced many hearts from the Bolsheviks, hearts that had previously considered them with favor, even with love. It demonstrated again the injustice, meanness, wickedness, and stupidity[7] through which party members sought to carry out their plans.

It was muttered quietly then that their real intent was to remove "dangerous" Lithuanians—estate owners, officials, kulaks, heads of wealthy enterprises—and that Jews had only been arrested out of fear of "what the gentiles might say"—that is, for balance. But there are two responses to this: first, balance could have been achieved with a far smaller number of arrested Jews; and second, why was this done with such overflowing fury,[8] vengeance, and cruelty? Prohibiting them from taking warm clothing, which ended up in the hands of the partisans,[9] was certainly unnecessary, as was seizing the prisoners' remaining property, the use of cattle cars, and the imprisonment of women and toddlers. There is indeed a shred of truth in the assumption that the Jews were imprisoned for balancing purposes. But in the end these "wise ones" could not see and anticipate the terrible consequences[10] for our country, a catastrophe like no other for the Jews.

When the Germans arrived, the Lithuanians blamed the deportation of their countrymen and the destruction of their families on the Jews, whom they identified with the Bolsheviks. This revived the age-old Jew hatred that had existed in the hearts of Lithuanians who, like others, see us as aliens and competitors. This hatred ignited like hellfire, consuming hundreds of thousands of Israelite souls in the bitter days that followed.

It is worth mentioning that Mayor Linkevičius, who was always mean and cruel, became a real Jew-hater after the Bolsheviks took his wife and his daughter while he was away from home. This was the last great undertaking of the local Bolsheviks, whose savagery and cruelty were to our detriment. It will never be erased from the memory of those who witnessed it. This was the final chapter of Bolshevism's record in Lithuania—a record replete with both light and darkness, positive and negative achievements, justice and injustice,[11] and the source of our later disaster[12] as it gave the Lithuanians an opening to take revenge on us during German rule.

Reaching a final verdict on Bolshevik rule in Lithuania raises too many sad thoughts to absorb.[13] If not for their sudden departure, the balance could have been positive: Jews had plenty of privileges, occupied respectable positions and could participate in cultural life, albeit a biased one. Our children could receive an education, although that too was biased. But when the Bolsheviks were forced out, they left us to our troubles, and the latent result of their rule was disastrous. In the end the damage done by this government exceeded its benefits. The initial shine of equality and liberty was tarnished quickly, and prepared the way for the terrible massacre of Lithuanian Jews. Whatever their motive, the Bolsheviks' actions regarding the Jews led the Lithuanian savages to turn their land into our valley of slaughter and add new pages, soiled with blood like none other in our sad history, to our book of tears, which was already full of lamentations, dirges, and woes.[14] Since we were exiled from our land, our lot has been destruction and injury.[15] In every generation they rise up to destroy us,[16] and we are the scapegoat[17] blamed for the world's troubles. Our pains never cease, and our mothers weep like Rachel[18] for their children, who are led like innocent sheep to slaughter. Yet our history, which is so full of troubles and disasters, has not seen such a bitter period as this, with no end and no escape in sight.

In previous times there were three barriers to catastrophe:

(a) **Faith**. It gave strength to the weary[19] and courage to the oppressed; enough, indeed, to let those being tortured ascend the Inquisition's pyres and die as martyrs. It gave them the patience to carry on through trouble and anguish, awaiting better days in this world and a reward in the next. In our era most of us, and most of our children, have lost these precious traits. Today even many former believers feel like Elisha ben Abuyah when he saw Hutzpit's tongue in a pig's mouth.[20]

(b) **Emigration**. Our ancestors used to follow the rule: "If we cannot find success in this land, we will find it in another" and would move in large numbers from a country where they were oppressed to another. During the Middle Ages they fled to Poland and Lithuania from the restrictions and killings in Germany. The Jews who were expelled from Spain found shelter in North Africa and Turkey. In the last century, refugees from the Russian pogroms escaped to America and South Africa. And now the entire world has closed to us, and we have no escape, no refuge.

(c) **Conversion**. In times past, to survive mortal danger many Jews converted, either genuinely or merely outwardly. There is a belief that even Maimonides and his young son briefly accepted Islam to escape those who wished to kill them. Maimonides is also said to have taught that our sages' decree "better to be killed than to transgress" referred only to paganism and sun worship, not to religions based on monotheism such as Islam. Yet now even this remedy is lost to us. Now comes the "little corporal"[21] who ruled that the racial theories of Chamberlain[22] and his ilk are true and valid and that malignancy is in Jewish blood, making Jews swindlers and cheats by their very nature. Therefore there can be no cure other than eradication, removal from under the heavens or through the Lithuanian partisans' bullets. These are our current savages.

Now all these former barriers have vanished, making our time unique among all our past bad periods.

The Bolsheviks did not appear to expect that they would soon be fleeing Lithuania in urgent haste.[23] They continued with their massive programs as if nothing was coming, preparing a new and much more extensive list of enemies of the revolution, whom they planned to deport from Šiauliai and its surroundings just like those who were sent to the USSR on June 17 [1941]. The famous Slavich, who is known to have said that the bourgeoisie needed to be swept away like dung,[24] intended to carry this out. And some who were in the know said the new list of counterrevolutionaries would include almost all physicians, except Jasaitis, Ubinsky, Levin, Brumberg, and Dr. Directorovich. The scandalous earlier night raids and deportations had not satisfied the Šiauliai [party] members, and their hunger to eliminate all bourgeois "enemies of the revolution" was insatiable. But they did not have the chance to execute these agitated schemes, just as they did not get to enjoy the property of those they deported.

It might indeed be a shame that the second deportation did not take place, because without a doubt the condition of those Jews who were transported to the vast forests and icy steppes of Siberia is much more pleasant and comfortable than ours. True, they certainly suffer from cold and starvation,[25] some of them have been tormented by bombs, and their youths have most likely been conscripted. Yet they certainly are not suffering humiliation, indignity, and death[26] at the hands of the murderers surrounding us.

THE START OF THE WAR

EVENTS IN ŠIAULIAI DURING THE first four days of the war, before the Germans arrived, illustrate the state of mind of the party and of the general population.

Among the Bolshevik regime's faults one can add excessive paperwork: orders, instructions, and demands flooded all their institutions almost daily. Add to that the questionnaires, statistics, recommendations, and general rules, all expressed in writing, and you can see how offices were literally "drowning in paper." At times the orders and instructions had nothing to do with the actual purpose of those organizations, leading to doubts and hesitation, which required inquiries and clarifications. Because of these doubts and questions and the various problems that required solutions, and also because of the desire to match the rules with those in effect in medical institutes in the USSR, Dr. Jasaitis, the head of the Šiauliai health department, decided to travel to Moscow for several days. Dr. L. was left in charge during Dr. Jasaitis's absence.

On the morning of June 22, a Sunday, a telephone order was received from Dr. L. that all physicians working in the central polyclinic and ambulatory clinics in the suburbs—the polyclinic's branches—should gather in the polyclinic. After some time, when all the doctors were finally assembled, Dr. L. arrived along with the city's deputy commandant. Both seemed agitated and a bit angry. They announced ceremoniously that war had begun between the USSR and Germany, that there had already been six aerial raids and that there had been injuries. As the polyclinic's director, I mentioned that there was no need to keep all the doctors here; if we did the rest of the city would be left without adequate medical help. I did not expect what happened next. Dr. L. immediately made it known that during times of emergency there needed to be military rule. He assumed an attitude of prince and commander[1] and announced loudly: "This is what I order. And that's it!" And that is how he made it clear that he was prepared to enforce his position, using a strong arm and the presence of the deputy commandant. His haste and militaristic tone almost made me laugh but I managed to keep it to myself. At that moment I decided not to challenge the authority of this chameleon in the presence of a military official. But after a few hours Dr. L. changed his mind, and heeding my advice, he ordered those doctors who weren't needed in the polyclinic to leave. He had been unnecessarily overwrought, and the war's outbreak caused confusion and panic. Even though he was supposedly one of the top leaders, he was not prepared to do his job. A king for a moment, he was among the first to bolt.

Meanwhile, Dr. Jasaitis had picked the right moment to return home. The day the war began he was already in Latvia, and he managed to cross the Lithuanian border to his homeland—a homeland that would forgive sins and forget the suspicious past of a son and citizen who knows how to adjust to the requirements of the moment. Jasaitis's past behavior toward the Bolsheviks evaporated like a cloud,[2] and he rose to greatness all over again: his old position was waiting for him as if nothing had ever happened, because after all, he was a loyal son of his homeland. All he did was in its name and for its sake. Yes! The homeland! How great is its value to the populace and to the individual!

The war went on in its full intensity across the German-Lithuanian front. Although the city of Šiauliai was happily not close to the front, several bombs still fell here, and frightening explosions could be heard. Several homes were set afire and their occupants injured by shrapnel, including some seriously, putting their lives in danger. Such patients were sent to the hospital, while those who were lightly injured were treated in the polyclinic. From its first day the war threw terror into the Jewish community: we felt there was serious trouble ahead, and many of us thought about hitting the road to seek shelter in the villages and towns along the Latvian border. Party leaders also started to fear for their own precious lives. But they were unconcerned about what would happen to those not in the party, and did not try to provide any means of rescue in case the Russians retreated.

The sounds of cannons firing and bombs falling intensified that evening around the city and its suburbs. Jewish residents, who were the most agitated, rushed to hide in the spacious basement of the Commerce Institute. A large crowd also gathered in the basement of the polyclinic, most of them carrying pillows and duvets for bedding. The crowding was intense, the lack of air was suffocating, and the fright overtaking all of us was terrible. Every shot caused panic. On the second day, rumors spread that the Germans had already captured Tauragė,[3] which was burning; that they were approaching Kelmė,[4] which had also been torched by the Russians; and that the Russians were retreating along the entire front. Party leaders trembled, realizing that if the Germans arrived, they would become the first scapegoats. Thus by the second day they had begun protecting the more important comrades and did not care for the lives of other officials, particularly Jews, who faced an even more serious threat. I decided to try to speak to Solovyov—one of the more honest Šiauliai Bolsheviks and a top leader—about evacuating Jewish officials who would be in grave danger should they fall into German hands. I went to the party headquarters but could not enter, as the guard was allowing only card-holding party members in.

I realized to my disappointment that members were worried only about their own precious lives and did not care about the other officials who worked in the regime's various institutions. As I left the headquarters with no results, I saw next to the building a large bus, filled like a cage with party servants and members of their households, and a large cargo bus, probably intended for the refugees' goods. I took a few steps toward Dvaro Street, and there on the corner with Aušros Avenue stood a light bus. At its door stood Dr. L. and Furman and also Petrauskas, the director of the Finance Department. As I approached them, the first two "jewels" rushed to board the vehicle. Furman, as usual, ignored me, a "damned Zionist." But Dr. L. honored me with a handshake, and when I asked about the fate of the polyclinic, he answered that the doctors could leave and go home. As we were speaking, the bus's doors closed—"Have a safe journey!" And I was left standing in wonder. These were your Šiauliai Bolshevik party leaders! This was like a captain deserting his sinking ship, leaving the passengers in God's hands. However, before reaching the border, Dr. L. reconsidered his hasty decision to flee the battle while the outcome was in doubt and decided to return to Šiauliai. In the evening, when he unexpectedly called the polyclinic, he realized that since we had received no official order we had not followed his advice and [had instead] continued carrying out our assignments. The polyclinic continued to operate.

In any event, fear of the Germans was growing among the Šiauliai population and particularly, of course, among the Jews. A panicked flight from town began. The comrades ran toward Joniškis, hoping to enter the USSR through Latvia. Others who had been scared by the bombs ran for their lives to the towns and villages surrounding Šiauliai. Many women and children attached themselves to Bolshevik family friends who were leaving town. On the third day even the military hospital left Šiauliai, taking Dr. Rakuzin and his family along. The refugees were terrorized by German aerial attacks on the trains and other modes of transportation, which caused many casualties. The railroad was also damaged at various points, increasing the danger. But this did not stop the flight from the city because there was no choice: as the Germans neared, fear kept intensifying. The escape was not organized at all; each wandered his own way.[5] But most of the refugees headed toward Latvia, following the comrades who as I said, cared only for themselves. Left to the beasts were even their most loyal men who merely had not possessed a party card, such as the director of the "Batas"[6] factory and the director of Šiauliai Fabrics,[7] Mr. T.S. The latter turned on the third day to the city commandant, asking for permission to leave the city because he had a high-level position and because his son, a leading Lithuanian Bolshevik and former political prisoner, was in mortal danger. Mr. T.S. was accompanied by several people, including me, all of us driven by fear of the Germans.

I would definitely not have left the city without knowing my son's whereabouts—he had remained in Vilnius without any means—but as the Russians say, "asking is not a catastrophe, and trying is not a sin." I just wanted to know if it would even be possible to flee. I had had an odd thought: since it would be impossible to get to Vilnius, maybe it was worth going to Latvia and trying to smuggle ourselves into Vilnius from there, going "all around the barn" to try to find our only son, about whom we were so worried we could neither rest nor sleep. The city commandant was confused, and he sent us with a military escort to the stationmaster. The latter promised to give us an answer about the possibility of leaving Šiauliai that evening, because at that moment the tracks were damaged and no trains were running. In the evening T.S. called. He had received a clear answer from the commandant: "There is no need to leave the city. Help is on the way and there is no longer a danger. Sit back and relax."

The commandant's calm reassurance, which proved illusionary and baseless, demonstrated the confusion and disorder that then existed among the Bolsheviks. This was shown even more clearly when Dr. L., who had reappeared to take charge, promised to get me a pass to be on the streets after the city's 8:00 p.m. curfew, something I needed as a doctor. On the third day, I stayed in the polyclinic in the afternoon, along with another doctor, who stayed to help out in case any of the injured required surgery. We both awaited the promised permit. Evening was coming. Eight o'clock passed, the permit did not arrive, and we remained, stranded, unable to leave the polyclinic without a pass. We called around and discovered that Dr. L. was in an endless meeting of the remaining party members, obviously trying to determine the best time and method for getting out of town. Hungry, thirsty, and impatient, we kept calling, asking that they give us a way to leave the polyclinic and go home. At half past eleven,

Dr. L. finally arrived, carrying some complicated permits, which he delivered to us ceremoniously. They were signed by the city's chief of the guard and were given on condition that we return them in the morning. The leaders obviously did not anticipate that by morning they would already be far from Šiauliai.

Dr. L. also had several permits for doctors at the municipal hospital. He headed there, and I accompanied him as far as my home street. On the way I asked him if the comrades had discussed a plan to evacuate Jewish doctors from Šiauliai. Dr. L. admitted that the question had not been brought up at all because it was impossible to execute such a plan and that if there were danger, it would simply be, as the French say, every man for himself.

At night, frequent blasts shook the entire city. The Germans were dropping bombs ceaselessly across the entire front, attacking the retreating Russians, but the terrible thuds reverberated as if within the city. Our neighbors, Dr. B. and the lawyer G., along with their families, lay on the floor in our hall the whole night, believing that it was safer to stay between the walls. We too moved from the bedroom to the dining room and lay on the sofa, which was farther from the window than our beds. Thus we all behaved, in our childish naiveté, without logic or thought, demonstrating the fear that overtook us all.

On the fourth day, after a sleepless night, I got up and went to the party headquarters. I intended to make an extra effort to see Solovyov to discuss the polyclinic's future. When I reached the headquarters, I saw a sad picture: all the doors were wide open and unguarded, allowing anyone who wanted to enter freely the innermost part. I stood there a few moments, wondering and amazed until a guard, an old acquaintance whose family I had treated, approached me. He too was amazed and told me that he had no idea what had happened here overnight. At my request he admitted me into the holy of holies,[8] Solovyov's office, where an ordinary person could normally never set foot. The office was well organized and in order, as if waiting for its owner: on the desk were a shiny typewriter, a telephone, and proper writing implements. Lenin's and Stalin's works were proudly displayed on the bookshelves along with other propaganda books in Russian.

Then the guard showed me the stairs leading to the central heating basement. The stairs were filled with luggage and suitcases, thrown around without any order. Most likely they were left behind for lack of room or time. The flight appeared to have been hasty and abrupt, leaving many documents undestroyed. Many of these later fell into the hands of the [Nazi-backed] Lithuanian secret police, bringing disaster on many people. As I mentioned earlier, the Communists also left behind many loyal people, sealing their doom at the hands of their tormentors. From all these events, particularly the passes that were to be returned in the morning, signed by the city's chief of the guard himself, you may consider for yourself how flawed was the information and organization of the Lithuanian Bolsheviks. They did not know what was awaiting them within even an hour or two.

Thus ended the Bolshevik period in Šiauliai (and in other Lithuanian cities). And so began the most terrible page in our history—a history already filled with mourning and moaning,[9] with torture, exile, martyrdom, and forced conversion. Some who fled with the Bolsheviks or followed them returned to Šiauliai with only their last breath to look forward to[10] after being turned back at the Latvian border or barred from entering the USSR because they were not party members. Along the way they experienced enormous dangers, putting their lives in peril.[11] When they returned home, they discovered their property looted, their homes left like empty vessels.[12] This was only a minority, however. The majority remained in Latvia, where they now are crushed by oppression, misery, and sorrow[13] in concentration camps.

It is worth mentioning how many common Lithuanian villagers began to bare their fangs as soon as they were freed from Bolshevik control. They stopped selling food to the refugees and, in one example, new self-appointed "rulers" from Lygumai[14] chased away all Jewish refugees within a half hour of that town. It is difficult to avoid a comparison here between the Jewish refugees' return to their demise and extinction and the return of Jasaitis to his homeland in honor and wealth. Jasaitis's past open Bolshevism was forgotten and forgiven while most of the refugees, merchants, and communal workers, who had suffered greatly under the enemies of the bourgeoisie, were later tortured brutally for being Bolshevik supporters.

That is how the Jews became caught in a vicious cycle that squeezes and chokes our souls: the present harassment, persecution, and deprivation of human rights increase Jewish sympathy for the Bolsheviks, who did not distinguish between Jews and other nationalities and who gave the Jews full human rights and safeguarded their lives. Such sympathy in turn inflamed the desire for vengeance and retribution[15] by those who hated the Bolsheviks, and on and on. In response to our persecution by the modern-day Haman, American Jews filed protests, which brought a new wave of persecutions as punishment for the protests. This is the vicious cycle that encloses the Jews, leaving us no shelter and no escape.

SIX

THE GERMANS ENTER ŠIAULIAI

WAR WAS DECLARED ON JUNE 22, and at dusk on the twenty-sixth, we suddenly saw Germans strolling on the sidewalk outside our window. We saw, and our eyes went dark! We knew their attitude toward Jews and what they did to our brothers in Germany and Poland; now our despair knew no bounds. The Germans' entry obliterated our hopes; our hearts stopped as if in mourning for one who died prematurely. We had hoped the Amalekites would get their just deserts from the Russians: in the event of war, they would surely be defeated by the glorified[1] Red Army, which was unmatched in its heroism, at least according to the pompous folk songs and the Bolshevik military anthems that we had believed wholeheartedly. Suddenly, such disappointment! Our agonized train of thought went as follows: the Russians prepared twenty-three years for a defensive war that could even become an offensive war. They lived in poverty, virtually naked and barefoot. They confiscated their citizens' property and spent its inestimable value to defend and arm their homeland, all the while boasting and threatening anyone who might dare touch the USSR.

We wanted to believe, so we placed our trust in the Bolsheviks and hoped they would protect and shelter us from the mad tormentor,[2] a psychotic who blames the Jews for everything. We consoled ourselves with such hopes, and suddenly they were gone, flown away like a dream.[3] After all their boasting, the arrogant Bolsheviks ran from battle like rabbits, and the bravery of the world's most celebrated pilots became less than nothing, a nullity.[4] Soon after the first clash we realized that to our pain, there would be no stopping the tyrant who had already occupied all of western Europe and would soon conquer the East as well. We were lost, fearing he would soon accomplish his monstrous goal of erasing the memory of the Jews from Europe. Our desperation was measureless.[5]

To this day we cannot understand the Russians' flight from the Baltics: was it a military maneuver to blind their nemesis, or were they simply unprepared to resist him? Nevertheless the USSR later demonstrated that it is not like the little states that collapsed like a house of cards before the German wind. Nor was it like France, which had atrophied in its affluence and placed its trust in obsolete defenses.[6] The USSR later demonstrated an extraordinary level of courage that largely justified the Bolsheviks' bragging. When the war finally ends, Russian courage will be inscribed in the world's annals and remembered by coming generations. (I am copying these words from a draft written in the eighth month of the war. As of today,[7] neither Leningrad nor Moscow are occupied. Yet the "great victories" on the Jewish front—toward our extermination—continue ceaselessly.)

When Amalek captured Lithuania it found a partner unique among all the countries that had fallen under its feet. The Lithuanians behaved like liberated slaves (essentially "a slave who becomes king"[8]), naturally crude and savage, removed from culture, primitive in commerce and industry. Their jealousy of the Jews was as fierce as death.[9] Particularly after declaring independence [from the Soviet Union],[10] this dormant beast awoke, baring its teeth and fangs in full force. Encouraged by the occupiers, who hated us in their hearts, the Lithuanians began slaying us, happy to rid themselves of "alien" competitors. Thus entire communities were wiped out, coldly and methodically, fifty or sixty people at a time, all in one day or over several days, the old and the young, women and children,[11] fathers in front of their children, children in front of their fathers. The murderers' hands did not tremble, and their eyes did not go blind. And we who have remained alive—for now—and are under the rule of Amalek and his minions, our fate is bitter! We are being roasted on a slow fire. The biblical prophecy of a precarious life[12] has materialized in all its horror. Our lives, stripped away from us, hang by a thread, our souls separated from our bodies. We are at the mercy of our slaughterers, clay in the hands of the potter.[13] At a whim they can end our lives or inflict all manner of torment on our souls.

From the day we fell under the oppressive German boots and became targets for the Lithuanian guns and fists,[14] our bodies, our property, and our labor all became cheap commodities. But it is useless to pile on words to express our pain. My pen is unable to describe even one against thousands[15] of humiliations that rain down on us, nor one against thousands of dangers we face, nor the torments renewed every morning[16] to embitter our lives at all times and in every hour.[17] That would require an artist like the poet of "Massa Nemirov"[18]

who could describe our agonies: the diktats intended to humiliate us and reduce us to dirt; the decrees intended to wear us out by starvation and over-
work; the edicts intended to impoverish us, to leave us with no property and
no resources; the beatings and blows to people, regardless of age or education;
the demeaning labor under the taskmasters' rod[19] forced on people unaccus-
tomed to physical toil. Who can list all the torments drowning us, with no way
out? Who will use words like sword thrusts[20] to record what the Lithuanians
did to us in collaboration with the Germans so that it will never be forgotten,
so our grandchildren can mourn the disaster that struck us in the old days
and can celebrate a new "Exodus" of miracles and wonders—an Exodus that,
even if it comes too late for us, will certainly arrive for our grandchildren and
great-grandchildren.[21]

As director of the polyclinic, I had two options: I could go to the polyclinic
and transfer the management to my replacement, appointed by the new regime,
or I could sit and watch events as they developed. I did not have to ponder this
question long. On the second day of the German occupation of Šiauliai, June
27, the dentist V.K. came and told me the Germans had seized the polyclinic's
facility and established an ambulatory clinic there without consulting anyone.
The German chief doctor had dismissed V.K. and the nurse L.T. for being Jewish. Then Dr. B.N. came and said that while at the polyclinic, he was approached
by the German chief doctor. When he learned B.N. was Jewish he ordered him
to "walk out as fast as he could and disappear." If that was to be the reception
given Jewish doctors, I thought it unnecessary to test the Germans' courtesy
and decided to stay home. That is how my tenure of more than six months as
polyclinic director ended. I was left like the other dismissed Jews, without a job
and without a livelihood.

We were also left with hardly any food or provisions, as the Lithuanians,
not waiting for the official decree, had essentially stopped selling food to Jews.
As soon as the Germans arrived, there was a general transformation in the
Lithuanians' attitude. Even their facial expressions changed: they rejoiced and
cheered. Most [of the Lithuanians] owned property, and they hoped the Germans would return their assets which had been nationalized by the Bolsheviks,
along with their country's independence. As they tried to curry favor with
their new masters by associating the Jews with the Bolsheviks, the old hatred
ignited in the villains' hearts and took on a cruel and savage character. No
longer restrained or civil, they showed few if any signs of sympathy, even among
the more educated of them, the so-called intelligentsia, or among longtime
acquaintances. They all rejoiced at our calamity; they all believed the Jews deserved punishment. Even later, when many among the Lithuanian intelligentsia

decided the Germans had gone too far and some began to show some degree of sympathy for the Jews, still they all agreed that some penalties were deserved.

On that same day the German chief doctor demonstrated how an intelligent German would treat Jews, even those who were his professional peers and colleagues. It was not enough for him to dismiss the [Jewish] doctors from the polyclinic, he went further: he sent a military man with the nurse Glovniska to the dentist V.K., the professional he had just dismissed, and ordered him to come back and spend the day performing "dirty work" around the polyclinic: cleaning the street and sidewalk, fetching water, repairing the entrance to the Lithuanian gymnasium's yard across from the polyclinic and so on, together with other Jewish youths who had been caught on the street and forced to work. Perhaps it was true, as some said, that Dr. V.K. had pestered the chief doctor for work, annoying him with his appearance and gestures. V.K was a persistent sort, doggedly undeterred when he wanted something. So it is possible that when the chief doctor found a troublesome little Jew bothering him with demands for a job, he gave him one—cleaning the street and fetching water. Still, it was not right for the doctor to humiliate someone who belonged among the organization's medical professionals. Perhaps it should be no surprise that our western neighbors could elect such a horrible enemy of the Jews as their leader if even their intelligentsia included people such as this, who might indeed make up the majority [of Germans]. Yet these events seem innocent compared with how they treated us later.

June 27 represented the calm before the storm. For the moment, [the Germans] were satisfied with eradicating Bolshevism: dismissing people from their positions, arresting suspects, and looting the homes of those who had left Šiauliai, either party members who had gone to Latvia or the USSR or simple Jews who had fled with their families to nearby villages and towns to escape the bombings. Many of the latter, as mentioned, were heartbroken when they returned and found their houses emptied of furniture, household items and anything else of value.

The real trouble began on June 28. That is when the deep began to swallow us, the mouth of the pit closed over us.[22] Would a miracle bring us relief and deliverance?[23] As long as we had breath, we would keep a spark of hope flickering in our souls' depths. Our nation has experienced both calamities and miracles. Although the evil in our era is without precedent, as mentioned, our salvation could also arrive unexpectedly, and our enemies' downfall could also be unprecedented, providing our strength and endurance does not break.

PART B

SEVEN

—ᴍ—

AFFLICTIONS

A. LOOTING AND ROBBERY

The Bolsheviks nationalized all of Lithuania's land, buildings, factories, and stores. They confiscated safes, bank deposits, and merchandise. They reduced the size of apartments. They arrested suspected speculators, detained middle-class people along with landowners and "kulaks," whom they deemed dangerous. In short, we endured our share of trouble and sorrow[1] under the Bolsheviks. But not only did they not discriminate against and persecute Jews, they also gave us full rights, respectable positions, and so on. Moreover they did not touch the property of middle-class people, nor even of the wealthy unless they were associated with suspect groups. How badly things changed for the Jews in our city with the Germans' arrival! The Lithuanian partisans went into a frenzy,[2] and their first attacks were on Jewish property, the fruit of Jewish labor. They behaved not like thieves or burglars who attack in the dark of night but robbed and looted openly in broad daylight. They strolled the streets, often with German soldiers, broke into Jewish homes and acted like they owned them. First, as noted they looted the homes of the "deserters" who had fled; afterward, they hit almost any Jewish home. Those they missed were the lucky exceptions.

But the Lithuanians' excesses were not all approved by the Germans. In one case, armed partisans and policemen arrested some Jews and forced them to carry belongings on their backs to the police headquarters. When they arrived, the Germans beat the partisans and police, and let the prisoners go home with their goods. They were probably upset because the Lithuanians had acted on their own without asking permission first. Subsequently the Germans issued an order forbidding looting and requiring that any robberies be reported to their police. Only the belongings of those who fled were transferred to the partisans. But the Jews were already so deeply depressed that none of us dared resist, let alone complain to the Germans when the thieves did not stop. Among the top reasons for that order was certainly the Germans' concern that the Lithuanians might not leave them any Jewish property, as well as the desire, mentioned earlier, to not give the Lithuanian leadership too much independence. It was evident that law and justice did not apply to Jews, and that sooner or later the Germans themselves would set upon us, making not only our property but also our lives free for all to despoil and ravage.

During one of these days of horror, several Germans entered my family's house and demanded mattresses. We gave them the mattress from our son's bed, which we had repaired for our former neighbor, the aviator Tzikin. We then suggested that they go to the address of my brother-in-law Zilberman, who as I mentioned had been deported to the USSR with his family, and whose house had been sealed up. These Germans behaved politely, and we thought that if we went along with them, we could open the door and retrieve a few items. We found the door already opened, possibly by other Germans or by the concierge, a singular thief and scoundrel who had speedily befriended the partisans. We gave the Germans a good mattress and several other things, and they, appearing to be upright[3] people, allowed us to take whatever we wished. Sadly, my wife and I were able to take only a few things from all that my wife's sister had left behind because of the following unfortunate incident:

My wife stayed behind in her sister's home, trying to put things together as best as she could, and I carried a suitcase full of dresses to our home. When I entered, I found four robbers in our son's room, each wearing a partisan arm-band, apparently halfwits from nearby villages who did not recognize me. They showed me a so-called document giving them permission to seize from the Jews five complete suits, which they interpreted to include shirts, socks, and shoes, to distribute to partisans who needed them. While we were absent they had opened our closets and picked three of my newest suits, one of which I had just tried on at the tailor's, as well as my son's only new suit. In addition, they took seven shirts, ten pairs of socks, and three pairs of shoes. When I entered the bedroom, everything was already piled up and tied in a bundle with a rope they had brought. The thieving idiots were acting like this was all legal, autho-rized by the license in their hand. The chief gangster even dared to leave behind an improvised receipt, stating that they had taken four complete suits from Dr. Levin, for the partisans' benefit. (We had spoken of Dr. Levin, who fled [with the Russians], which explains his error.)

Why did they take four suits? Because they already had one suit, stolen somewhere else, and their idea of a complete suit included shirts, socks, and shoes. As far as that goes, they took more shirts and socks and fewer shoes than allowed, because they could not find more. But I did not think it appropriate to negotiate with four large, threatening young men. I was also afraid they would open a small leather suitcase that stood in the corner, which was full of silver and gold jewelry that had belonged to our brother-in-law. One of them eyed it but, seeing my business card attached there, must have assumed it was full of drugs. So much the better!

The robbers left, giving the German salute as befit upstanding supporters of "H,"[4] and I lost clothes and other things which I certainly would not be able to replace for a very long time, and with which, if I had them to sell now, I could probably survive for more than six months. Further, because this event had taken so much of my time and peace of mind and because the day was waning, I did not have a chance to return to our brother-in-law's place to continue salvaging his belongings. And by the next day the partisans had rushed back, probably invited by the evil concierge who appropriated a huge quantity of coats, dresses, linens, rugs, duvets, household and kitchenware, etc., etc. A wealthy household, a lot of loot! Some of what the thieving concierge obtained "knowingly or unknowingly," she offered for sale in her own home, which became kind of a store where loot was sold. That is how nearly all the Jewish homes were devoured, either by Lithuanians accompanied by Germans or by Lithuanians operating on their own.

On the night of June 30, six people—five Lithuanians and one German—entered the apartment of Dr. R.K., our brother-in-law's former tenant, and stole his pocket watch, a table clock, fountain pen, eighteen rubles,[5] and some of our brother-in-law's son's clothes, which my wife had tried to hide in their closet. Then they took him, saying he was going to prison. It is easy to imagine how this weak and fearful person was affected. On his sick legs, his knees trembling[6] for fear of being shot (as he later told us), he walked with them until they reached Darius and Girėnas Street,[7] where they met an officer who ordered them to let Dr. R.K. go. It seemed to me the whole thing had been staged, a tragicomedy of simple robbers who were prepared to get their hands dirty for a mere eighteen rubles and some items of little value, and that the so-called officer was part of the act, coordinated in advance. But the phony arrest scared Dr. R.K., who of course did not dare protest or file a complaint, particularly since he thought he had been saved from mortal danger.

Obviously there is no way to describe even a fraction of all the stealing and pilfering, since as I mentioned, hardly a single Jewish homeowner was not robbed multiple times: "What the cutter has left, the locust has devoured; what the locust has left, the grub has devoured; and what the grub has left, the hopper has devoured."[8] They returned to Dr. R.K.'s home and took his only dining table and three chairs. It did not concern the thieves that without these, their owner could not live normally. Why should they care about a Jew's normal life? We also were visited by robbers several times: first by the mattress seekers; then the suit robbers, as I described; then Germans came and demanded that we and our neighbor Getz hand over our radio sets before they were confiscated officially from all Jews. One of them also wanted to take one of our few suitcases, but a German told him they should remain "decent." (He was of the older generation.) The fourth time, Lithuanians and Germans came and took one of our two beds with the mattress. The fifth time, just before our departure for the ghetto, we experienced the epitome of thievery by a committee that decided which items physicians could take into the ghetto, as I will describe in the following pages.

The Germans and partisans found a trove of loot in the homes of Drs. Brumberg and Savich, who had successfully escaped to the USSR. Being members of the committee that had examined military draftees allowed them to obtain entry permits. These two doctors had earned nice incomes as did their wives—one a dentist and the other a pharmacist, who didn't do badly[9]—and they had spent all they earned on clothing, food, and medical instruments. So their pantries, closets and basements were full of produce of all kinds,[10] and their medical clinics had supplies enough to last many years. For example, Dr. Savich's clinic had a decade's worth of material for casts and bandages, things that now are priceless. In addition they found such a quantity of clothes and fabric in his home that the Germans who seized the property said he appeared to be more speculator than physician. At these doctors' homes, they found a variety of foodstuffs, all of which was looted by the Germans and Lithuanians. Their books and medical instruments were transferred to the polyclinic warehouse, which became the repository for the huge "treasures" of Jewish doctors (discussed later). Another warehouse was also set up in the home of Dr. Levin, who had also earned well and owned a rich library and a variety of medical instruments. One of the pillars of Bolshevism in Šiauliai, he also fled to the USSR with his family, leaving his vast wealth behind. Indeed, there were many Jews who made good livings and had had enjoyed beautiful abodes, beautiful vessels,[11] and a rich cultural life. And suddenly the storm came and uprooted everything. Once again, we learned that all our accomplishments in lands of exile amount to nothing more than spiders' webs.

B. SUFFERING AND FORCED LABOR

This persecution, whose edge has subsided recently, was initially horrific and terrible. They would hunt Jews like dogs on the streets, break into homes and with shouts, threats, and beatings drag people out to perform arduous, humiliating jobs without pay and even without food. "The parasitic Jews, who live off the nation, sucking its marrow, now must pay with their sweat for the privilege of living in this country, breathing its air, even if they live like dogs and ravens.[12]" It was terrible to watch the Jews' terror when the kidnappers showed up. Those who could would hide in a closet, in woodsheds or under beds to escape the oppressors' crude cruelty, brutal fists[13] and whips. If not for these no Jew would have shrunk from physical work, since the times had turned us into hewers of wood and drawers of water[14] and our wives into cooks and kitchen maids.

The forced workers did not know at first whether they would be sent home or to prison. I remember that while I was still living in town, two partisans entered and told me and my neighbor, whom they found in the corridor, to take up brooms and go clean the street, etc. I told them I was a physician with more important work to do, and they left me alone. In time things got a little better: the Germans recognized the value of Jewish professionals, and consequently their treatment of such workers became more humane. Jews were given more appropriate jobs and even wages, although less than half as much as Christian day laborers. Still, they were paid for their work and not exploited for free. Now ghetto residents work in the city hall, in hospitals, and perform menial jobs in various institutions, at the aerodrome,[15] in the peat mines and on the streets. Artisans such as watchmakers, hatmakers, leather smiths, tailors, glove makers, etc., work in shops they were allowed to set up in town under the ostensible supervision of Christians. There are Jewish servants in purely German institutes, in the homes of their officials and their kitchens. These Jews work willingly as their jobs give them some protection against transferal from Šiauliai, and because they have become settled in the ghetto and at the various work sites, avoiding potential calamities. By contrast, those who remain idle face constant danger from the Germans and Lithuanians, who reluctantly keep the remaining few alive because they need our labor, particularly for skilled jobs that Lithuanians cannot do.

There is one other reason everybody seeks work outside the ghetto: the chance they may find food to smuggle back inside, where there is great hunger for bread and even more for meat, butter, and so on. Due to the general protection that work provides, and because of the advantage mentioned previously that will be discussed in detail later, many respectable women devised fictitious contracts with acquaintances among the Christians to work for them as maids. Interestingly, some actually worked as maids, and their husbands treated it as normal: given the privileges that these erstwhile positions brought, why shouldn't they become real maids in fact, even at no salary? After all, the Jews are now anybody's to claim or use, and many among the Lithuanian intelligentsia accept it as fair that their Jewish acquaintances should serve them. But these arrangements were ended in recent days, as the Germans discovered the ruse and began cracking down on Jews found wandering about the city; they decreed that from 8:00 a.m. to 4:00 p.m., no Jew may be seen or found[16] on city streets.

I want to recognize Dr. Jasaitis for his actions on behalf of several Jewish physicians. He took great pains to obtain permission from the district commissioner[17] for six doctors to work as "lab technicians" in various city medical establishments. It was forbidden for Jews to treat "Aryan" patients, but the commissioner was more lenient regarding laboratory work, and permitted it. I was among those lab technicians. I should mention that Jasaitis regarded me highly, as he had previously appointed me director of the central polyclinic. Still, it is hard to believe that his attempt to obtain these permits was made solely out of affection for the Jewish doctors; a variety of reasons were at play. Jasaitis had been known as a generally honest man who treated Jews fairly, probably influenced by his wife, the daughter of well-known "leftist" (the lawyer Lukauskis[18]). She was among those of the Lithuanian intelligentsia who believed the Germans went too far in their treatment of the Jews, and that the latter are being punished far more harshly than their sins justify, assuming they sinned at all.

One can also assume that Jasaitis is the wise one, able to see that the Germans are not assured of victory and wants to arm himself with Jewish endorsements in case those become necessary in the future. Should there be punishment and retribution,[19] he would be able to show he worked on the Jews' behalf. But we need not probe his motivations. The fact is, he acted as a helper and protector of the Jews at a time when our past friends feared to even smile at us. His actions merit special recognition because, as a former Bolshevik official, he is already suspect and could catch the Germans' attention as an advocate for the Jews. And yet he did not shrink from trying. Of course it may also be that this is why he did not follow through by requesting that we get paid even a meager salary for our labor, which benefits the establishments that employ us. It could be this is why he did not fight harder against the evil mayor Linkevičius, who objected to paying us salaries, arguing that the city's budget had not anticipated such an expense. Nevertheless, six doctors started working, wearing out their shoes for no pay, yet more or less content because of the reasons suggested here: we avoided forced labor at the aerodrome or elsewhere and had a chance of finding food in town—a preoccupation of nearly all ghetto residents, who are physically declining from undernourishment.

And the jealousy of our Jewish physician colleagues was too much to bear! This even though we tried to set up a walk-in clinic in the ghetto, a place for doctors to practice who could not work in the city. But working in the ghetto clinic had less "status" than work in the municipal medical establishments and so offered less protection against being transferred by the Germans to other jobs or liquidated altogether, as happened in Kaunas, where several doctors were killed.[20] Work in the ghetto clinic would be a weak reed to lean on during those days of wrath and fury[21] that have not been infrequent and would offer no possibility of going to town to bring back contraband—bread, butter, meat, and vegetables, which are more available and cheaper in town than from the ghetto speculators (as I will discuss later). The other doctors have grown especially jealous since we started receiving salaries, thanks to an order of the labor police that no Jewish worker may work for free, but must be paid a fraction of a Christian worker's salary.

Regarding Dr. Jasaitis, it is worth noting that he always treated me well because he knew me as the director of the internal medicine and infectious disease departments in the municipal hospital for sixteen and a half years (and for a time he worked there under my supervision as a lab technician) and also as a "noted" medical lecturer and author of scientific papers. Also, while he was in Moscow he learned about my brother,[22] a well-known professor there (although at that time he was heading a scientific mission to central Asia to study silicosis among the miners as part of his occupational-health research). Jasaitis had also conveyed warm regards to me from an old friend, Dr. Tagievski, with whom I had prepared for anatomy exams in Paris and who is now deputy director of the hospital in Moscow named after the famous Botkin.[23] These two facts might someday be of significant benefit.

The Joniškėlis Event

A disaster related to the forced labor disturbed our peace of mind for about two weeks. Our son is not very enterprising: he inherited his character from his paternal ancestors, yeshiva students, and from my wife's parents who were sluggish, passive people. He could not find a proper job and settle in the city like many of his friends. He chose instead to become a house mover, helping Jews relocate into the ghetto. He was doing this for several weeks, from the time of his miraculous return from Vilnius until our move to the ghetto, when I got out of prison—which will be detailed later. Long enough have we endured our bitter tribulations![24] By the time our turn came to move to the ghetto, we were exhausted. For nine days thereafter, we moved from one place to another, unable to find home and shelter (and this after my tortures in prison). Our belongings were scattered about in the open and in a woodshed, open to the hands of thieves. I slept [during that period] at the home of the teacher Zilbershtein, being the seventh [person] in a single room. My wife found shelter "under the roof" of the Vanover family, her relatives, where the roof truly was right overhead, and our son was somewhere with his friends.

Even during that period, our son could not find a job because he was dragging behind us, ready to help us settle in a home—which the ghetto council kept promising would be found any day—and collect our belongings, which were scattered in various locations. Finally, we were shown (by outsiders, not our [Jewish] police) a somewhat decent home that was already occupied by some despicable people[25] from Tauragė, who were then offered a different home. After some drama and a lot of negotiating, we managed to get this home for 200 rubles (and a cup of butter!) over the objection of the son of the woman who lived there previously, who tried to take advantage of us.

This "jewel" later got back at us in a way that caused a lot of pain. Here is what happened: after helping us move into our new resting place, Tedik,[26] our son, was planning to go to the city the following day to seek a job, or at the very least to work on repairing streets and sidewalks. But on that same day, police and partisans came into the ghetto to round up laborers and take them to the outskirts of Joniškėlis,[27] where the rail line to Žeimelis was being repaired. Naturally I, and particularly my wife, preferred for our son to work nearby, where he could come home to eat and sleep every day. And so we were pleased when the police skipped our small home, which is located behind some others. But our happiness was fleeting.[28] Suddenly the scoundrel who had tried to cheat us when we took over his mother's dwelling showed up with a policeman and pointed out our son as a young man fit for work. The policeman added him to the list of those ordered to report for work in Joniškėlis.

The parting was very difficult, particularly after the terrible torment we had suffered when our son was stranded in Vilnius at the start of the war, leaving us in the dark about his fate. We were somewhat comforted when the council promised that the Joniškėlis work would last only five days. When our son left he did not take much clothing or gear, since it would only be five days. But five days passed, then ten days, and there was no word and no response![29] The council began to say reluctantly that the work there might last two months. My wife, whose condition had been aggravated by her family's calamities as well as our own private predicaments, could no longer bear it, and her illness became severe. Our distress increased when some of the Joniškėlis workers sent notes home describing conditions and complaining about the hard work, but at least indicating they were still alive. Still there was no word from our son. Our worries kept us awake at night: maybe he was sick, maybe he was transferred elsewhere, maybe someone informed on him, and besides he did not take enough clothes and underwear or enough money. The council told us that on Sunday, October 5, they expected a few of the Joniškėlis workers to return to pick up enough supplies to see everyone through the length of the job. Still the prospect that those in Joniškėlis would stay there even longer was quite depressing. We felt it was a tragedy to be kept from our only son so long with no news from him, particularly after almost losing our minds when he went missing in Vilnius. Our life had become a daily series of tests of endurance and patience. How long could we hold ourselves together and not explode?

Suddenly there was an unforeseen miracle! The Germans decided to start work on the aerodrome and demanded laborers, forcing the Lithuanians to bring back the Jews working in Joniškėlis. Rumors suggested that had it not been for this order, the Joniškėlis workers would have stayed there indefinitely and been fated to perish forever.[30] Their living conditions were far worse than in prison. For thirteen days, they slept on straw scattered on the floor of a partially demolished house, full of mold, fifteen or twenty to a room. The well was far enough away from the dwelling that water became precious, and it was difficult to wash. They lacked wood for the stove and were without heat for several days. They were short of underwear, but even if they had had enough, the conditions made it impractical to change or even store the clothes they removed. In short, hygiene was deficient, food rations were grossly inadequate,[31] and the work was so hard that they would not have survived long.

And then suddenly, after thirteen days, they brought all the workers back to Šiauliai.[32] Interestingly, they were taken first to the aerodrome, but from there they were sent home on condition that they return every day to the aerodrome for work. So our son returned in one piece and healthy. He was missing only two good leather mittens, which the partisans pickpocketed, and his good pocketknife, which I had received as a gift from the pharmaceutical lab "Garmafa"[33] and gave to my son when he left. When the workers left Joniškėlis, their oppressors, the partisans, demanded a "tax": watches, pocketknives, in one case a new leather coat. That is how they were sent off and thanked for their work. After our son, the apple of our eyes, returned from Joniškėlis, he worked for a time at the aerodrome. The long walk and the hard work finally exhausted him, so we tried to find him a job with the ghetto council. Our efforts were successful and he was hired as a policeman, a keeper of order. The job requires him to be strict and to occasionally coerce and threaten people, aspects that our idealist son finds difficult, so he is not very happy. Still we are glad our son is with us, and as he comes home many times each day we can tell the work is not too hard. He worked as a mover, as a laborer in Joniškėlis and a laborer at the aerodrome, so he deserves a bit of rest. But he isn't satisfied with being a policeman and seeks a more substantial job.

C. ARREST AND IMPRISONMENT

Our troubles with those who rule over us have been like a malignant eruption,[34] eating away at the Jewish population since the Bolshevik days. The best of our Zionist leaders and publicists were arrested [by the Soviets]. Reputable merchants who dared to spend their cash were arrested and their merchandise seized. Suspected speculators and counterrevolutionaries were arrested, including many Christians who truly were reactionaries and pogromists. Anyone whom the Bolsheviks deemed dangerous was arrested and deported to the USSR. Their guiding purpose was: enemies of the revolution deserved to be punished and removed from the community. Finding these enemies required some intelligence, some investigation—not always quite legal, of course. But there was at least a rationale, a basic program handed down by the leadership. This is not the case with the Germans or their partners and servants, the Lithuanian partisans. Their program requires no investigation or selectivity. It is as basic as can be: every Jew deserves extermination, if not right away then imprisonment, and not merely imprisonment but mental and physical torment, a foretaste of the extermination to come one way or another. Thus Jews began to be hunted on the streets or in their homes as soon as the Germans arrived, without regard to age, from teenagers to the elderly. All were imprisoned after being tortured, as a cat tortures a mouse.

The Germans, as mentioned, arrived in Šiauliai at dusk on June 26. On June 27 and 28, there were few arrests. But beginning on June 29 they began in earnest. It is estimated that in Šiauliai alone, they imprisoned about one thousand men, both old and young. On Saturday June 28, I saw Rabbi Nochumovsky[35] on the sidewalk near our house, dressed for the Sabbath, surrounded by policemen and partisans, being led to jail. I was later told that on that day they also arrested Rabbi Baksht[36] and his son-in-law Rabbi Rabinowitz, and Rabbi Nochumovsky's son, a sickly youngster with symptoms of pulmonary tuberculosis. It seems the murderers chose that day specifically to torment religious leaders: Orthodox, God-fearing Jews who would be forced to violate the Sabbath. On June 30, when the arrests had really taken off the Germans collected eighty Jews in the courtyard of the former Shogam Brothers' store, lined them up facing the wall and, after torturing them extensively and scaring them to death by pretending they were about to be shot, led them to prison. A small fraction were released after various organizations interceded for them, but the majority remained confined.

Unspeakable mental and physical anguish awaited them under the Germans and Lithuanians, who delighted in degrading and humiliating Jewish prisoners, beating them for any reason or no reason, making no exceptions for educated professionals such as doctors or lawyers. It is impossible to describe the hard labor; the whips and fists of the heartless oppressors; the scarce rations, barely enough to sustain life; sleeping on hard iron or wooden beds without mattresses or so crowded on the cold floor that no one could turn over without everyone else doing the same. Add the mentally oppressive military discipline, the humiliations directed specifically at Jews such as cleaning latrines, which in the early days had to be done with bare hands. And who was forced to that? Professional people: lawyers, pharmacists, school principals, even a doctor who ended up there inexplicably. My guess is that when they entered Dr. Getz's home and ordered him to work, he was confused and failed to tell them that he was a physician, as I had done in the same situation. Instead he followed the "kidnappers" like a sheep being led to slaughter,[37] and after his work they took him to prison. There he most likely argued, as is his nature, in the yeshiva style, with typical Jewish gestures. But it was too late. He was ensnared in their traps[38] with no escape or shelter.

Along with all these insults, the Germans forced prisoners to perform calisthenics—a clever invention to laugh at the ridiculous Jews and their awkward movements, particularly the elderly who had never done such exercises.

They also ordered the prisoners to sing Jewish folksongs before bed, after long days of hard physical labor and endless humiliations had broken their spirits, as in the psalm: "For our captors asked us there for songs, our tormentors for amusement, 'Sing us one of the songs of Zion.'"[39] And they sang "as one who sings songs to a sorrowful soul."[40] In the prison they mercilessly tortured Rabbi Baksht and his son-in-law and Rabbi Nochumovsky: they were put in with some crooked characters, who hadn't been hard to find among the prisoners. Then they clipped their beards and hair and posed them for a group photograph, something to delight the readers of "*Der Stürmer.*"[41] Pictured front and back, they made a caricature that would make Germans laugh and say, "These are the teachers of Israel, Talmudic frauds and con-men; these villains are the Jews' spiritual leaders!"

After several weeks of insults and humiliations, trouble and suffering, they deported the Jewish prisoners from Šiauliai to an unknown location, whose secrecy added to the fear and terror. Where did they take them? Are they still alive?[42] Were they sent to work in Prussia, or the Klaipėda region, or near Trakai[43] as some rumors suggested? Everything was shrouded in fog and secrecy, which added to the fear and suspicion in our hearts. Indeed, they left behind many widows and orphans and many bereaved fathers whose spirits yearn for any shred of knowledge about the fate of their providers or sons.

But yearning and hope may be better than learning the stark truth of their fates. To begin with, it cannot be assumed that the disappeared Šiauliai prisoners were sent to another work place: Rabbi Baksht is old and sick, Rabbi Nochumovsky and his son with tuberculosis are incapable of physical labor; they therefore were most likely viewed as merely extra mouths to feed and disposed of. Once the permission was given to the Destroyer to destroy,[44] he would spare neither the young nor the old, nor extend a hand to one prisoner over another. Indeed! If we cry over those who are gone, our tears will not be in vain.

And who were these prisoners? Among them were the best of us: activists, intellectuals, and lawyers—people in their prime, with initiative and drive. The Šiauliai community has been reduced almost by half: from nine thousand Jews before the war, only five thousand remain. The rest have disappeared, been "deported," or died before their time like most of our brothers in Lithuania, which has become the valley of death. They were butchered for no sin or crime. Our woe is such that we have given up hoping for salvation or justice from Israel's God, who is bankrupt, defeated on all fronts. Our present torments have no precedent in our entire cursed history, and there is no one in heaven or on earth to avenge us. Even the Americans are unwilling to take revenge on those Germans who live there. For us there is "no law and no judge."[45]

D. MY OWN IMPRISONMENT

My imprisonment was unusual. I was not among those Šiauliai Jews who were hunted like beasts and imprisoned just for being Jews. I was an actual sinner, one whose transgression was so great that only prison could absolve it. I dared to approach Stankus, the "king of the Jews,"[46] and confront him over his treatment of Jews. I said some harsh words, and he put me in jail, as Ahab did the prophet Micaiah ben Imlah[47]—although the comparison is merely superficial. Even if Stankus is indeed "king of the Jews" as Christians say, I am certainly no prophet, though I am presumptuous enough to believe I was punished for trying to act in the public interest and for tilting at windmills like Don Quixote.

It was September 5, a sad, ominous day. We had received bad news about the fate of our remaining brothers in Kelmė,[48] and of the death by gunshot of my wife's cousin Buria (which I will detail). The news worsened my wife's disease, agitated my spirit and frayed my nerves, which were already strained by worry and fear over the Germans' daily edicts, invented to make our lives ever more miserable. This was all in the background that day when I entered the office of the official named to oversee Jewish affairs. He was a thin young man, short, with a gypsy's face. He sat at his desk looking weak, either drunk or tired from lack of sleep, both of which were normal for him. He typically did not look his visitor in the eyes or offer a seat. Although he knew me well (I believe I once treated one of his children in the hospital) and I had visited him in his office several times, he treated me with the same indifference he showed any other visitor, obviously to demonstrate his power or show his disdain for Jews.

I had come to request that a young woman already living in the ghetto (we were not there yet), who had worked as our maid, be allowed to leave the ghetto daily for a few hours to come care for my wife, who was bedridden. "No need," Stankus replied. "Soon you too will move to the ghetto." "So be it," I replied, "But for now we are still in the city, and I cannot cook for myself. More importantly I cannot care for my wife." "Not necessary!" he mumbled with typical Lithuanian stubbornness and signaled that our conversation was over. Straining to hold back my rage, I replied as calmly as I could: "What is the point of this unnecessary strictness? Even if you wipe out three quarters of us (I thought I was exaggerating; sadly, I was not), a quarter will still be here. I don't know what will happen with the Germans, but Lithuanians will certainly have to live with the Jews."

When he heard those words, which I did not get to fully clarify, the minister jumped up as if bitten by a snake and banged his fist on the desk with such force that his ink bottle jumped. "So you are threatening me!" he yelled angrily. "Officer!" he called. "Come write this man up for making threats!" I started to apologize, saying I had not meant to threaten him, merely to emphasize that Lithuanians and Jews will have to live together, but he would not bend his ear to listen.[49] Again he called for the officer, who walked in from the adjacent room to prepare a report. The officer ordered me to follow him to his office, where he shrugged when I explained what I had said to Stankus, how he had interrupted me in midsentence and did not let me express it clearly. I said I thought the harsh treatment of the Jews was unwise because whatever happens, even if we assume that Germany, as a developed nation, doesn't need Jews, Lithuania is still underdeveloped in commerce and industry and will still need the talent and initiative of Jews who remain.

After writing his weird report, the officer called out to ask Stankus what to do with me, but Stankus had left the office. So the officer let me go. As I returned home, my spirits lay in the dust[50] from measureless[51] anger and desperation. My heart was telling me I had gotten myself into something that would not end well. I concealed the matter from my ailing wife but told my son what had happened. We both were terribly confused and deeply depressed. There had been talk then about permitting doctors with certain types of medical equipment to continue operating their clinics in town, confining them to the ghetto only at night. As the owner of an X-ray apparatus I was among those doctors hoping to obtain such a permit, and Stankus had promised me one explicitly—a promise I was counting on because neither Stankus nor I expected that the Nuremberg Laws,[52] which prohibit Jewish doctors from treating Christians, would be imposed here as well. I thought then that my chance to obtain the coveted permit depended only on Stankus, and that I had squandered it by arousing his anger. With the hope of keeping my office in the city gone, I would have to prepare to move into the ghetto. That meant dismantling my library, which included books in six languages and which I had hoped to keep along with my clinic. Now this misfortune had erased that hope, and I could not possibly take it in its entirety to the ghetto. I had begun to select the more interesting and useful books to take along when suddenly the doorbell rang. When it was opened, the clerk who wrote up my indictment stepped in and asked me to go with him. I immediately understood the calamity that faced me,[53] but I tried hard not to show my distress to my sickly wife. Instead, I looked at her briefly, mustered a fake smile, and, without a word, left with the clerk.

A car waited outside with a second clerk and a police driver. I sat where they told me, next to the clerk who had written the report. We drove from my street through Venclauskas Street to Tilžės Street and toward Joniškis. When I asked where we were going, the clerk replied, "To Stankus at the German security police." My heart trembled inside me like a caged bird. I surely need not describe my state of mind when the clerk led me into the corridor of the German security office. My world turned dark, and I could barely breathe. I was shivering and my thoughts were confused, unable to analyze what happened or what awaited me. I knew only that I was headed for disaster in the hands of our mortal enemies.

While I sat in the corridor, Stankus arrived. I hurried to apologize to him, but he paid no attention as he rushed by me, muttering that it was all up to the security police now. After a short time I was called into the office, a spacious room. In one corner sat a German clerk; next to him stood his assistant. Stankus sat across the room along with two other people, apparently detectives. My knees trembled as I entered, and I stopped in the middle of the room, embarrassed and confused. I was approached by the clerk's assistant who, if memory serves, had been speaking Lithuanian and who now said mockingly in German, "Middle of the room!" and pushed me unceremoniously toward the head clerk. After his assistant said that I understood German (probably assuming that any intelligent Jew would), the clerk looked at me angrily and asked in an accusing tone, "What did you say today?" In my exhaustion and my confusion I replied briefly: "The Lithuanians would still need to live with those Jews that survive."

Then Stankus handed him a note, apparently with my words translated into German. Despite my confusion I quickly understood that Stankus had dangerously distorted what I had said about the Germans, making it seem as though I had doubted they would win the war. The chief clerk read the translation aloud and then chastised me, asking: "And what did you say about the Germans? That you don't know what will be with them?" Because of my dizziness, I did not think I was capable of an extensive explanation. I might have said that I did not mean anything about the Germans but spoke only of the Jews. I might have voiced my opinion that, with its developed culture, Germany may need no help from Jews, but not so the Lithuanians, who in commerce and industry still have a lot to learn from us. Yet in my weakness and dizziness I answered only that I certainly did not say such things about the Germans and that anyone can make a mistake. "Like who?" the clerk asked me. "Even Mr. Stankus," I answered with a slight hesitation. "And you?" "Of course. Me, too."

We made small talk for several minutes. Then the clerk asked my occupation. When I said I was a physician, Stankus added, "And a good one." Then the clerk

asked about the polyclinic: was it private or public? After receiving the necessary answers from me and Stankus, he ordered me to wait outside. I turned to
Stankus and began to say, "Please, for old times' sake, try to reduce. . . ." Then I
stopped. I realized I was asking to have my sentence reduced and, thus, in effect
admitting that I deserved some punishment. This naivete was also the result
of my confusion. I walked out to the corridor, and with me came a German
soldier who closed the door. "A bad sign, it means I am arrested," I thought, my
heart in a vise. I sat and waited, fretting and anxious. Every minute felt like an
eternity.

After some time a young policeman, a Lithuanian gunman who worked at
the prison, appeared and in a crude voice ordered me to follow him. I thought
we would leave through the front door as we had entered, but he pushed me
aside and ordered me into the yard. Here I experienced a psychological moment
I will never forget, which illustrates my state of mind at the time. As the policeman pushed me out to the yard, my eyes fell on a soldier with a rifle standing
by a wall. I thought at that moment that they had sentenced me to be shot and
that my sentence would be carried out right there. I was already in terror of
Germans and Lithuanians, so I had good reason to think this. But I did not have
time to sort out my feelings, because the policeman yelled at me to turn left and
get out to the street. My sense of relief was brief as he began barking orders:
"Hands to the back!" "Walk at the edge of the road, not on the sidewalk!" "Do
not look to the side!" "No talking!" When I obeyed, he added, "Fast! Faster!"
On Trakų Street we passed Abramovich the photographer. I whispered to him,
"I have been arrested. Tell my wife!" He had recently become somewhat deaf
and did not hear what I whispered. Still wanting to know what was going on,
he approached the policeman with the polite flattery of an old *shtadlan*,[54] an
expert in dealing with officials. But his skills were of no help this time. In a moment I heard a fearful cry and saw the policeman holding a soft leather whip,
flogging Abramovich for his audacity. So he never understood my situation and
of course did not tell my wife of my arrest, leaving her to anxious and sleepless
nights as she worried about my fate.

The policeman took me to the Šiauliai "forced-labor" prison.[55] Its gate
seemed to me like the maw of a giant wild beast, able to swallow victims without a trace. I was brought into a small intake office, and the night watch[56] clerk
started writing down my information. By coincidence this clerk was the husband of a hospital orderly from the old days, who had known me well and always
addressed me with respect. He inquired about the reason for my arrest, and I
told him I had had a dispute with Stankus the Jewish affairs overseer, who decided I had offended him. I handed over my money, my papers, watch, fountain

pen, and other small items from my pockets. Then I entered an adjacent room where another official demanded my comb, tie, belt, suspenders, shoelaces, and socks; evidently this was done to prevent the prisoner from committing suicide by cutting his own throat with the comb (?) or hanging himself with the other items. Then he carefully patted down my clothes to make sure there were no forbidden items hidden there. I was later told that many were beaten during this ceremony to give them a taste of what was to come. I was led through a second gate to an inner court where the prison's main building was located along with the warehouse, kitchen, bathhouse, etc. In the inner court were many [Soviet] prisoners of war, mostly Mongolian in appearance, with their slanted eyes and short stature. Their beaten,[57] cowed appearance was depressing. After being defeated in battle, which alone would be painful, they had been starved, over-worked, and viciously beaten for any slight infraction of the rules, as I myself witnessed later. I was told that many had been killed by various diseases or their oppressors' bullets while working. In one case, some of them had protested or resisted at the airfield and were shot by the Germans in full view of the others.

The "delightful country that fell to me"[58] in prison was cell number nine or eleven; I'm ashamed to admit I don't remember which. My spirit was too crushed to stop and read what was written on the door. I had barely entered the room when I was surrounded by seven Jewish prisoners led by Widzinski, who had been the secretary of the Šiauliai kehilla and of the "Ezra" charity[59] during the years when I chaired its board. They had heard rumors of a doctor's arrest but they did not expect to meet me, a senior physician known and respected as an official in the municipal hospital. The prisoners began bombarding me with questions, asking the reason for my arrest and for news from the city, the ghetto, and the front, since no outside information could penetrate the prison's walls. I tried as best as I could, given my own confusion, to satisfy their curios-ity. I was pleased, if I can use that word given the situation, to find Widzinski here. He was a good friend and a man of action. Indeed he immediately began to teach me the rules of life in prison, which he had mastered after being there for a month. First he explained it was necessary to find a place to lie down, because the night inspection had already happened and the room would soon be dark. Two large sleeping shelves were mounted on the wall, upper and lower bunks. Widzinski and his neighbor, also a Jew, prepared a place for me to lie down between them on the upper shelf. They recommended I use my clothes as bedding, with my suit as a mat and my coat as a blanket. If I recall they lent me one of their own small straw pillows. I followed their advice, cushioning my spot with my better suit, which I happened to wear the day of my arrest. I also tucked in half of my summer jacket, using the other half as a blanket. It was all in vain: my bunk remained rock-hard and my entire body ached, and there was no sleep to be had.

Even if the bed had been deluxe I would not have slept because all that night I loathed myself[60] as I recalled my ways and acts. First, I should have been more careful about arguing with Stankus, who had power and dominion.[61] The timing had clearly been bad: before entering his office I had overheard Dr. Rosenthal arguing and pleading with him about something so intensely that the back of his neck reddened. Stankus had remained cold and stony until he grew impatient and showed signs of blazing anger.[62] After Dr. Rosenthal left, red-faced and anguished, I entered, another troublesome and impudent Jew who then dared to chastise him. Second, I surprised even myself by mentioning the Germans in my moment of anger, a dangerous move that could easily shorten one's days. Third, I blamed myself for being devoid of sense[63] and not properly explaining to the German security officer what I had truly wanted to say. I had offered what might have been taken as a compliment to German culture when I noted it does not need the Jews, but the essence was missing. When I had said, "I don't know what will happen with the Germans," I should have added, "relative to the Jews." Had I done so he might not have taken offense at my words, and this disaster with its unknown outcome would not have occurred.

As I tossed on my hard bunk, my heart ached with oppression, misery, and sorrow.[64] My grief was intensified by the thought of leaving my wife sick, perhaps brought to her deathbed[65] by her family's afflictions and our son's troubles before his miraculous escape from Vilnius. The news of her cousin's death had aggravated her condition, and I was sure that my night in prison would depress her to the point that she would never leave her bed. Worry about my wife's health overcame my personal distress, along with the sense that I had failed her. I already blamed myself for her worsening condition; now I was lying here sleeplessly while she was in far greater danger, maybe on her deathbed. It also pained me that she would be unable to plead for me or come to my aid, while our son was too young and impractical: what could he possibly do for me? To whom would he turn? It looked like I had bought myself a long stay in this place—or worse, until my demise, which wouldn't be far off.

Meanwhile, dim light began penetrating the two windows, which had iron bars inside and wooden shutters outside, blocking our view of the yard. It was explained to me that these barriers were a Bolshevik invention. But through the top we could glimpse a bit of the sky, and that is where the dim light of a gloomy morning came through. After a little while a loud whistle sounded, then a second and third. The prisoners left their bunks, disheveled and sad, and started to dress. As Widzinski explained, this was the routine every morning at 5:30. In a while they let the prisoners out to do their business and wash. That is when I had the pleasure of seeing the famous latrines that the earlier Jewish prisoners had been "honored" to clean with their bare hands. The latrines were still filthy, and cleaning them was still the Jews' job, but now there were rags and water. Finding water, though, was not so easy. With all the prisoners of war there it was sometimes impossible to get enough water not only to clean the latrines, but even to wash hands. There were only a few latrines, moreover, and therefore necessary to wait in line. It may be of interest, by the way, that at prison latrines the most valuable item, "worth its weight in gold," was paper! Newspapers and books were prohibited, letters could not be delivered or written, and Jews were not permitted to receive packages, so where to obtain paper? The shortage often led to great torment, as I can attest, so I decided to use one of the handkerchiefs in my pocket and immediately wash it under the faucet whenever water was available.

The prisoners returned to the cell, and soon the whistle sounded again, [indicating] the morning inspection. The prisoners lined up in two rows like soldiers, to wait for the clerk who came each evening and morning to count the prisoners. He came in and counted eleven Lithuanians and eight Jews; then he looked at us briefly and left. The prisoners remained at attention until a short whistle indicated the inspection was over, and the day's routine began in the cell. Waiting for breakfast, which came at 6:30 a.m., some prisoners paced back and forth like caged animals, others busied themselves obtaining smoking tobacco. This preoccupied nearly all the prisoners, prompting a variety of schemes. I did not study them all in detail, but one involved making contact with the prisoners of war in the yard through open windows and cracks in the shutters. There was a Russian lad of sixteen in our cell, a shepherd whom the Germans had seized along with his flock. Since he was not a soldier and was younger than the other captives, they thought it inappropriate to leave him with the other prisoners of war and put him in our cell. This boy was an expert at negotiating with the prisoners of war. He would knock on the window, and in a soft, murmuring voice,[66] call, "Comrades!" When the answer came the exchange began. From the cell, a slice of bread was thrown over the shutters into the yard; in return, through cracks in the shutters, came bits of tobacco taken from the Germans' dropped cigarette butts or wherever. This Russian boy also had a talent for eating as much as three grown men. He and other prisoners kept busy hunting for the lice that proliferated in clothes and underwear when the water shortage closed the bathhouse, and the guards said underwear could not be dropped off at the laundry until the bathhouse reopened.

All this I learned from Widzinski, who had become knowledgeable after a month in the prison. Breakfast took place at 6:30: each prisoner received four hundred grams of wheat bread and twenty grams of sugar. (The actual amounts were less, because evidently there is no shortage of people able to benefit at prisoners' expense.) Along with the daily ration they provided coffee, or rather hot water colored with chicory, but as much as we wanted. This was brought in a large kettle, and the drinking was unrestricted.[67] At first I did not have a cup like the other prisoners, but Widzinski managed to find me one.

Work started after breakfast. First it was necessary to peel potatoes for lunch and dinner. This was a voluntary job; each day up to ten prisoners from cells on the first floor were allowed to enter a room adjacent to the kitchen. Two of the stronger prisoners would bring up two sacks of potatoes from the basement, and the potato peelers got to work, using pieces of broken knives. During the three days I participated in this, nearly all the potatoes were rotten—black and full of eyes from sprouts and roots. We would throw three-quarters of a potato away to find one small piece fit for eating. These pieces we dropped into a large steel barrel half-filled with water. When we finished, we washed our hands in the same barrel, and some of us raked the skins and rotten potatoes back into the sacks to be tossed into the garbage bins. We were told that the prisoners of war picked them out of the trash, cooked and ate them because they were always hungry.

The real work started after this volunteer job. This was a forced-labor prison, after all. A policeman entered our cell on my first day after the potatoes were cleaned, and took me and another Jewish prisoner (Levin) to the guards' residence to clean a dirty vacant apartment. In one room, two women were washing the floor. When they saw us they shook their heads, and nodded toward me in apparent recognition. The policeman led us to the other room and ordered us to clean a bathtub that was filthy with many years of grime, and to remove stains from white tiles on the stove, which also showed neglect from years of old.[68] Finally, we were instructed to tidy up the toilet. The guard was a reasonable man who treated us politely. He even found us some powder to help remove the filth from the tub. We cleaned the rusted tub together; then I cleaned the stove while my companion cleaned and tidied the toilet. We returned to our cell afterward, but did not have long to rest.

I had yet to taste the real flavor of the prison, which had actually improved markedly since the first days after the Germans arrived. After a few minutes, a short gunman came in and ordered six Jews, me among them, to haul lumber. Outside in the yard I received a terrible blow to my right kidney that made me recoil and scream in pain. I managed to cry out, "I'm an old man!" but was ignored by the villain who hit me, probably for falling behind and not marching in lockstep with my fellow prisoner. Even today my blood boils at the memory of this blow. I was even angrier at the time but had to keep walking, quietly bearing the pain and insult. The gunman led us, dragging a cart, to the adjacent second yard. The lumber was down a slope; to load the cart we had to fetch the lumber and carry it uphill. Then one of us had to get between the cart poles and pull it, like a horse, with the others pushing from behind or the sides. This job was hard, particularly under the supervision of the gunmen and local partisans who did not know us. They tormented the Jewish prisoners and hit them for no other reason than cruelty and hatred. Presumably these were the same partisans who participated in the terrible killing and destruction of entire [Jewish] communities in Lithuania, so what was one more beating? There was one armed gunman at the lumberyard with a permanent smirk on his cretinous, evil face, who harassed us continuously to carry more logs. With the lumber finally on the cart, Widzinski pulled from the front while we pushed from behind. As a well-dressed, older, intellectual-looking man, I must have attracted the attention of this gunman, who decided I wasn't working hard enough. To change his mind and avoid being branded a slacker, I leaned in with all my strength and pushed the cart with my shoulder. But suddenly I received a blow from behind that made me straighten up: the gunman had honored me with his boot, just to brutalize an intelligent Jew. So I was hit twice in one day, for the first time since becoming a man. And that was in addition to the hard forced labor which I had never experienced until that day.

After hauling and unloading several carts of lumber in the prison storeroom, I returned to the cell, shattered in body and spirit. The pain, the insults, my inability to protest or resist, all had such a depressing effect that it was a miracle I did not go out of my mind, especially since my mind was buzzing like Titus's gnat[69] with the recognition that this calamity was not an accident. I had brought it on myself; I was to blame. My mental torment began all over again as I was visited by the same hallucinations of the previous sleepless night. This was interrupted when a guard came to take me and several new prisoners to the storeroom to fetch our prison gear. Each of us received a cup, a bowl, a rusting spoon (all made of tin), a small pillow filled with hay, an empty mattress sack, a towel, and, most importantly, a clean, warm blanket.

Widzinski told me it was hard to believe how much conditions had improved. The first ones to be imprisoned here after the Germans arrived slept on the cold, hard floor, or on iron beds without mattresses or hay sacks as cushions. Those beds, attached to the walls opposite the sleeping shelves, were now upright, and prisoners could use them to hang coats, hats, and towels. The Germans had also tortured the first prisoners with immense cruelty and starved them. Now the situation was much better. I put the bedding I had received on the lower shelf near the window, claiming it as my bed as my friends had advised me. My dishes I put in the closet, which was attached to a long table, like a grocer's counter. Besides this, the beds and sleeping shelves, was the famous device described by Dostoevsky in his "House of the Dead"[70]: an iron barrel placed in the corner for use as a toilet. So there you have a tour of the cell.

We were given lunch at 12:30. Two prisoners from the ghetto—one who served as the prison's cook and the other a "forewarned"[71] thief—brought in a large vat filled with soup, either cabbage soup with potatoes or beet soup, and prisoners approached one by one, bowls in hand, to receive their portions. I did not get to taste the beet soup, but the cabbage soup was tasty after the hard physical work, although it seemed to lack meat or butter. (It may have been flavored with a little lard.) After lunch we rested a bit, then work resumed until dinner at 4:30 (cooked grits one day, "farfel"[72] the next). Sometimes work resumed after dinner but not for long. The prisoners were left alone for an hour or two until the evening inspection, which was identical to the morning inspection. Some lay on their beds, jumping up at any sudden sound because lying down was forbidden. Some played at checkers, hiding the game under a blanket when a guard entered. Some paced back and forth like caged animals. Some chatted with each other or sat idly, lost in their thoughts. Some searched for lice in their clothes, and some prepared cigarettes from the collected butts. Preparations for sleep began after evening inspection.

The routine was the same, with only small variations, during the four days I was in the prison. I was not beaten again, possibly because after the first day a guard accompanied the partisans and curbed their aggressiveness. One day, instead of lumber we had to haul flour and grits from the storeroom. And on another, I think my last day in prison, we were "privileged" to be given a job we could not have had the strength to do[73] without help. We were ordered to haul a garbage bin from its place by the prison gate to the adjacent yard, where the lumber was; empty it; and haul it back. When we tried to lift the bin onto a cart, it refused to budge as if nailed down. Of we six laborers, only three were young men with strength in their loins.[74] The rest—me; the dentist from Tauragė, also an old man; and another weak Jew (Friedman)—were of questionable use. Then one of the Germans serving in the prison approached us and, together with our guard, demonstrated the value of Esau's hands.[75] Only with their help were we able to execute the order. We loaded the full bin on the cart, carried it out to the adjacent yard, and emptied it. In the meantime, however, some prisoners of war took the cart away to haul lumber. So we were left to carry the bin back with our hands, which we were barely able to do, because it was made of thick oak boards and very heavy. I think this was the hardest job of all I had to do while in prison. It was even harder than being forced by the evil gunman to play the "horse" between the cart poles as punishment for my supposed slacking. When he made me do it again the following day and I felt my strength diminishing I decided to defy the oppressor, no matter the consequences. I dropped the poles and announced I could no longer play the horse. That was when Widzinski, the strongest among us, took my place and I joined the push-ers. Indeed, this was like a prophecy of my impending release, setting me free from the oppression of this villain. If not for that, he would surely have found an opportunity to take revenge for my audacity, which thanks to the guard's presence went unpunished.

On my fifth morning in prison, before breakfast a guard entered, called my name and ordered me to return all my issued gear to the storeroom. This meant I was free! I quickly collected my dishes and bedding, wished my cellmates farewell and rushed out, my heart aching for the other Jewish prisoners, who were rightfully jealous since their own offenses, as I will explain, were trivial.

To my pleasant surprise I had underestimated my wife. I thought my im-prisonment would crush her because she was gravely ill, unable to rise from her bed. But in fact after spending a sleepless night filled with bitterness and worry, she gathered all her strength and demonstrated exceptional courage, initiative, and drive. The next morning she began knocking on the doors of Dr. Jasaitis, Stankus, Kozlovska, Dr. Daugirdienė, and officers of the secret police. And her efforts were crowned with glorious victory! On the fourth day of my imprison-ment Stankus himself went to the office of the Jewish council with a note from the secret police ordering my release and told the members to "take your doctor back!" Shapira, from the council secretary's office, immediately rushed the note to our home. Our son, Tedik, rushed it to the prison office, but it was late so I was not released until the following morning. The office holding my personal belongings was still closed, and I could not take my personal belongings that were taken when I entered. I decided to go home immediately without waiting for my belongings. It is hard to describe my wife and my son's joy when they saw me. My wife's efforts probably saved my life; she took up the task with all her remaining strength and succeeded! A little while after I returned, a messenger came from the Jewish council's office to ask that I go there immediately. I did not understand why, but when I reached their office they told me that Stankus had been there a few minutes earlier and had said, "I was too angry, but Dr. Pick was also very angry. I wish to see him." I rushed to his office and he greeted me with a smile. "Did you like it?" he asked. "Not particularly," I answered, adding that I bore him no ill will and would not forget his kindness. I offered my hand and thanked him. That is how we parted, and thank God I have not seen him since. From there I walked back to the prison and retrieved my personal belongings and money. (Not all freed prisoners were so fortunate.) By order of the prison superintendent, I had to go to the secret police and notify them of my release. That was the last unpleasant moment of this sad affair. I entered the office where I had been shaken to the bone five days earlier and announced that I had been a prisoner but was now released. To which I received the brusque reply: "All is in order." That is how this terrible incident, which I will never forget to my last day, came to an end.

As I left the office, I reflected that I still was walking the same "road of suffering," but now I was as free as a Jew can be. I also recalled what one of the earlier prisoners had said: "Better to be shot than to land in prison." And then I remembered the story of my jailing as a youth, when I was student at the Slabodka yeshiva.[76] To avoid breaking the rules of the Sabbath I had gone out without my identification card and been caught. I thought about the difference between my situation then and now, between the servants of the tsar and those of the "supreme source of evil."[77] Some fifty years had passed since then, and how far had humanity declined! When will history end this deviance and return to the path of progress and improvement? The situation does not give my heart much hope.

As I finish my notes on the sad chapter of my imprisonment, I think it necessary to describe the Jewish prisoners who were my cellmates.

(1) Widzinski: Applying for a job during the Soviet period, he had emphasized his inclination toward Bolshevism, which was appropriate at that time. His application fell into the hands of the German secret police and he was arrested. Lithuanians were forgiven such sins, but Widzinski had already been in prison for an entire month before I arrived, with no investigation or review. When I left he still had no hope of getting out soon. I am so sorry for him. He himself told me that desperation had begun to eat at him, and his strength to resist was diminishing. Someone told me that once he was being transported from the prison to a job location; standing in the truck, he saw his daughter on the street. When he nodded to her, a Lithuanian or German guard hit him so hard that he fell down, with his daughter watching. She screamed and fainted. Yes! The Jews are abandoned, anybody's to abuse with no law and no judge!

(2) Tovir, a simple country Jew, wrote up accusations against six of his village's kulaks, rich farmers, and also identified himself as a Bolshevik on a job application. This fellow caused us plenty of grief: day and night he cried to himself and refused to eat, trembling at every sound at the door or down the hall, thinking he was about to be taken out and executed. He also had several episodes of epilepsy which in normal years might have prompted his release, since someone with this condition cannot be responsible for his actions. But now an appeal on those grounds could prove dangerous, because the Nazis have no need for sick Jews who cannot be turned into slaves. They think it right and proper to shoot such a person.

(3) Friedman, Israel, about forty years old, a truly God-fearing man who during his entire stay in the prison nourished himself only with bread and "coffee." He would not allow himself to be tainted [i.e., violate the kosher laws] even with soup. As a doctor I ordered him to eat the cabbage and grits, because if he continued to limit his diet like that he would undoubtedly have dropped under the burden of the hard labor. This honest man had gotten into needless trouble for allegedly trying to bribe an official to permit an artisans' cooperative[78] to continue, or to revive it—the matter is still not quite clear to me. I only know that he had nothing to do with it and that the true culprit was (4) Abramovich, a young hoodlum and con artist, yoked to deceit[79] who began the affair and when caught, assumed wrongly that his sentence would be reduced if he named others. So he said that Friedman and another prisoner, Levin, were his partners in the bribe. This young swindler admitted in the cell, in front of Widzinski and Tovir, that Friedman was not guilty, but then recanted and threatened Tovir if he mentioned the confession.

By trying to win vindication by involving others in his guilt, this Abramovich also dragged down (5) young Levin, whom I mentioned earlier. He is a full-fledged Hebrew scholar who read and studied [traditional Jewish texts] and is also familiar with secular literature. He asked me to do him a favor after I was freed: to speak of him to Feinstein, Gorgil's brother-in-law, who was his partner and who has contacts with the authorities. But this was in vain: Feinstein had suffered a great calamity and could not even help himself. When I left prison I learned that while Feinstein was away from home, the Germans had come and grabbed his young wife and two children along with his in-laws, and took them from the ghetto to that unknown, mysterious place[80] from whence none have returned. The husband tried with all his might to find his wife and children, but it was for naught. They had disappeared as if the ground opened its mouth and swallowed them.[81] Indeed! No one returns from the depths where they were certainly put by the partisans. Obviously I could not bring up Levin's case to Feinstein at such a time, and so the matter ended there.

This incident with Feinstein's wife created a huge problem for the doctors, arousing the anger of the ghetto's Jewish population against them. What happened was this: after several families and a few other individuals were taken from the former Feinstein house at 2 Padirsiu Street, Dr. B.N. and the dentist V-sky[82] took apartments in that building. The latter worked in the hospital for prisoners of war. The German chief doctor at that hospital, a kind man, protected the Jewish doctors who worked under his supervision. Among other things, he obtained notes for them signed by the district commissioner, ordering that they be provided apartments in the ghetto. Normally this is harder to do than parting the Red Sea, but thanks to these notes the council rushed to get them apartments—which caused the catastrophe [the Feinstein family's abduction]! That is what is being said in the ghetto.

It is hard to know how much of this terrible accusation is true. However, when V-sky the dentist wants something for himself, he digs and gnaws like a mouse and can penetrate cracks like a troublesome flea. It is hard to believe he would finagle the authorities for an apartment that was already occupied by others. On the other hand, this is a wily and selfish man who is unstoppable when he wants something, so it is possible that his actions led indirectly to the tragedy as he was unable to see the consequences of his wheedling. Since then, people have grown angry with the doctors because of this terrible business of relocating people to synagogues[83] and from there to their destruction. People thought this resulted directly from the need to clear spaces for the doctors! There were no apartments for six or seven doctors who were late to arrive in the ghetto, so families were taken from the ghetto to the synagogues that became corridors to the grave for at least five hundred [Jews]! It is an interesting calculation, but let us return to the story. Because of this issue I could do nothing for the innocent Levin, because his partner Feinstein was himself immersed in unspeakable grief.

(6) The sixth Jewish prisoner, the dentist St-b. Mt-n., was a very uninteresting character who became a burden to us all with his incessant chatter and empty and stupid questions that he repeated daily. He had apparently joined some Bolshevik committee in order to be seen as an activist and progressive in keeping with the spirit of those times. Now he is accused of being a communist, although he's as much that as is the emperor of China.

(7) The seventh Jewish prisoner was a young cobbler, approximately eighteen years old, careless but alert, who had taken part in his town's "komyug."[84] In my first days he was helpful to me, removing my shoes, tucking in my blanket,

and so on. He managed well in prison and was our cell's "cook." His clothes were in tatters, and I promised to get him decent ones when I was freed, but I never had the chance to fulfill that promise. And now who knows where he is, because none of those who were with me in the cell are still in Šiauliai. All were taken away except Tovir. Because his crime was so serious he was initially not allowed to work outside the prison's walls, and so was not taken away with the other prisoners. For quite some time he remained there alone. I used to see him on my way to work, being led to labor together with Christian prisoners. Now he too is no longer in that prison. Where are they all? Who knows? They probably suffered the same fate as those imprisoned earlier. All have disappeared.

(8) The eighth prisoner was me, the eldest and most educated, known to nearly all the prison's high officials as a well-regarded physician, a public officeholder jailed for a minor infraction. I was thought of as a guest in the prison, but I was in deep despair for the reasons mentioned. That is, I was to blame for my disaster, I had undermined my wife's fragile health, and her illness would certainly make it impossible for her to lobby for my release. An interesting psychological note: I spent five nights in prison. The first two I absolutely could not sleep. But over the last three nights the edge of my grief dulled to the point where I could distract myself and force sleep by trying to mentally translate my Hebrew novel "Summer Flowers"[85] into Yiddish. I never got beyond the first page before sleep took me over. But it was only a short respite from the struggle with my melancholy thoughts.

I should mention here that the Christian prisoners displayed no overt anti-semitism toward the Jewish prisoners, and that peace prevailed among us during my stay. There was one minor scuffle between Widzinski and a Christian prisoner after Widzinski mistakenly took the latter's cup. But the disturbance ended quickly, particularly when Widzinski realized his mistake. It is interesting to note that not only the political prisoners but also the general prisoners behaved decently to each other. Among the Christian prisoners was a red-haired young man, the secretary of the Bolshevik committee in his village. He received a package from home (something forbidden to Jews), with a large cheese, which he distributed among the prisoners, including the Jews. He made a good impression. I did not have the chance to engage him in conversation or to get to know three other political prisoners. One was a young man who had only recently finished the Lithuanian gymnasium, a handsome, well-dressed lad who had memorized Latin and German poems in school and showed off by reciting them.

Among the general prisoners was a repeat thief, a recidivist who was happy to be receiving free housing and food in prison. Another man there had murdered his wife, who had made his life miserable with her bullying, and after the murder he took some of her things from their house. The thief, who was an expert in criminal law, told him: "Killing your wife means nothing; it was her fault. But you will be punished for taking her things." Another interesting prisoner had previously been employed as a cook in the prison and "emerged from a dungeon to become king."[86] He pretended to be a secret police official and began searching passersby. When the hoax was discovered, he was sentenced to year and a half. He was among those distributing meals in our cell, and he treated everyone with a dismissive smile.

There were two other young men: the Russian lad who communicated with the war prisoners in the yard and had a huge appetite, eating everyone else's leftovers as if he had had nothing else to eat that entire day. He was also a voracious smoker. The other young man, a handsome fellow with a nice shock of hair and a pleasant voice, would walk about the room immersed in his thoughts and singing to himself. Widzinski told me that he was one of those Lithuanians who had gone to East Prussia to work on German farms. As luck would have it he ended up working for a farmer who overworked, starved and occasionally beat him. One day when the young man's patience with this cruelty was at an end,[87] he attacked the German with his knife and injured him, then fled back to Lithuania, where he was arrested and jailed. I do not know how long he had been in our cell, but one evening a guard ordered him to come with him. A bad sign: he was not ordered to take his belongings as I was when they freed me. The young man never returned to the cell. Later, in the latrine, the cook said some prisoners said that they had heard an order come by telephone that this young man was to be shot. It is hard to forget a victim of German cruelty.

E. "FOR THESE THINGS DO I WEEP":[88]
THE ANNIHILATION OF ISRAEL IN LITHUANIA

"*Pogrom.*"[89] How often in our history have we heard this sad term! The horrific acts for which it was invented: rob and kill the Jews *en masse*, and not because of any immediate crisis. It happened as far back as Alexandria in Egypt, became more frequent during the Middle Ages and was revived in modern Russia and Poland. To such pogroms we must add the killing of Jews during wars and national uprisings such as during the Black Plague, the Crusades, the Khmelnytsky uprising,[90] the Cossacks, etc. The common denominator is that they all begin with heated emotions and an awakening of dormant, beast-like instincts to spill blood, and are forged by propaganda and other forces that arouse and incite the masses to insane acts, typified by the savage attacks of an inflamed crowd on its victims.

But alas, what horrors befell us in Lithuania! Would our grandchildren and great-grandchildren even believe that a peaceable, stolid nation, not given to anger or easy incitement, had put its heart into the cruel murder of tens of thousands—hundreds of thousands of Jews, coldly and deliberately? Hair will stand on the backs of their necks, blood will freeze in their veins, when they hear of the massacres of Jews in Lithuanian cities—of the old, the young, of women and toddlers, of pregnant mothers. Their skulls were crushed and their hearts pierced by the bullets of the Lithuanian partisans and gunmen, all in an orderly fashion! Methodically, one group after another was brought to the slaughter; each group waited its turn. The pits were ready; the victims were forced to undress to save their clothes, and then fathers were murdered in front of their children, and children in front of their fathers. The murderers' hands did not tremble; their eyes did not flinch, and their hearts did not fear[91] at the moans of the fallen as they breathed their last, or at the pulsating earth that covered those not yet dead. Indeed our brothers' blood cries out to us from the ground[92] of Lithuania, which has become our valley of slaughter, our gallows, its sons our executioners.

Can we forget what was done to us? Will we ever be reconciled with the members of their "intelligentsia" who led the murders: people such as the lawyers Požela and Koloksa,[93] and schoolteachers, gymnasium students, and others? They will be remembered in our history books as Amalek's partners and their crimes will never be expunged. We now know they received whispers from above that exterminating the Jews would be welcomed by "Samael,"[94] the supreme source of evil—and that was all the encouragement they needed to destroy hundreds of thousands of innocent Jews without question or hesitation. The Germans themselves have attested that nowhere else have they found such intense and wild hatred for Jews as in Lithuania. We cannot be consoled[95] when remembering the communities that have been erased from under heaven. A wave of Jew-killing washed across the countryside and no Jew escaped,[96] everywhere except for Vilnius, Kaunas, and Šiauliai. Here I will list the communities whose destruction was described by eyewitnesses, in the order that the testimonies were collected.

Kelmė.[97] The town of Kelmė was put to the torch on the third day of the war. Only outlying barns and granaries were left standing. And then came the Lithuanian partisans, who acted like conquerors. They selected 190 young and strong Jews to labor in the barns, while the remaining Jews were sent to work on farms outside the town. They remained there for about a month: meanwhile the murderers conspired with their cronies from other Lithuanian towns and "on the third day before Tisha B'Av"[98] the fate of Kelmė's Jews was decided. There were brick kilns about a half a kilometer outside the city, and nearby were quarries with large ditches. These became the graves of Kelmė's Jews. This is where Dr. Kagansky, his wife, and two daughters were butchered; it is where they ended the life of my wife's aunt Mrs. Sheffer, a healthy and beautiful woman, with her two daughters, one of whom finished the Lithuanian gymnasium. One of her friends said to her: "We are innocent, yet we are ordered to die. I die without fear!" Here they pulled my wife's young, sickly cousin from his mother's arms and killed him. She survived miraculously, as they were then still keeping many women alive. Here perished the leaders of *musar*[99] in Kelmė, those righteous and God-fearing ones who would not harm a fly. The Divine Presence[100] turned away from His faithful servants who walked with Him[101] their entire lives, abandoned the sons of Israel and disappeared. Gone!

From the family of Sheffer, my wife's uncle, only two young sons remained after he was killed in Raseiniai, and his wife and two daughters died at Kelmė. The boys were saved by Lithuanian acquaintances whose farm they had worked on. Ten days after the massacre in Kelmė, the lads and the farm owner showed up at our house. We gave them what we could (after having given many of our things to my wife's sister Zilberman and her family when the Soviets deported them from Šiauliai). We gave the two young men shirts, shoes, sugar, soap, and a "Gillette" razor with blades for shaving. Several weeks passed and on September 5 the farmer showed up again at our house, but this time he came alone.[102] The first thing my wife noticed was that he wore one of our son's shirts with his initials in Hebrew, "D.P." stitched proudly on the chest. We had given this shirt to one of his cousins. The farmer told us that of all Kelmė's Jewish residents only fifty still lived, scattered and isolated on various farms. On a day when the older Sheffer son happened to be in Tytuvėnai,[103] partisans came with Germans, collected the remaining [Kelmė] Jews as one gathers abandoned eggs,[104] including the younger Sheffer son, and shot them. The farmer sent his son to meet the older Sheffer brother to tell him what happened and give him a cross and a Catholic rosary. The boy may have escaped because he speaks Lithuanian and is blond like an Aryan. That is how a mother city in Israel,[105] famous throughout Lithuania for its God-fearing Jews, was destroyed.

A few days before these events my wife fell ill. In the face of all her family's catastrophes (nationalization, appropriation, and deportation to the USSR), her heart began to fail. When she heard what had happened to her cousins, her heart quaked and leapt from its place,[106] and she turned as white as a sheet. To a large extent, this is what led to my imprisonment: it was on that day when we heard about the extermination of Kelmė's Jewish community and my wife was unable to leave her bed, I became agitated and decided to ask Stankus, the "king of the Jews," to permit the maid who had been helping my wife to leave the ghetto. That is how the storm began that picked me up and threw me in jail.

Krakės near Kėdainiai. The Jewish community within this small village was not large, but it was the hub of seven neighboring communities (Grinkiškis, Dotnuva, etc.). Here 1,500 Jews were collected in a detention camp and a ghetto. The camp held men aged fifteen and older; the ghetto was for women and children younger than fifteen. On September 3 partisans accompanied by soldiers (one of whom spoke German) came, about sixty in all, and collected 355 men, lined them up in rows of four and led them out of town under the ruse that they were being taken to work, even though some were elderly or sick. At some distance from the town they were ordered to lie on the ground face down. (Apparently the murderers used these moments to prepare for their evil acts.) After a short while they were ordered to stand up and strip to their underwear. Old men and youths, weak and sickly, all fearing death, began with trembling limbs to follow the order. Suddenly sixty guns opened up, splattering death in all directions. Many tried to run from this lethal mayhem, but the partisan bullets caught them as they fled. One young man of fifteen managed to hide among the potato plants in a field and remained there until evening. Then he crawled like a worm to the house of a peasant who took pity on him and gave him some rags to wear and temporary shelter.[107]

For several weeks the youth wandered from village to village. His fear was great and he suffered much abuse from the farmers and the secret police until finally he found rest (!) in the ghetto of Šiauliai, where he had been a student in the Yiddish gymnasium. Later they murdered the women and children, annihilating in all some 1,500 Jews from Krakės village and its surroundings. Our spirit is crushed by oppression, misery, and sorrow.[108] Who will compose new lamentations for the destruction of these communities? An order from above was enough to turn the Lithuanians into unhesitant, methodical murderers, determined to squash us like flies.

Šiluva (near Raseiniai).[109] Here the partisans called for a rally of traitors and arrogant evildoers.[110] They invited partisans from Raseiniai, and the festivities ended with the sacrifice of nearly four hundred Jewish men and women from the town and surrounding area.

Tytuvėnai (near Raseiniai).[111] While the entire Jewish population was being murdered, the local physician was away visiting a patient in one of the nearby villages. When he returned home and found his family no longer among the living, he wanted to end his own life as well. He did not need to ask twice: his request was granted with precision and expediency by the Germans' willing tools of destruction.

Pakruojis (near Šiauliai).[112] The Jews were wiped out here in the same fashion as throughout Lithuania. Lies about being taken to work, undressing, shooting, and done! The physician Schreiber and his family became apostates and were saved. It was a difficult conversion, however, as the priest did not want to admit them into the covenant of the "merciful savior," whose followers emulate his virtues like wolves who present themselves as sheep. The daughter of Dr. Yochelson was with them but was not as fortunate. Rather than being admitted into the covenant of the Catholic Church, she was granted direct admission to the "Kingdom of Heaven" without delay and without the priest's help.

Panevėžys. A mother city in Israel![113] One of the most important cities in Lithuania. At first they allocated several streets for the Jews without putting up walls or barriers. This did not last long, however. First, they killed the men; then they eliminated the women and children. Doctors were among the first to be killed there, because of the following events: during the Bolshevik regime a nurse in the regional hospital was accused of mistreating Bolshevik patients. When party officials attempted to arrest her, she was hidden by Christian doctors. Eventually she along with two of the doctors were executed by [Soviet] firing squads. When the Germans arrived, partisans rushed to take revenge, first killing the Jewish doctors and then eliminating the entire Jewish population, wiping out an important community that had produced excellent Jewish institutions and leaders. "Alas for those who are gone and no more to be found!"[114]

Šaukėnai (near Šiauliai).[115] The oppressor Kolokša, the right hand of Požėla whose arm was outstretched[116] over the Pakruojis district, had a feast here. The two are lawyers and presumably intelligent men. They organized the slaughter of Jews in and around the Šiauliai district. Their hands were defiled with Jewish blood,[117] which they spilled like water. Half the town's Jewish population was killed and the other half was sent to Žagarė and met their end there. Two young women whom the drunkard Kolokša fancied were saved by him. One lost her mind, the other stayed on his farm for a while until his "mistress" found a way to get rid of her. The one who had been a local dentist and her family accepted the Catholic religion; after their murder the Catholics buried them in choice graves in the Catholic cemetery.

Tryškiai. On the twenty-fourth of Tammuz,[118] a Sabbath day, seventy-five men were massacred, led by the rabbi and his two sons. The victims were forced to dig their own graves and then undress.

Žagarė.[119] Many tents were prepared in Žagarė for Polish refugees. Later, Jews from Šiauliai, Papilė, Šaukėnai, Vaiguva,[120] Užventis, and elsewhere were sent there. Rumors about the Jews' fate there horrified us for quite some time. Then we heard about events there. We were told the partisans collected a large group, intending to actually take them to work. However, knowing that it was standard procedure to pretend to take Jews to work when they were to be murdered, they panicked and began to run. The partisans chased them, shooting and killing most. Some of the details are in doubt, but it is clear that not a single Jew was left in Žagarė. They were all killed—men, women, and children. Indeed, how great is our disaster.[121] Even our feelings have dulled so that we record these terrible stories of our brothers' bloodletting indifferently, using ordinary words because our minds cannot grasp the truth.

A Lithuanian patient told me innocently, when I asked if there were still doctors left in Žagarė: "There are no Jews in Žagarė. The partisans and the volunteers brought shame and dishonor on us by their actions. They turned Žagarė into a 'slaughterhouse.' All that became loathsome to us."[122]

Radviliškis (near Šiauliai).[123] This comes from a well-known dentist who had many acquaintances among the Christians. On Sunday [June 22] when the war broke out, her acquaintance, the Lithuanian commandant, advised her to move to a certain village. He warned her that the town of Radviliškis was an important military center with an important weapons factory nearby at Linkaičiai[124] and a principal train station with a large gasoline storage facility. Because of this they expected aerial bombardment, artillery attacks, and armed clashes. On his advice she took the best of her jewelry and clothes and went to the village, leaving her maid at home. On the second day another forty Jews arrived at that same village. The commandant's prediction came to pass: on Monday, attacks began on the town and its surroundings. This made it impossible to obtain food from town, and hunger began to torment the refugees, since the village lacked sufficient bread for so many. On Wednesday there was an enormous battle and the refugees had to lie for eight hours in a ditch full of water. On Thursday the battle resumed, and the refugees again had to hide in the waterlogged ditch to escape the bullets and bombs. During all of this the refugees saw Russian soldiers fleeing on foot or horseback. By Friday the Germans had occupied the town and region. That is when the dentist dared[125] to return to the town.

Not a single Jew was on the streets, as they did not dare leave their looted and burglarized houses; the mood resembled the eve of a pogrom, and anyone caught on the street had been quickly arrested. The dentist was not arrested because her acquaintance, the commandant, protected her, and at noon she returned to the village. But at three o'clock the partisans came and forced all the Jewish refugees back to town. They also issued a warning that any Christian who allowed a Jew to stay in their house would be shot. The partisans pressured the refugees, giving them only half an hour to leave the village. When they approached the city they saw Jews being led into town from all directions. All Jewish men were arrested while the women were let go. Meanwhile they were spreading false rumors as a provocation that Jews had killed two partisans and one German. The Germans killed a Jew on the street, and the Lithuanians threatened to kill one hundred Jews for every Lithuanian harmed. On Saturday at three o'clock they released all the prisoners, who said they had been subjected to a night of torture and forced labor.

On Sunday the Germans seized the best Jewish houses and, along with the Lithuanians, ransacked and looted them. After taking everything they could find, the Lithuanians demanded that Jews turn over any hidden jewelry, threatening severe retaliation if they did not. On Sunday they again began abducting Jews supposedly for work, but in reality just to torture them: they trimmed their beards, put dung on their heads, or poured water on the sidewalks and ordered Jews to dry it with their stomachs. They made them run while being poked from behind with bayonets, stabbing whoever fell behind, ordered them to jump over fences and obstacles, and so on. The community's rabbi was beaten, his beard was cut off, and he was tormented all day with other Jews before being released in the evening. This was all repeated on Monday. On Tuesday they assembled the Jews in the market square and drove them from there at dusk like a flock of sheep with whips and sticks, to the area near the train station where they were put into an old barrack with three filthy rooms and shelves to sleep on.[126] The men, under German supervision, built an iron-wire fence. Directed by the Germans, they elected "order keepers" and a camp commandant; only then were they permitted to go into town to buy bread. The filth in the rooms was terrible; there were not enough sleeping shelves so some had to lie on the muddy floor. There was no kettle to boil hot water, and no bowls to wash with. Hungry and thirsty children cried; women passed out.

There was one helpful feature there, which all the prisoners made use of: a freshwater well, convenient for washing. A German guard was bribed to allow them to bring kitchen utensils from town, while several others became "traders" and sold dried fish to the residents. Conditions improved for a time, but then "a new king arose":[127] new Germans came and brought with them a Lithuanian translator, a sadist who caused the camp's inmates endless torment. He forbade them to see doctors, go to town for food, etc. An extraordinary incident took place here: a young Jew named "Jaška" arrived. No one knew where he had come from. He began to befriend the partisans, drank with them, played cards with them every night, abused the camp's young women . . . he did terrible things. Even the Lithuanian sadist was surprised to see how badly he treated his own people. He was an exceptional villain and assumed to be a German spy. A woman in the camp gave birth to a child, and "Jaška" would not permit a midwife to be brought. So the dentist played midwife, using hot water from two thermos bottles they found. Another woman suffered a gallbladder attack (probably a gallbladder stone and an infection of the bladder ducts). Because of Jaška, no doctor was allowed, and the woman died. This "Jaška" also introduced the wearing of yellow stars of David, as is common elsewhere.

Eventually all the local Jews as well as those who came from elsewhere were transferred to another barrack further from the city, and this camp was closed. One group was transferred to Žagarė, a second went to Šiauliai, and a third was lost in the wilderness.[128] The Radviliškis camp held not only Jews from the town and its surroundings but also from other places. Either by German order or on their own initiative, police would arrest and bring to the camp any Jew who passed near Radviliškis, either on foot or in a cart. It is therefore a miracle that my son and his friends, when they traveled from Vilnius, were not arrested when they passed near Radviliškis.

Telšiai.[129] A city famous throughout Israel's diaspora, Europe, and the world for its yeshiva, which produced so many great sages. Admittedly, this yeshiva was home to the most narrow-minded, orthodox opponents of the new ideas animating our people.[130] Nevertheless it gave the world a great many students of the Torah, one of the pillars of our existence. The history of this community, which was as filled with scholars and those who seek the welfare of the faithful in Israel[131] as a pomegranate is with seeds, is a story unto itself, a depressing and shocking tale that deserves to be inscribed in eternal memory. Let all the details of the ruin of the Telšiai community be recorded by a master scribe, one who can trace all the details of the terrible events there and recount them unto the last generation. Here as well the God of Israel hid His face from his servants and abandoned them. They always trusted in God—and oh what disappointment! What anguish! The heart and the soul are as empty as a dry desert.

This is the story of one woman who survived the concentration camp in Telšiai: after their store in Skaudvilė was confiscated by the Bolsheviks, they moved to Tauragė, where they lived for two months. (The Bolsheviks gave her husband a decent job there.) On Sunday, June 22, when the war began, the entire city was set ablaze, so they fled to Upyna, which was already in German hands. The partisans there detained the local rabbi, cut off his beard and made him build a fire, planning to burn him at the stake. But the square was narrow, and the surrounding houses were in danger of catching fire, so the plan was called off at the villagers' request. Instead they ordered the rabbi to run while they shot at him, injuring his legs. The rabbi's wife found a chance to get away, and took the injured man to a town that had doctors. Nothing else is known about the rabbi's fate. In Upyna the mood resembled that on the eve of a pogrom. So this woman and her family—her husband, in-laws and her small child—headed from Upyna to Tryškiai. But the partisans captured them fifteen kilometers from Tryškiai near the village of Luokė, stole everything, and brought them to a concentration camp in Luokė, where there were already about 150 people.

Their treatment there by the partisans was terrible. The prisoners stayed in a barn. A guard was always present. They were beaten ceaselessly with whips for the slightest offense or for nothing. They were given forced labor, pulling weeds from between street cobbles, washing floors in houses and so on. Five kilometers from Luokė is the village of Kaunatava. Two Jewish families lived there. Those two families were also brought to the camp in Luokė. The partisans did their customary search of their homes and found amid the Ziv family's belongings a red flag left over from the Bolshevik days, which in their haste they had failed to destroy. That day they brought in twenty other people from around the village. They took all these new arrivals, led by the Ziv family, accused them of Bolshevism and beat the men with whips until they bled. Then they put them in a damp, cold basement and left them there. During the days they sent people to work in town, where they attempted to find food since there was none at the camp. On July 16, two Germans from the S.A.[132] arrived and took all the men to a field and for about an hour tormented them sadistically, interminably: they were forced to crawl on their bellies, and to hit each other in earnest. All the prisoners received terrible blows before being sent back to the barn.

It turned out that one of the Germans was actually a Russian (Itamlinski), a family acquaintance of the woman who told this story, who apparently committed himself[133] to the Germans when the Bolsheviks arrived. He announced that an order had come from Berlin to kill all the Jewish men because the Germans were suffering many casualties, but there were no casualties among the Jews. That night starting at midnight they led small groups of men to the basement for "work," and the following morning took them about two kilometers from Luokė, where they shot about 80 men and buried them in pits prepared ahead of time. Nine men fled but only two survived according to one of the partisans. The women remained in Luokė three more days, then were taken to Viešvėnai, about fifteen kilometers from Luokė, where there already were many women. There they remained for four days in open barns, filthy, full of mold and water from the rain that was coming down. After four more days they took them to Geruliai, about fifteen kilometers from Telšiai.[134] About 2,500 women and children from Telšiai and its surroundings were collected there.

After the men were wiped out, the women began to organize: they established a committee under the supervision of a Lithuanian official. He allowed them to work in the fields and the women received bread, butter, grits, and milk. There was also a physician there, Dr. Blat, who took care of the camp. He was supposed to be the only man there but in fact there were ten men in the camp, dressed as women. Their ruse was later discovered and, except for one, all were put to death. A rumor spread that the women would be killed as well. So a delegation was sent to the district minister and to the commissioner, Gewecke,[135] who was then visiting Telšiai once a week. The delegation asked that a ghetto be set up for the women. On September 30 the partisans came and ordered the women to hand over all they had, otherwise they would be shot on the spot. The partisans said they would be taken to their ghetto in Telšiai but were forbidden to take money or jewelry with them. The next day at 6:00 a.m., the women were led outside. The district minister told them carts were on their way for them but that they had only ten minutes to gather their belongings. They even suggested that the women not wake their children but leave them notes; the children would be brought to them later.

Ten minutes later all the women reassembled in the field, where they were divided into two groups: one, of five hundred women with daughters, was ordered to walk to Telšiai. The other two thousand, with male children, were left in Geruliai. The belongings of those walking to Telšiai were loaded on carts. In Telšiai the five hundred were allocated two streets, which were fenced in with wooden boards. The women could see immediately that the ghetto was only meant to be temporary, because no firewood had been provided even though it was already getting cold, particularly at night. A Lithuanian liaison collected the salaries of the women who were sent out to work and distributed their rations of bread, grits, and potatoes.

Meanwhile Christians spread a rumor that the Telšiai ghetto was about to be eliminated, prompting a wave of escape attempts. Many women perished from cold and starvation in the forest; many fell at the hands of the partisans, and a few are still hiding in different farmers' houses. Four women, including the one who recounted this story, obtained permits to enter the Šiauliai ghetto. Their escape was fortunate because the women who had been sent to Telšiai heard shots during their walk and passed by prepared pits. That is when the extermination of the two thousand women in Geruliai began.[136] After being forced to undress they were murdered with machine guns and hand grenades.

The partisans got drunk and then finished the job with precision and serious-ness. On December 27 they killed the remaining women—more than four hundred—and children. And that is how the Telšiai tragedy ended, a tragedy we will never forget. The victims of Telšiai have an eternal place among the holy and pure ones,[137] all those who fell victim to the supreme source of evil.

A "Brand Plucked from the Fire":[138] How a Man Dressed as a Woman Survived Telšiai

On June 28, the first Sabbath after the Germans arrived, the Lithuanians in the "Rainiai" forest found seventy-three corpses of Lithuanian "nationalists" who had been prisoners of the Bolsheviks. The corpses bore signs of terrible brutality: body parts cut off, eyes gouged out, etc. (Some say the partisans themselves inflicted these atrocities on the corpses to emphasize the brutal-ity of the Bolsheviks and Jews.) They sent fifteen Jews to exhume the bodies and a photographer to document it. These people returned after midnight, and from their account of the Lithuanians' mood the Jews realized they were facing trouble. On Sunday and Monday, the partisans made some fifty Jews wash the victims' bodies and kiss them. They were forced to do this twice a day with threats and beatings, and one of them was shot. On the second day they prepared an "arch of triumph," and on the third day, they brought the victims to town. One hundred people were kept busy digging a mass grave in the cem-etery, and then the "funeral" took place, accompanied by terrible speeches of incitement against the Jews.[139]

The torment of the Jews of Telšiai had begun even before the victims were found. On June 26, the Lithuanians arrested 150 Jews and sent them to the Rainiai estate, about six kilometers from the city. On the twenty-seventh, the Germans broke into the Jews' houses and took them all to the marketplace. There the German major called up the local rabbi and ordered him to tell the assembled crowd to select three women to negotiate with the pro-Russian fighters who were attacking Germans from the forests. He promised that if this happened he would treat the Jews more gently. The rabbi said that in his opinion Jews were not likely to succeed at this, but he conveyed the major's words to the assembled crowd. After several hours, all the Jews (about 1,700) were assembled near the lake; there the major announced that the Germans were about to test a new weapon and sent the women, children, and elderly people home. The men were kept there until morning, and the sound of machine guns firing could be heard—but this was just a ruse to torment the elderly and the women. It was only a rehearsal for what was to happen later on.

On Saturday they sent all the Jews of Telšiai (about 2,000 people) to the Rainiai estate, leaving the town "cleansed" of Jews. After several days they began bringing in Jews from the surrounding area: Plungė, Rietavas, Varniai, and elsewhere, some 1,500 in all. These were sent later to another estate, Viešvėnai, about eight kilometers from Telšiai. They began organizing both areas, electing committees, opening kitchens, etc. They sent people from both estates to work, cleaning barracks and streets, etc. The committees recommended that the commandant allocate cars for the workers, who would provide drivers and gasoline, but the commandant refused. His argument was that the work was not really needed by the Germans, and their intent was merely to torment the [Jews] and make them suffer.

On July 6, the Jews were ordered to turn all their money over to the committee, which would deposit it in bank accounts on their behalf. A sum of six hundred thousand rubles was collected. The officials explained that their Russian currency would become worthless in coming days.[140] A lot of cash was lost during those days: money was thrown around, even dumped into latrines by people who were afraid to keep it but also did not want to surrender it. That caused great damage because until then they were able to buy food from villagers passing by the estate. After all the men assembled in the Rainiai estate were slaughtered there were still women remaining in Geruliai, plus ten men who managed to escape and hid, dressed in women's outfits, among the women in Geruliai. As we know, however, the cup of wrath[141] was passed also to the women of Geruliai: all were destroyed, except the five hundred who were sent back to Telšiai—and of those more than four hundred were killed and the rest scattered in all directions. Some perished in the cold as they fled through the forests, or were massacred by farmers whom they had trusted and to whom they had given everything in hope of being rescued; instead they were killed by those who took all they had. Some survived by hiding in farmhouses or with priests, and some managed to get to the Šiauliai ghetto.

As for the ten men who put on women's dresses, they were discovered even before the women of Geruliai met their end. All were killed except for one who managed to escape. The adventures of this "brand plucked from the fire" are a story on their own, and I could never detail them all. It will suffice to cite just one example: for six days, this survivor hid in bushes alongside a farmer's barn. At night he would steal grain from the barn to eat, and he quenched his thirst by sucking on icicles he broke off the edge of the roof. He survived all these adventures through extraordinary courage and endurance. It seems like a fable[142] that an ordinary Jewish man would have the strength to bear and suffer all this. Yet all of us who still survive demonstrate day by day that the Jews are as hard as rock. No nation in the world has as much forbearance,[143] endurance, thirst for life, and resistance to adversity. Without these traits, we would have been doomed to perish[144] under the burdens piled on us by our mortal enemies.

Raseiniai.[145] The native town of my wife's family, home of her uncles, brothers, and their families. It appears that they too were caught up in the Lithuanian sweep of extermination. How can it be that we will never see these beloved and cherished ones[146] again? Were the children of my wife's brother Leib really annihilated? Hard to imagine! One cannot believe it! But our bitter fate cries out: "Believe and know! Believe and hang your heads! You were unconcerned about the future! You did not seek to become a nation like all others, a people tending our own vines in our own homeland!"

Kėdainiai.[147] My native town, where my mother and her ancestors were born. An elite city stuffed like a pomegranate with Jewish scholars. The ancient cradle of rabbis and Torah sages who spread to all corners of eastern Europe. (And even to the west, e.g., Yehezkel Katzenellenbogen.)[148] My eyes flow with tears[149] for the destruction of the ancient town where I spent my youth and where my memories cling to every step. The native town of Shneur Zaks[150] and of Lilienblum,[151] my next-door neighbor. The entire community was erased from under heaven within a few hours.[152]

Šiauliai, Kaunas,[153] and Vilnius.[154] Three oases, three cities of refuge![155] In all of Lithuania, only here do Lithuanian Jews survive! What portion is left? And [what has been] the fate of those taken from your midst and from your prisons? Is it true that they were all put in graves before their time? An innocent question that arises from the inability to believe the horrors that occurred here. How many bewildering and frightful rumors petrified us until the bitter truth came and smacked us in the face? "Do not delude yourself with false hope: eighty thousand Jews perished in these three cities alone! And in all of Lithuania more than two hundred thousand Jews found early graves. Perhaps one in ten remain." It is quite possible that fate's cruel arm is yet outstretched, and that the prophecy "But while a tenth part yet remains in it, it shall repent"[156] will come horribly to pass. The tragedy is that we, the remaining few, cannot even now be sure of survival, that the murderers' hand will not stretch out over us, that the supreme source of evil will not unleash his rage on us if he fails [in his war] or erase us completely from Europe if, God forbid, he wins.

And if we do survive, how will we exist in a land saturated with our blood? How will we reconcile with people who turned on us like beasts? How can we forget what they did to us? Is it possible that the slaves did not dare defy their harsh masters, who certainly ordered them to eradicate us? But their ready "we will do and obey,"[157] their diligence in carrying out the order, the cruelty and the tortures, without leniency or compromise, never turning a blind eye to those trying to escape—all that weighs against them and will not be forgotten nor forgiven. After these events is it possible that the few surviving communities will arise from the ashes and revive? What will they consist of after all the men of initiative and action were wiped out? The future will tell, in words like sword-thrusts!

Addendum to the killings in Kėdainiai. For a time a ghetto existed in Kėdainiai, on Smilga Street.[158] Then they took all those in the ghetto and lined them up on the road to Dotnuva. When they realized what was to happen, several young men rebelled. It is said that they dragged one of the partisans into a pit and killed him.[159] It is easy to see the futility of an uprising by a few youths against hooligans armed with rifles and other weapons. The wish to "die with the Philistines"[160] must have come from utter desperation.

THE EDICTS

THE GERMANS HAVE A SINGLE goal: to embitter the lives of the surviving Jews and make them unbearable. They do this by issuing edicts, a torrent of decrees that rain down on us daily, ceaselessly. Some aim to humiliate us, to demonstrate that we are inferior and do not deserve to be in the community of the exalted Aryans, that we are unworthy of property or culture. Then there are edicts intended to further our physical and mental decline, to impoverish us, starve us, and spread deadly infectious diseases among us. It would be impossible to list all these countless decrees, which are like needles stabbing live flesh, enveloping our lives in pain. I will therefore write what I remember, chronologically if possible.

BEFORE THE TRANSFER TO THE GHETTO

1. Jews may not be outdoors after 8:00 p.m. Christians could stroll until 11:00 p.m., but that was later changed to 9:00 p.m. The one-hour difference was maintained to emphasize that Jews are not the equals of Lithuanians.
2. Jews may not display the Lithuanian flag on national holidays. This decree was designed to demonstrate that Jews are not full citizens, equal to Lithuanians. But it also served incidentally as a convenient way of identifying Jewish homes.
3. Selling food to Jews is barred. Even before the official order and the introduction of [ration] "tickets," Christian shopkeepers began preventing Jews from buying certain food items, particular-

ly butter and milk. It was said that Dr. R's wife was standing in a line to get milk when a Lithuanian ordered her to leave. Since she is hard of hearing,[1] she did not respond, so he grabbed her neck and shook her violently, nearly causing her to fall. Later, two stores were designated where Jews could obtain small rations[2] of certain food items. But very soon there were serious shortages of foods essential for health: meat, milk, butter, cheese, bread, flour, and sugar.

These restrictions reached their climax in the ghetto, as I will discuss in detail later.

4. The "badge of shame." The Middle Ages, with all their abominations and revulsions,[3] have returned. What was an outrage when we merely read about it in history books is again a reality! First, they ordered us to wear a yellow "Star of David" on the left side of the chest. But then the district commissioner added an embellishment of his own: a second Star of David on the back so that Jews could be recognized both from the front and behind. My wife and I experienced the effect of this for ourselves on September 13, the day we left for the ghetto, when my wife had an episode affecting her nervous system. It happened like this:

After the inspection committee confiscated my office and equipment, my furniture and library, after most of what we had built and accumulated over twenty years was gone, we collected the remaining fraction of our furniture and goods into two carts. The day was turning toward evening[4] as we left, our hearts heavy, for the ghetto. Suddenly my wife felt a terrible pain in her legs, a new sensation that nearly paralyzed her. It was impossible for her to continue walking. As she sat on the sidewalk to wait out the problem, I was desperate. Using a driver was forbidden, walking on the sidewalk was forbidden, and it was getting late. We had yet to enter the ghetto, find a place to sleep, and store our belongings. Our desperation was measureless![5] Finally, my wife's pain eased a bit, and I started leading her on my arm slowly. Near Dr. Ivansky's house, I decided to use the sidewalk because the pain in her legs had intensified. Suddenly it was as if we were both struck by lightning: we had each been punched in the head, leaving us stunned. A stem of my glasses broke, and when they fell off my nose I was unable to make out the face of the villain who had hit us. He seemed to be a common worker who was apparently defending the sacred honor of the sidewalk from the filthy Jews. As I tried to fix my glasses I protested, "You have no right to hit us!" Through clenched teeth like a mad dog, he answered, "You want to see my permit?" He seemed about to attack me again, but perhaps he recognized my face, and at that moment a German approached, and I started to complain that this villain had struck a sick woman. The German did not respond, but the villain rushed into a neighboring courtyard and disappeared. The point is, was it not the "badge of shame" on our backs that had prompted this vile deed? The Germans are being extremely strict: they even dictated the size of the badge, its width and where it should be sewn.

5. Walking on the sidewalks is banned for Jews. This is a terribly offensive and insulting edict. The Jews walk like shadows at the edges of the streets, and honest Christians watch and are ashamed. The feet stumble often on loose or protruding stones, helping ruin the soles of shoes that cannot be repaired due to leather shortages, and overshoes that are hard to replace. Naturally the question arose of how to manage this in winter, when snow piles up on the edges of the streets. Moreover it appears heaven is against us: this year winter came early. In November the cold intensified, and with it came plenty of snow. We experienced the pleasure of stumbling into the snow piles as we struggled over ice and slippery roads; like the righteous, we fell and rose seven times.[6] But no problem! If they leave us alive we will endure this too.

6. Restrictions on science and culture. We are barred from enjoying the inventions that largely enable civilized life. It is forbidden to use radio, telephone, telegraph, mail, or any modern mode of transportation such as trains, automobiles, buses, or bicycles. It is painful to recall how Jews contributed to the development of the radio, the telephone, and the airplane or our general role in contemporary life. We were enjoying these scientific advancements before the Lithuanians ever saw them, and when they did encounter a train, bicycle, or automobile, they saw it as the devil's work, believing that demons must be hiding inside the engine. Indeed, a telephone receiver in a Lithuanian's ear is "like a gold ring in the snout of a pig."[7] Now they are permitted to enjoy these inventions and we are not.

7. We are barred from public spaces. We were presented with a full bouquet of edicts to exclude us and shoo us away like lepers. We are forbidden to enter theaters or the cinema, visit city parks, sit on street benches, or stroll about the city. (This decree evolved and solidified when we were already in the ghetto, details to follow). Any petty official or any German soldier may begin an investigation into the activities of any Jew they meet on the street. Where is he coming from, and where is he going? If the answer is not satisfactory, it means at least a beating, if not arrest and imprisonment.

Recently, Jews who work in the city have been terrorized when they encounter prisoners of war. Those guarding the prisoners seize any Jews they happen upon and force them to help their weak prisoner "comrades," or even carry them on their backs all the way to the prison (their place of rest!). And they are beaten on the way to motivate them. Some inventive guards order the Jews to kiss their "Bolshevik friends." It is said that one educated Jew was ordered to kiss a prisoner not on his face but "somewhere else . . ."[8] Even if that isn't true, it's "at least a good story" as the damned Italians say.[9]

Yet all these restrictions were nothing compared with the ghetto decree, which reshaped our entire existence and marked our lives. Who would have thought that this historical anachronism, which went extinct hundreds of years ago, would be revived in the twentieth century, that the ghetto, with all its humiliating and depressing aspects, would return? And who better to re-create this than the Germans, with their passion for historical romanticism, their love of Wotan,[10] which inspires them to return medieval darkness to the world?

The enduring questions are "why and wherefore?"[11] Did the entire German nation lose its mind by attaching itself to the psychotic lunatic, who convinced them that Israel was to blame for everything, that Jews aim to destroy the Aryan nations and control the world? These stupid, sick, and crazy notions provided the motivation to attack us when we had done nothing wrong. It is true that until he became embroiled in his sad war with Russia, this madman with his boldness and initiative bestowed many benefits on the German nation. That is why they overlook his faults and worship him like a god in this classic birthplace of "scientific" antisemitism. The swallow went to the crow for a reason; they are of the same species.[12]

8. Before discussing the ghetto—the central point of these notes—I must mention another important prohibition that was imposed even before we moved in. This was the ban on using Christian services: horse cart drivers, barbers, porters, storekeepers, servants, etc., because it is improper for the superior to serve the inferior. Unthinkable that the Aryans, creation's crown jewels, would work for the loathsome Jews, members of an inferior race whose defect[13] is in their blood. Indeed, you can see this literal blood feud expressed in the signs on storefronts, horse carts, and barbershops, which proclaim "No service to Jews." From Stankus I obtained a written permit, written in Lithuanian and broken German, to travel by horse cart to see patients (before physicians were banned from treating Christians). It was like sitting on a scorpion:[14] the cart I rode on had a sign saying, "No service to Jews."

Figure 1. Dr. Aharon Pick with his wife, Devora, and their son, David (Tedik),
undated. Courtesy of Dvora and Amir Shatz.

Figure 2. Dr. Aharon Pick (*left*) with his friend Boruch Chaim Cassel, ca. 1900. Courtesy of Andrew Cassel.

Figure 3. Dr. Aharon Pick in his private clinic at home, ca. 1935. United States Holocaust Memorial Museum, courtesy of Haia Nudel Pick.

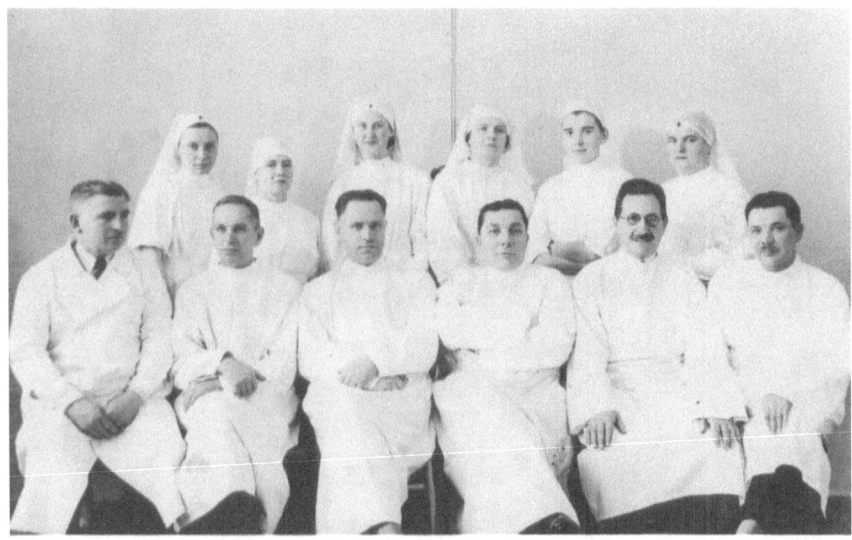

Figure 4. Dr. Aharon Pick (*sitting second from the right*) with his staff in the Šiauliai municipal hospital, undated. United States Holocaust Memorial Museum, courtesy of Haia Nudel Pick.

Figure 5. Dr. Aharon Pick (*sitting fourth from left*) hosts a dinner for the Jewish dramatist Nathan (Bistritski) Agmon (*sitting center*), who was visiting from Palestine, undated. United States Holocaust Memorial Museum, courtesy of Haia Nudel Pick.

Figure 6. A holiday gathering of friends in Dr. Aharon Pick's house (*Pick sits fourth from the left*), undated. United States Holocaust Memorial Museum, courtesy of Haia Nudel Pick.

Figure 7. Dr. Pick (*third adult from the right*) among the group welcoming Bialik (*to the right of Dr. Pick*) in the Šiauliai train station, undated. United States Holocaust Memorial Museum, courtesy of Haia Nudel Pick.

Figure 8. A group of Jews under SS guard, standing by the gates of the so-called White Prison in Šiauliai, before they were murdered in the Kužiai forest. In the first row on the right is Rabbi Nochumovsky, the city's religious court judge. The second from right in the first row, with a beard, is Rabbi Aaron Baksht. First on the left is the attorney Azriel Abramovich. Yad Vashem Photo Archives 2502/1.

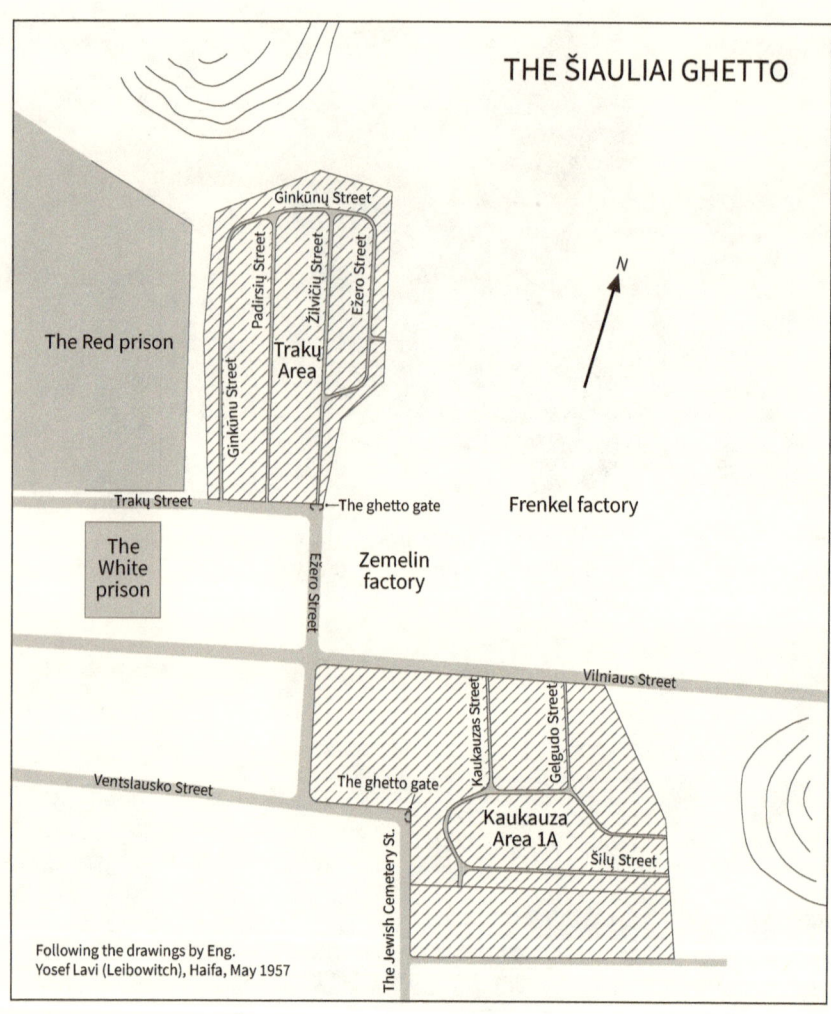

Figure 9. The English version of a map of the Šiauliai ghetto. Hebrew original Yad Vashem Photo Archives 3461/5.

Figure 10. Jews digging pits, apparently in the Kužiai forest, not far from Šiauliai. The Einsatzgruppen would later use these pits to bury the Jews of Šiauliai after they were murdered. The photograph was taken by a member of the SS. Yad Vashem Photo Archives 4216/22.

Figure 11. A group of Jews before their murder in the Kužiai forest between June 26 and 29, 1941. Yad Vashem Photo Archives 4216/26.

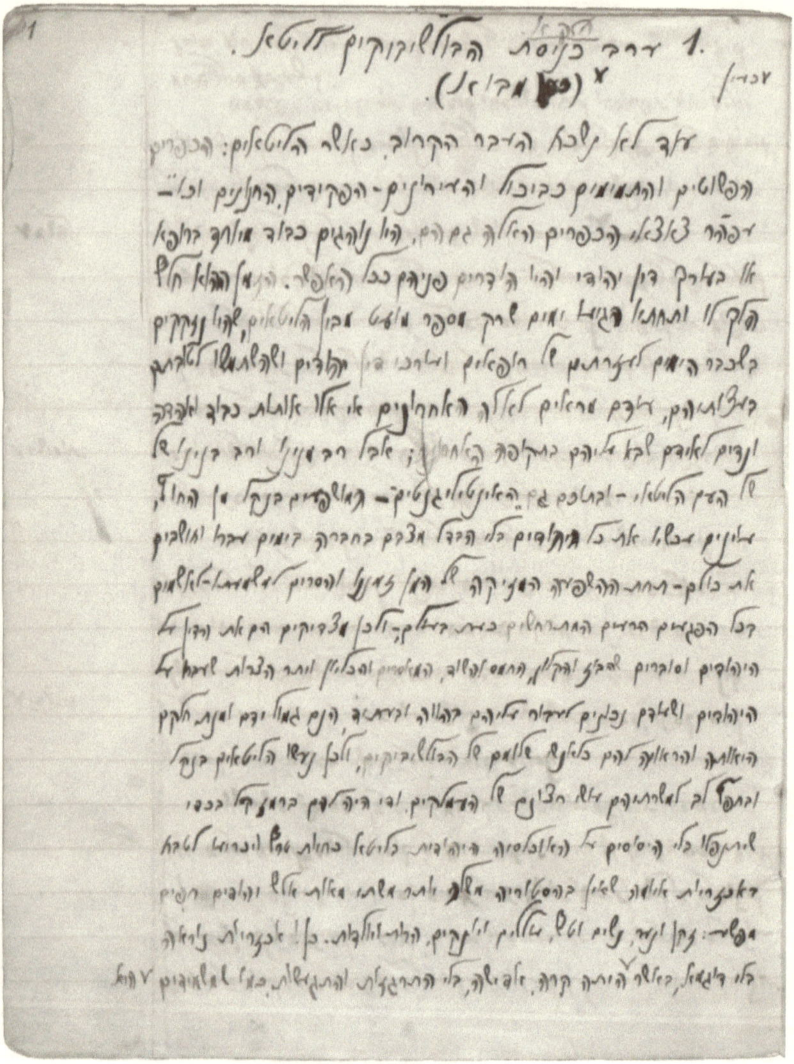

Figures 12 and 13. The opening pages of Aharon Pick's journal. His dense handwriting almost suggests that paper was precious and had to be used efficiently. His manuscript (now held at the US Holocaust Memorial Museum in Washington, DC) consists of three notebooks, one of them apparently a draft, sections of which were copied to the other two. Shown here is Pick's table of contents (*right*) and the opening of his journal describing the years leading up to the war.

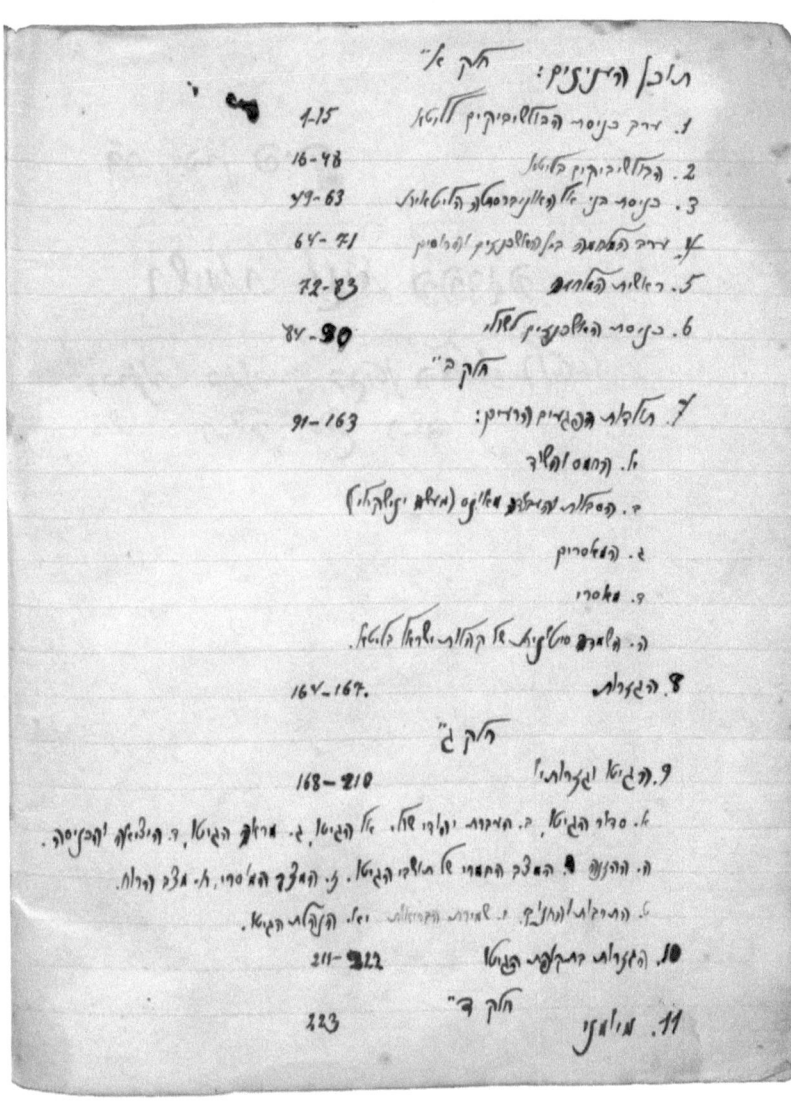

Figures 12 and 13. (*Continued*)

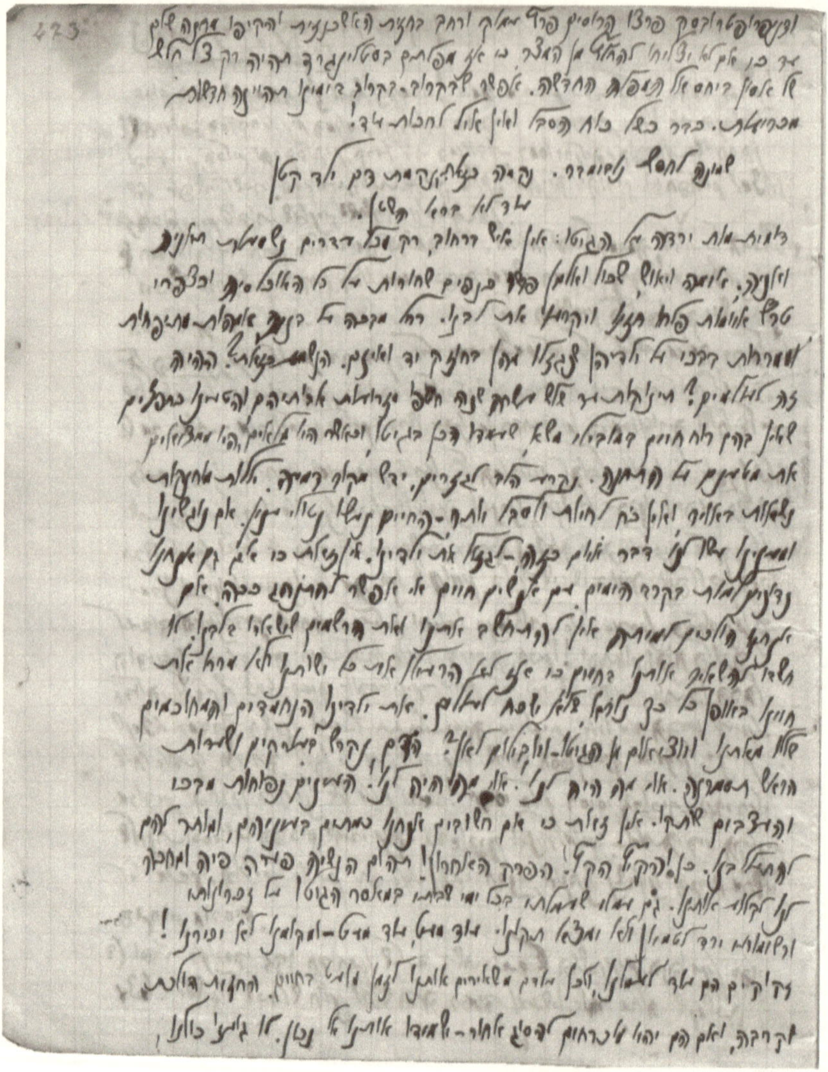

Figures 14 and 15. The right-hand page focuses on events that occurred late in October 1943, including the murder of a Jewish worker and news about a meeting of Allies ministers in Moscow. On the following (left-hand) page, the fifth line starts with a quote from Chaim Nachman Bialik's poem "On the Slaughter" (Al HaShechita): "Vengeance like this, for the blood of a child, Satan has yet to devise. . . ." Pick then describes the horrific November 5 *kinderaktion*, in which hundreds of children were taken from the Šiauliai ghetto and sent to Auschwitz.

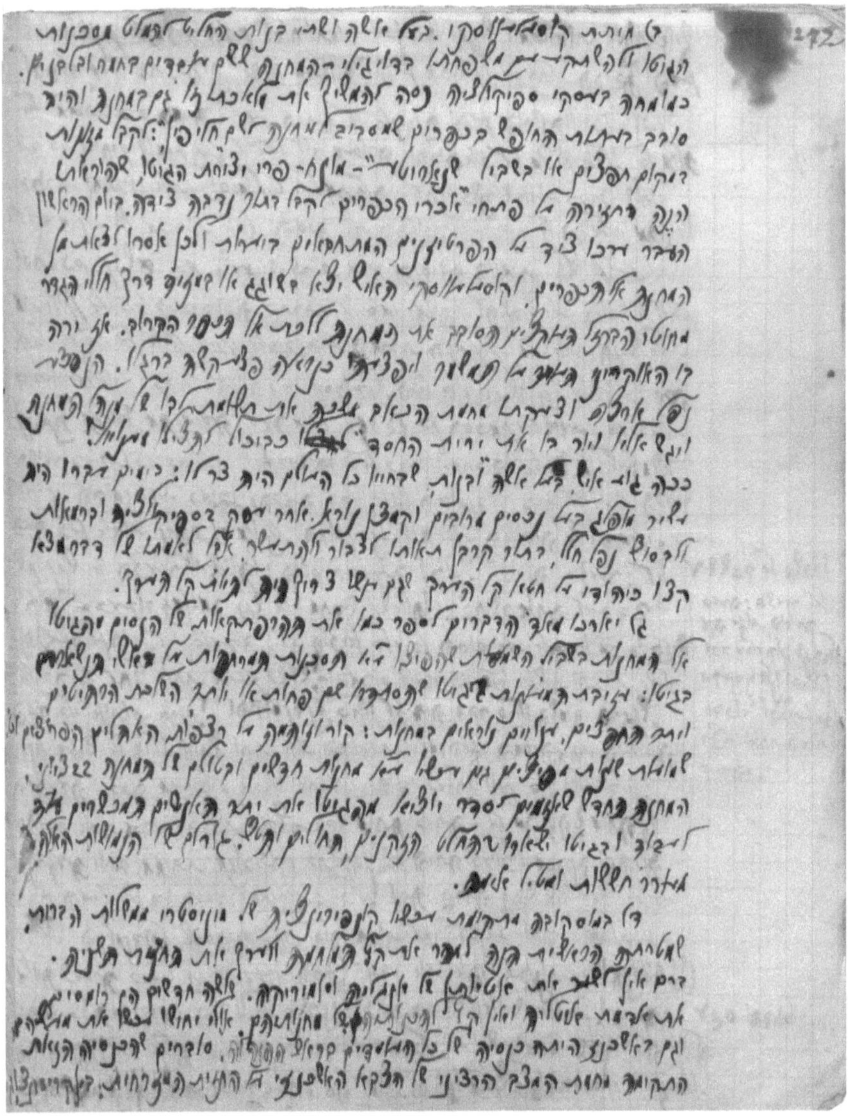

Figures 14 and 15. (*Continued*)

PART C

NINE

—ɯ—

THE RULES OF THE GHETTO

IT IS IMPOSSIBLE FOR ONE person to describe in all its fullness and detail this evil decree, which continues in force and is still evolving. The ghetto—that is our entire tragic, confined existence—has various aspects and details that merit study, observation, investigation, and research, requiring specialists in many fields. This is why my notes will be somewhat incomplete, merely an outline of the anguish and distress[1] we encountered. But at least they will provide our descendants with a sketch, albeit a blurry one, of our situation in the Šiauliai ghetto.

A. THE STRUCTURE OF THE GHETTO

Rumors of a ghetto began soon after the Germans entered Šiauliai, frightening us like a violent wind, like a deadly pestilence[2] troubling us day and night. The Germans began immediately to deal with the "Jewish question," in which their knowledge and expertise was unmatched. First, they created the position of "administrator for Jewish affairs" and gave the job to Stankus, a young drunkard who had been a "major" in the Lithuanian army.[3] The title "bane of Israel" would have fit him better, and his band of deadly messengers[4] got straight to work. Stankus pressured leaders of the Šiauliai kehilla to nominate Jewish representatives, people who had been active in community affairs. Almost all declined, citing various reasons, but in reality because they feared attracting the attention of the Germans, who in other places had arrested and tortured local leaders first. After some negotiation, several people with inclinations to public service volunteered to take upon themselves the task of representing the Jews of Šiauliai. They included Leibovich, Kartun, and old Rubinstein.[5]

At the same time rumors began to startle and haunt us, changing daily and contradicting each other about the establishment of a ghetto. One day the rumor spread that all Šiauliai Jews were to be sent to Žagarė—a little place[6] not far from Šiauliai. The following day another rumor said this decision was canceled, and instead we were to be sent to the village of Šimšė[7] and kept in peasants' mud houses, which even in summer are surrounded by muck and swamp. On the third day a new rumor circulated that Šiauliai Jews would be divided into two camps: one for experts and professionals, and one for ordinary workers, tradesmen, and artisans. The "specialists" would be settled on Trakų Street, and the rest would be sent to a hilly, muddy area of the city known as "Kaukazas." Then on the fourth day, our anxiety was relieved by news that for now the ghetto idea had been set aside, and joy filled our homes.[8] Thus did rumors shift from day to day.

What actually happened was this: Stankus one day summoned the Jewish representatives and suggested they travel to Žagarė to see the place designated for Šiauliai's Jews, in buildings put up to house Polish refugees who had fled to Lithuania at the start of their war with Germany.[9] The representatives had the courage to turn him down, saying they had no authority to visit grave sites for their brethren, since five thousand people could not possibly survive in a remote town like Žagarė. There isn't even a railroad there; moreover, the deportees would likely have to abandon their property and take only what they could carry. When we heard about this we were mortally afraid. We realized the ghetto idea was alive and well and that our transfer from Šiauliai to a place of calamity was likely in coming days. Bizarre, contradictory rumors about a ghetto continued; their only common denominator was that they embittered our lives and left us in fear of the terrible future we faced.

Finally, those in power decided the ghetto would be created here and not in another town, because Šiauliai has plenty of "holes and dens" of its own. Its suburbs are filled with shacks, dilapidated houses and mud huts on "chicken legs"—filthy places that could quickly shorten the lifespans of affluent Jews who had been spoiled living in their comfortable, well-furnished homes. At the same time another hopeful rumor circulated, that skilled workers and specialists would get to remain in town, but that one was quickly refuted. Instead, it was announced that all Jews, without exception, would be required to live in the ghetto. Only medical offices with electrical equipment would remain in town: doctors would be allowed to continue their practices there during the day and only forced to spend nights in the ghetto. My clinic, with its X-ray lab, was at the top of the list, along with Dr. Wolpert's clinic, the clinic of Dr. Peisachowitz[10] with his cardiograph, and several others.

The agile and opportunistic Dr. Peisachowitz (who thinks he's the crown of creation) lobbied Stankus and obtained a real permit. I did not rush to acquire such a permit because Stankus had assured me that I would receive one eventually, and that for now there was no need for it. But when I finally realized what was happening I gave Stankus a written request for the permit, asking to keep my clinic in town as he had promised. To my surprise, unlike Dr. Peisachowitz's, my case became complicated. Stankus sent my request to Dr. Jasaitis, asking him to concur that my clinic was necessary, but Jasaitis hesitated. Probably he had learned that the Nuremberg Laws, which prohibit Jewish doctors from treating Christians, were about to go into effect here, which would void all the permits anyway. So when I asked Dr. Jasaitis to sign my request, he said, "Let's wait a few days." He likely already had some vague information about a ban on treating Aryan patients. Meanwhile I was put in prison, and of course my permit request remained pending.

And so the creation of the ghetto began. In the Trakų area they allocated the following streets: Ežero, Žilvičių, Padirsių, and Ginkūnų, which branch off Trakų. And in the Kaukazas area they allocated Gelgudo, Šilų, Krymo, and Kaukauzas streets and small portion[s] of Venclausko,[11] Vilniaus, and Ežero streets. Around each of the areas they placed equally spaced fence posts, filled in the gaps between them with barbed wire, and installed two gates in the fence. So the Jews of Šiauliai were given two German-style compounds to separate this underclass from the superior Aryans, including the "preeminent among ten thousand" Lithuanians, who once had been slaves and doormats to the Poles but now were so exalted that they required a wall to separate them from those impure and dangerous Jews, who by chance had survived in their country, the valley of slaughter.

B. TRANSFERRING ŠIAULIAI'S JEWS TO THE GHETTO

After the two ghetto areas were designated, their previous occupants—factory workers and the poor—were forced to leave their decrepit and filthy homes while preparations were made for our transfer. Several committees were appointed to appraise the Jews' property and to determine which of their belongings could be brought into the ghetto and which would be taken for the "common good." In most cases the committees were extremely harsh, even cruel, often but not always under external pressure. They acted on the premise that whatever the Jewish slaves owned actually belonged to their German and Lithuanian masters. They acted as if all Jewish property was rightfully theirs, and whatever they let the Jews take into the ghetto was out of charity. Thus the committees appropriated the best furniture, clothes, jewelry, and gold and silver objects, allowing Jews to take only a tiny portion.

O, how much of Israel's treasure was lost! The committees also determined how much money, food, clothes, underwear, and shoes a family could have, which further diminished the Jews' property. We began to "smuggle" our own belongings, hiding what we could in the homes of our Christian acquaintances. Nearly all the more affluent Jews did this, which led to some disastrous results, as I will explain further on. There were also committees that were not as strict and allowed more belongings to be taken into the ghetto—a reason that even today many items of furniture and others are scattered in the ghetto courtyards under the open sky due to a lack of space in the small, crowded dwellings. Indeed! Since the Bolsheviks first laid their hands on Jewish property, followed by the German and Lithuanian thieves, and now with our departure to the ghetto we are impoverished, destitute, sunk to the bottom.

After the property was inspected and confiscated, with items marked that could not be immediately carried away in their carts, the departures to the ghetto began gradually, street by street. Soon they realized that the two ghetto areas would not accommodate all the Jews still in Šiauliai. Despite the Bolsheviks' deportations, the flight when the war started, and the many arrests since then, some five thousand Jews remained out of nine thousand in Šiauliai before the war. Even with severe crowding there was not enough room in the ghetto for all of them. So they decided to add another area—"Kalniukas," near the edge of the large lake. But the residents of Kalniukas protested and sent delegates to the district commissioner, asking for protection lest the impure Jews defile their beautiful houses (which are definitely not superior to those in the two other ghetto areas, filled with fleas and cockroaches, and infested by countless rats). It is said that Stankus supported the Kalniukas residents because he also has a home in that area. The district commissioner listened to the residents and canceled the decision to add that area to the ghetto. So crowding in the ghetto worsened unimaginably, and many families were left sleeping in the open, unable to find shelter for rest and sleep.

Then the Germans and the Lithuanians decided to "kill two birds with one stone"[12]: they would reduce crowding in the ghetto by reducing the number of Jews in Šiauliai. Of course, all that had happened to the Jews at the end of the Bolshevik regime, and even more after the Germans arrived had significantly reduced their number in Šiauliai. But to the Germans that was a benefit, not a problem.

The scheme devised by the Germans and their Lithuanian servants to alleviate crowding in the ghetto will remain written in blood forever, as one of the saddest chapters in our history. It was no less cruel and violent than the murders of Lithuanian Jews elsewhere. Without exaggeration, as long as the Jews of Lithuania and their descendants live, we will not forget the Lithuanians' evilness and their abominations against the Jews, who built their cities and brought commerce and industry to their country. We will remember what they did in every Lithuanian city where the children of Israel were encamped,[13] after the Germans arrived and particularly during the ghetto period.

In the end, the Lithuanians, led by Stankus under German supervision, prepared a list of Jews they considered redundant: the old, the sick, the feeble, single women without skills or professions. (Except for those whose skills they need and cannot easily find among their own citizens—such as hatters, watchmakers, glove makers, furriers, etc.—all Jews are redundant.) To those listed they often added their relatives and their young, healthy children. Some believe they also added a few single women who had managed to hide valuable articles with influential Christians, and that the latter, hoping to inherit their valuables, pulled strings to have them eliminated. When the list was complete, they started transporting those on it, some from town and others from the ghetto, to an unknown location, under the pretense that they were going to Žagarė. After a while they stopped taking them out of town. Instead they were put at first in one of Šiauliai's synagogues,[14] perhaps so the children of Israel could fulfill the commandment to "redeem the captive"[15] for their captors' benefit. Those who were not "redeemed" were eventually also taken to that unknown[16] place. . . .

Where? A terrifying and silent question mark hangs over the great deep[17] of tears and blood. As I said, those on the list were told they were being taken to Žagarė, but the truck carrying the victims returned far too quickly to have made such a trip. In fact they were taken to one of three places near Šiauliai: near Kužiai, a place of past calamity, where in Tsar Nicholas's time Jews had been accused of betraying the Russian military to the Germans, near the village of Šapnagiai, and to the Bubiai forest.[18] A Christian girl said she happened by the Bubiai forest and from a distance, saw an arm, adorned with a bloody bracelet and a watch, rise out of a pile of corpses in a pit. A partisan rushed over, tore the bracelet and watch off the arm and pushed it, still convulsing between life and death, back into the pile of corpses. Thus the villains showed their unbounded cruelty, while we at first believed that those taken from the city and ghetto had actually been taken to Žagarė.

Their blood cries out to us from the ground.[19] Our ears burn,[20] our hearts shrink, and our souls cannot rest! How can we forget the pharmacist Meirovich and his wife; the teacher Goldstein[21] and his wife, and last but not least, Professor Kravitz and his wife? Dear people, good-natured and affable, honest beyond compare! How can we forget them? We cannot be consoled when we remember them. We had hoped to continue meeting often with Professor Kravitz, a frequent visitor to our house. We looked forward to many pleasant and interesting conversations in the ghetto with this educated man who had a clear, logical mind. An irreplaceable loss! Of course his son's tragedy dominated his and his wife's minds, filling them with a despair that only death could relieve. These sickly people had an only son, strong as an oak and educated in the law. Under the Bolsheviks he had an important job with the police; if I am not mistaken, he was head of municipal administration. When the Germans arrived his parents thought it wise for him to leave Šiauliai, so he went to the village of Linkuva. There he reportedly identified several partisans who planned to attack the Jews. After they took power, the partisans stopped a train full of Jewish prisoners on its way from Linkuva to Pakruojis. Among the passengers was Munya Kravitz. They took him and two other Jews, and a few minutes later, travelers in the car heard gunshots, which ended the lives of the three Jews. Among the witnesses was the engineer Rafaelovich, who told me this story. By his nature, Professor Kravitz was a great optimist and never complained about his misfortunes. But recently, even before learning of his son's terrible fate, his heart had foretold disaster and he was in a state of sorrow and agitation, often shedding tears. Indeed, death released him and his wife from their endless tribulations. Pity for those who are gone and will not return! A sea of tears, a sea of blood engulfs us.

As for the doctors who toyed with the idea that they could keep their clinics in the city, and believed Stankus's and Jasaitis's promises, they met only disappointment and heartbreak. The infamous Nuremberg edict relating to doctors went into effect, and everything turned upside down. After the prohibition on Jewish doctors treating "Aryans" was issued, the idea of allowing Jewish clinics in the city, where most of the Aryans were, died on its own. Further the committees were ordered to seize all doctors' clinics, together with their equipment, furniture, and books. A special committee appointed for that purpose, which included one Christian doctor, did precisely that. A fortune that Jewish doctors had built over many years with the sweat of their brows[22] and endless sleepless nights, was stolen and handed over to our enemies. All the medical equipment and libraries had been held in the polyclinic or in a warehouse near Dr. Levin's physiotherapy clinic. The Christian doctors who worked in the hospital or other city institutions shared in the looting. The wasted Jewish assets were invaluable, particularly now that it is difficult to obtain medical equipment. The sad outcome is that the doctors who had comforted themselves with the idea of keeping their clinics in town did not secure their equipment and belongings in time. They were also late relocating to the ghetto while it was still possible to find lodging. I was among the laggards, not just because I was waiting for my permit but also because of my imprisonment.

The murderers' radical plan to clear out apartments in the ghetto by reducing the Jewish population deepened our wretched poverty.[23] Not only were we filled with endless torment when our friends and loved ones were taken away, but the crowding in the ghetto eased only minimally. For those who were late to arrive in the ghetto, obtaining a home was like parting the Red Sea. It is hard to describe the tribulations of these "invisible" souls who wandered all day along the ghetto streets, stumbling desperately through the offices of the Jewish council, and at night were thrown into remote corners of their friends' narrow and crowded homes, finally finding a resting place in some remote hole in the wall.

On the third day after my release from prison, the committee came to inspect my belongings and seize my clinic. After my imprisonment, I felt I had been delivered from a great danger; having avoided the fate of earlier prisoners, I put less value on possessions. My attitude was "all that a man has, he will give up for his life."[24] Therefore, I was almost indifferent to the seizure of my office equipment. "After the fire, it turns out you were rich." Now I appreciate how rich I was before I was robbed! The X-ray machine, "the Mountain Sun," "Solux," the Diathermia,[25] my gynecological chair, instruments of all kinds, furniture, and above all my library, in six languages: Hebrew, Russian, French, German, Yiddish, Lithuanian. Over how many years had I accumulated and nurtured it! How much money did I spend on these books! I did transfer a good portion of them to the ghetto, particularly the Hebrew books that my son took care of, and I left many medical books in the attic of my previous home. But the majority of my books I abandoned for three reasons: (1) my indifference after my imprisonment, as mentioned; (2) a lack of packing materials or the means to transfer my entire library; (3) being misinformed by my colleagues, who said I must turn over my library along with my office equipment to the committee. In fact, the physician who participated on the committee that seized clinics was Dr. Doctoraitis, who had been my student in the municipal hospital and who treated me as his "rabbi and teacher,"[26] with deference and respect.

If not for these reasons, I could have arranged to take as much as I wanted. But to my regret, because of my imprisonment and my hope of staying in the city, I missed the chance to properly see to my office equipment, as I did with my household and kitchen items, which I managed to hide with Christian acquaintances. Obviously I could not smuggle my big machines. But a doctor from Kelmė promised me he could obtain a permit to buy my X-ray machine, along with the new tube I purchased, for about eighteen thousand rubles, an amount that could lift me out of the distress and poverty I now face. This all resulted, as I said, from Stankus's promise to let me keep my city office, a promise that became a stumbling block.

We received the committee graciously. My dear "student," who likes to drink, as do the other two committee members, accepted our generous gifts of liquor and other items. And after they had drunk their fill, they prepared a list of items from my office and library, ignoring the rest of my belongings to the point where I could have taken along whatever I wanted. Unfortunately, I had hidden most of my belongings and my clothes before with my Christian friends and now, due to other reasons, it is hard for me to retrieve them. So now I am missing things I could have sold to support myself and my family, because I ran out of money long ago, and our income (fifteen rubles a day for my work and ten rubles a day for my son) is not enough to purchase the food we need, even using the ration card. The Germans allocated our income as a couple, but it was barely enough to provide us with meager bread and scant water.[27] Because of the chronic bread shortage in the ghetto, one loaf may cost as much as eighty rubles. Tea disappeared long ago, and sugar—who can even remember it?—was replaced by saccharin, which is very expensive.

Thirteen days (a "devil's dozen") into September, at dusk, after my wife's nerve attack and the two punches we received, we had the "good fortune" to arrive at the Trakų ghetto. There was no home made ready for us, no place to put our remaining furniture, books, and other belongings. This is when our real trials began. We did more than our share of wandering; for nine days we drifted like vagabonds. In vain we pleaded with the Jewish council to find us a home, stressing that I was exhausted from my imprisonment and my wife was sick. The bureaucrats just kept putting us off, day after day, with promises that were never kept. Because doctors were still being blamed for the deportations from the ghetto to the synagogues, they were hesitant to take serious steps to find us a home. Finally our friends directed us to a "nice" apartment occupied by a family of "losers"[28] from Tauragė who had moved there soon after the ghetto was established. That's when the ghetto officials came to our aid and offered the family a different apartment, one that was no worse than theirs other than its location (near the gate) and more difficult access (down a hill) which were inappropriate for a doctor's apartment.

Our difficulties with that family—"the poor of another city"[29]—are too long to describe in detail. After many arguments and complications and the older son's desire to take advantage of us, we gave that family 200 rubles (and a cup of butter) as compensation and got the apartment: a small room, a narrow kitchen, and a small corridor with more holes than wall. The place was filthy; cracks in the walls were full of fleas and yellow and black cockroaches, and the wallpaper was saturated with dirt. We cleaned up as best as we could, tried covering the walls with carpets to hide the bugs, and are now living in this apartment, which is confined, crowded, unclean, full of mice who raid our food—and we are happy! There is a place to sleep, room for a pantry, and, most importantly, the kitchen is all ours; we don't have to share it, something that causes many quarrels and feuds in other apartments.

The scoundrel son of the previous occupants took revenge on us by bringing a policeman to take our son to forced labor in Joniškėlis, which caused us an endless agony. We suffered even more because of what the previous residents left behind, namely the teacher Y.R.'s sister, a neurotic girl, bordering on insane. She was a gossip, a snitch, probably a kleptomaniac; and her presence in our kitchen at night, grumbling endlessly, angered us immensely. Finally, after many fights and a broken kitchen window, we kicked her out because she started stealing from us. Her belongings remained in our corridor for a long time however, which gave her an excuse to show up occasionally and swear at us. We finally got rid of her when she was transferred to the Kaukazas area. I am telling this to further emphasize the hardship and unpleasantness of daily life in the ghetto, the crowding, the proximity to dishonest people, etc.

C. THE GHETTO'S APPEARANCE

The two ghetto areas (see map, fig. 9), large tracts enclosed by barbed wire, spread across slopes that descend to the Šiauliai lakes. The streets here are steep, unpaved, and lacking sidewalks. Although boards were laid down along the edges of some streets, the rotten and narrow planks are of little help when the snow melts, or after a pouring rain when the streets flood and puddles fill with ankle-deep mud and muck. Things also become difficult when ice coats the streets. Walking becomes perilous, and the danger intensifies when youngsters, the "children of Israel's children," slide down the slopes on their sleds, making them truly slippery. The youngsters enjoy indulging in what was always a privilege given to Christian kids, and now they "rejoice to exultation."[30] But who can predict the future of these children, who are growing up like wildflowers, without school or education? Is there any hope for their future? Will they get to become adults? Or will they meet an untimely end at the villain's hand?

The ghetto architecture is quite primitive. All the buildings except for a few are one-story wooden structures, low and crowded. The apartments are mostly one or two small rooms, much smaller than rooms in ordinary farmhouses. The ceiling is typically very low. The walls are covered with low-quality decorative wallpaper or simply newspaper. The stove is meant to serve both for cooking and heat, but in the winter it fails to properly warm the apartment, and in summer it is difficult to vent the heat from cooking. The people who used to live here were mostly workers from the Frenkel factory[31] and other poor, troubled people, who likely frequented bars in their spare time. Their wives also worked in addition to overseeing their households[32] and caring for the children. In short, the residents did not properly maintain their homes, and the neglect shows; on the outsides "the breached is greater than what stands,"[33] and the insides are filthy and filled with insects.

Another serious problem plagues the ghetto: mice, large and small, dominate with all that implies. Small rodents often steal the last crumbs from the ghetto-dwellers at a time when finding food is harder than parting the Red Sea, so provisions must be guarded vigilantly. But guarding against these little pests is not easy at all. We once managed to buy an edible piece of meat and smuggled it back into the ghetto in a basket beneath some potatoes. A guard at the gate caught us however, and we had to pay another fifty rubles as a fine. A day after we hung up this meat, which cost us a fortune, in the corridor, we discovered that the pests had stolen most of it. They probably entered the corridor through holes in the ceiling. The bold vermin also gnaw through bags of food that we hang on the walls in our room. The profusion of mice in the ghetto may be explained by the proximity of the leather factory, whose products feed countless battalions of mice, which then spread through the area. In the old days, Frenkel's factory was renowned not only in Russia but also in western Europe. Now its glory has dimmed, its fame faded, but the factory continues to operate, with even the same manager, Mordil.[34] As much as they would like to, the Germans cannot fire him because he knows every inch of the factory. But now the entire world is closed and the factory's output, now redirected to war production, has declined significantly. But its mouse population still grows.

How many sad thoughts does this factory, which abuts the Trakų ghetto area, bring to mind? A living testimony to the talent and initiative of a Jewish man. Long ago the elder Frenkel wisely acquired the swampland near Šiauliai's large lake. There he set up a small tannery and began working there himself with just a few day-laborers. His success was astonishing: business increased almost daily, and the factory flourished, eventually becoming world famous. When the elder Frenkel became a multimillionaire he treated his family and many relatives generously by installing them in respectable jobs at the factory, unlike many others who became wealthy only to "ignore their own kin"[35] as a way of erasing the past. He was philanthropic and did a lot for the Šiauliai

Jewish community. His only son[36] was less talented than his father, but the immense fortune he inherited could make even the simple wise.[37] Less generous than his father, he was notably stingy toward organizations promoting the Jewish national cause.[38] He was more open-handed with those of a religious or communal nature, particularly if such acts gained him publicity and acclaim, because he craved respect. Yet how hard did we have to negotiate with him to get a contribution to the capital campaign of "Keren Hayesod"[39] or another Zionist institution! He put us off with the excuse that he was not a Zionist. So much this Lithuanian Rothschild could have done for his people! And how happy he would be today if he had bought himself a possession of fields and vineyards[40] in the land of his ancestors, which he could easily afford! Ha! If he had only spent for the benefit of his people just a tenth of what the Bolsheviks seized! And now it all belongs to the predators and destroyers who rule over us. In our ancestors' land he could have created steady jobs for hundreds of workers and created institutions to buy himself eternal fame. Ha! How much Jewish wealth has been lost in Germany and the other countries occupied by our mortal enemies! We have been left empty-handed.

But the younger Frenkel, his wife and sons were fortunate in their timing, departing for America before the Bolsheviks arrived. They went when the global exposition[41] opened and settled there. How much trouble did he avoid by leaving the confines of Lithuania for the land of freedom! Had he stayed here this sickly man would have died in a concentration camp, a prison, or in the ghetto, right next to his own property that had fallen into alien hands. That was the fate of his old mother,[42] who died in the ghetto not long ago. She drained the cup of wrath to the dregs! Once immensely wealthy, she was impoverished, living on a meager bread ration and forced to sell her last belongings to live. The wife of millionaire Frenkel died in a stranger's house, a small room filled with mold in the Šiauliai ghetto. A powerful lesson for our affluent brethren who believed their wealth safe in a country not their own, and were certain their money would shield them from harm. This would be humorous if it weren't so sad. The woman was famous in her day for parsimony: it was said she would turn out the office lights at night so as not to waste electricity, and that her employees who lived in factory buildings could not stay up late for the same reason. Thus did she protect her millions!

Regarding the ghetto's appearance, one positive detail should be mentioned. Nearly every house has a garden, small or large. In spring and summer, these gardens provide a certain beauty to the area and give it the appearance of a pastoral village. But we have not yet seen this ourselves. By late fall, after the gardens were harvested and winter approached, the view was quite sad because next to every house was an empty lot, muddy and black. Recently, many of the previous residents demanded payment for the cabbages, potatoes, and so on that were left when the ghetto was established and that the new tenants supposedly enjoyed. These demands are mostly exaggerated, another way to drain Israel's resources. By the way, the owners of these houses apparently miss their former homes very much. They petitioned the district commissioner to return the houses and gardens, which in summer provide vegetables and flowers that serve as a source of income. The district commissioner turned them down, so they retained two lawyers to take their appeal to the regional governor[43] in Kaunas. We do not yet know the outcome of this.

The larger question—will we survive?—torments us constantly, an indication of how bleak our lives have become since the Germans arrived. And if we do survive, will it be here in the ghetto? Maybe they will move us somewhere else, like they did recently with Jews from western countries, moving them to Latvia and other occupied areas. Perhaps I am overreacting considering such unlikely events. Perhaps our relief and deliverance[44] will arrive early and by spring we will be free to leave the ghetto. "Is there a limit to the Lord's power?"[45] For now it is hard—so hard—to believe our salvation is coming. It is true that the Bolsheviks have performed miracles and wonders at the front that no one expected, holding out against the most powerful army in the world, unmatched in technology, discipline, and boldness—but how far are they still from decisive and total victory! Of course we should not rely on miracles,[46] but the war must end at some point. If we can make it to that day, we will be insane with happiness! Who could contain their joy after so much suffering, after doubting our survival for so long! Most survivors will sell everything they have to the last needle or shoestring and rush to make *aliyah* to our forefathers' land.

Will this wonderful dream come true? Will the Arabs go along? Will the empires that rule over the Jews in [Palestine] support us? Although surely the Arabs need no lessons in murder from the Lithuanians; those desert savages are no less brutal than the savages of Europe. Still, what a difference there is between the Arabs' victims and those of the Lithuanians. Here we were innocent lambs to be slaughtered,[47] and there we were heroes who gave their lives for their country. There we fought back against our enemies; here they slaughtered us like mute sheep and we were helpless, unable to resist. We pray to stay alive so we can offer our lives for our forefathers' land, bring salvation and victory, become like all nations in our own land, citizens with a homeland and not foreign "competitors," thorns in their eyes.[48]

It is true that there was a time when the people of this land greatly needed us. In those good old days, we were ranked as merchants of the third guild:[49]

traders, artisans, and intermediaries between the nobles and peasants. But now that they have begun to develop their own commercial class, they suddenly decided we are redundant and no longer needed, although the facts show that even today they are still not ready to take our places in commerce and craftsmanship. Those who dwell in cities or wish to, and especially storeowners, thought our role was finished and we should disappear. Others began to accomplish this for them. First the Bolsheviks and then the Germans quickly did what would have taken the Lithuanians a lot of work—getting rid of the Jews to the extent they have. Indeed! Others did their work, but they are unlikely to enjoy the result, and it is doubtful that Lithuania will benefit from the current situation. Recently the Lithuanians have begun to complain and protest, and it is said that their representatives presented a memorandum in Berlin, raising three issues. They complain that they have not been given independence; that they do not receive enough food; and that . . . they have been turned into killers, whose names will be forever cursed.[50] God have mercy on the poor, victimized Cossacks! Who would have believed it? Recently the Germans have begun to placate the Lithuanians, giving them and the other Baltic states some degree of municipal and commercial autonomy under their supervision. Apparently they need the manpower of the Baltics, although the latter have so far received only heartbreak and disappointment.

I will end this description of the ghetto's appearance with a short comment about how it looks at night. (These notes concern the fall and winter—we have not yet been fortunate enough to experience its fair-crested[51] spring and summer beauty.) The ghetto streets lack lights so the nights are dark. A few faint rays emerge from behind the required blackout window curtains. Then the ghetto resembles a remote medieval town, a place from another era: there is no pavement, no sidewalk, no lights, and the houses have no form or beauty; darkness conceals them.[52] Light can be seen only at the two ends of the Trakų ghetto: a dim one to the right and a bright one to the left. The Frenkel factory is on the right, where every night the guards and servants clean and ready the workshops for the next day. And to the left, floodlights on the towers of the prison, where the guards serve as reminders that the ghetto is also a prison to thousands of oppressed Jews, beset with troubles and living in terror of starvation. They have no money left, prices have risen enormously, and any attempt to bring a few potatoes or slices of bread into the ghetto means imprisonment, should such a dangerous criminal be caught at the gate. We can be grateful to those former residents who installed electricity in their homes. How awful it is in homes without power! There is no kerosene; candles are very hard to come by, and now it is impossible to install electricity due to shortages of materials and their high cost. Those in such houses must spend the long winter nights in the dark, just like those in prison.

D. ENTERING AND LEAVING THE GHETTO

As mentioned, the Šiauliai hard-labor prison borders the Trakų ghetto. To a large extent the ghetto is itself a prison, but inside the inhabitants are more or less free, and in some matters we are allowed a degree of independence. We have a council of representatives,[53] who can even tax us. We have a court (but without rabbis or religious judges,[54] who were all exterminated). We have officials, policemen, storekeepers, who are supposed to support us and take care of our needs, etc. But even these operate under the watchful, hostile eyes of our enemies, and numerous bizarre restrictions and decrees shackle us daily in iron chains. I will give details in what follows. First I will describe the rule we face that reminds us every day that we are indeed in prison. I am talking about the rule on exit and entry.

As mentioned, barbed wires and guards encircle the two ghetto areas. Our own "monitors"[55] stand inside near the gates, and policemen on shifts stand on the outside. The monitor's job is to check those wishing to leave and make sure they have the necessary permits. Such permits are obtained from the German "labor police," which, besides the director and another official who visit the ghetto almost daily, also includes several clerks from the ghetto's [Jewish] council, who administer these matters along with officers of the labor police.

At first, matters were more complicated: many people received permits inscribed with, "may leave at any time." These went to those with privileges: a few doctors, acquaintances of the officials, and those with "recommendations" from the police. There was also an allowance made for "servants" of Christian families in town who pretended to hire their Jewish women friends as maids, submitting fake contracts to the labor police for approval. This was popular because it provided Jewish women the chance to bring different food items into the ghetto. But such arrangements have now been nullified, and without those permits women are unable to bring in extra food, a matter that presently dominates our miserable lives.

Lately permits to leave the ghetto have been given to those working as craftsmen, whom the Germans to their chagrin cannot replace with Lithuanians. So they allowed shops in town to hire Jews as hatters, harness makers, blacksmiths, leather craftsmen, watchmakers, glove makers, and furriers.[56] There are also women's fashion shops selling corsets, belts, shirts, dresses, purses, etc., where many [Jewish] women, including former "maids," work now. Doctors now working as lab technicians are included among these specialists, as are pharmacists who work in various offices as translators and letter writers in German, etc. Permits to leave the ghetto are also given to simple day laborers who work at the airfield or on the roads, in the kitchens of Germans, in the hospital as hewers of wood and drawers of water,[57] etc. Workers at the Frenkel factory and the "Batas" factory, a small group, are also in this category.

The need to see a doctor is also a reason to leave the ghetto and return once or multiple times. Officials of the Jewish council take care of all these details under the supervision of the labor police. Ghetto officials also provide workers when the Germans request them to clear snow at the railroad station, unload cargo trains, etc. It is worth mentioning that when the Germans demanded many workers to clear snow off the railroad, the council reassigned people from the workshops and elsewhere; even three young doctors spent a day doing this lowly work. Finally, the Jewish police inside the gate check the permits of all those who leave and warn them to follow the German rules: walk in twos and threes as much as possible, and don't be seen on city streets between 8:00 a.m. and 4:00 p.m. Those who leave must therefore do so by 7:45 a.m. in order to be inside their shops by eight, and must stay inside until four, as mentioned. They cannot be on the street between 8:00 a.m. and 4:00 p.m. without a special permit from their shop supervisor, unless necessary for their work. The policemen outside the gate play a more critical role. They can reexamine permits if they wish, and they carefully scrutinize those returning from town, asking if they are bringing anything prohibited into the ghetto (which I will discuss further). Many Jews have been arrested recently, either for trying to leave the ghetto without permits, or for being caught on the streets at the wrong time. The German rulers want to keep the damned Jews from defiling the city's beauty and keep them constantly afraid whenever they venture out. People are also arrested daily when watchful policemen find them carrying any kind of food, including slices of bread, potatoes, etc.

E. NUTRITION IN THE GHETTO

Our oppressors have deprived us of all cultural and spiritual pleasures: they have left us only our material existence, uncultivated like weeds. But then food shortages waste away our physical being as well. We often lack even meager bread or potatoes, and hunger torments us. The Jewish council established two stores in the ghetto to provide for our needs. At first those with ration cards could purchase bread, potatoes, turnips, cabbages, and groats, but nothing else. Protein, which is fundamental for physical health, was missing altogether.

Meat, fish, milk, butter, cheese, eggs, and so on were nowhere to be seen. These shortages began to have an effect: significant and visible weight loss affected nearly all ghetto dwellers. People often meet and cannot recognize each other's thin faces, although much of that is also caused by unceasing emotional torment. But the chronic lack of food is certainly the primary cause. After a while the stores expanded their offerings: sugar began to appear, along with artificial honey and small portions of flour.

Recently things have improved somewhat, possibly because our representatives heard the complaints of ghetto residents about those running the stores. These shopkeepers were true leeches, sucking the blood of their brethren, operating the stores as if they were their own private businesses rather than public institutions. They were trading for themselves and inflating prices for their own benefit. Sometimes they would acquire small amounts of scarce commodities, such as sugar, honey or flour, and people in the ghetto would never see them, because the store workers would divide them all up among themselves and their friends. They ignored their responsibility to provide food to the ghetto, and abused their privileges by bringing in various goods, some permitted, others not, but only for their own benefit. They enriched themselves at the expense of the poor. It is rumored that some shopkeepers hid away commodities to sell in winter when there were shortages and prices rose. The council finally listened to these complaints, put new people in charge, and set up new rules for the shops. Now meat, fish and butter, things that previously were never seen in the stores, are being sold to ordinary people, although infrequently and in small quantities.

Still nutrition is insufficient, particularly since the daily quota of bread is two hundred grams per person. With potatoes and flour usually unavailable, this amount of bread leads to physical deterioration and eventual starvation;[58] thus, most people in the ghetto are entirely focused on overcoming hunger and take home rations for their starving households.[59] During our first days in the ghetto we were still allowed to bring in potatoes, vegetables, and a little bread; other foods were restricted, particularly meat, butter, sugar, and flour. But many of the guards were not strict, and turned a blind eye to prohibited goods or made only superficial inspections. There were then several ways to avoid malnutrition: first, we still had money and could obtain prohibited merchandise—for double or triple the price, of course—that speculators were clever enough to bring in. Moreover, the number of men and women permitted to enter and leave the ghetto was still large, and they could visit their acquaintances or get food from stores or speculators. The difficult part was getting it back into the ghetto, past the police. When no policeman was in sight, they would pass packages to their relatives or friends through openings in the fence and wires; or they would hide meat, butter, or eggs in their pockets, under their coats, tucked in their pants or in their boots. (Women used their chests or armpits.) They prayed that the police would not investigate too rigorously and not reach into private areas. But this did not always work out. Sometimes they used the simplest method, covering forbidden items in baskets and sacks with potatoes, onions, and other vegetables that they were allowed to bring in. Other times they used peculiar methods that would take a long time to describe.

Yet despite all the clever schemes, many were caught, and offenders would be hauled before the authorities and fined as much as the officials saw fit. Later the policemen became smarter, and rather than taking the smugglers to the office to be punished, they would "settle" with the offenders themselves for considerable sums. The risk was not that high, and the contraband, whether known or not to the policemen, kept coming in. Speculators multiplied like mushrooms among the Christians in the city, trading butter, fat, etc., not for money but for goods such as clothing and shoes.

The German secret police who watch us constantly (including, it is believed, through spies and informers) learned of the smuggling by ghetto inhabitants. Recently, due to the ongoing war and the many demands of the army, the Germans imposed food restrictions even on the Christian population, cutting back especially on proteins and fats. This has made them less tolerant of Jewish smuggling, and they began to come up with ways to combat the "criminals." First, they tightened inspections of those entering the ghetto and said certain items would not be allowed, even in small quantities. Violators would no longer be merely fined but jailed, and occasionally even put to death. Second, they strictly barred Jews from city streets between 8:00 a.m. and 4:00 p.m. and prohibited visits to Christian houses or stores during free time. Third, they began to search farmers coming to town, particularly on market days, because they too were engaging in speculation, trading food for various goods, which they hid from the Germans. Finally, they closed some of the workshops and ordered the essential ones that stayed open to replace half their workers with Christians. And so 300 people lost their permits to leave the ghetto, and the amount of food coming in was severely reduced.

The new edicts have resulted in many arrests, which is very worrisome. The heightened fears and suspicions around the new inspection regime (searches and arrests in the Kaukazas area were likely prompted by informers) caused speculators to disappear from the ghetto. The only ones remaining were Christians, a lesson for our enemies that speculation is not a uniquely Jewish trait. After they barred visits to Christian homes and stores, the Christian speculators started coming to the workshops to barter with Jews. But now that the number of Jewish workers in these shops has been cut in half, and with inspections at the gate more rigorous, the quantity of contraband has diminished, and the lack of food is felt even more acutely. Many ghetto homes face the prospect of starvation in coming days, even though food smuggling has not fully ceased. The hard work that strains the body, and the worries and fears that depress the soul, can only be alleviated with a healthier diet. Yet here the bread is spoiled, and the vegetables are scarce, and the spirit is dry and hungry! So those ghetto residents who still have contacts in the city risk their lives to try to bring food to their homes, helped by speculators at an unbelievable price. The smuggling continues and so do the arrests. Although many prisoners have been released recently, they were severely beaten, presumably as part of their punishment. Perhaps some of the Lithuanians, who recently gained a degree of municipal autonomy, feel guilty for their sins against the Jews and decided to atone by releasing some of those imprisoned by the Germans.

We have included some details here that may not be very interesting in order to paint a picture of life in the ghetto, and of the factors that rob us of energy and initiative and turn us all into thieves and fabricators. Although our own conscience is clear because we are dealing with matters of life and death, nevertheless we still suffer a great deal from the conditions that have brought us to this.

F. THE ECONOMIC STATE OF THE GHETTO

Jewish wealth passed through the tight Bolshevik sieve, which trapped and seized factories, workshops, and large stores from their owners. Industry, trade, and real estate could no longer produce private income. Livelihoods were blocked[60] for a large portion of our people. Only day laborers, clerks, doctors, and others who lived on fixed wages with no side income were unaffected. Little savings remained because bank deposits were seized, leaving mainly jewelry and other goods that some owned. By the time the Germans arrived, Jewish merchants and property owners had already lost much of their assets, but many remained comfortable, even wealthy, possessing real estate, furniture, household and kitchen items, clothes or jewelry that the Bolsheviks did not get their hands on. But how things worsened when the Germans arrived! First, the occupiers and their partisans began a wave of theft and robbery. Then came the ghetto edict, accompanied by the inspection committees that decided what goods could be transferred to the ghetto while confiscating the "lion's share." Rumors spread that bringing certain goods into the ghetto would be strictly forbidden, that only one suit, a few old shirts and a few shoes would be allowed along with two kilograms of sugar and two thousand rubles, and that all else, particularly newer goods, would be seized. So Jews hastened to use up their food supplies while arranging with Christian friends to hide their best clothes, linens, and especially jewelry, since silver and gold objects would not be allowed in the ghetto. They also gave the Christians large sums of money—huge fortunes—to hide. The outcomes varied: many Lithuanians began to immediately use the goods they were supposed to safeguard, behaving as if the original owners were already dead, and they had just come into a windfall. There were also some Lithuanians overcome by temptation who, if they had influence, arranged for the owners of these goods to be quickly moved to the "synagogues" or to that mysterious place from which none returned, making them the legal inheritors. There are also Lithuanians who can be trusted to return everything when the time comes. But for now, for reasons that will be explained below, it is difficult to get things back.

From all of this it should be clear that ghetto dwellers have been left naked and lacking everything,[61] and will soon face abject poverty if they don't already. But what sources of income remain in the ghetto? The German labor police decreed that every worker must receive wages. On the surface this seems just, but in practice it has become a stumbling block for many Jews. For the privilege of going into town and avoiding forced labor, many men and women in the ghetto had been willing to work for free in shops or Christian homes. But now every worker's salary must be deposited every month with the police, who end up keeping half of it. Specifically, the order states that every employer must deposit wages according to the general pay scale "irrespective of religion." But Jewish men receive only fifteen rubles per day, and Jewish women, thirteen rubles per day, Sundays and holidays excluded. The remainder—that is the difference between the Jewish salary and the Christian—is kept by the police. Thus, many Christian employers, who formerly could pay their Jewish workers little or nothing, were now forced to turn over significant sums on each worker's behalf. Usually it is not worth it to the employers; therefore this edict led to many workers being fired. As for the specialists who continued to work because their services were valued by their employers, they receive fifteen or thirteen rubles per day, a laughable salary considering that prices rise daily, particularly for food, the most basic of needs. Of course the intent is to reduce us to bread and water, like in prison, and make us the hewers of wood and drawers of water for the Germans and Lithuanians.

It is worth emphasizing that even skilled workers receive the same wage. For example, I work in the municipal polyclinic as an X-ray technician, using my own X-ray machine that was taken from me. For this work, which often brings hundreds of rubles a day to the polyclinic, I receive fifteen rubles per day, the same as all ghetto inhabitants, except for a privileged few whom I will discuss later. So what do those who "earn for a leaky purse"[62] do to make up for their deficient incomes? The answer is simple: those who can, sell what remains of their belongings—clothes, shoes, linens, etc.—or trade them for food. Obviously, the restriction on entering Christians' homes and the reduction in permits to enter the city present big obstacles. Moreover, sometimes the practice of hiding things with Christians has very sad consequences. The Germans put out a warning that whoever holds Jewish assets, no matter how they were obtained, must notify the authorities before a certain date. A few Lithuanians obeyed this order, fearing searches and punishment, but most ignored it and kept what they had. Still they fear that if Germans see Jews carrying things out of their homes they will be in jeopardy. Therefore, even if goods are safe in the hands of upright Christians, it is difficult now to get them back and extract whatever benefit or money they could bring.

And who can guarantee that we will live to see our property returned to us? Will we live to bless him "who sustained us and enabled us to reach this occasion?"[63] Time will tell. Nevertheless, some will survive, and they may learn that whatever they build in a foreign country is like a tower in the air; whatever they own there is like a cobweb, liable to fly away at the slightest breeze, "like chaff whirled away from the threshing floor."[64] The only solid things that will stand forever are territory and structures in the land of our ancestors. Even "a people that resemble a donkey"[65] will not face trouble like ours if it lives in its own country, if it is not alien, if it cannot be accused of swallowing native wealth and ordered to spit it out.

To sum up, the economic situation in the ghetto is generally pathetic and will get worse due to ever-increasing prices and a lack of decent sources of income. The situation for doctors is also very bad, except for Dr. D., who fortunately remained the only internal-medicine specialist in the Kaukazas area, and Dr. P., who suffers from delusions of grandeur and will dare to visit Christian patients in the city until he is brought down by calamity. The other doctors earn no more than day laborers when they treat private patients, and the six doctors who work as lab technicians, thanks to the efforts of Dr. Jasaitis, receive the wages of simple workers as determined by the German labor police. We should thank the villains for even this much because the Lithuanian city government, headed by former judge Linkevičius, was prepared to take our services free without payment.[66] Indeed, until the police intervened we worked in the municipal medical institutes with no hope of payment. The mayor's excuse was that the budget did not foresee paying lab technicians. Of course, like any budget, the city budget had a line item for "unforeseen expenses," and it could have been very easy to allocate a salary for us. But this cruel man, the mayor, always a cold and strict bureaucrat, became a fierce antisemite the day the Bolsheviks deported his wife and children from Šiauliai. (A shame he was away from home at the time.) He delayed paying our salaries, which depended totally on him, as long as he could. And who would argue against him?[67] Jasaitis indeed did us a favor by lobbying to get us jobs when most of the Lithuanian intelligentsia did not even dare to smile at us. But he would not go further and argue for giving us a salary, perhaps because even then he was starting to be labeled a "friend of the Jews" in certain circles, which would not endear him to the Germans. By the way, it is worth noting that when Jewish workers asked to be paid for building a fence around the ghetto, Mayor Linkevičius, a Lithuanian intellectual, lawyer and former judge, replied: "After all, the Jews built the ghetto for themselves!" And he did not allow payment.

For the doctors now working as lab technicians the future has become unclear, since the Germans closed some workshops and cut the number of Jewish workers in others. Once the permission was given to the Destroyer to destroy, he does not distinguish between essential and excess. I and Dr. P. could not be replaced as X-ray specialists, so how could they remove us? The answer is simple: the Germans care about the Lithuanians' health as much as they care about last year's snow. The Jews must be exterminated because the Leader has ordered it, but it is no problem if the Lithuanian pigs die in the process. The Lithuanians are pulled between their hatred of the Jews and their concern for the health of their own people, so it would not be surprising if they decided (this is an autonomous government, after all!) to dismiss us. It is clear why even doctors, who used to be among the better-compensated Jews,[68] now face enormous economic pressure and, like their brethren, must scheme and scam to find buyers for their possessions to finance their daily bread.

One group of ghetto residents is exceptional regarding their economic situation. These are the self-employed artisans and speculators, such as tailors, cobblers, brush makers, etc. Since they are not employed in shops the general law on salaries does not apply to them, and they earn well. They have money and therefore are among the speculators' best customers, prepared to pay 250 rubles for a kilogram of butter, sixty rubles for a kilogram of bread or flour, 10 rubles for an egg, three hundred rubles or more for a chicken—one artisan on the eve of Passover paid 850 rubles for a turkey—prices that a common worker, or a physician, could not even dream of paying. The speculators' heyday has passed because of the new edicts, but during the early period, they managed to fill their pockets with silver and gold.

Besides the former clerks in the council's cooperative stores, there were others who grew rich after they managed to find large quantities of butter, meat, or flour, which they smuggled into the ghetto. One Jew made a connection with an official of the wholesale firm Lietūkis,[69] and through him obtained barrels of butter weighing 100 kilograms each. He would pay this supplier forty rubles per kilo, double the official price of twenty rubles. The official, who wrote up the order in the name of a fake cooperative, earned two thousand rubles per barrel; the Jew, who then resold each kilo for fifty rubles, and later for sixty, earned a similar amount. Of course he had partners, and obtaining permits to smuggle in the merchandise must have cost a sizeable sum, but still there was enough left to get rich on because how many are the foods our people received?[70] Thank God there is now flour, meat, potatoes, sugar, salt—goods that would bring substantial amounts of money. Some meat traders once dared to bring a live cow and a heifer into the ghetto. This was at a time when the Germans were registering even the chickens in farmers' homes, so the speculators could have brought disaster on us all. The council fined them three thousand rubles and barred kosher slaughterers from handling the animals. The result was that the speculators charged an additional forty rubles per kilogram for the meat. In short, thanks to their past brilliance, they enjoy comfortable lives while the rest of the ghetto inhabitants face imminent starvation.

As an appropriately gloomy end to this account of the ghetto economy, I will describe the terrible edict issued on October 13 [1941]: the "contribution" tax. After the Bolsheviks, the partisans, the Germans and the inspection committees; after hiding away our goods leaving us empty-handed; after our sources of income were stopped except for the scant laborers' salary and speculation, which was still going strong; a decree went forth that residents of the two ghetto areas must pay the regional government half a million rubles! Jews were also ordered to turn in all silver, gold, electric kitchen equipment, furs, leather suitcases, and more. Thus they decided to suck the last drops from us and turn us into beggars with nothing. In apportioning shares to be paid, the [Jewish] council ordered W.T. to pay 7,500 rubles, and the dentist Dr. W. to pay 7,500 rubles (later reduced to only five thousand rubles). Drs. K.R. and D.N. had to pay 1,500 rubles each, while I and Dr. B.L. were each ordered to pay two thousand rubles.

I had been unemployed since the Germans came, and also had not been paid for my work during the Bolsheviks' last days (as chairman of both the sanitary commission and the committee for driver certification—that was all for naught). In July I was hired to work in the ambulatory clinic, but that closed soon thereafter. My private practice was not doing badly, particularly since patients would bring me various food items as gifts, but it did not last long because in early September I was imprisoned, and five days later I was transferred to the ghetto. Here I earn very little. For various reasons which this is not the place to discuss, I have not had many Jewish patients. So I was no longer receiving a salary, and during the first few months in the ghetto I survived exclusively on the money that my brother-in-law Zilberman gave me when the Bolsheviks deported him and his family from Šiauliai. If not for that money we would have already starved, because my savings were used for the move to the ghetto, which cost us a lot, and for other necessary expenses. We have a lot of "cash equivalents," but it was impossible then to convert those into actual money because the clothes, shoes, etc. that could be sold were not in our possession but in a hiding place. It goes without saying that two thousand rubles was my "enduring wealth."[71] My wife tried to plead with the council to reduce the amount, but she did so quite meekly because, to speak frankly, although I knew that the allocations had been arbitrary, often wrong and done with favoritism, I thought that disputing our share could prolong the process and possibly cause the collection to miss the imposed deadline. So on October 16 we paid the requested two thousand rubles, and also turned over a silver box with Hebrew engraving, which had been a wedding gift to my wife.

So I was left needy and destitute,[72] so short of money that I was forced to borrow from my Christian physician colleagues certain sums, which are barely enough. Now I have no idea whence my help will come[73] if I cannot sell some of my belongings. I am severely depressed, and a growing desperation is overwhelming me. Indeed, if the war lasts a few more months and the situation does not improve, we are doomed to perish as we will not have enough money even for dry bread. Moreover my wife is sick, and we need to pay the young woman who helps us from the little we still have. Indeed our fate is bitter, and for now there is no escape. We do retain a spark of hope that we can sell some of our belongings for a decent sum, a few thousand rubles. On the other hand we would like to believe that if spring and fall pass without a decisive victory by the Germans, then the war could finally end, with [German] army officers removing the supreme source of evil. Peace would come and we would be freed from our imprisonment and live again like human beings, and then . . . then we would try with all our might to leave this valley of slaughter, this land saturated with our brothers' blood. Is our hope real, or are we merely dreaming? It is hard, so hard, to believe the world is entirely dark, that we are lost without hope, that evil and injustice will rule forever.

G. THE STATE OF MORALITY IN THE GHETTO

Despair with no prospect of salvation. Disappointed believers who put their faith in God. Doubts about a creator who is silent while we suffer as never before. The forced desecration of the Sabbath and holy days. The chronic shortages of kosher meat and of food in general. All this brought a notable drop in religious observance in the ghetto. Who among us does not sin now by eating unkosher meat? Who is not forced to desecrate the Sabbath in his own home, and who does not do so openly, without even being forced? Who among us does not routinely violate the commandments? Such indifference and apathy regarding the faith has overtaken ghetto dwellers! Yes, some remain devout amid the deepest gloom,[74] refuse to change their ways and follow the law as strictly as before. But their numbers are so miniscule, a child could count them.

It is true that fear of God is not always correlated with justice and honesty, morality and ethics. Yet while many thieves and crooks are also God-fearing believers, one still cannot deny that for certain people there is a connection between religion and morality. Here in the ghetto we sadly see how the pillars of morality have been badly shaken as faith has declined. Indeed besides the reasons already cited, several additional factors brought a decline in morals. Traumatic stress, fear and anxiety about a tomorrow that might bring loss and annihilation; the personal difficulties that everyone has and which absorb all one's attention—all these fostered a self-centeredness that became extreme and shook the foundations of morality. Each one is fully immersed in his own troubles, which are as vast as the sea, and no one else matters. And thus grows the desire to benefit at others' expense. The shearers came because there was a flock. Speculators multiplied, inflating prices, skinning the poor. Theft became common: stealing food, stealing belongings, stealing firewood. Artisans refuse to return items they received for repair. Informers have leaked details of the council's meetings to the Germans. Some have kowtowed to the Germans, hoping for concessions at others' expense. Certain deceptions regarding apartments had terrible consequences, such as families being evicted to make room for the more privileged. Although rumors have greatly exaggerated this, with baseless stories blaming doctors for some of the deportations, they may contain shreds of truth. Some were surely removed from the ghetto solely because of self-interest and criminal indifference. But who would have thought that such unparalleled misery would aggravate division among brothers and cause such a lack of sympathy between a man and his friend? Relationships among doctors these days are a clear example. Jealousy, hatred, "strife and contention,"[75] even physical violence within our supposedly intellectual cohort. We are taught that

"Torah scholars increase peace in the world."[76] See what peace these scholars bring! And if the (supposedly) upright cedars burn,[77] is it any surprise that scalpers, swindlers, crooks, and cheats grow as plentifully as mushrooms and moss?

Our experience was typical. We bought potatoes in town from our Lithuanian landlady, paying her in full and agreeing that she would have them delivered to us by one of the ghetto's coachmen. At the same time, she also promised to send some potatoes to one of her other acquaintances in the ghetto. That man sent his neighbor, the coachman, to pick up his promised potatoes. When the coachman arrived and asked for the potatoes, the landlady thought that he came for those we had bought, and asked, "Did Mrs. Pick send you to get her potatoes?" He quickly answered "Yes," took the potatoes and delivered them to his neighbor, who started to eat them. The coachman, a former cook, and his neighbor were considered honest people. But now in the ghetto, everything is permissible! So the landlady had to come into the ghetto, and we managed to pry the food out of the cheat's mouth and shame him.

When they wanted to transfer one of my doctor colleagues to another apartment, he shamelessly said, "If they try to harm me, you should know that half of the ghetto will be deported." Although this fool never caused the deportation of even a single person, his careless statement, at a time when this fate hangs over all our heads, testifies like one hundred witnesses to the egoism infusing this man's entire being. Indeed, he received his punishment after being indicted and tried by the council.

This doctor was also slapped by a colleague whom he had cursed at, and he is planning to sue him before the people.[78] What scorn and provocation![79] The reputation of doctors in the ghetto is already tarnished. And the doctor who took it upon himself to be the leader has already transgressed, God forbid, by informing. Jealous of his colleagues who received jobs as lab technicians in town, he blurted to the head of the labor police that the lab work was a sham. Of course these words, stated in his excellent German, could have caused the technicians to lose their jobs. But in fact our jobs are useful and necessary, and therefore his hopes went unrealized. Similarly, when I fell ill with the flu, the polyclinic doctors were in a very inconvenient spot because they were short one radiologist and could not find a substitute.

Moral decline in the ghetto is also evident in a lack of politeness and courtesy. An absence of hospitality and kindness can be seen everywhere as inhabitants follow the negative example of our rulers. The ghetto police go around in storm and tempest,[80] always angry, yelling and even beating those who break discipline.

Even the [Jewish] officials behave as if they are permanently upset, responding crudely and harshly to questions if they deign to answer at all. In most cases they literally turn their backs. Of course the burdens and the bickering[81] of the "holy community"[82] weigh on their nerves. But the council's officers must realize that those turning to them suffer as much as they do. Moreover, the reasons they turn to these officials should bring forth feelings of sympathy and pity. Well-to-do people, former homeowners, humiliate themselves often by begging for a corner to lay their heads, or a little firewood to warm their shivering bones in their cold, drafty, filthy apartments.

H. THE MOOD IN THE GHETTO

It may be presumptuous to say much about this topic, but as it affects many aspects of ghetto life, we will consider it. It is not hard to understand how ghetto dwellers feel: people who were previously well-to-do are now downtrodden and wretched. People of initiative and drive are forced into idleness or to work as laborers. People who not long ago were free citizens now are deprived of rights, their persons and property not their own. People whose souls crave healthy and nourishing food now hunger for bread, of which there is never enough. The oppressive restrictions, the threat of bitter death,[83] and the constant struggle for food rattle the nerves and depress the spirit. The various tricks to deceive the police at the gate have one common feature: they all involve risk and thus are accompanied by agitation, stress, and tension—so much that one may say without exaggeration that the toll on mental and physical health outweighs the value of the smuggled food.

But we may also say that all these troubles are as nothing compared with the bereavement and loss[84] that have struck nearly every family and individual. Those calamities began under the Bolsheviks with the deportations of the bourgeoisie, and reached a climax with the arrival of the Germans. Many pitiable, bereaved orphans were left behind when their parents and relatives were deported to the forests and tundra of Siberia. The chaos and confusion in families was multiplied when people started to flee the war. How many parents lost touch with children who ran to Latvia, hoping to enter the USSR? How many young men and women studying in Kaunas or Vilnius panicked when they learned of the Germans' approach and lost their way in trackless deserts,[85] leaving their parents bereaved, with no hope of ever learning their children's fate? Many other parents grieve even though their children never fled, because Jews are now forbidden to travel by train or communicate by mail or telegraph, and thus all contact between them and their children has been cut off.

Still, nothing compares with the harm done to families by the deportations and disappearances through the "synagogues" under German rule. Partisans went house to house, arresting both old and young, whoever they chanced upon, leaving parents without their children and children without their parents. How many were left widowed and orphaned after these arrests! How many young wives mourn their husbands with no one to console them? And the tragic deportations, first to the synagogues and from there to the killing sites: who can describe these horrors and the painful and depressing impression left deep, deep in our hearts? Our language has no words to convey the feelings of people led to slaughter for no crime,[86] their mood as they were locked inside the synagogues, weeping through the night before an open, empty ark[87] (from which the Torah scrolls had been taken and hidden earlier), bitterly beseeching the God of Israel who had turned His back—a divine spirit that left them long ago. From there they were taken to the valley of slaughter, forced to undress with blows from rifle butts, and then killed without mercy—the innocent, the saintly, and the pure. Kravitz and his wife! Terrified and trembling, I am trying to imagine their last moments, their eyes radiating mortal fear, their emotional distress when they saw how their lives would end. Beloved and cherished,[88] pure as God's angels, how could I forget you?

Three places were turned into our gallows, near the villages of Ginkūnai, Bubiai, and Kužiai.[89] The latter was a place destined for trouble since the [First] World War: it was there that the rumor emerged that Jews had disclosed Russian military positions to the Germans—a bitter twist of fate!—which was why they were sent into exile by the destroyer Nikolai Nikolaevich.[90] The partisans prepared, locating places where pits and caves were available for ready burial. To make sure the bullets would damage only bodies and not clothing, they forced victims to undress before being shot. Recall the shocking story of the arm with the watch, reaching up from the pile of the fallen. We also remember how a partisan asked to have gold crowns put on his teeth, not realizing his dentist was Jewish. When the dentist asked where he would get the gold, the partisan said he had an ample supply, taken from the teeth of murdered Jews.

The mental state of family members who drank from this poison cup, seeing or hearing about these horrific events—that is to say, everyone in the ghetto—can be readily imagined. In their few free moments amid the suffering, the forced labor and the struggle to find food, people fade away like lengthening shadows,[91] their faces lean from hunger and darkened by sorrow. When they meet they cry, moan, complain, discuss the situation at the front or in the ghetto, sharing any good news without conviction or faith. They "meet without joy, part without sorrow." There is no present and the future is uncertain.

We are being roasted on a slow fire, and the spark of hope, which still flickers deep inside, is slowly fading. Will that faint spark endure? Will hope reappear, and become a bright torch to illuminate the long night for those feeling their way in darkness? Will it bring help and salvation? Could we be the last Jews of Lithuania? Or are we doomed like the other victims of this time of distress?[92] For us now the worst of the bitter prophecy[93] has come to pass: "Cursed shall you be in your comings and cursed shall you be in your goings"[94] (as if referring to passage through the ghetto's gates). "You shall be constantly abused and robbed, with none to give help"[95] (the thieving partisans come to mind), "until you are driven mad by what your eyes behold."[96] (Is this not a reference to our brethren's deportation and slaughter?) "You shall be in terror, night and day, with no assurance of survival. In the morning you shall say, 'If only it were evening!' and in the evening you shall say, 'If only it were morning!'—because of what your heart shall dread and your eyes shall see."[97] (An accurate summation of our mood in the ghetto).

The prohibition on being outdoors after 8:00 p.m. applies also in the ghetto. Therefore when eight o'clock arrives, the entire population moves indoors and windows are covered, occasionally with shutters but mostly by black fabric and rags to prevent light from escaping. The unpaved roads are covered with fog during the dark fall and winter nights. Here and there a flicker of light between curtain edges and window frames gives the ghetto a mysterious appearance, as if sorcerers and alchemists were hiding behind the windows.

The medieval darkness affects the ghetto dwellers' mood, accelerating the dark rumors that circulate endlessly through the air. Beyond what has sadly actually happened, beyond the frequent edicts and the undisputed news about massacres of Jews in Lithuania and persecutions abroad, unceasing fear prompts the imagination to create dreadful images, "embroidered cloths."[98] Terrible rumors spread easily, and some sadly turn out to be true. But most are baseless and contradict each other. Their common feature is that they leave us numb, anxious, and depressed. We were tormented by a series of rumors about the ghetto arrangements even before our transfer here; some were encouraging and some dismaying. After we moved into the ghetto came the rumors about Žagarė:

- –"There are Jews there who were deported from Šiauliai."
- –"There are no Šiauliai Jews there."
- –"All the Jews were killed there."
- –"The Jews there are free and able to buy food in the market."
- –"Many Jews were killed there for no reason on the street in broad daylight as happened elsewhere in Lithuania."

–"Jews there were killed because of their mistake: they were being taken to work, and they thought the partisans planned to execute them (a notion completely foreign to the Lithuanians!). So they began to flee, and for that the partisans shot them."

Thus were the events described in various versions. In fact, none of it happened.[99] They later wiped out more than four thousand Jews collected in Žagarė without reason or excuse, as they did throughout Lithuania, wherever the children of Israel dwelt.

Rumors about the partisans began to circulate as well:

–"Partisans, led by Požėla the slaughterer, have arrived in Šiauliai."
–"The partisans have left Šiauliai."
–"Partisans are gathering for a meeting."
–"Partisans have finished slaughtering the few that remained."
–"Partisans are refusing to continue shooting Jews."

Particularly rampant were rumors about when Šiauliai Jews were to be killed. At first it was claimed that all Šiauliai Jews would be eradicated on October 12 [1941]. Then the mass killing was postponed to the fifteenth. When that day passed without incident, rumors said the slaughter would happen on the eighteenth, and then the twenty-second. Finally, it was agreed that November 7 was the date, based on other supporting rumors: "Požėla has moved to Šiauliai." (This was true.) "Stankus said his name will be inscribed in gold letters in the pages of Jewish history." "The wife of Gewecke, the district governor, bought underwear from a Jewish seamstress, demanding that it be ready in three weeks," indicating that the Jews would not be killed for three weeks. Some said the "contribution" tax and the demand for valuables were a pretext to search Jewish homes prior to eliminating all Šiauliai Jews. Others argued just the opposite: if they wished to exterminate the Jews,[100] they would not demand money but simply would kill them all and take everything.

Reports about the front also differ wildly, as those with creative imaginations as well as outright liars construct castles in the air out of a whispered word or two. "The Germans are advancing." "The Germans are being pushed back." "The German army is surrounded."

One day a rumor spread that Göring[101] had sent a memorandum forbidding further harm to Jews. A few days later the newspapers published a speech by the supreme source of evil, who, like a dog returning to his own vomit,[102] repeated his psychotic claim that Jews are to blame for everything and should be eliminated from Europe. Sometime later, some seventy people who had stayed too long in the villages were rounded up and killed, the imaginary Göring memo notwithstanding. Among those was Zeigernik's wife[103]—without exaggeration a woman of valor[104]—who in her life had managed to accumulate a large fortune. She was killed, along with her two children[105] and her sister's children. Then another rumor claimed that the Lithuanians had complained to the German government that they were being forced to become killers and would thus be condemned for eternity.[106] Suddenly the rumor is revived that Jews will be transferred from the ghetto to Žagarė or to Zokniai (where the airfield is located), etc. Thus do conflicting rumors spread in the ghetto. Some are hopeful, others depressing, and nerves are stretched and stressed more and more. One day, all the pessimistic ghetto-dwellers walk around stooped and faces turn ashen,[107] frightened by a bad rumor. The next day, that rumor is found to be false. The clouds disperse, faces brighten, and postures grow more erect. One winks at another, "I have a secret." Thus are lives lived in fear and terror, with the violence and catastrophe that is our fate imprinted deeply on the minds and spirits of the ghetto inhabitants.

We learned something of the mental state of bereaved parents through our own experience with our own son. He was to finish his first-year final exams at the university in Vilnius and return home at the end of June. Then the war broke out. He had just enough money to remain in Vilnius until the end of the month and return home, but no more. Since all communication was cut off, we had no idea of his whereabouts: did he try to flee to the USSR? We greatly doubted that this young man, who inherited a timid passivity from his yeshiva-scholar grandfathers, would take such a bold step, particularly without any resources. But in an emergency he might have thought about looking for my brother and our other relatives in Moscow. My pen is inadequate to describe our emotional torment, caused by the lack of news and our only son's unknown fate. Fear and worry about his whereabouts troubled us day and night: had he found shelter? Was he free or in prison? Was he hungry? In forced labor? If he escaped from Vilnius, had he managed to cross the border? These thoughts frightened us endlessly, particularly after rumors reached us that Vilnius had become a hell, with Jews dying there from starvation. We abandoned all hope of seeing our son before the end of the war, and grief was stamped on our existence. The bitter question, "What are we working for?" plagued us, and we literally did not want to live anymore.

We later learned the truth: our son had actually remained in Vilnius and found shelter at the home of his schoolmate's family, who took care of him as best as they could. Quite a few students from Šiauliai, male and female, stayed with him in Vilnius. The situation worsened over time as food became a problem, forced hard labor began and the outlook darkened. At that point six young people from Šiauliai who were in Vilnius met, along with the father of one of them, and found a Pole who agreed, for a considerable sum, to take them to Šiauliai in his horse cart. The money allowed the Pole to buy himself an excellent "Rocinante,"[108] a mare that after the second day lay down beside the road and decided that should be her burial place. The Pole walked to a nearby village where he managed to buy another horse, not much better than the dying mare. But after a few hours' rest on "holy ground," the first horse recovered a bit, and since two are better than one,[109] the two "eagles" began to drag them along. They went by roundabout paths,[110] avoiding larger towns, which could be dangerous. The travelers hit the road in early morning and found shelter in the evening in the barn of a hospitable farmer, a few of whom still remained in the villages, or slept in the open if they found a convenient grove (and the weather allowed).

In short, after six days of adventures they thankfully reached Šiauliai. They experienced a great miracle passing Radviliškis, where there was a concentration camp. The Jew-hating commandant there and his evil deputy, Jaška, were seizing any Jew who passed nearby on foot or in a cart and sending them to the camp, which was noted for its exceptionally cruel treatment of Jewish prisoners. Our son and his friends miraculously avoided these kidnappers and passed safely through this minefield. Although our son had left nearly all his belongings in Vilnius—clothes, underwear, suitcases, books—he returned home in good health, and our eyes lit up.[111]

On the same day my son and his friends left Vilnius in the cart—which they pushed more than it pulled them—two other students, Savich and Epstein, persuaded a young woman to get them two tickets on a train heading for Šiauliai through Radviliškis. Near that stop, other passengers spotted them as Jews and had them thrown off the train. Partisans then shot them, ending the lives of these two young men, one of whom—Savich, a student in the drama department of the university—would have become a top-rated actor. Even as a gymnasium student he had been an excellent orator. Pity for a talent lost but never forgotten! "Weep for this beauty that will decompose in the earth."[112]

A unique and terrible phenomenon that significantly affects ghetto dwellers are the rumors about people who have disappeared. Those now gone include many who were imprisoned, among them the best of Šiauliai's sons—the unfortunate ones[113] taken from the city and ghetto to the synagogues and from there to a mysterious place or directly to that place, from which they never returned—and finally, those who were collected from the villages and vanished. Where were they taken? Did they go to their graves in Lithuania? Were some sent out of the country? Are any of them alive? "Desire begets belief":

many of their relatives want to believe they are still alive, and it serves them to think they are in a concentration camp or something similar abroad. Painfully, however, we must admit that the hope for reunification after the war is a naive self-delusion. Were they different than all the other Jews whose blood was spilled like water, saturating the land of Lithuania like gushing rain? How could we forget the people of initiative and drive, the scholars and intellectuals who left us, never to return? Their unknown fates disturb and shock us more than those of our known dead whose end is undoubted. "Do not weep for the dead. . . . Weep rather for him who is leaving, for he shall never come back."[114]

I. CULTURE AND EDUCATION IN THE GHETTO

In his speeches, the supreme source of evil talked often of his decision to eliminate the Jews of Europe. He also claimed more than once that he has already eliminated Jewish influence for the next one thousand years. From this it is clear that even if he did not intend to butcher all the Jews of Europe, so that none escaped,[115] he meant to leave those few survivors no discernible role in human society. Consistent with this objective, he ordered that the children of Israel be deprived of education, like animals in the wild. Schools were to vanish in the ghetto, and even study circles are forbidden. Initially a small elementary school was set up unofficially, based on Stankus's promise to turn a blind eye. Without a classroom large enough to accommodate all the pupils, they found a porch where small groups could be taught. The rest were divided into smaller groups and studied in their teachers' small, crowded homes. Since there was no formal permit for this arrangement, there was a danger that this ruse by the deceitful, criminal Jews would be discovered.

At the same time it was decreed that anyone without a specific trade or profession should move to the Kaukazas area. Since officially there were no schools, and therefore no need for teachers, teaching no longer qualified as a profession. So the teachers stopped teaching. One who had headed the informal school began work as a belt maker; two others joined a chemical materials shop; another turned overnight into a painter, and so on. With these jobs they did not have to register as unemployed, and therefore did not have to relocate to the Kaukazas ghetto along with the unskilled and elderly, a prospect that had greatly frightened all the residents of our ghetto. So organized schools in the ghetto were canceled in favor of private lessons. But not every parent could afford tuition for their children, and many in the ghetto are now growing up without Torah or education. Things were even worse for older children, since there are no middle or high schools. For former university students, of course, their studies are set aside for now. And how long will "for now" last? For as long as the hand of evil rules us. As long as we are trampled like mud and shunned like lepers, our sons will remain illiterate and ignorant, enslaved at hard labor. An appropriate fate for a defective and inferior race that is to be blamed for every trouble of humanity, that wishes only to live off others and raise conflict among the nations! Why would children of such a race need education?

And what sort of culture exists for adults? Would anyone organize a club in the ghetto? Would anyone arrange lectures, when hearts are full of suffering,[116] when there is no free time or space? What could interest people preoccupied with finding food, who live in constant dread because of the rage of an oppressor,[117] for whom the fear of death is a constant? Those with a shred of attention left for cultural matters could read books, but of course there is no library in the ghetto. The Hebrew public library, which I helped found and which was named after me, was lost during the Bolshevik days. Hebrew books made up the bulk of that library, followed by books in Yiddish. The latter were seized by the Jewish "comrades" and put in a Yiddish-Russian library set up by the MOPR.[118] The Hebrew books were archived in one comrade's attic after a teacher in the Hebrew gymnasium, who had become an enthusiastic Bolshevik, recommended that they be burned. Right now I have no knowledge about the fate of these books.

The rich Hebrew gymnasium library was taken to feed the central heating furnaces, where the labor police office is now (the commerce institute also moved there), and the furnace of the district commissioner, although the Jew who worked for the labor police rescued many of these books and transferred them to the ghetto. Many individuals, my son among them, also brought some volumes, so there are actually a fair number of books in the ghetto. But readers are few. Everyone works from 8:00 a.m. to 4:00 p.m. and therefore must get up early, and they return to the ghetto after 5:30 p.m.[119] With lunch and dinner, the little time left is devoted to reading the newspapers that circulate in the ghetto. Obviously, all are interested in the situation at the front. Although these newspapers are a "muddied spring and ruined fountain,"[120] there is no alternative. The best is a German paper published in Riga,[121] which has some style and is decently written, but its news reports are full of baseless falsehoods[122] and propaganda, boasting endlessly of victories and success. The audacity! The Germans never tire of it, announcing daily that they have pushed the Russians back, caused innumerable casualties, destroyed so many tanks, but not a word of their own damages and losses, as if the Russians are throwing snowballs and potatoes at them. So enthusiastically do they spread these lies that someone who recently counted found that the reports put Russian losses at 20 million people! The falsity of this math should be obvious. Even discounting its occupied regions, from which soldiers could not be drafted, the USSR still has a population of 160 million. Of that, at most some 15 percent could be drafted, or twenty four million. So based on the German reports, only 4 million should be left in the Russian army, which has been attacking the Germans and holding them back all winter.

Aside from the false news, this newspaper is full of poison and incitement against the Jews. Reading it causes disgust. There is also a German daily in Kaunas[123] that imitates the Riga daily, and the filth from these two German outlets drains like sewage into the Lithuanian press. There are two Lithuanian papers: a daily in Kaunas[124] and a weekly in Šiauliai. The latter[125] is a "pogrom" rag. Its front page carried a purportedly "scientific" article, with quotes from books that have never existed, drunkards' tales about Jews using Christian blood in the Passover celebration.[126] Here in the twentieth century they revived all the lies and libels of medieval times, endangering our existence. The character of this rag was made clear in its first issue, which included an article clearly calling for anti-Jewish riots and inviting Lithuanians to hold a "popular court" to indict Jews for all their troubles under the Bolsheviks. The writer enumerated "murders" of Lithuanians and their bodily mutilations, amputated limbs, breasts, eyes, etc. And in a revealing detail the writer claimed that some of those murdered by the Bolsheviks had their hearts cut out of their bodies, "according to the ritual," that is, following Jewish religious practice. In other words, Jewish Bolsheviks murdered Lithuanians to fulfill a Jewish commandment. So the atheist Bolsheviks included devout Jews, sufficiently committed to religion to want to practice ritual murder! And even to cut hearts from bodies! Surely these lies have no legs. And now we can see just how much substance these reports of murders committed by the Jews have. The tone of the article is consistent from beginning to end, and supports the view of Ahad Ha'am[127] that the recurring "blood libel" illustrates the falsity of most accusations against the Jews. They arise not from reality but from the accusers' evil spirits. To summarize, cultural life in the ghetto is quite feeble. Our focus is mainly on painting a more or less complete image of life here.

J. HEALTH AND MEDICINE

A principal requirement for physical health is hygiene, which requires a bathhouse or a bathtub, or at the very least a full-body wash. These are nearly out of the question in the ghetto. The overcrowded conditions, along with the

constant anxiety and fear that distract the mind and erode good habits, make
it impossible for most ghetto dwellers to maintain personal cleanliness. Obviously a bathtub could not possibly exist in the ghetto, but the real hindrance
for residents is the lack of a bathhouse. Even our sages understood the importance of this, saying that "a Torah scholar may not reside in a city without a bathhouse."[128] It is notable that the [Šiauliai] municipal bathhouse is idle two days
a week. The Jewish representatives lobbied city hall and the district commissioner's office to allow ghetto residents to use it on those two days. They noted
that since it was only a short distance away, visitors to the bathhouse would
need to cross only one side street, not a main road. But of course, appealing to
the wicked was in vain: permission was denied. We are talking moreover about
a formerly Jewish bathhouse, which the kehilla and its successor, the "Ezra"
organization, spent huge sums to maintain and repair. Indeed the prophecy has
been fully realized: "If you build a house, you shall not live in it."[129] How much
of Israel's fortune was lost! How much of our labor and energy are consumed
by others!

   An aside: from the laboratory windows in the municipal polyclinic, where
I work, I can see across the square to what was once the Hebrew gymnasium,
which now houses the commerce institute (now closed to Jews), and the German labor police. Every day I look at this building, which cost us so much. From
its newer bricks I can tell that the third floor was added only recently, before the
Bolsheviks' arrival. I look and my eyes weep, and my heart is faint. Each of us
donated significant amounts to add this floor. How much labor and difficulty
was required to execute this project, and also to buy the adjacent plot, so students could use it for play and exercise! As a member of the parents' committee,
I was aware of all the tribulations associated with building the gymnasium and
extending the square. And now what had been our own proud achievement
belongs to our murderers and mortal enemies! And its fate is like that of the
bathhouse, another of our community's properties, the fruit of our own labor
whose benefit is forbidden to us.[130]

   As the saying goes: "A dirty house is a troubled house." If those in the home
are in pain or anxious, they pay no attention to its cleanliness. The truth of this
is plain to see throughout the ghetto, where all are overwhelmed by grief and
worry. Add the effects of overcrowding and it is easy to imagine the state of
sanitation. Egypt's third plague[131] has already spread alarmingly, even through
the houses of the better-off and educated, so imagine what must be happening
among the poor? Further, all the yards overflow with piles of trash, muck, and
mud. And the latrines are filled to capacity with human feces because there are
not enough horses and carts to haul the filth away. When spring comes and the

sun's rays begin to warm the earth, it will be difficult to breathe the air, because of the stench emanating from the yards.

It is thus easy to see that hygiene in the ghetto is lacking and that any communicable disease here could quickly turn into a deadly epidemic. This danger increased when typhus, which we know is spread by lice, appeared in the city. This terrible disease was carried by prisoners of war and soldiers returning from the front and transmitted to the city from the prison and military hospital. Many were sick. Had the epidemic penetrated the ghetto, with its poor hygienic conditions, it would have overwhelmed us, prompting our "friends" to "cure" us by burning the place with all its inhabitants, as they did with the Jewish hospital in Kaunas.[132] There were in fact a few isolated cases in the ghetto: several young people who worked for the Germans became sick. But there were no deaths, and the disease did not spread. The council tried several methods to contain the problem: it organized a small hospital for those with communicable diseases. Barbers shaved the heads of boys and girls with lice and ordered that all pillows, duvets, and other bedding be put outside to air, an effective treatment as the cold intensified. In the end the danger passed over the ghetto, and miraculously we avoided an epidemic. The "inferior" race demonstrated vigor, resilience, and more practicality than did its supposed superiors. But miracles do not happen every day, and many problems remain: unhygienic conditions and insufficient nutrition significantly reduce the body's resistance to disease in general and to communicable diseases, such as tuberculosis in particular. They await us around every corner. The weakened body is susceptible to all the triggers of communicable diseases and is a fertile ground for parasites that can establish themselves in various organs.

In contrast with the hygienic situation in the ghetto, which is not only unsatisfactory but also dangerous, the state of medical care here is far more acceptable. Two ambulatory clinics were established, one in each ghetto area, to provide free or affordable care to all. There are also dental clinics. In addition, in the two ghetto areas there are more than 20 doctors, midwives, and nurses available to provide treatment. Although six doctors work in the city, after 4:00 p.m. they return to the ghetto.

Any discussion of the ghetto medical facilities must emphasize three points, which will be discussed in more detail in a chapter on the new decrees. First, hospitals and medical offices in town were forbidden to accept Jewish patients. Second, Jews were forbidden to buy medications from pharmacies in town. And finally, the unprecedented and infamous prohibition against Jewish women giving birth to sons, thus forcing them to abort their pregnancies. How could a heart not break on hearing this? Are we made of stone that we can accept such things? "Pharaoh only decreed against the males,"[133] but the supreme source of evil, may his name and memory be wiped out,[134] sought to annihilate an entire people! Will he succeed? Will there be no salvation for all the children of Israel? Will there be no final redemption for all Israel?[135]

In light of these details, the council decided to set up a small hospital in two buildings of the cemetery:[136] the "cleansing room"[137] and the custodians' dormitory. This facility is able to care for those who need treatment and also for women who must be relieved of their pregnancies due to the harsh punishment promised by the German police if they bear a live male child. Of course we lack an X-ray machine and other instruments. But in a time of need, this modest hospital could substitute for the municipal hospital, particularly since the chief surgeon of the municipal hospital, T.K., has softened toward the Jews and begun visiting the ghetto hospital to perform surgeries too complicated for our own young surgeon, H. Though an antisemite, the chief surgeon is among those educated Lithuanians who believe that even though the Jews needed to be taught a lesson, our persecutors have gone too far. So he has grown more willing to put up with Jewish patients and is willing to work in the ghetto, particularly since he is being paid for it. Payment precedes action.

Dr. B.N., who arrived recently, was quickly chosen to be the ghetto's chief physician. A native of the Memel region, he speaks German well and volunteered to make an appeal to the district commissioner, along with Mrs. L., who was educated in Germany. Their mission failed, but his good intentions won him the position of chief doctor. While this job carries no privileges, neither is it a disadvantage, and he likely is deriving some material benefit from it. This doctor bore a significant grudge against me. When Dr. Jasaitis returned from Moscow [on the eve of the German invasion, June 1941], he resumed his position as director of the Šiauliai health department. He learned then that I had been left without a medical job in town—this was before the Nuremberg laws were imposed on our area—while the newer doctors, B.N. and G-sky, were working in the city's ambulatory clinic. Dr. Jasaitis, who had known me for years, decided to let Dr. B.N. go and gave me his position. B.N. then also worked in the prisoners' hospital, which prevented him from being drafted for forced labor, while I, after running the polyclinic and managing departments in the hospital for more than sixteen years, desperately needed a job to avoid conscription. I also did not turn down Jasaitis's offer because I thought I deserved it more than a newcomer, particularly one with a job already.

So what did B.N. do when I took the job, which had been mine by right as the previous institute director? He spread the story among our friends that I had coerced Dr. Jasaitis into giving me the position, as if that were possible. After that, Dr. B.N. turned hostile toward me; when various groups held meetings at his house, I was not invited. So I distanced myself from community work. Thanks to my lobbying with Dr. Jasaitis, I was among the six doctors hired as lab technicians in town; B.N. was not, and moreover his job in the prisoner-of-war hospital was eliminated. So his fury burned within him,[138] and he was planning to tell the labor police and the ghetto council that our jobs were phony, a fiction. Once, at a meeting of ghetto doctors, we confronted him: Dr. G. slapped his face, saying that if the Memel horse-trader who runs the labor police[139] is reexamining our positions in the labs, it must have been due to B.N.'s prompting. B.N. jumped out of his chair as if bitten by a snake, and after insulting Dr. G., he rushed out of the meeting. He realized then that I do not particularly like him,[140] and since then, he has avoided me even more.

When they began to organize the ghetto hospital and needed a director, they turned to me, as a physician who had managed the municipal hospital's internal medicine and infectious disease departments for more than sixteen years, and as one with significant knowledge and experience. The chief doctor kept hopping between two opinions,[141] but finally offered me the position and promised to obtain a permit for me to leave and return to the ghetto with no time restriction, so I could go to the lab after morning rounds at the hospital and leave the laboratory early to visit the hospital again in the afternoon. I would work the same total number of hours, since I am currently staying in the laboratory longer than required. Moreover, the inclination to public service is in my blood. So I agreed to take the hospital director position, but my wife objected, reasoning that it would be difficult for me to walk to the hospital on dark winter nights. I too began to have doubts: I worried that the labor police would not allow me to hold two positions and would take away my job in town, which is very important for me, particularly since there I receive at least a meager salary for my work, while the hospital job is without the expectation of reward.[142]

My second and larger concern was that in those days, for various reasons, people were being transferred from one ghetto area to another. If I had to go twice a day to the Kaukazas area, they might reconsider and transfer me from the nest I had made with great difficulty in the Trakų section to Kaukazas altogether. That settled it: I withdrew my acceptance, and the director's job was given to Dr. P.,[143] whom I recommended because he is much younger than me. I had doubts at first, but in retrospect I do not regret it because my work in the hospital would likely have compromised my work as a radiologist in the polyclinic, where surgeons send me their patients up to 4:00 p.m. In addition I now have some free time to study the English language, and I have made quite a bit of progress, more than I expected, and I can now understand a simple story. If we are fortunate enough to leave the ghetto alive, we will try to make aliyah, and my knowledge of English will prove useful.

The ghetto pharmacy should also be remembered favorably. It has had an important role, particularly after pharmacies in town stopped dispensing drugs to Jews. There is also a great value to the chemical laboratory, managed by a first-rate specialist, Zeigarnik,[144] where herbal mixtures are prepared that serve as substitutes for tea, dental powder, various cosmetics, and so on.

K. GHETTO MANAGEMENT AND GOVERNMENT

"How fair are your tents, O Jacob, your dwellings, O Israel."[145] The ghetto streets that stretch over hills and slopes are unpaved and have no sidewalks. When the snow melts or after a pouring rain, they fill with mud and muck. In summer they are filled with dust. The houses are small and low, without form or beauty;[146] the homes are crowded and cold in winter and unbearably hot in summer because the cookstoves are in the living space. They are also filthy, filled with fleas, cockroaches, and mice. The inhabitants are depressed and tormented; they lack sufficient food; the restrictions are hard and ever-growing, and bereavement saturates us all with sorrow and grief.

Yet despite these substandard and excruciating conditions, the people of the ghetto deserve praise for establishing an honest, effective system of administration and policing. The ghetto is managed as follows: at the top is the "representation," the council of community elders,[147] which intercedes between the ghetto and the authorities—that is, between the Jews and Stankus, the "king of the Jews," the administrator for Jewish affairs, the sewer pipe that discharges on our heads all the decrees of the Germans and their Lithuanian lapdogs. Below them is the "administration," the various officials who execute the council's orders through a battalion of young women, who work in the office keeping and managing the books, and through the Jewish policemen, the "security service" who also act as the ghetto's investigators.

The council consists of Messrs. Leibovich, Kartun, Rubinstein, Rabbi Hiller, Attorney Abramovich, and the chief secretary, Katz (who had been the director of the Popular Bank).[148] "In a place without men, they strove to be men."[149] Some seasoned former activists avoided community work (for various reasons, mainly fear of the Germans and insufficient German language skill). But those mentioned did not shrink: they picked up the load and continued to work on behalf of an anxious and traumatized people. Their task is endless, difficult, and fraught with consequences. More than once have they stood in the breach[150] and vigorously protested [German] edicts. That is how they managed to prevent the deportation of Šiauliai Jews to Žagarė, where they would have met the same fate as those Jews from other cities who were sent there and disappeared. The council's job is multifaceted, requiring them to deal with the many needs of the ghetto. They organized two food stores, an ambulatory clinic, a pharmacy and a hospital, a sanitary department to oversee ghetto hygiene, a heating department to provide firewood, a department to support the needy, and a department to negotiate with the labor police for those who work both in the ghetto and the city, regarding exit and entry permits, wages, etc.

The council has the power and dominion[151] to levy taxes on ghetto residents, punish those who disturb the peace, and rule in civil disputes: a court was set up for this purpose. Among those brought to trial there was the physician who in a moment of anger, said that if the council tried to move him out of his apartment, half the ghetto would be removed. This was an inflammatory statement, as many in the ghetto already believed several families had been sent to their deaths because of the doctors. (He was the head of the ambulatory clinic and was suspended from his office for three months.) There were a number of other trials, but there is not space enough here to discuss them, although they are interesting as snapshots of ghetto life. Perhaps I will return to them in coming days.

One task, as difficult as parting the Red Sea, was apportioning the "contribution" tax among the residents. I will say that the council nonetheless managed this satisfactorily. The administration also resolved, as well as could be done, the very difficult and complex ghetto housing problem. It managed to find room for those who had escaped various hells and apparently considered our ghetto a heaven. But it is also appropriate to mention the many mistakes the council made, often serious ones. They bear responsibility for a number of grave injustices: some people were unfairly overtaxed and others undertaxed. Apartments were sometimes distributed peculiarly; they did not properly care for some people who deserved better. They claim not to have favored relatives or other insiders who received larger and more comfortable apartments and paid much less than they could afford. But when the job is so complex and exhausting, especially in such difficult conditions, it is impossible to avoid mistakes. We should not complain because they are drowning in a sea of troubles, and they work hard for little reward. We must forgive their errors and thank them for their extensive and often dangerous efforts.

However, it is difficult to accept the bureaucratic rudeness and inflexibility that prevail in the different administration offices, where the rule is to show no deference to anyone. No distinctions are made between the old or learned and the ignorant or simple-minded. It is the Bolshevism of small-time revolutionaries who think that elevating the downtrodden necessarily means reducing the value of everyone else to zero. But the one does not always imply the other.

The council must also be credited with another valuable initiative: establishing workshops in the ghetto, which provide jobs and income to many who would otherwise be unemployed. Foremost among these are the lab for chemical materials, the fabric repair shop, the laundry, a paper bag and box workshop, a shoe repair shop, etc. They should be recognized for these enterprises, without which many would be labeled idle and worthless by our oppressors.

As an appendix to this chapter, let me mention some of the other cases tried in the ghetto court besides that of the doctor who misspoke in anger. (His case was heard behind closed doors):

(a.) There was a young man whose father became ill at 2:00 a.m. The doctor he summoned had returned home late (it is rumored that he was playing cards until 1:00 a.m.) and did not want to get out of bed so soon after lying down. The young man said that if he did not get up quickly, he would break the doctor's windows. And that is what he did! The doctor filed a claim against the young man, which they eventually settled themselves. However, the head of the Jewish police filed one complaint against the doctor for refusing to help a dangerously ill person and another against the young man for disturbing the peace. The doctor was reprimanded, and the young man was ordered to pay thirty marks: fifteen for the damage and fifteen as a fine to the council.

(b.) There was a young woman, a skilled speculator who came from Galicia[152] with her husband and child. She made her income selling the goods of ghetto residents in the town and taking a percentage as commission or whatever she could get above the agreed-on price. One day she obtained several items to sell, but decided to keep them for herself and claimed she had never received them. The court investigated on behalf of those who had been harmed, and the woman was forced to return the items, fined and jailed.

It should be noted that there is a jail in the ghetto that is used often. Strife and contention[153] that end in violence find resolution there. Also, minor theft and resisting administration or police orders land people in jail. Even Germans who catch Jews stealing food prefer that they go to the ghetto jail rather than the general prison.

Among the more prominent cases were two involving doctors. Following the edict prohibiting pregnancy and birth, a woman went to see Dr. G., who performs abortions and specializes in "premature deliveries." But this man's carelessness has led to several disasters, including a doctor's wife who suffered sepsis during a hard labor, and a young and beautiful woman who lost her life because of him. Such cases are often forgotten; explanations and excuses are found, and patients return to the same doctor. In this case it is unclear whether the doctor was eager for a fee, or if the woman pleaded with him: the fact is that he agreed to terminate her pregnancy using a method common among peasant women called "the midwife of angels." In a crowded room he inserted a "zonda."[154] She aborted but then developed a uterine infection and lay for months in hospital. When she left and was asked to pay for the treatment, she filed a claim against Dr. G. The court could not decide whether her illness was due to his negligence, since she had remained free of symptoms for several days after the abortion. He received a reprimand but was not fined.

That was not the end. The director of the gynecology department where the woman was hospitalized is a longtime enemy of Dr. G., and Dr. G. thought this rival had persuaded the woman to file her claim. Seeking to get even, [Dr. G.] looked for an opportunity to file a claim of his own, to trigger a court investigation [of the gynecologist]. His chance arrived when the gynecologist, who is also a surgeon, operated on a young woman above her left eye, and the operation failed. For an unknown reason, a fistula remained discharging pus. The young woman is foolish and ignorant, but her older sister is intelligent, and she works in Dr. G.'s household, helping his wife manage their home. At Dr. G.'s apparent urging, the patient filed a claim against the surgeon, Dr. L. It ended when the city surgeons' council determined that the operation was done properly, and so the court rendered no judgment. But these trials do not reflect well on the doctors, who already do not enjoy much respect in the ghetto.

L. EDICTS CONTINUE IN THE GHETTO

The angels of destruction[155] gather and confer, saying "let us deal shrewdly with them."[156] Our mortal enemies continually try to embitter our lives with edicts of all types: first, to end the Jews' scheme of buying or trading for food from acquaintances or speculators, prohibit them from walking alone in the city and from visiting Christian homes and stores. They scrutinize to a hairsbreadth those trying to bring food into the ghetto, and throw them in prison. And so the following edicts were issued for ghetto dwellers:

(i.) Those working in the city must leave the ghetto by 8:00 a.m. and be back by 4:00 p.m. They shall not be seen or found on city streets without special permits. It is bad enough to have to see Jews going to and from work: we will tolerate no more than that.

(ii.) Workers must leave the ghetto and walk to their workplaces in groups and in military order, in platoons led by a Christian who will see that none split away and, God forbid, enter a private home. Groups of up to five must march like geese in single file; of up to fifteen in pairs in a column; of more than fifteen people three abreast, in one column. The Germans are fond of military order; this is also a way to humiliate people, reducing them to the level of prisoners.

(iii.) A circular that was distributed later made the main purpose of these directives plain: "Purchasing anything in the city is forbidden." Along with the decrees about marching in platoons, with a leader, and the prohibition on walking alone in the city, this edict confirmed the intention to starve us, by eliminating any chance that the provisions of the superior Aryans might fall into the hands of filthy Jews.

(iv.) All working Jews belong to a single category, irrespective of education, expertise, and experience. A Jewish doctor, laboratory expert, radiologist, engineer, etc., is in the same category as a lumberjack, ditch digger, or other day laborer. All receive the same wage! One and a half marks per day for a man, one mark thirty pfennigs per day for a woman.[157] And wages are paid only for days worked; Sundays and holidays do not count. The simplest Christian laborer or housemaid receives double or triple that amount and is paid by the month, not the day. No long explanation of this order is needed: it aims to diminish us, reduce us to dirt, and slowly starve us, since prices rise daily, leaving us to subsist on dry bread and hot water (assuming food and firewood can be found).

(v.) Workshop owners and managers of the different offices that employ Jews are not permitted to pay them their wages directly, hand to hand as used to be common. The employers must turn over their pay to the German labor police—this is an interesting fact—at the full rate for Christian laborers of the relevant category. But the labor police pay Jewish laborers their one-and-a-half marks, or one mark and thirty pfennigs, and keep the rest for themselves. They make significant profit at the Jews' expense because the Germans' only objective is to impoverish and demoralize us and return us to dust.[158]

The order imperils Jews who work in town. Until now, Christian shop owners could benefit from cheap Jewish labor; now they must pay the police the same wage for a Jew that they would pay a Christian worker. Why then hire Jewish workers at all? Not only that: many Christian managers registered their Jewish acquaintances as workers fictitiously so they could escape forced labor at the aerodrome and retain the ability to go into town—but now all the fictitious workers and those not truly needed will be dismissed. Only essential workers, the specialists in various fields, will be kept. Presumably, of the Jews working in the medical institutes, only the dental technicians, radiologists, the one neurologist, and the essential lab technicians will remain—about twelve people. And Drs. G. and L. will lose their jobs as lab technicians.

Speaking of Dr. G., I remember the ordeals he experienced building his house, a splendid, gated structure on the main street, that now houses the city maternity hospital. His rival and competitor, Dr. L., had beaten him to an apartment in a nice building that Dr. G. had intended to buy and turn into a private maternity hospital. While Dr. G. was bargaining for the place, Dr. L. had come in like a rich Jewish bigshot, topped his price and turned the house into his own maternity hospital. Their competition for the property spawned arguments, fights, threats at gunpoint, arbitration, and lawsuits until finally Dr. G. spent a fortune to buy a plot in town for himself, where he built a marvelous home, even more splendid than the house that Dr. L. had "snatched" from him.[159]

Thus Šiauliai came to have two maternity hospitals, and things quieted down—though not for long! Soon afterward, the Bolsheviks arrived and nationalized both hospitals. They turned Dr. L.'s house into a children's hospital, while Dr. G.'s house became a maternity branch of the municipal hospital. Dr. G. was given a license to work as an assistant in the hospital that he established, and he became reconciled to his fate.

The truly horrible changes began when the Germans arrived, bringing the Nuremberg Laws, which prohibited Jewish doctors from treating Christian patients, and creating the ghetto. Dr. G. was driven out of his own possession.[160] That is when Dr. Jasaitis came to the aid of a few of his physician colleagues and, for his own reasons, lobbied to get them jobs as lab technicians in different medical institutes. His efforts bore fruit, and the district commissioner granted permits for six Jewish doctors, among them the honorable Dr. G., who surely reminded Dr. Jasaitis of his moral right to the building he had built literally with his own sweat and blood. But if the municipality has to pay the labor police his full price, then the parsimonious, antisemitic mayor, Linkevičius, will weigh in, and Dr. G., whose work is not particularly essential, will be fired again. And so the terrible prophecy comes true for Dr. G.: "If you build a house, you shall not live in it," but with an even more terrible addition: "Bow low to him for the sake of a silver coin and a loaf of bread."[161] Because the effort to obtain one of these lowly positions for such a meager wage is like bowing for money and bread. "A sorrow shared is a sorrow halved"[162]—the curse applies to all Jews who have built their homes on foreign soil. But this is cold comfort.

(vi.) The "contribution" edict sucked out our remaining strength and essence. After most of our assets were seized, first by the Bolsheviks and then by the Germans with the help of the local thieves, leaving us empty-handed, this struck like a lightning bolt. Who could imagine that a half million ruble tax could be levied on the impoverished, downtrodden ghetto? Quite a few tears were shed by those forced to raise this money by selling assets, which is very difficult these days, or by other schemes to pay their allocated portion. In addition to the tax, which despite the council's effort they would not reduce, they also demanded our remaining silver and gold items, those that miraculously survived those committees of official thieves who "inspected" our assets when we were transferred to the ghetto. Even now many ghetto residents remain in debt, enslaved to those who loaned them money to pay the contribution. I too experienced this: I was forced to borrow my allotted share of two thousand rubles since for quite some time we have lived on what we can get by selling our possessions. This is the lot of most ghetto residents, other than the speculators, whose numbers are diminishing due to the edicts and restrictions.

(vii.) All the thieving and robbery—blatant and subtle, official and unofficial, through inspections, confiscations, and now the contribution—has still not satiated the leeches who gulp our blood in mouthfuls. Suddenly after all these horrors a questionnaire arrived, asking for details about our clothes, furniture, money, jewelry, dishes, etc. A new rule was published requiring that "excess" household goods be declared and registered. If there is more than one chair per person, more than six shirts, more than two suits, etc., they may only be kept if they are old. All new items must be registered, with no exceptions or appeals. Also, good beds and mattresses, leather suitcases in good condition, furs and "Karakul" hats,[163] all kinds of jewelry and more must be registered so that they can be handed over to the leeches. This order terrified us because it showed how we had been left naked and empty-handed. We feared they would search our homes to verify our responses, with unpleasant consequences if they found "excess" or prohibited items. In truth, this decree remained on paper only and was never implemented. It appears they recognized that, after robbing us 101 times, skinning us bit by bit, leaving us with no source of income, paying us wages too meager to live on—after all that, it wasn't worth the masters' effort. Even if we are crooks and liars, we are not magicians and cannot create something from nothing. This latest attempt to steal from us that which was devoured long ago was probably the invention of the "donkey nation"[164] because the real villains are too smart to waste money printing senseless orders that could be foreseen to fail. Those evil people give us trouble enough in more efficient and effective ways.

(viii.) The municipal hospital's ban on [Jewish] patients with communicable diseases is one of the cruelest and most scandalous edicts of all. It was issued as the typhus epidemic began spreading in Lithuania and reaching Šiauliai. Our rulers clearly knew there was no hospital in the ghetto and no space to quarantine[165] patients with communicable diseases. The epidemic frightened everyone in the ghetto, where lice, known to spread the disease, multiply in the crowded and filthy housing. Indeed, it might be no exaggeration to say that this order was issued intentionally to spread the epidemic and thus provide an excuse to eliminate the ghetto and all remaining Šiauliai Jews in one blow. The Germans and Lithuanians would rid themselves of a major headache, and no one could object to ending an epidemic. But what need is there of an excuse to exterminate a few thousand Jews? All it takes is a small hint, and the execution could be carried out in short order, as the savages with whom we lived for hundreds of years have already shown more than once.

However, "blessed be changing times."[166] There are signs that some sectors of Lithuanian society have begun to look for reasons and excuses for their condemnable actions. In Kaunas, an office has opened to collect information about the wrongs supposedly done by the Jews to the Lithuanians! Abroad, the Lithuanian intelligentsia (to whom we will present a special IOU when the time comes to collect on debts) defend themselves by saying their hands did not spill Jewish blood and hang the blame on the [German] conquerors. It is rumored that that Lithuanian representatives gave the German government a memo and that among various requests and complaints they expressed their annoyance for having been turned into murderers. Also, that [Lithuanian] priests apologized to the Pope. In short, many Lithuanians feel they overreacted against the Jews and worry that a day of reckoning will come, in particular since things in the front are not going well. Moreover the conquerors show the Lithuanians no signs of affection or gratitude for carrying out their wishes so diligently. Thus they seek an excuse to eliminate those of us who remain. The need to destroy the source of an epidemic is an excellent excuse and would raise no complaints.

So how wonderful it is that our [Jewish] council members took serious action to halt the epidemic's spread in the ghetto, by shaving the heads of children infected with lice, airing out bedding, and especially by setting up the ghetto hospital. Thanks to these actions, only a few cases of typhus were seen in the ghetto and no deaths. That the epidemic did not overwhelm us despite the wretched ghetto conditions and lack of hygiene is a real miracle, and at least a minor consolation that must be recorded and remembered. The villains' wish to see the plague overwhelm the ghetto was dashed. Indeed, the inferior race had the last laugh as the superior Aryans died like flies while we had no fatalities at all.

The municipal hospital's prohibition against Jewish communicable-disease patients was soon expanded to a general ban on all Jewish patients, even for childbirth and surgery. Simultaneously, pharmacies were barred from selling drugs or anything else to Jews. And how good is a timely word![167] Our representatives performed marvels, establishing the ghetto's hospital and pharmacy at just the right moment. In this at least we were not defeated, and our enemies erred by taking with one hand and giving with the other, closing the hospital's doors to us while permitting us to open our own hospital. All their evil scheming brought them nothing, and they did not dare to leave us with no hospital at all. Of this charity of theirs, infused with ill will and attached to a villainous edict, it may be said: "Sin is a reproach to any people."[168]

The oppressors' surgeon, T.K., seems to be among those educated Lithuanians who realized that they overreacted "a bit" and are now turning in repentance. In his dealings with Jews he has lately become more humane, and he agreed to operate at the ghetto hospital for a generous fee. Now free from competition with the Jewish doctors, the Lithuanian physicians have seized the opportunity to fill their pockets with gold, although some prefer their peasant patients pay them with butter, eggs, poultry, etc. They also ask their urban patients for "items of equivalent value."

(ix.) Recently a new, terrifying edict has ordered a population transfer from the Trakų ghetto area to the Kaukazas area and vice versa. For ghetto residents hoping to settle down at least for a while, this came as a shock. The assembly of angels of destruction plotting ceaselessly against us decided to transfer all the manual laborers to the Kaukazas ghetto along with the weak, elderly, frail, and handicapped who were spared miraculously from the synagogues, and to move specialists, artisans, and professionals from the Kaukazas area to Trakų. Those professionals who have to stay in the Kaukazas ghetto for lack of space in Trakų will have a street allocated to them in Kaukazas.

This entire matter is strange and begs for explanation. The transfers could be an attempt to concentrate the two classes of workers so that they can be found quickly if needed, without an extensive search as now. But why transfer the elderly and the weak to Kaukazas? And what is the relationship between them and the laborers? A frightful suspicion grows in the heart. Is this not like the infamous deportations to the synagogues, with their awful consequences? Is this not a corridor to the netherworld? Some say the real transfers will start after January 6, when their holidays are over.[169] Then they will bring about the end.

An update: this fear did not materialize. As of spring [1942], the exchange has not had dire results. The only consequence was anxiety and displacement.

(x.) The ban on Jewish farmworkers affects relatively few, but it is no less cruel than the extermination of entire Jewish communities during the months of Tammuz and Av.[170] We were deluding ourselves with the belief that nothing bad would happen because Göring ordered them to stop murdering us. Although no one saw such an order, even clerks in the district commissioner's office swore it existed. But "the mouth that prohibited is the mouth that permitted,"[171] and it is possible that the order was made and then rescinded.

In any case, while we were under the illusion that we were safe, disaster struck. Seventy lives, mostly women and toddlers, were cruelly cut short, just as had happened with most of the urban Jewish population in Lithuania. About seventy people, mostly young men and women, and women with children, had contracts to work on farms near Šiauliai. Living in rural villages provided many advantages: first, food could be obtained directly from producers. Second, village life is quieter and calmer, removed from the ghetto's orders, fears, and dangers, particularly for those who managed to find shelter with a "friendly" farmer. That is how the young woman, Mrs. Zeigarnik, with her son and daughter, ended up in the house of a young woman farmer in return for some past favor. Mrs. Zeigarnik, the wife of the chemist who was known as an excellent professional and scholar, was truly a woman of valor. She was the one who established a chemicals and pharmaceuticals warehouse that grew, under her management, into a gold mine, earning her and her family a fortune. After marrying the chemist Zeigarnik, her business flourished even more. He established a chemistry lab and bought half of the city's largest pharmacies. They grew wealthy and built themselves two gated homes in the city center, which generated more income in rent. If not for the arrival of the Bolsheviks, they would have become immensely rich in time, all thanks to Mrs. Zeigarnik's initiative and acumen.

This woman had an instinctive fear of the ghetto: under no circumstance did she want to move there. She settled in a village with some farmers and insisted that her daughter, who was living with her father in the ghetto, be sent to her. She also arranged places in the village for her sister's daughter, a young woman, and her two brothers. In similar fashion seventy people settled in various villages, blending in, pretending to be Christians like Marranos.[172] These people lived quietly working for the villagers for several months. Then suddenly an evil spirit[173] came upon the district commissioner, and he had all the tenants of these villagers arrested! Why? Had someone whispered to him that these temporary workers were fake? Did they deserve punishment for that? Was their guilt sufficient to warrant taking their lives? For a while they were kept as prisoners in various barns and stables. Eventually an emissary was sent [from Šiauliai] to Stačiūnai,[174] where they had arrested Mrs. Zeigarnik, to learn of the prisoners' fate. The man returned with sad news: "The prisoners are no longer in the village." They had vanished, just like those deported from the ghetto. Then came horrifying news: an order had been sent to kill them all, and it had been carried out to the letter. Our friend Zeigarnik, who worked in a German pharmacy, tried his best to save his family, but all his efforts came to naught. It is being said that the district commissioner ordered the Zeigarnik family be kept alive, but the local police chief was in a hurry to murder the Jews and apologized later, saying the commissioner's order had come too late. Since the error was not his fault, he believed he would face no punishment. Thus this family died.

For a man bereaved and widowed, our friend Zeigarnik shows extraordinary resilience and strength. He now fills in as prosecutor in the ghetto court and is totally dedicated to this job. He also manages the ghetto chemistry lab that he set up. His face looks worn, and he is very thin. He walks like a shadow, bent forward, sad and depressed. But he does not complain to others about his immense loss: his lovely family, and his huge fortune, all gone!

(xi.)   The childbirth decree. Pharaoh only ordered the male children killed, but our modern-day Haman intends to annihilate all. One day our representatives were summoned by the security police and instructed to make an announcement in the ghetto.[175] There are no words to describe our feelings upon hearing this decree: helpless rage, disgust, desire for revenge, aggrievement toward heaven. This was the announcement:

- Childbirth in the ghetto is undesirable.
- Artificial termination of Jewish women's pregnancies is permissible, and required(!).
- Jewish women giving birth will be severely punished.

Was anything like this ever heard of in our long and bitter history? Never! Unprecedented villainy! It wasn't enough for them to smash our babies against trees in Telšiai; now they want to destroy embryos in their mothers' wombs, so that Israel will become extinct in Lithuania, giving them no further trouble. It appears they are worried about America, where news of their cruelty toward the Jews has caused outrage and created a storm in the press. But they can continue humiliating us covertly, treat us like mud and speed our demise. They will continue to murder us, one by one or in small groups, but to completely exterminate the Jews they need to violate universal norms forbidding forced abortions, which carry risks for the mother at all stages of pregnancy and jeopardize the chance of future births.

How could these people so harden their hearts that they became like wolves and slaughtered more than 200,000 innocent people? And still not satisfied, they want to immiserate and exterminate us? No shame, no regret, not a shred of humanity toward Jews because Jews are not humans! The supreme source of evil could manipulate Germany, the land where modern antisemitism was born. There was a reason this murderer was elected: the shepherd resembles his flock. Had the Germans not been ready and willing, he would not have found means to bring upon us this endless disgrace and sorrow. We are the scum of humanity—fleas, lice, and worse. We are not human. The date of this decree reducing us to beasts must be remembered from one generation to the next: it was February 5, 1942. They have not yet ordered men castrated.[176] When they do, the decree will be complete. We are halfway there.

(xii.) Miscellaneous decrees and additions to earlier edicts that sting like needles:

1. Drivers may not sit atop their horse carts when carrying cargo.[177] Decreed by Strenge,[178] the head of the labor police. It appears that this "father of mercy"[179] felt pity for the poor horses that have to haul the loads of Jewish corpses. Not fair.

2. Stars of David must be stitched to clothing at all six corners. They used to be satisfied with fastening the stars with pins, but there were problems. Some Jews would remove these badges of shame when entering Christian homes to buy food, which offended the esteemed masters. Now those conniving Jews can no longer do that, and so have to find another way to alleviate their hunger.

3. The edict regarding Jewish patients was extended and completed: Christian doctors are forbidden to treat Jews, period. So from now on, those who are seriously ill or urgently need an operation have no recourse. The Christian surgeon has come into the ghetto to operate several times. Now, should there be a case of appendicitis, clogged intestines, lung cancer requiring surgery, the outcome will be a painful death because we do not have a Jewish surgeon. Similarly, we lack a Jewish expert in eye diseases. The de-

THE RULES OF THE GHETTO

cree also covers the ambulatory clinic, dispensaries, hospitals, and pharmacies.

4. Several workshops in town, where Jews made up the majority of workers, were closed. This of course left them unemployed. It was also decreed that in those workshops remaining open, at least half the employees must be Christians. After they learn their jobs from the Jews, it will be possible to get rid of those Jews altogether.

5. The strict prohibition on leaving the ghetto and returning alone without a Christian "escort" is intended to prevent Jews from entering forbidden places, such as stores and private Christian homes. As always, food is the main issue. Now Jews wait every morning for Christian escorts to take them to offices and shops, and wait every evening for the same to walk them back home.

6. All city streets and public institutions must display a "beautiful" poster, featuring an ugly face looking out from a Star of David, winking deceptively with a long, wild beard. A disgusting, revolting face. Beneath this image is a list of questions, such as: "Who destroyed the land of Lithuania?" "Who violated the daughters of Lithuania?" "Who destroyed the factories in Lithuania?" "Who lives in the nicest apartments and put you in a hole in the wall?" "Who ate the choicest food and starved you?" "Who is to blame for the war?" and many more tasteless and baseless questions. And to all of them a single answer: "The Jew!" This poster has not been all that successful, and its exaggerations have drawn laughter from Christians.

7. Horses, carriages, and harnesses were all ordered confiscated in the ghetto. There were ten horses in the ghetto, and their owners made a decent living offering transportation. At the start of this year they seized the horses and carts from their owners, eliminating the livelihood of this entire group.

(xiii.) Shrinking the ghetto. Even though ghetto residents are well experienced with calamity, this decree caused desperate confusion, comparable to that which overcame us when they began taking Jews away to be massacred. Our enemies, whose daily edicts aim to make our lives unbearable, decided to reduce the area of the Trakų ghetto by moving the gate and fence three buildings further in. That meant taking three houses from each of the three ghetto streets and reassigning them to their previous owners or to other Christians. Their excuse—the housing shortage, which was also used to justify shrinking the Kaunas ghetto—is invalid, as many Lithuanians are being drafted, leaving more room in and around the city. Their conscription caused protests. They say that in Kaunas, students broke into a theater and rioted, causing bloodshed and casualties. The Germans, who badly need the Lithuanians' help, thought to appease them by allowing a few Lithuanians to return to their homes, needlessly squeezing the Jews at the same time. As a result, four hundred people were left homeless, and finding them shelter in this overcrowded ghetto will be nearly impossible. The fear continues, and at the time of this writing (May 16, [1942]) those who had to leave the houses cut off from the ghetto are still looking for places to live. Some who have found spaces are moving there, but in most cases they have had to scatter their belongings in different places because their new apartments have barely enough room just for them.

It is worth mentioning how this decree was announced. Early one morning, a German military official appeared at the gate and ordered the Jewish policeman on guard to summon the community elders immediately. When the head of the council, L.,[180] heard the order, he tried to explain that the terrible overcrowding made it impossible to further shrink the ghetto. The German pointed toward the lake in the distance and said, "There is plenty of room for you there!" He added: "You wanted a war, so here you are!" A short while later, thirty armed Lithuanian partisans showed up, terrifying the Jews beyond words. People were sure they came to take residents from the ghetto to the "synagogues"—that is to be killed as in the first days of the ghetto. Women and children began to wail, and some climbed through holes in the fence to escape the murderers. Also, some workers returning to the ghetto were told by Christians that something dangerous was happening there. The workers turned back in fear and remained in the city for several hours, until it became clear that for now there were no deportations, only a reduction in the ghetto's size.

(xiv.) Forced labor in the peat mines. The fears sparked when the ghetto was shrunk have not yet faded. The sighs of those who were displaced continue to be heard as they search for new rooms. And now we have a new trouble, which is far worse because it affects most of the ghetto and particularly our sons. The band of evil angels continually seeking new ways to afflict us has found a new way to "deal shrewdly with us"—a diabolical one, magnified eightfold, that hits multiple birds with one stone. This latest edict, conscripting Jews to labor in the peat mines, will destroy families that depend on their sons' income to live, and debase and humiliate professionals by forcing them to perform dirty jobs. It will separate parents from their children and husbands from wives, since the work site is far away from Šiauliai, in the region of Radviliškis. It will force Jews, particularly the educated ones, to do unfamiliar work in difficult conditions, resembling a concentration camp: living in tents and, in these days of food restrictions, subsisting on a questionable diet. The treatment is likely to be harsh and antisemitic as is typical for Jewish workers under the Lithuanian or German rod. The work will be hard, exhausting, and wet, exposing bodies to colds and rheumatism and certainly having a negative effect on those already suffering or inclined to such illness.

The conscription list for the mines was strange and astonished everyone: they called up fathers of large families, specialists in various professions, doctors, pharmacists, chemists, workers in public bureaus, even German ones. They included old people, who were afraid to disclose their true age for fear of being deported from the ghetto. (One man who is seventy-three years old claimed he was fifty-nine. Now he has been drafted.) They are even drafting people who are sick and incapable of hard physical work. It is worth mentioning that they are not even excluding the doctors who, thanks to Dr. Jasaitis's efforts, work as lab technicians. One of them has already been drafted. In vain did they believe that a permit from the district commissioner would protect them from forced labor unrelated to their profession. Our "masters'" plan to conscript eight hundred men and four hundred women; that is, nearly everyone capable of this hard work between the ages of fourteen and sixty for males and sixteen to fifty for females. Only the old men and women, toddlers, the handicapped, sick, and maimed will remain in the ghetto. This raises worries and numerous suspicions. What will happen to those incapable of the work? In these days of acute food shortages, even for those working hard, our tormentors might easily decide to no longer feed those who do not produce. We all worry that after separating out those fit for slave labor, they will find some simple way of eliminating the "excess baggage." Whether or not that happens, this edict, demanding hard labor on an insufficient diet under the oppressor's rod, is on its face a terrible disaster for those who remain behind, with potentially terrible consequences.

Tomorrow two hundred people will leave on foot for Radviliškis to work in the peat mines. And on Wednesday a second list will be published. I am certain I will not be among their number because I am over sixty years old, but my son will certainly be called. I worry that even my wife, who is seriously ill, could be called, and then I will have to plead for her. If they are willing to take the word of a Jewish doctor, I should be able to succeed without much effort.

The fear that this conscription might be a prelude to the elimination of one ghetto area is, I think, unfounded, because the workers will need to return to the ghetto at some point. Still, the terror this edict created is real and enormous: some think it signals the beginning of the end. It is rumored today (May 17 [1942]) that the conscription will total only 450 men and women combined from both ghetto areas, and not 1,000 as was declared yesterday. Let us see how things turn out.

(xv.)   The scrap-metal decree. A bulletin was issued calling on all residents to donate aluminum and copper scrap to the Germans. They need this so the German army, which fights to free all humanity including Lithuanians from the yoke of Bolshevism, can manufacture sufficient arms to continue its battle. When the Germans collected warm winter clothing,[181] they did not turn to the Jews. At that time the Germans sought to show all of Europe and America how much they are loved, as demonstrated by generous donations of furs, woolen socks, etc. They took nothing from Jews so as not to spoil the impression of their citizens' commitment to the German army. But with metal it is a different story. Here necessity sets the rules: when their general scrap drive fell short they turned to the "scapegoats" to make up the difference. One morning police and partisans entered the ghetto and seized not only scrap but serviceable metal items: samovars, Primus stoves,[182] pots, anything they could find or that could not be hidden in time. Apparently this collection did not turn out well either, satisfying neither the Lithuanians nor the Germans. So a second act of the tragicomedy began with forced "donations." One morning an entire company of police and detectives showed up to thoroughly search the ghetto's dwellings. The Jewish police took it on themselves to deliver all metal pieces still in Jewish homes. They walked the streets, announcing that Jews should turn in all their copper and aluminum items for the army. Those who tried to hide anything could pay with their lives.

The panic was terrible. Everyone rushed to bring out objects of all kinds. In no time a mountain of metal goods was piled in front of the council's office. As it kept growing, the detectives realized that this time the Jewish "donors" had overreacted, and they allowed some items to be taken back. The fear provoked by the Jewish police was so intense that homes were stripped of all samovars, pots, and pans, and people thought they could keep only those of clay and iron. The officials themselves decided to relent. Meanwhile beggars from Tauragė and elsewhere, of whom there are many in the ghetto, took the opportunity to appropriate various household items and so ended up benefiting from others' misfortune.

This review of the latest bloody period is done. How much blood was spilled! How many tears have our eyes shed over the past year! How many have met untimely death, and how few Lithuanian Jews remain! Our strength fails[183] amid the suffering and torment that surrounds us. And who can foresee the end? Terrible desperation overwhelms us when we see no escape or shelter from the evil one who wishes to annihilate us without exception. Eleven months have passed since the start of the war. And the state of emergency continues in full force! There have been no decisive victories on either side, so our troubles continue. How long until the end of these awful things?[184] Will our tortured and tired souls find respite? Will we live to see the war's end? For now, news from the front keeps us between hope and disappointment, without peace or solace. Our strength is ebbing; soon we will collapse under the burden of our troubles.

The overview of this most terrible period in our bitter history is complete. From now on, I will record events in the form of a diary. It is necessary to leave some pages blank for new edicts, which will continue to arrive for as long as we remain under the German boot and have not yet suffocated.

Will my account have a happy ending? Will I be so fortunate as to record an "epilogue" after we have been spared and are secure? When will the miraculous end come? So much darkness envelops us that we no longer can believe that one day the clouds will disperse, and the light of a charitable sun will melt the terrible ice in our souls.

I finished this on May 18, 1942 (I do not have a Hebrew calendar, and therefore, I cannot state the Hebrew date),[185] a day of distress and chastisement, sadness and sorrow, measureless tears and sighs. The first group of workers left today on foot toward Radviliškis and will be gone for two months. They were surrounded by police armed with rifles, led like prisoners of war. What will be their fate?

PART D

TEN

—ᴍᴍ—

FROM MY DIARY

18 May, 1942 (Evening)

Those who went to work in the peat mines near Radviliškis sent back greetings and a message via a member of the council who accompanied them. The first impression of their workplace and their supervisors is much better than we expected. Even their journey[1] worked out well: they were not beaten or harried; they had opportunities to rest and were fed well in the villages and also at their "desired destination." We can reasonably believe things will go well[2] at that location. The dread and fear[3] that gripped the whole community yesterday has diminished significantly. At least now we are certain they were actually taken to work and not, like those earlier, to be killed.

19 May

Today they published a new list of workers to be sent to Radviliškis. Young women and girls are included on this list. Of course it caused an uproar in the ghetto.

20 May

Another 50 people left today for Radviliškis, while 250 women who were also scheduled to go were excused for one week. Probably there were no rooms ready for them.

News from the front is not encouraging. Despite denials by England, the harbor at Kerch[4] was finally occupied by the Germans. And the city of Kharkiv, despite the intense attacks, is still in German hands.[5] Their strength has not yet diminished, and they remain very aggressive. Who knows when the end will come? Yet despite all the unsatisfying news, rumors are spreading in the ghetto that salvation and consolation[6] are near. More than once have we been misled by such stories. More than once have we deluded ourselves with false hopes, which up to now have brought us nothing but disappointment. Still, let us have faith that redemption, even if late, will certainly come one day. The question is, will we be fortunate enough to reach that glorious day? It is completely impossible to assume that the black triple alliance[7] will triumph. History cannot allow such injustice.

21 May

"Not a day passes that is not more cursed than the one before."[8] My neighbor the dentist in the polyclinic stopped by today and said that her father, who works in the Frenkel factory, told her the ghetto was surrounded by German police and military, who are searching all the houses. We thought they were looking for food and hidden metal items. Our dread was beyond imagining because one cannot find a house that does not hold something prohibited: a samovar, an electric iron, some food, etc. I was terrified for my sick wife, whose hair has turned white in the last few weeks as her heart condition worsened. If she were to be arrested she would certainly die. At the same time, the daughter of Verbolinsky from the denture laboratory also came, trembling, as she had heard the same news. We waited nervously,[9] desperate to hear some definitive word, having sent one of the laboratory's students to the ghetto for that purpose.

Suddenly my son arrived and told us that the ghetto is quiet and peaceful. It turned out they were looking for seventy escaped prisoners of war, and had no interest in anything else. They left when they realized there are no "refugees" in the ghetto. His words were like a balm, restoring our peace of mind. Yet what we had felt was merely a shadow, a fraction of what those in the ghetto had experienced, since hearsay is not the same as seeing.[10] Imagine the anxiety in the ghetto when people saw the police and the Germans searching. People hid many items in wells and hurriedly buried food.

I just learned that today is the eve of Shavuot. The day our Torah was received! There are no signs of celebration—no milk or butter, no eggs or meat.[11] We expect only the indignity of starvation.[12]

20 June

I have written nothing for a month. Since I have no desire to regrind flour,[13] what is there to write? Lamentations, dirges, and woes![14] There has been no news, and our troubles continue. The work in the peat mines is hard, and they treat the laborers like prisoners. Their food is substandard: two hundred grams[15] of bread per day; gruel with wheat or barley flour; beatings and blows; terrible crowding in the rooms; fleas and cockroaches, etc. The pay is as before, fifteen and thirteen rubles per day.[16] They are toying with us, mocking the poor.[17] This wage won't even pay for what is allotted by the ration cards. All ghetto residents can think about is trading their belongings for food. Smuggling food into the ghetto continues; many fall into the hands of the police and are beaten mercilessly and imprisoned. In prison they are tortured with starvation. I saw prisoners bloated with hunger. News from the front is very depressing. The English have proved themselves worthless as soldiers; they have no hope against the Germans. They had the upper hand at first when they fought the Italians and captured Abyssinia,[18] but when the Germans showed up they suffered one defeat after the other: Norway, Dunkirk, Crete, Greece, Africa. The Russians are incomparably better fighters: they have held out against the Germans for an entire year and are still not defeated, while the more celebrated and famous nations—the French, Belgians, Poles, etc.—were beaten within weeks.

The ghetto's economic situation continues to worsen. Its moral state has declined precipitously as well. Thefts and altercations occur daily; even doctors are involved in strife and contention. Among them are characters who bring reproach and disgrace[19] upon us all. Tomorrow marks one year since the war began. To our chagrin the Germans can point to some "brilliant" recent victories: capturing Kerch, capturing Tobruk,[20] capturing the enormous and imposing Sevastopol fortress. Such victories empower the Germans, bolstering their courage and their hopes. We meanwhile are immersed in despair, frightened and worried for Eretz Israel:[21] if God forbid it falls into the hands of the Germans, our last hope will be dashed. Who then will build our homeland? Surely not the Russian Jews, who are like a "withered arm"[22] on our nation's body. The Jews of Europe are vanishing. Only one source will remain, the Jews of America. Antisemitism is on the rise there as well, and ultimately, they too will need to find a haven so our hope will not be lost. If the Americans and the Allies win, they will need to find someplace to send their unneeded and troublesome Jews, so they do not remain a nation in exile, a foreign element, and a burden on their citizens.

8 July

The villains have turned us into cheaters, thieves, beggars, and food smugglers. O what has become of us! What will become of us! How long until the end of these awful things? Our energy is gone. We are terribly afraid of having to spend another winter in the ghetto. Cold and hunger, crowding and filth, physical and emotional torture, who can stand it? The Germans are advancing in the USSR.

They captured Voronezh[23] and are heading to the Caucasus after capturing the Crimean peninsula. Who can foretell the future? One little comfort: the [German] offensive in Egypt has been halted, for now. Maybe they will not reach the land of our ancestors. If they are beaten decisively there, their morale will suffer.

11 July

"Because you drowned others, you were drowned. And in the end, they who drowned you will also be drowned."[24] The simple view of life seen in the "Chad Gadya"[25] song is realized often in history and in individual daily lives. Society cannot tolerate injustice it seems, and sinners receive their just deserts. Who would have expected that Stankus, the overseer of Jewish affairs, the servant and instrument of German will, who had thousands of Jews arrested and liquidated—who could have imagined that he would be fired and imprisoned? True, after several months he was set free, thanks to his attorney, Stankevičius: the Germans acquitted him at trial on various charges that are not quite clear to me. So now he too has had that taste of prison he asked me about after my own four days in jail, which ended after he himself arranged my release. Although he caused us a great deal of trouble, once when he was "merry with wine"[26] he bragged that the Jews of Šiauliai would have to inscribe his name in their books "in gold letters." And after all, in places such as Panevėžys they liquidated all the Jews, with no survivors, while in Šiauliai they left about five thousand Jews alive.

A better example is the case of Požėla. This villain spilled Jewish blood like water. He had a hand in killing the Jews around Pakruojis and Žagarė, and filled his home with Jewish property—money, gold, and furniture. The Lithuanian governor[27] once bragged that he had an excellent advisor, the attorney Požėla, who had dedicated his whole life to fighting Bolsheviks and Jews. Suddenly, a disaster no one expected: in an NKVD archive, a document was found that the comrades had not gotten around to burning, showing that Požėla had been among the servants of the Bolshevik secret police! This murderer was arrested; his property was seized; he was beaten savagely in prison and finally executed by firing squad. The lawyer Kolokša, the murderer of the Šaukėnai Jews, was also arrested, but he disappeared, his fate unknown. It could be that he was sent to the front. So may all our haters and killers perish.[28]

19 July

The peat mine workers returned on Sunday. Their faces were tan, and their appearance not too bad. A few looked as if they might have gained weight. But their stories of how the police and the guards treated workers in Radviliškis are shocking: beatings with clubs and whips, flogging to the point of bleeding for minor infractions, such as walking to the village to look for bread. Guilty and innocent alike were beaten. The guards are the same partisans who took part in murdering Jews. One of them reportedly bragged that "beautiful Jewish girls were hugging my legs; one bullet to the head, and into the pit." They apparently believe the old myth that Jews are lazy, and treat them as prisoners sentenced to hard labor. Food rations are meager and insufficient, and there is no one to complain to. For us there is no law and no judge, and all who increase our torments are praised.[29]

Last night there was a scare: Airplanes of a foreign country (probably the USSR) passed over our city and graced the area with bombs. Details are not yet known.

For our torments in the ghetto last winter, we have been rewarded this summer with an abundance of food. The sewage and feces have been buried deep and green gardens have appeared next to each house, a joy to the eyes. The seedlings that were planted and those that grew wild both flourished this year, and ghetto residents have their own green onions, lettuce, radishes, and so on. Later there will also be cucumbers, turnips, cabbage, tomatoes, etc. The weather is not bad, although the climate changed during the month of Tammuz:[30] there were perhaps five or six warm days; the others were cloudy with cool breezes. Soon summer will end, and the terrible fall and winter will arrive! We are horrified at the thought of spending another winter in the ghetto. And it will be a hard winter with shortages of firewood and food. Cold and hunger will be our lot. The Germans are advancing on the eastern front, but to date there have been no decisive victories. Both the real and imaginary German victories hurt them in the long run: Partial, temporary and passing, such victories encourage the Germans to continue fighting, spilling the blood of their youth. Without this encouragement the military establishment might have ended the war last year by removing the supreme source of evil, the main obstacle to international peace. But for now they continue to trust him and hope to emerge victorious. In the end they will weaken themselves severely, and America will keep its promise to be ready in 1943 and will bring new strength, a fresh army and new weapons, and will put an end to the war and the barbarian tyrants.

22 July

The Russian army has held out against the Germans and their allies for thirteen months. Could its strength now be failing? Is it in retreat, unable to stop the German advance? Frightening rumors are arriving from the front. Our enemies are holding their heads high while "we are crushed by oppression, misery and sorrow."[31] A "second front" would bring relief, but there are not enough supplies because the German submarines have sunk innumerable British and American ships. Such a front might be established next year, but will we have the strength to reach that moment? My spirit is crushed[32] today over these events, and I cannot continue writing.

30 July

The Germans boast endlessly of their victories. I am reminded of how they vowed last year to finish off the Russian army. Although they are advancing and winning battles,[33] their victories are not decisive. If they cannot end Russian resistance in the next four or five weeks, fall will arrive and then winter, and there will be no resolution until spring. If we do not die, maybe we will be blessed to see salvation and consolation. For now it is bitter, bitter.

1 August

An article in today's Lithuanian newspaper says, "Bessarabia has been freed of Jews." The meaning is clear: the Jews of Bessarabia were liquidated! How many? Probably several hundred thousand. And in Poland, it is said that a million Jews were wiped out. In all more than two million Jews have been massacred in Europe! Will history not avenge our blood? Will evil win? Surely the endless war is weakening the Germans, and aerial attacks also spill their blood, but this is not the revenge we seek: only their decisive defeat will satisfy us. When that occurs, we will finally leave the European lands saturated with our blood, to settle in our own territory and "dwell apart,"[34] far from the murderers. May our dream become real in the land of our ancestors!

I have omitted two important items: the death of lawyer Abramovich and the Palanga affair. The lawyer Abramovich[35] was a unique character: despite being seventy-two years old, he was so full of youth it was as if he mocked old age, giving it no control over him. On the beach in Palanga two years ago, he demonstrated some gymnastics exercises that testified to his physical flexibility and muscular strength. His greatest pleasure was bathing in the sea every summer. He would frolic in the water like a young lad and really splash around. And then a time of distress[36] came, and he fell ill, with an enlarged prostate. If the times had been normal, and we were not shut up in the ghetto, he could have turned to specialist surgeons abroad, and since his overall health was good—particularly his heart, which was normal and healthy—it would have been possible to operate on him. But now that no one may leave or enter,[37] this irreplaceable man was lost. He was a person of rare persistence and talent: Torah, wisdom, and experience were combined in him. While occupied as a teacher, husband, and father, he studied for the exams and earned his baccalaureate, then enrolled in the university, completed law school, and became a lawyer. Even in old age he continued studying, reading every day. In recent years he prepared for aliyah, studying English and achieving significant mastery. He was dedicated to both religious and secular studies: besides a deep knowledge of the Talmud, he was also well read in European literature. Besides being a scholar, he was dedicated heart and soul to public service. Despite his many work obligations, his devotion to his family and his studies, he gave much of his time to community work, as head of the Lithuanian *Mizrachi*[38] association and chair of the Šiauliai kehilla and then of "Ezra" and "*Knesset Israel.*"

I worked with him for several years when I chaired the "Ezra" council; thus I felt obligated to give one of the eulogies when he was buried. Here is what I said:

> In the repository of our traditions, our ethics and our past ways of life—that is to say in the midrash—a story is told about a certain rabbi. It is related that when R[abbi] Ammi was about to die, his sister's son visited him and found him weeping. He said to him: "My master, why do you weep? Is there a single law that you have not learned and taught? Indeed even now thy disciples sit in your presence. Is there any kind deed you have not performed? But more important than all the virtues you possess is the fact that you have restrained yourself from acting as a judge and have refrained from overseeing the needs of the community." Whereupon he replied: "My son, that is why I weep. Perhaps I shall have to account for the fact that I refused to serve as a judge in Israel, although I was able to do so."[39]
>
> This story clearly shows how our forefathers' viewed the obligations of our nation's elite. That is, Torah and good deeds, not just for the individual, but also for the public.

Torah and public service are our two pillars: The Torah is our culture. It put its unique stamp on us and kept us from assimilating and wasting away among the gentiles. And public service led us to organize, establish, and strengthen the institutions that enabled us to survive in exile and aspire for revival in the land of our forefathers. After that I spoke about the deceased, his superior ideals of Torah and public service. I highlighted his dedication and his unbiased approach to working for the public and the nation. I stressed his irreplaceable loss in times so troubled that, God forbid, Israel might forget the Torah and that the loss of its best sons will be felt most acutely when we arise from the dust of the ghetto and live again.

I will put off the Palanga affair for another time. The story began during the Bolshevik time and ended during the German invasion. There is no serious news now, but I still feel it necessary to record several details.

15 August

A brief pause in the diary. I am tired of depressive thoughts, of moaning most pitifully[40] and of rehashing old news. There has been no improvement and no spark of hope for the future. Darkness envelops us; anguish and distress are our lot and the threat of death hovers over us with no respite. For now there is no news worth mentioning. The situation on the front is depressing. Russia's south, joy of all the Earth,[41] including the fertile Ukraine, the iron-rich Donetsk, the beautiful Crimea and Caucasus, all fell to the murderers, and the Russian army seems broken. A bit of good news flew around the ghetto, that a second front has been opened, but this is likely a rumor someone invented to make himself feel better. Who can predict the war's outcome? It will be bad for us if they win, bad for us if they lose. Yet we still hope for their defeat, even if it means our end.

Our treatment is worsening: those trying to smuggle in food are being arrested more often at the gate and also on the streets in town, as the prohibition against walking without an escort became stricter. In the Kaukazas area, doors and windows of houses facing out from the ghetto were boarded up, in addition to the barbed wire to prevent anyone smuggling in contraband. There are constant rumors about the persecution of Poles in Lithuania and of Lithuanians of Polish origin. Let it be so! Beaten and chased like dogs, the Poles managed to bite us no less than the Lithuanians. They too have annihilated hundreds of thousands of Jews recently, as their hatred of us, dormant during their own time of repression, returned in even more virulent form.

The Lithuanians we trusted with our belongings do not wish to return them. The scoundrel Mrs. R. took various things from us hoping to "inherit" them; after hearing from her German acquaintances that the Jews were to be exterminated she assumed we would be among them. She came to us in person, demanding we give her some of our belongings. To my surprise she brought along a heavy suitcase. She then left Šiauliai with her German lover and our goods were irretrievably lost. Recently I was told that she is back to Šiauliai for a few days and is considering moving to Vilnius. It is interesting to note that she could not stay in Baranovichi[42] because of threats to her life by Russian partisans. I thought that asking her about our belongings might not be worth it. I was also warned that it might be dangerous, because she is involved with the Germans and might inform if we demanded she return what we gave her.

The fate of the things we gave to D.S. is also notable. Showing no concern whatsoever, he notified me that the fox fur, the new portfolio, my camera and other items were lost! Supposedly, a dishonest tenant and their neighbor, a policeman, stole all of it, and so we lost property worth thousands of marks that could have kept us going for many months. But what can we say if even Dr. Pr., a truly honest man, lost our shoes, shirts, and my new suit, the only one left after the partisans robbed my four better suits? They entrusted some of our things to their relatives, and there was a theft, and our things were taken. I suspect his relatives are themselves thieves when it comes to Jewish goods. It is being said that many supposedly honest Lithuanians now refuse to return the "foreigners'" property. "Even the best of the gentiles should be killed!"[43]

Our attention is now focused on the news that yesterday, Zeigarnik was arrested and beaten to the point of bleeding.[44] He is one of the ghetto's treasures[45]: a true Torah scholar, an expert in chemistry, full of initiative and energy. His fortune betrayed him: his wife, a woman of valor, and his lovely children fell into the villains' hands when they murdered those [Jews] who remained in the villages. For the moment, the reason for his arrest is unclear. Presumably, it had to do with his "partner" in the pharmacy, the whore[46] K., who holds some of his huge fortune, and wanted to eliminate the entire family.

The news of his arrest hit us like a lightning bolt. Job's troubles pale in comparison. His entire fortune, his wonderful homes, his excellent laboratory, and pharmacy were lost, then his family was annihilated, and now the hands of the wicked have reached him as well. Terrible, terrible, who could bear it? Surely the council will do all it can to free him. Aside from acting as prosecutor in the ghetto court—a job at which he excels, thanks to his talent as a speaker and his knowledge of both Jewish and European literature—he manages a chemistry lab in the ghetto, which produces necessary and useful items and provides a living to many ghetto inhabitants.

Just now my ear caught a whisper[47] of the reason for Zeigarnik's arrest, along with the happy news that he hopefully will be released on Monday. It is rumored that many silver and gold items belonging to him and his friends were found in his lab at the bottom of a barrel filled with herbs, enough to last for several years, until the end of the war. A maid discovered the "treasure" unexpectedly and informed the security police. I am sure this sad matter will be cleared up in a few days. How happy we will be to have him back among us!

Yesterday I had to say the "Vouchsafe"[48] blessing. I purchased about eight liters of "black seeds"[49] from the laboratory, which I use as a remedy for my intestines. Recently my intestinal problems have worsened, making me ill, so I was very happy to find these seeds. But then I had a problem: how to bring such a large quantity of seeds into the ghetto, since it is forbidden to buy such medicines in the city, or even to receive them as a gift. Further, the "colleague" from the dentures lab who accompanies me on my walk home left work early, and it could be dangerous to run into a policeman who doesn't know me. A young officer stands by the gate at 3 p.m. who can be "appeased and conciliated"[50] with a gift in secret.[51] He also has had his teeth fixed by Dr. V., who walks with us. We started out early, so [as] to arrive at the ghetto at 3:00 p.m., dragging our feet slowly, and arrived just as the guards were changing. We hoped to find our preferred policeman there, so we were terrified to see the "tall one," a notoriously vicious guard, walking with another officer toward the booth at the ghetto's gate! We could no longer turn back because they had already seen us from afar, so we decided to count on a miracle and kept walking. We approached the gate just as the tall one entered the booth to greet his friend from the earlier shift. Our little convoy, loaded with provisions, passed through unchecked, and we sighed in relief. After the tall one took up his post, he started with his despicable deeds and arrested seven people for carrying small quantities of butter, flour, or eggs. Even after receiving a nice gift (500 marks!), he continued to torture the inmates. We would have certainly been among them, but we had timed our arrival well and we entered the ghetto safely.

26 August

The cucumber leaves have begun to show spots, and the sunflower stems are wilting and drying up. The days are appreciably shorter. Morning mist rises from the earth—fall is approaching—and still we see no salvation. It is the end of a summer in which, even at its peak, we saw few very hot days. Now however, the days are really warm and clear, like a real summer. Surrounded by gardens, we can sometimes feel like we are on vacation in the country—but fear and trembling return when we recall that we will still be here next winter. Crowding, filth, cold and hunger will be our fate. The Germans will take everything for their army, and we who get half of what the Lithuanians receive will truly starve. Even now we are often short of bread, and the inspections at the gate grow ever stricter. We suffered from the cold terribly last year; it will surely be worse this winter when they seize all the firewood for the troops. Last winter the potatoes under our bed froze and turned into rocks. So what can we expect this year? What new edicts will they impose on us?

The news from the front is shocking and infuriating. In the south, the German army has captured Ukraine, Crimea, and the northern Caucasus, and is advancing in giant steps while the Russians are unable to stop them. The English army's raid in France[52] was defeated decisively, adding to our disappointment.

Although they failed this time, at least they showed it is possible to land on the shore no matter what Goebbels[53] claims. Perhaps the next time they will bring more soldiers with the right weapons. For now the war news is very painful.

Zeigarnik was freed after ten days, thanks certainly to the efforts of the council. That too is for the good! Details are still unknown. His mood is not too bad. Despite all his troubles he is far from despair and retains his optimistic Jewish character. Too bad that my own optimism is waning, and in its place a bitter disappointment has settled in my soul.

Yesterday there was a major scare at the gate. After he finished his shift in the afternoon, the "tall policeman" reported that ghetto residents were smuggling in food. As a result, German police showed up at the gate and started searching men and women who had not been warned about the danger. The Germans arrested seven people, but in the end they proved more decent than the Lithuanians, and released all those arrested, including one man who had a rooster. They took the rooster but let the man go.

4 September

It would be fitting to write in detail about the latest events in the ghetto, our experiences and frame of mind, so they may be remembered to the last generation. However, because of the bowel ailment that has hit me quite hard recently and my weakness, I have put off writing until now, when I am setting them down after the fact and in brief. Future readers will surely have hearts sensitive enough to imagine, even without many words, our bitter lives and our emotional tribulations. They will marvel at the extent of our endurance at how much suffering this weak creature called a Jew could bear.

Indeed, this past week truly saw days of distress, chastisement, and disgrace[54] for us. Last Saturday the district commissioner[55] himself showed up in the ghetto (he has been our guest rather too often lately) with some cheerful news: once again the two ghetto areas are to be reduced in size, with dwelling spaces removed from all streets, including Žilvičių Street, in the center of the "cage."[56] The overcrowding is terrible. Many families were already squeezing into "upper chambers"[57] [attics] and will have to find other shelter come winter. There are four or five people in every small room, and it is hard to imagine how they all will find places. And the commissioner also took the trouble to notify our council of a new edict, issued only to make us like the dust under his feet.[58] He claimed that there is more food in the ghetto than in town and that ghetto inhabitants are enjoying a bounteous diet. The council members tried all they could to dispel this slander and to calm the "master" by whose orders so much of our brothers' blood had been spilled, and to whom the life of a Jew appears utterly worthless.

The great master was just leaving the ghetto when he met a "column," as we call it, of ghetto residents who work in town, returning home at noon, unlike other days when they return in late afternoon. Lately the guard at the gate between 9:00 a.m. and 3:00 p.m. has been a decent and forgiving policeman who will turn a blind eye to those bringing in food. The one who follows him, however, is harsh and strict, harassing those coming back from work at 4:00 p.m. Naturally the speculators and those planning to bring food into the ghetto wait eagerly for Saturday, when the workers return at noon and the easygoing good policeman tends the gate. Accordingly, after lecturing our council members about the ghetto's luxurious food supply, the district commissioner met a group loaded down with groceries: butter, eggs, lard, vegetables, bags of flour, some of which they dared to carry openly. Enraged, he stopped the column and ordered everything dumped onto the street not far from the ghetto. A large pile accumulated, which was carted from the scene of the crime to the police station. The district commissioner, who had been accompanied by high-ranking officers of the secret police, left fuming at the impertinent Jews for so brazenly attempting to feed themselves. The guards wrote down the names of all those in the offending column, and with the food confiscated, the matter appeared to have been settled.

The absence of individual punishments, however, raised suspicions among those of us who understand these matters, and this incident, along with the reduction of the ghetto's size, worried us greatly. On Monday the district commissioner summoned the council to his office, and they returned looking somber and anxious. They did not reveal what had been said, but we felt certain that a new wave of decrees and orders was imminent, that the wrath of the murdering commissar at those sinning individuals would go forth[59] upon the whole community. The representatives sat up all night with a few residents whom they invited in to consult about the mysterious situation while the rest of the ghetto trembled in fear. On Tuesday morning as we left for work, the council chairman, Leibovich, and the chief secretary, Katz, were leaving as well, their faces ashen.

But then at noon, some of the council members showed up at several workplaces in the city and began to congratulate each other, smiling and saying "mazel tov!" As the full story spread around the ghetto, we all sighed in relief. The details must be inscribed, so their memory shall never perish among our descendants[60] and the memory of the murderer Gewecke shall remain to everlasting abhorrence.[61] What did this enemy of Israel attempt, in order to punish the ghetto? He demanded that the council, by noon on Tuesday, present him with a list of fifty souls to be put to death by firing squad! All that previous night our representatives had pondered, considered, and reviewed a variety of responses, and had finally assembled a list of fifty people to be executed. At the top of the list were the names of the council members, the ghetto managers, and the Jewish policemen. This was the list they turned in. But then Dr. Günter, the head of the labor police, who has a positive attitude toward Jewish work, intervened.[62] He argued that a massacre of the Jews' representatives and advocates, or of Jews in general, would seriously hinder the ability to use Jewish labor, which was then essential.

In short, we do not know the details of the negotiations, only the result: the commissioner canceled his barbaric decision and generously agreed to accept, in place of a human sacrifice, a fine of twenty thousand marks. And in the ghetto there was happiness and joy![63] All that a man has he will give up for his life.[64] A contribution in two installments! Thank God! And what will they say when the first payment is due? After all, the entire ghetto survives by selling off possessions, which grow fewer, and selling them is becoming more difficult because buyers already have enough Jewish property. Moreover, the Lithuanians in town are preparing for shortages this winter by stocking up on food items rather than clothing and jewelry. Also, many more Lithuanians are refusing to return the things they were given for safekeeping and hope to keep them. In any event, apportioning the tax will be a challenge both for those who collect and those who pay. Since we now must pay two-fifths of the first "contribution,"[65] it would be appropriate for everyone to pay two-fifths of what they paid the first time. But much has changed since then regarding ghetto dwellers' finances. Some prospered and grew rich,[66] but their number is small: most have been impoverished and are wretchedly poor.

I should point out that among the policemen selected to be fed to the beasts was my son. Had the commissioner not rescinded his bloody order, I would have offered myself in his place. My young son has not yet had a chance to live and see the world, whereas I am old and sick. I truly want to live to see the end of this war and of our torment, which will certainly come; yet I would not have hesitated to take my son's place among those slated for death.

12 September, Rosh Hashana[67]

A somber holiday! No meat or fish, no white bread, no fruit or vegetables. And the gloom! If we were to write, we could not say it all.[68] The lingering emotional shock from the commissioner's demand for fifty souls to be offered up to Moloch;[69] the tax payments that amount to ransom for the condemned, which will further drain our resources and will not be made up by selling belongings, our only source of sustenance; the constant worry and stress caused by the decrees and restrictions imposed on us; stumbling over loose stones in the middle of the street; passing through the ghetto gate under the hostile, suspicious eyes of the police; working for a mockery of a wage; derision and contempt from all sides; requiring some gentile, even a deaf-mute, a lunatic, or a child[70] to accompany us anywhere; malnutrition, the endless effort to find bread and bring it into the ghetto; being cut off from all sources of culture, such as radio, cinema, etc.

And to top it all off, depressing rumors come from near and far: the torment of the workers at the Radviliškis peat mines, who are beaten until they bleed for no reason; the fear that they will be kept there through winter to dig a canal; sad news from the front, that the Germans are advancing in southern Russia with the Russians unable to stop them; the deportations of the Jews from France, Belgium, Holland, etc. From France they took eight thousand children of Israel! Where? Why? Once we might have assumed this was in order to convert them to Christianity. But now that the main concern is "impure" Jewish blood, perhaps they are being slaughtered. Or perhaps they are being turned into slaves and servants, since Samael believes he is establishing a "thousand-year" empire and is bent on erasing the Jewish presence in Europe. Poor soul! And what will he do with Christianity? As long as it exists, it will carry traces of its Jewish origin. Even drained of its basic values and perverted despicably as it has been, Christianity will not be easy to get rid of.

Fall is coming nearer: The days are getting short and the nights long. Mornings are dark and foggy; evening comes early, cloudy and cold. The days are still pleasant: "The mellow season, with her glorious beauty," to use Pushkin's[71] words, but the coming rainy season and the harvest's end can already be felt. The gardens are still full of produce, but the days of cold, hunger, and want are approaching. And still we are not saved!

Rosh Hashana, Second Day

Reflections for the holiday: "There is a tsar in the world, a merciless tsar; his name is—Hunger!"[72]

This cruel king has already imposed a ransom on us, and we feel his heavy hand: faces have grown thin and pale, stomachs are empty and wanting. Even stale bread is frequently scarce and even more so meat, fish, butter, milk, or sugar. And what dark days can we expect this winter? Tsar Hunger will force us to search for food and sneak it into the ghetto, and the inspections will be meticulous and strict. Many will fail and fall into the hands of the Lithuanian and German police, very likely to be shot as promised. So the fear that we are all in mortal danger persists. The district commissioner already has plenty of experience spilling Jewish blood.

The hard labor at the peat mines is barely done, and a new task begins: building and renovating a munitions factory at Linkaičiai. They promise that conditions there will be comfortable, and that there are enough living units. We will see how things develop. At first they also praised conditions in Radviliškis, which turned out to be incomparably awful: workers were beaten senseless there for no reason, even at night, and the guards were always threatening to shoot. Indeed, it was a wonder that those who complained about the frequent sleep interruptions between days of heavy labor were not shot. Their vicious partisan slave drivers really intended murder, and only a miracle saved them.

The Germans demanded that a physician accompany the Linkaičiai workers. The doctors discussed it and decided to go in two-week rotations. Dr. Rozovsky was excused because of his feebleness and advanced age. I was excused due to my bowel disease. The other doctors were obligated to go, starting with those who had not been in the peat mines. The problem is that those who were forced to leave their positions, such as Dr. Lichtenstein and the technician, Levin, were not given back their former jobs by the labor police. A similar risk awaits doctors Feinberg, Peisachowitz, and Wolpert. When they are away, the labor police may request substitutes from Kaunas, and then they most certainly will not return to their jobs. The Christian doctors who run the offices where these Jewish doctors work are surprised that the council gave up trying to find an arrangement for these Jews. They think the council should have tried to ensure them their positions, which were so hard to obtain. This strange fact can be explained in my opinion by the council's hostile attitude toward doctors in general, whom they regard as arrogant and aloof. Our representatives are from that group of intelligentsia who look for ways to quash the doctors' smugness and humiliate them to the point of disgrace.

The fear of God overtook a good portion of the ghetto ahead of the Days of Awe.[73] Repentance, community prayers, and observance of the Sabbath and kosher laws preoccupied many of our Israelite brothers. On the Sabbath before Rosh Hashana most ghetto households lit no fires, left stoves off and prepared no hot dishes; first to thank the Lord for the fifty souls who were rescued from destruction, and second as a sign of repentance before the holidays. Their boundless troubles were not enough to prove to these Jews that there is no law and no judge, and that their God cares as much for them as for last year's snow.

What a difference between this New Year and those of the recent past! On Rosh Hashanah 1939,[74] we were free and had everything we could want. We had just returned from a vacation in Palanga. The war between Germany and Poland had just started, and we were amply stocked with food—bags of sugar, flour, salt, etc. We did not appreciate our situation and could not foresee the troubles awaiting us. At this time in 1940, I had traveled to Vilnius to plead with the rector to admit my son to the university. It was the time of the Bolsheviks, and I was the director of the polyclinic. There were some unpleasant moments, but in general we were happy, respected, and full of hope for the future. And by Rosh Hashana 1941,[75] our world had grown dark, with most of the Jewish population arrested and deported. We could not possibly have known, nor could we believe that they would slaughter innocent people in such huge numbers, and we entered the ghetto humiliated, tortured, and robbed.

This year the waters have reached our necks,[76] and desperation engulfs us, with not a ray of light or spark of hope. Our only comfort is that the Russian line is holding, and autumn is coming, with clouds, wind, rain, mud, and muck. One more month, and the German advance will have to stop. Meanwhile the Americans and English are gathering strength, making it possible that the Germans will be defeated or will choose to end the endless war, and put an end to the murderer's rule of bloodshed and destruction.

May it be so that by next Rosh Hashanah our exodus from slavery to freedom will occur, allowing us to leave this valley of slaughter and go up to the land of our forefathers. Certainly our brothers in America will be eager to help us, setting up a generous assistance fund to provide financing.

29 September (Chol HaMoed Sukkot)[77]

A terrible tragedy happened yesterday. One of the women working on the railroad was killed, another had her right hand and right foot crushed, and a third had her right foot and the toes of her left shattered. The women were collecting bits of coal beneath a freight car, when suddenly a locomotive arrived and pushed the car abruptly, running over the women. The first was killed instantly, the other two seriously injured, and several others were slightly injured. The injured lay bleeding for quite some time with no help. After much negotiation, the district commissioner finally allowed the injured women to be brought to the municipal hospital for surgery. In the hospital they amputated the shattered limbs, on condition that the women leave the hospital a day after the operation! Be appalled, O heavens, at this![78] The women were hurt working for the Germans, yet because they were Jewish the commissioner felt no shame setting despicable conditions on their treatment.

When will our troubles end? The blood freezes in our veins to think about how the Germans treat us. For now we have nothing but disappointments. Last year we placed our faith in the Russian winter to wipe out the murderers, like Napoleon in his time: our hope was dashed. We hoped spring would bring decisive events, a second front—again, bitter disappointment. We thought that their winter ordeals would wear the Germans down, and that a Russian counterattack would shift the war's momentum in the summer. Instead, the Germans advanced in giant steps, capturing the regions of southern Russia. Now they have reached Stalingrad, entered the city and are about to capture it, although they must fight for every house, and the fighting is harder than anything seen since the Verdun siege[79] during the last war, where the German strength was broken. Here as well their losses are innumerable, but their might did not dry up[80] and they will most likely capture the city. The blow to morale will be decisive. The great city, named for the "father of nations,"[81] will fall into enemy hands! So winter passed as did spring and summer, and we were still not rescued. The English and the Americans are not ready to open a second front, and who knows whether they will ever be ready if so many of their cargo ships are sinking? The enemy and its allies are so strong, but the Russians demonstrate wonders! They are holding up against all of Europe! But eventually their strength will fail if the English and Americans don't hurry up and help. How terrible! We will spend the winter here in hardship and want, waiting expectantly for next spring, when England and America promise to show their strength. Will our hope finally be realized?

One encouraging development which many talk about and claim to have witnessed firsthand: German deserters. Soldiers are seen almost daily at the rail station, passing through without their military belts and epaulets. A good sign! If it increases it could change the commanders' attitudes, with unexpected results. We are tired of waiting; tortured and oppressed, we cannot continue to hope that there might come a day of freedom, a day of salvation!

The gate police pay no attention to our catastrophes; they only add to our torment. Yesterday, the day of the [railway] tragedy, they made seven people kneel and beat them with rubber truncheons, then sent them back to the ghetto. What was their sin? A few potatoes and crusts of bread! They also took out a number of Jews from the prison to make examples of them. They included several speculators who had removed their Stars of David and gone looking for food in the city, but as usual, most may have done wrong for a piece of bread.[82] It is rumored that they were shot. They also shot many Lithuanians who refused to work in Germany or go to the front. It also could be that some refused to give up the best of their harvest: livestock, milk, butter, and eggs.

An interesting directive: people from Kaunas staying in the city have been declared nonessential and told to vacate their apartments to make room for returning German soldiers.[83] How can they determine whether such people are essential or not? Almost all the residents work as professionals in the city: doctors, merchants, craftsmen, etc.

Rumors are spreading of disorder at the front and in German cities. Hopefully these rumors will prove accurate and not merely the product of the imaginations of those seeking comfort in fairy tales.

Simchat Torah[84] [4 October]

A day full of sadness and despair. The district commissioner, who had not honored us with a visit for a whole year, now appears in the ghetto frequently, and each visit leads to a new edict. Shrinking the ghetto twice, demanding fifty victims after inspecting those returning to the ghetto and finding food in their pockets. The victims were replaced by a contribution—but no peace! The ghetto dwellers continue to search for food because their hunger forces them on.[85] Their rations, half the amount Christians receive, are inadequate even for a child. And the commissioner has gone to war against the Jews[86] over a handful of potatoes and some bread. He summoned the council again and warned them "for the last time" that he will no longer go easy on those who smuggle in food. "We live on our rations (so he claims!), and you should live on yours." Before the council members could reply, he declared the meeting over and told them they would be held responsible and that the blood will be on their heads[87] if any ghetto residents are caught. Since then the Jewish policemen have been making gate inspections. Yesterday they patted the pockets of everyone returning from the city. I myself was inspected yesterday and today. How humiliating! Our son, too, will have to search for contraband food in the pockets of those entering the ghetto because he is a policeman. He is suffering in his soul from this job, which he holds because of my wife's pleading.

Smuggling food into the ghetto has become impossible for now, and the result will be very sad: we all will starve because one hundred grams of bread per day is below starvation level, a mockery of the poor.

The latest speech by the hell-demon[88] left us feeling terrible. His old song about how Jews want to exterminate the Aryans would be laughable if not for the fact that more than two million Jews have already been wiped out because of it, and his arm is outstretched still.[89] "The Jews will laugh no longer!" he vowed. Indeed, he is keeping his promises regarding Jews, 100 percent! Ignoring his ridiculous rhetoric about his supposed love for humanity and brotherhood among nations and so on, there were still several parts of his speech worth noting. First, he ridiculed England and America, mocking their military failures and inability to endure a war, and listed the German army's magnificent victories. Then he added that he will show no mercy to traitors and saboteurs within his own country. This clearly indicates there are many inside Germany and even within the army who have had enough of the war. A notable trend which, if it continues to progress, will become a major headache for the Führer. Still the speech left a sour taste, since it mainly bragged about things that sadly we cannot deny are real.

Isru Chag[90] [5 October]

On Shemini Atzeret,[91] an event in the Kaukazas area demonstrated the perils of trying to bring even a handful of potatoes into the ghetto under the latest decree. That day the Jewish policemen at the Kaukazas ghetto gate were following their orders to check those returning home and seizing even tiny amounts of food. Some wretched people live in that area, and encouraged by the speculators, they attacked the policemen, injuring them. Their fellow policemen came from the Trakų area to help them, and a battle broke out across the entire Kaukazas area. The Lithuanian police heard about it and intervened, punishing all those involved with beatings. Investigations and trials are still to come. "King Hunger" has taken charge!

Yesterday was Simchat Torah, normally a day of joy and celebration, but the sun has set on all our joy.[92] The council called an assembly outdoors in the street and warned us to not try bringing anything into the ghetto because of the mortal danger hanging over all our heads. Many useless things were said as well, but they nevertheless left us depressed. The message was that we must tolerate constant hunger in order to spite our enemies until our salvation comes.

8 October

The story of Dr. Peisachowitz illustrates the extent of our enemies' cruelty. The doctor, who works in the tuberculosis clinic, happened to walk by the German security police. He was accompanying a Jewish policeman from the ghetto[93] who is infected with tuberculosis and needs treatment for a collapsed lung. Dr. P. was preparing his treatment in the clinic when suddenly two German policemen came in. They arrested both the doctor for violating the ban on treating Jewish patients in public medical facilities, and the patient for daring to seek help there. Dr. P. did not deny that he was offering medical help because a Jew is permitted to treat a Jew, and besides, the labor police routinely give written permission to treat workers. Even now he is sure he can obtain such a permit but has not yet had the chance because it is hard for a Jew to move about the city. The Jewish policeman had been in town on official business and thought to use that opportunity to get the medical treatment he needed and get the permit later. The German officers were satisfied with this answer and did not punish the doctor. But when they questioned the patient, he became confused and said he had come not for treatment but on behalf of the ghetto hospital, where Dr. Peisachowitz is the director. When his story did not precisely match the doctor's, they slapped him on his face twice, which startled him. But that was not enough for them: they took him to the basement and gave him twenty-five lashes! That is how they treated a sick man with a collapsed lung who was afraid to tell the truth.

Still, they would have punished him even if he had told the truth because if there is even a slight fault in a Jew's behavior, the slightest reason for criticism, the villains do not let him go. No matter that he is seriously ill; what do they care if his condition worsens or even if he dies? We should be thankful that they did not kill him. The sheep cannot find justice with the wolf. And now is not a good time for the Jews. The chancellor of demons keeps returning to his dog's vomit about Jews wanting to destroy the Aryans and promises that the struggle will end when Jews are eliminated. This mad refrain is repeated constantly in his speeches and the newspapers, and the villains' anger grows with their lack of success at the front, particularly at Stalingrad, which is beginning to look like the siege of Verdun. Let us hope they receive their just desert.

After a delay Dr. Peisachowitz obtained the permit from the labor police, to be delivered by the clinic director to the security police. For now the storm has quieted. But Dr. P.'s carelessness might become a problem for all of us lab technicians if the German police grow interested in our work and decide to look at us more closely. That would not be helpful.

10 October

This is our fourth day without firewood or potatoes. We cannot prepare a hot dish, and we have nothing to eat. It is a foretaste of the coming winter, when some of us will die from cold or hunger. How important wood is for heat and cooking! One benefit of working at the polyclinic is that I still have a little food there and can bake potatoes in the oven. Last week my son ate lunch with me in the polyclinic twice. Indeed, how many benefits has the polyclinic bestowed upon us:[94] food, sometimes a little money beyond the absurd wages, and especially eating lunch at 10:00 a.m. I keep a little bread, eggs, butter, and sugar there, but bringing them into the ghetto is impossible now, and the ghost of famine has begun to haunt us there: There are no potatoes in our house, no eggs, no butter, and today our neighbors have no bread. And everyone feels the lack of wood.

24 October

The past week is one that even we who are experienced in calamity will not soon forget. Two German officials burst into the ghetto, entered the homes of people known to have been wealthy or able to acquire food, and stole whatever they found: food, furniture, clothes, anything that caught their fancy—suitcases, mattresses, sewing machines, baby strollers, etc. All this was accompanied by random beatings of men and women equally. They took all they could carry, noted down what they couldn't, and sent carts back to take the loot away. Their guide was the new "administrator for Jewish affairs," a wicked man who vowed to bring the looters back to all the homes in the ghetto, to end what he said was Jewish speculation. Gripped by fear, we all waited a few days for another visit from these guests and were deeply depressed. We are accustomed to dread surprises, but this time the fear and trembling were boundless. The thieves, who overlook nothing, not even buttons and chess pieces, would certainly find something to take in every home. And along with seizing what is left of our food, they would surely beat us mercilessly because their cruelty is infamous. Fortunately, Dr. Günter of the labor police has some regard for his Jewish workers. As he has done several times in the past, he intervened and held off these wild beasts over whom we had lost several nights' sleep. In the end they forbade the murderers and robbers from entering the ghetto without a special permit.

Our spirits had barely recovered from that experience when a new incident shook us once again. A German became furious when a young Jew, a hard worker,[95] failed to answer some trivial question precisely and struck him on the head with a wooden cudgel. The beaten man dropped to the ground, unconscious, and the murderer kept beating him. Doctors later found his skull was broken in one location and that he had suffered a major concussion. He had surgery and now this strong young man hovers between life and death, with the outcome very much in doubt. No further proof is needed to show how little the Germans value Jewish life.

Stalingrad has not yet fallen! Dissatisfaction and quiet dissent are spreading. Who would have thought the Russians could hold off the Germans, Italians, and other European gangsters? Critics of the Bolsheviks maintain that their regime leads only to "poverty and destitution"[96] and indeed, their shortcomings are well known and beyond doubt: excessive and unnecessary cruelty, incoherence and inconsistency, a lack of professional leadership, the abrupt destruction of an entire class, ideological errors, etc. But it must be admitted that when it came to defending their homeland, arming and preparing the military, the Bolsheviks performed superbly, and for now they are saving humanity from the crushing boot of the German barbarians. Decisive events that will end the nightmare of this war are likely in the spring, when America is prepared and ready.[97] But our strength is diminishing, and we cannot wait much longer.

27 October

Sorrow and sighing![98] Horrible rumors about the fate of the Jews in Poland terrify us during the day and keep us awake at night. The cup of poison that was passed to us last year is now theirs: annihilation of entire communities, massacres of hundreds of thousands of Jews. It is said that tens of thousands of our brothers were killed by poisonous vapors, like fleas and cockroaches—a lovely death! We had deluded ourselves into thinking they had grown tired of killing us, and now the storm rises again, and the pledge to eliminate Jews from Europe is nearly fulfilled. The depth of the Führer's madness regarding us is shown in his telegram to Il Duce[99] on the twentieth anniversary of fascism. Even in this formal and celebratory greeting, he found it necessary to mention that "Judaism, plutocracy and Bolshevism will be defeated in their war." Among all this villain's enemies, the Jews are first! What destruction this madman's insane fantasies have wrought!

And here we sit without wood, shivering in the autumn cold and damp and hungry for a warm bowl of stew. Most of the ghetto is hungry all the time. Our pantries lack meat, milk or fish; we live on bread, cereal and potatoes. Protein has vanished from our diets and there is nothing to replace it; thus we are constantly hungry and malnourished. After the news from Poland arrived, two questions torment us: Will they exterminate all the Lithuanian Jews, so none escape or get away,[100] seeing how after this disaster in Poland the propaganda not only has not subsided but only intensified? And second: Will we survive the cold and hunger, the terror and fear, the mental and physical torments expected this winter? For now we see no hope that our situation will improve.

7 November

It snowed lightly yesterday, the first snow of the year. It brought cooler weather, which today has intensified. It appears that winter is coming early, which could be an advantage at the front. But here in the ghetto, we sit without wood and the cold tortures us. Cold and hunger came entwined[101] since if there is no wood for heating, there is none for cooking. All the yards in the ghetto stand bare and open, as all the fences and posts have been taken down that they may be ravaged[102] and burned for fuel.

Some good news arrived from the Egyptian front: the official German army announcement reluctantly admitted that for strategic reasons, German and

Italian forces have made an orderly retreat to positions prepared earlier. It is rumored that they suffered a major defeat. We so hope it is true that the Italian army was defeated and that a sizable portion of the German army was captured.[103] Each defeat of theirs has huge consequences, material and moral. The city of Stalingrad has also not fallen—and winter, the friend and ally of the Russian army, has arrived.

9 November

Morale is high. Encouraging news is reaching us from the African front. The Americans landed in Morocco and the French did not object, so the German and Italian armies were attacked from both front and back, caught in a pincer. The American and English air forces are far superior, and their enemies are fleeing the battlefield in urgent haste.[104] It will take time, but the hope that the Italians and Germans will be pushed out of Africa is already lifting our spirits. Then the Mediterranean will be open, and a second front will become possible in Italy. For now we cling to such hopes. Meanwhile the oppressor gave another disgusting speech and again vowed to destroy the Jews of Europe.[105]

21 November

Again mortal danger looms over us. An incident occurred in the ghetto that could have unknown consequences. A Lithuanian informed on a friend for selling beans to a Jew. The Germans rushed into the ghetto and found the farmer with his goods—three *zentners*[106] of beans and other provisions stored in a warehouse near a workshop belonging to the Jewish council. The beans were intended for the privileged gang who distribute food among themselves without sharing with the rest of the community. But all are to suffer for it. The district commissioner and his minions warned that if ghetto residents are caught smuggling food, there will be no mercy; unlike the first time, when they graciously agreed to spare fifty lives in exchange for a tax, they would not be so tolerant. The times are already hard, and now the oppressor and his lackeys promise to wipe out the Jews of Europe. Rosenberg[107] says that as long as even one Jew remains in Europe there will be no peace. Now the district commissioner can make good on his threat and demand new human sacrifices, so we are all consumed by fear.

In the evening we heard a more comforting rumor: The business with the beans will not be held against the entire ghetto, only the speculator who bought the provisions (Dubkin[108]). He was arrested and now faces great danger.

Encouraging news keeps arriving from the African front: The Germans and the Italians are retreating from the places they captured earlier, and the

Americans and English are advancing and doing well. Important things are also happening in France: Pétain's deputy, Darlan,[109] betrayed the Germans and joined their enemies. Giraud[110] now commands the French forces fighting the Germans. The German general Rommel is preparing for a battle in Libya, but there he will be attacked from two sides. One can assume that the Germans will not be able to stand their ground[111] in Africa—and then the real second front will open! For now, the Americans and English are destroying Italy's cities. "Happy the one who waits!"[112]

Our only son left yesterday for Pavenčiai[113] to unload beets at the sugar factory. Sorrow, boredom, and distress. He had been taking care of all our needs and chores, and I am unable to replace him in this.

23 November

The inspections at the ghetto gate have again become strict and thorough. When I leave in the morning, I worry that I may be arrested before I can get back home, because if I manage to obtain some food in town, I have to try to bring it in, which is dangerous. I have been caught only once: last year when I carried meat in a basket under a layer of potatoes. I escaped by giving the policemen fifty rubles. Since that incident I have not been thoroughly searched and have managed to get by, but I am always nervous when I carry "contraband." Thus we live in fear, cursing our tormenters and our miserable lives.

A notice in big letters was posted by the council office,[114] announcing that the defendant Dubkin was sentenced to be hanged in the ghetto. (In Kaunas there was a trial for a similar case of speculation.) But because it was his first offense and he was not profiteering from this purchase, his sentence was commuted to hard labor at Linkaičiai. Of course there were warnings and threats of the death penalty for future cases, etc. None of that will matter because the ghetto is hungry, and hunger will force us to continue trying to bring in food. And meanwhile the speculators will "neither slumber nor sleep."[115]

4 December

The business of potatoes torments us. The cooperative made a point of telling residents to hurry and pick up their allotted rations of potatoes. These tubers are frozen, rotten, and wet: After throwing away a third of them because they were useless, we apportioned another third to be cooked and eaten as soon as possible, and set the last third on the floor of our small, moldy room to dry. The potatoes release a vapor that chills the room and adds to the mildew, of which we already have plenty. And the potatoes we set aside to eat stink and will be thrown out in the end also, because my wife and I cannot enjoy eating bad potatoes and our son is gone. And although the maid is a big eater, she will not be able to finish them all. Sorting the potatoes, cleaning them of mud and hay, smelling their stench, having no room left to sit or stand: all these seem like small complaints, but after three days of dealing with the potatoes we were ready to end it all. Just another small illustration of our accursed lives in the ghetto.

The war has likely entered a new phase, possibly a decisive one, but how long it will last is hard to predict. The allies have a fresh, well-equipped army, but the Axis armies are courageous, experienced, and superbly disciplined. There is no way to know who will win. It is arguable that the two sides could fight to a stalemate, and that a third party—the Pope, Sweden, or Switzerland, who can say?—would show up to mediate between them. Such an end would not resolve the Jewish question, unlike if the English emerge victorious. Then they could show their power to the Arabs, who are rebelling against them, and give us back the land of our forefathers. That is the only solution for those who survive[116] the slaughterer's plans for our extermination. Indeed he has succeeded in his war against the Jews, overpowering the world forces of history, integrity, and social justice. Will those forces rise again, even belatedly? Let us believe so, and hope.

19 December

Horrifying and heartbreaking rumors say that the extermination of the Jews is nearly complete. There were millions of us, and now the few survivors are vanishing. Here the job was done by Ukrainians and Lithuanians. Now the Poles are finishing the destruction of our brothers there after dormant hatreds were reawakened. The Germans sent many Polish workers to Germany, replacing them with Jews, so the masses believe the Jews bribed the Germans and that Polish Jews were profiteering on the black market. Begging has proliferated along with disease and filth, and for all that the Poles blame the Jews, helping the Germans make them into sheep for slaughter.

23 December

There was a scare by the gate yesterday. The policemen need money for liquor, etc., ahead of their holidays, so they began inspecting those returning from the city especially closely, even patting down women head to toe, front and back. People on their way home were warned that the line at the gate had slowed because of the thorough checks, so they started dropping contraband by the side of the road: butter, fat, eggs, turnips, etc. Some, who either ran out of time or did not want to give up the items they had obtained with great difficulty and for inflated prices, took their chances, were stopped by the police, and had to pay large sums to avoid jail. I should note that I also was committing the crime of hiding prohibited items: I had two quarter-kilogram soap bars in my long underwear above my boots. The guard patted me down casually and did not notice my contraband. For the most part my age, my profession and my past positions protect me from harassment and disrespect.

My son Tedik returned from Pavenčiai. The work there was truly hard: unloading sugar beets from the cargo trains and moving them into a factory warehouse, mostly with handcarts, straining body and soul. But the eating was good: hot stew twice a day and opportunities for the workers to prepare their own meals. Moreover, groups were allowed to go into nearby villages and beg for food, which was successful most times. The farmers did not turn them away and either fed them or gave them provisions.

The news from the front is more encouraging. For the first time the Germans have acknowledged that they suffered a decisive defeat near Voronezh. The British say more than twenty thousand were killed and nearly thirty thousand were taken prisoner. Other signs indicate that all is not well in the German camp. We frequently see deserters transferring through the Šiauliai train station. The German morale is very low. Let them all fall to the depths of hell.[117]

27 December

A party was held in the ghetto the other night, marking one year since the establishment of the ghetto hospital. A year ago they prohibited Christian doctors from treating Jewish patients and ordered the council to immediately remove all Jewish patients from all departments of the municipal hospital, even those who were critically ill with fevers above forty degrees.[118] The meanness and cruelty after all our other troubles did not surprise us. The council did not panic and found a way to prevent disaster, although with some difficulty: They immediately set up an isolation ward "outside of camp"[119] to house the critically ill. The only available space was the cleansing room in the cemetery, a room with a concrete floor that was very cold in winter. There were no medical instruments, no furniture or bedding, but there was a need, initiative, generosity, and flexibility. The council showed courage and overcame all obstacles, and in a short time the cemetery cleansing room and the Burial Society[120] dormitory were turned into a hospital—a tiny one, but given our current living conditions, respectable and even elegant. "How fair are your tents O Jacob, your dwellings O Israel!" Even in the ghetto, despite our enemies' efforts to turn the last survivors[121] into the dust under their feet,[122] our vigor is unabated.[123] Our stamina, initiative and ability to adapt say a lot about us. This suffering and oppressed people, broken and bowed, will rise up, shake off the dust, and take action as soon as their salvation comes and they are freed from the ghetto and their enemies. This was the first celebration since the Germans invaded our city, and it left a pleasant impression like a ray of light on a dark night.

12 January 1943

There has been much recent news in the ghetto, and much could have been written both of a personal and general nature. But on the first of Shevat[124] (7 January) the cold intensified, dashing our hopes that this winter would be easier than last. The cold is penetrating and depressing in our home, which is not properly insulated or sealed against the weather. Heating is minimal due to the lack of wood, and this increases our tendency to sit, hugging ourselves,[125] bundled and motionless in the cluttered, damp room. One day we decided to freshen up the room a bit, air out our pillows and duvets in the yard and sort through the potatoes stored under our bed, throwing out the rotten ones and removing the shoots and roots that had sprouted in the damp air. We also took our clothes down from the walls where they were hanging to find they had grown mold. I took them out to the yard to clean them, but I was not dressed warmly enough. The cold was intense, the wind blew fiercely, and as a result I caught a cold, which is unusual for me. I developed pneumonia, which is dangerous at my age, and was in bed for two weeks. I recovered in time and returned to work in the city, but I still feel a terrible weakness in my legs and am still coughing. Thus our accursed lives in the ghetto bring us almost to the pit of hell.[126]

A new development in the ghetto has turned our lives upside down. The villains who are constantly scheming to make our lives miserable came up with a strange new idea: impose a "communist" order in the ghetto. Here are the details: Ghetto residents who work receive a monthly wage between 37.5 and 40.5 marks. Since the official price of the monthly food ration amounts to 7 marks (!) they decided to give the workers' wages directly to the council and make them responsible for covering all the ghetto needs: food, heating, housing, health, etc. The council will give each worker with a family 5 marks and each single worker 3 marks per month for miscellaneous expenses.

Clearly this will improve things for the poor, who will now receive for free those necessities whose current prices, as set by the council, far exceed their wages. Those absurd wages have not been a concern for the better off who can continue to sell or exchange goods they own for food, although such exchanges grow more difficult day by day. The burden of this change will be felt by the council itself. It has many expenses that cannot be disclosed such as [payments to] the German and Lithuanian officials and policemen whose grace and goodness are bought with hard cash. It also must cover the cost of the hospital, management, etc., and has been doing so through surcharges at the cooperative and the pharmacy, etc. But now this will be much more difficult.

5 February

Stalingrad! Stalingrad! The name will remain etched in world history in all ages to come.[127] The city bearing this name controls the Volga, the main artery of southern Russia, connecting the center of the country with the fertile south and the Caucasus oil fields. The Germans tried to capture it to sever those connections, and particularly to interrupt the flow of oil, an essential commodity in wartime. They sent their best divisions, the Sixth Army, along with Romanian and Slovakian legions.[128] They spared neither manpower nor weapons to conquer a place bearing the Russian leader's name, and the German leader promised with immeasurable confidence that the city would certainly be taken. In fact a large section of the city was nearly occupied with enormous losses, but they did not have the strength to completely drive the Russians from the city. The Russians demonstrated unprecedented heroism, turning every house into a fortress from which to attack, entrapping and crushing their enemy. Here the German advance was broken and their fortunes turned in a way they had not foreseen. The aggressors were put on the defensive and were surrounded by a large Russian army, with no way to escape. Driven by their pride and their crazed Führer, they still refused to surrender until they ran out of supplies and ammunition. Twenty-four generals, about two hundred officers and eighty thousand soldiers surrendered to the Russians. The siege trapped 330,000 people in the city, and 250,000 died there, beyond those who fell during the first phase of the German attack.

The defeat has no precedent in the modern German history and has shocked the entire German nation like a lightning strike. They declared three days of mourning and ordered a general mobilization of the entire nation! And the German press produced mountains of twisted arguments about how defeat would finally bring victory, and how the Stalingrad experience will harden the German nation like a hammer hardens steel. This defeat will not soon be wiped out of their memory. For the murdered Baltic Jews, this represents revenge, but for the more than six million Jews of Europe who have died,[129] revenge has not yet come. The victory brought honor to the Russians and a new spirit of courage and initiative. And now they go from strength to strength.[130] Who knows? Maybe it is the beginning of our deliverance, when Jews can say a blessing for being allowed to witness the defeat of our enemy and receive some comfort in our affliction.[131] But the outlook is still troubling: the general mobilization of the villains who live by their swords[132] could awaken their ancient warlike spirit and enable them in desperation to push the Russians back and retake the cities they have abandoned. The coming days will tell, but our strength is failing,[133] and we are impatient for our tardy salvation to arrive.

26 February

Since Stalingrad, the Russians have achieved more brilliant victories: they captured Kursk, Kharkiv, Rostov, and some other fairly important areas. Their defeats have terrified the Germans—terror and dread descend on them[134]—prompting official periods of mourning, a general mobilization, and an acknowledgment of the coming danger. They portray their enemy as a bold deceiver who managed to conceal his real level of preparedness until now (!) and plans to destroy all of Europe and erase human culture, of which Germany is supposedly the guardian. At the same time, the Germans have grown even more brutal and wrathful, and they are prepared to exterminate even the remnants of our people. Now they want to show that their problem is all Europe's problem and that danger looms over the entire civilized world, and so they are seeking to enlist all the peoples of Europe. Here they have restored assets that were seized by the Bolsheviks to their owners, and at the same time announced a conscription of young men between the ages of nineteen and twenty-four to work initially and then go to the front. Presumably the poorer Baltic people will try to hide or will quickly turn themselves into prisoners of war because they know the Germans are lying about the Bolsheviks; under their regime life was far better than it is now.

News! Every resident must draw up a list of his belongings and paste it on the door of his dwelling to make inspection easier when they come to verify it. The point of this edict is not clear. How far down have we fallen, unable to rise! A common policeman hit Dr. D. in the face because he dared to walk on the sidewalk! When it comes to the Jews they do not consider age, education, or previous social position. For Jews there is no law and no justice.

Another policeman came out of hiding and attacked Dr. K. after a Lithuanian woman passed him a package of food, which his brother had sent, through a hole in the ghetto fence. The policeman demanded one thousand marks and wouldn't budge or show mercy. Toward Jews, "the law has no mercy."

A new edict: Jews may not buy newspapers in kiosks. This comes after an incident that occurred in Kaunas during the excitement after Stalingrad fell. The Germans understand that Jews rejoice at their downfall and look for news that is bad for them and happy for us. Unfortunately, the Russian advance seems to have paused recently.

Chol HaMoed Pesach,[135] Second Day

Strength waning, nerves stressed, troubles persist; no hope for deliverance soon. No decisive events at the front; resilience is wearing down. There is much I should be recording, but lethargy is taking over. I have little desire or energy to write, and my mind is tired with worry; I am a helpless man.[136] Beyond these excuses, there are more serious reasons for my negligence and silence. Our only son, whose good health was our pride and our solace during my wife's and my own illnesses, succumbed to the ghetto conditions and developed an infection of the pulmonary pleura.[137] The disease is certainly caused by Koch's microbe[138] and is very dangerous. He needs time in a health spa, a sanatorium—but these are things we now can only dream of. We did all we could, and he is recovering, but it is the third month since he fell ill. His illness has taken my free time since I visit him daily in the hospital and give him my full attention.

Aside from this, a number of events indicate we are in a transition period, a process that has yet to play out.

(a.) After their defeat at Stalingrad, the Germans announced a nationwide mobilization, and also tried to enlist the peoples they have conquered. The Lithuanian nation showed unexpected resistance and unity: no one responded to the call for recruits. The Germans reacted with various repressions, and after certain concessions, a conference representing various [Lithuanian] groups concluded that it is necessary to fight the Bolsheviks and help the Germans. Few are volunteering for the front, however.

(b.) Following Stalingrad, the Germans face a second major defeat in Africa. If that occurs they will be forced to evacuate Tunis, with many casualties likely from the English and American airplanes and submarines.

(c.) The Germans' defeats increase their blazing anger,[139] and they take it out on us. Their propaganda is intensifying, blaming us for everything.

(d.) The English and American air raids on German and Italian cities are intense and powerful: suffice it to note that the attack on Antwerp[140] (they are also attacking Germany's allies) caused two thousand casualties! The city of Essen[141] was almost blotted out from the earth.[142] Berlin has suffered much as well. Rosenberg claimed that the hand of Israel was behind it all and told Germans to remember and react with "hatred and revenge."

(e.) Near Smolensk the Germans discovered mass graves containing twelve thousand Polish army officers whom the Russians captured and killed.[143] The propaganda is extensive, and the Poles' rage is immeasurable. Whenever the Bolsheviks are condemned, the Jews are mentioned too, so it appears that even in this case, which is still in dispute, the "Jew-Bolsheviks" were responsible.

(f.) Terrifying news from Poland, more than the heart can bear. From the radio in Warsaw come reports that the ghetto there has been burning for several days[144] and that the Jews staged an uprising with rocks and axes against the Germans, who were forced to bring tanks into the ghetto to exterminate the last remnant. This is not yet confirmed, but bad news should always be believed these days.

Chol HaMoed Pesach, Third Day[145]

Today the temperature was unusually high for April, making it feel like July. The first troop of ghetto residents leaves to work in the peat bogs at Bačiūnai.[146] This time the German head of the "Arbeitsamt"[147] selected the workers; ignoring the advice of the doctors' committee he decided to send all those eligible, excusing only those who fall ill on the job. Two doctors were also sent as common laborers.

We can take as a lesson the story of M.L.,[148] one of Šiauliai's richest men, the director of the [Frenkel] factory. He managed to accumulate substantial wealth, enough to permit him to settle abroad, but he was satisfied with life in this world and intent on increasing his fortune. He believed his wealth would always protect him[149] from harm. I recall a conversation where he tried hard to convince me that Lithuania was in a good location and faced no danger, because it is between two giant countries that would want to ensure its neutrality as a barrier between them. Convinced of this, he started constructing a four-story building with three apartments on each floor. He invested most of his fortune in the building, which was the most splendid in the entire city. He was hoping to generate a healthy income from his tenants. But before he could complete the building, the Bolsheviks arrived and threw him out of his own home. And his troubles have multiplied in recent days. The Germans arrested him twice before. The second time he was in serious danger because someone revealed that he had given a Pole a letter to deliver to the Vilnius ghetto, raising the suspicion of espionage. Pleas for his release were successful, but today he was arrested again, because he had dared to sell his piano. He returned home in such a condition that he could only lie on his stomach, because his back was covered with wounds. This is how the civilized Germans treat a man advanced in years,[150] a respectable Jew because they do not consider a Jew a human being. Moreover his position in the factory, which was very important because he knows all aspects of the work there, is lost; and his downfall means the downfall of the other Jews who work there. Thus the assets of first the factory owner and now its director have been lost to our people, along with the benefits they could have provided to our ancestors' land.

Chol HaMoed, Fourth Day[151]

Talk in the ghetto yesterday focused on the size of the German losses in the last four months. If the numbers are not exaggerated, their losses are enormous: 338,000 taken prisoner, 840,000 fallen, more than hundred thousand vehicles, etc. etc. Stalingrad, Tunis, the eastern front, the aerial raids—none will be forgotten soon.

One of the sadder things happening in the ghetto is the rise in tuberculosis among the younger generation. Overcrowding, a lack of hygiene in the homes, hard labor, malnutrition, unceasing stress and worry, all promote the spread of disease, particularly tuberculosis. Notably deaths among the elderly have also increased disproportionally since last year. Exhaustion and weakness affect all ghetto residents. Signs of old age come on prematurely as trouble and misery push us to the wall.

5 May

I am sick of writing about our troubles, tired of rehashing endless woes. The ghetto remains hard to enter and exit. Bringing in food is sometimes less dangerous and sometimes leads to imprisonment and flogging. The latter has happened twice in public, and this must be recorded and remembered—but we have already experienced so many worse disasters that our sensibilities have been dulled. Certainly all faces turned ashen[152] the first time residents were summoned to attend a public beating of workers caught carrying food home. But the impression dissipated quickly. Similarly, the urgent need to record the shameful flogging of elderly people for smuggling food also faded because what does this punishment amount to, when the life we face is precarious[153] and we know not what a day will bring?[154] How important is this when we have been sold into slavery, our bodies wasted and worn out by hard labor, day after day?

Today however, an event occurred that has shaken the ghetto to its core and forced me to break my silence and take up my pen: today a Jew was hanged in the ghetto.[155] He was sentenced to die by hanging after they found in his possession more than thirty packs of cigarettes, a half pound of chocolates, a new coat, and a sum of money. For this they tried him as a speculator and ordered him to be hung. All appeals failed, and the sentence was carried out today. These are the tragic details:

Mazovetsky and others were leaving the courtyard of the bakery (Petersons) where he worked, carrying the prohibited goods. Suddenly a German police car arrived on the street along with the Lithuanian policeman Belkštys, a well-known Jew-hater. Frightened, Mazovetsky retreated into the yard, which caught the attention of the police. They chased and caught him, and when they found the prohibited items they arrested him. He sat in jail for a few days and people thought this would be his punishment, since all they found on him were low-value items, some candies for his little daughter and some fat.[156] His only real crime was the cigarette packs and the money. No one expected this would bring the death penalty! But the murderers had been looking for a reason to execute a Jew in public, with the ghetto watching. Now they found their victim and could satiate their thirst for Jewish blood.

The prisoner did not know his verdict until today. The Jewish police went house to house and ordered all residents to gather in the Kaukazas ghetto to witness the execution, warning that the Germans would check to make sure the residents obeyed. So a large crowd gathered in Kaukazas, including some Lithuanians, and in front stood about fifteen Germans from the secret police and the commissioner's office. The gallows was prepared in a park. The prisoner appeared in chains. Everyone thought they would commute the sentence at the last minute and, after scaring him, merely put him in prison. The Germans were gloating at the prospect of seeing a terrified Jew dragged against his will to the gallows. And yet the man who appeared was young, handsome, solid as an oak with a smile on his lips. On his own he climbed onto the small table that stood beneath the gallows, put his own head into the noose, and nodded farewell to those around him. He then fixed his gaze on his executioners, smiled so as to give them no satisfaction and died a hero, astonishing all who witnessed it.

This man, though frightened at the appearance of the police car, showed extraordinary courage at the time of his death, impressing even the Germans. He wanted to say goodbye to his wife and mother, but the villains would not let him. In his last moment, he said, "Stay calm! I will plead for all of you!" Thus did a thirty-year-old Jew die, an innocent victim of these times and of the beasts whose thirst for Jewish blood is insatiable.

We do see evidence that our enemies are suffering, and each day brings us a little comforting news. Since Samael assumed command of his army he has led them from one defeat to another: Stalingrad, the flight from the Caucasus, and the Allied victory in Tunis that they will never forget. Our enemies have never suffered such defeats before. We should be pleased, but each of their defeats worsens our situation. To distract the masses from their military setbacks and the flood of aerial attacks on their country, they tear into the "Jewish question" like mad dogs playing with their own feces, chewing it over and over, endlessly. The incitement has climaxed and our lives hang by a thread; there is no knowing what will happen tomorrow.

10 June (Second Day of Shavuot)

The air is bright and clear; spring is in full swing. Every house has a garden in front, unfenced since the fences were burned early in winter for lack of firewood. Last year people treated their gardens casually, but by the end they realized their value to those who tended them well. This year residents have been serious about raising vegetables, and as a result the ghetto is dressed in the colors of spring. Green grows everywhere, but gloom remains in our hearts. We are overcome with desperation and our spirits are depressed, because the outlook shows no sign of hope and the propaganda against us, filled with asps' venom,[157] does not end.

26 July

Today we received great news that filled the whole ghetto with a joy[158] we have not felt since the modern Haman got his hands on us. Mussolini has fallen![159] Finally even his own gang realized he had driven Italy to the edge of the abyss.[160] He chose with the encouragement of his lackeys to become Amalek's partner; now his defeat is absolute! Italy lost its colonies, poverty is widespread, its best soldiers were lost on the Russian front, and its enemies are before its gates, *ante portas*![161] Sicily will fall, and its defeat will drag all Italy down. Amalek's partner fell from the heights, all the way down, hopefully like his mentor, H., never to rise again. May his downfall be contagious. Such a hopeful sign, perhaps the beginning of our redemption! All the poor, downtrodden ghetto residents are happy and breathlessly awaiting further news.

30 July

Mussolini and his cronies are in jail! The Fascist Party has ceased to exist! The new government has made a show of declaring it will continue the war. But the masses demand peace! And it will get no help from its former partner. The Allies make three demands: unconditional capitulation, passage through Italy for their armies to keep fighting the Germans, and the abolition of the Fascist Party.

4 September

I did not expect to have to add another notebook to this journal.[162] I was sure I would end my volume with good news and that our redemption would arrive before I filled it. My hope has been dashed for now: Redemption is still far off,[163] and the long wait is a torment. Who knows if even this new notebook will suffice? Events unfold slowly, the war drags on, and we are exhausted. The enemy remains fierce, showing stiff resistance despite defeats, and absent a miracle he will hold out for a long time. Those defeats have been significant, beginning with Stalingrad. Then followed the expulsion from North Africa and the loss of the colonies that Italy drove itself to destitution to acquire; the occupation of Sicily, Italy's pride and its breadbasket; the destructive air raids; Mussolini's defeat and the end of Fascism! Italy resembles a slaughtered and plucked chicken; it continues to fight, given no alternative by the devil. That devil has been wounded, will never recover, and may even have to drink from the cup of wrath soon.

We depend on miracles, which now happen daily. That we were spared our brothers' fates and are still alive is a miracle. The German defeats are miracles. The downfall of sycophantic and evil Italy, which stabbed France in the back in her time of troubles[164] is a miracle from heaven. And we await the final miracle, which will put an end to the German butchers and bring us all relief and deliverance.[165]

New things[166] lifting our hearts: the English and the Americans have landed in Italy. Our friends in the battle-tested Eighth Army showed their strength[167] again, with prompt results. The English have already captured three cities and three beaches. They broke the German defenses, destroyed the bridge leading from Austria to Italy, and the Italians are eagerly surrendering. Miracles and wonders! And on the Russian front, how many miracles and wonders are occurring there! Who would have expected[168] the comrades not only to hold out but to push the enemy back? There is good news from there as well: the Russians are advancing, and the enemy is in retreat! Miracles and wonders!

The leader of the Amalekites is now seen by all as a liar and empty braggart! Two years ago, he predicted that the remnants of the Russian army would soon be destroyed and that the Bolsheviks would never again raise their heads! He bragged that a German army that had marched across eastern Europe would easily cross the last ten or twelve kilometers to Leningrad. About Stalingrad he claimed the city was already in his hands and that the part that remained unoccupied was insignificant and did not interest him. In haughty language he boasted that German soldiers would never surrender or retreat. He told endless lies, and now he has gone silent! The war has passed its fourth anniversary, and we are also past the opening day of "Winter Aid" events, on which he habitually rattles off an empty speech for his minions. But now he is mute and has nothing to say, like the dog that didn't bark. It seems his cronies are advising him not to speak. "The front will speak!" Come summer, he promised to strike back: "We will beat the English wherever we meet them." So many lies, which now have come back to haunt him. He probably beats his head against the wall—"Vare! Vare! Where are my legions?"[169]—a historic cry that certainly terrifies him and keeps him awake. May his distress only grow and intensify.

His only victories have come against the Jews. There what he prophesied has nearly come to pass because he acted when he had the power. But even there his prophecy may not be fully realized. This false prophet predicted that all nations would thank him for revealing the source of all their troubles—the Jews—and for destroying them. But he has not destroyed all: a remnant survives, and when the time comes, we will avenge the blood of our brothers who were executed for no sin. And even if deep inside the nations are glad he has solved their "Jewish problem," they did not openly join the murderer and did not thank him. Just the opposite: his crimes are the justification for their aerial raids, which have caused innumerable casualties among old people, women, and children. They cannot accuse the Allies of barbarism and cruelty after their own boundless cruelties, such as the Telšiai partisans smashing the heads of Jewish babies against tree trunks, etc.

If our situation were more secure; if rumors from the Vilnius ghetto[170] were not terrifying us; if extinction did not hover over our heads day and night, we would be rejoicing openly to see revenge and retribution.[171] The defeats in Russia and Africa, the aerial attacks, the defeat in Sicily; all these fill our souls with joy, a sign that their defeat in western Europe will be total. Finally, a second front! Finally, a light in our darkness, showing a way out of our misery. Let us hope! Let us hope!

9 September

Such news! Such news! It opens new horizons and fills the soul with pleasant hopes. Italy has surrendered! It is handing its arms and its navy over to the Allies. England and America can now deploy their airplanes and ships in the

Mediterranean and use their armies on other fronts. Hungary too will likely quit the battlefield; the Balkans, Yugoslavia, and eventually all of Europe will shake off German oppression and break their grip. Redemption nears—we can hope to be free from our imprisonment in the ghetto by the new calendar year. Who could contain their joy? Living to see salvation who would not go crazy with happiness? Let us hope! Let us wait!

11 September

The Germans are raining sulfur and salt[172] on the [Italian] turncoats! They overran several strategic locations in Italy. Amazing: Their fierceness and resilience are boundless, enabling them to put on hold, at least temporarily, the Allies' hopes to occupy Italy. The Germans claim to have reinforced and plugged all the weak points and breaches. One hopes they will fall soon. But they have succeeded in postponing victory and peace, probably for a long time. A pity!

The bread mixed with straw and hay, the lack of healthy and digestible food, the crowding, the filth, the moral anguish, the endless edicts, the battles against fleas, cockroaches, and bedbugs, etc., are eroding the ghetto population's health. Pulmonary tuberculosis and other lung diseases have multiplied. A rising number of young men and women have high fevers at night with no clear anatomic basis. It could be latent or hidden tuberculosis. It could be that some imbalance in the bodily system is causing fevers to rise, or the ill effects of hard labor are suppressing normal physical development in young people. I too have been quite sick lately: my old stomach and intestinal ailments reached a new peak, and my condition is critical. But how strong is the desire to live! In this historic moment full of critical events, we so wish to see the outcome of the "battle of the titans," the battle that caused the destruction of a third of our people. We want to see them avenged and witness the start of a new life. For all the Germans' bravery and stamina we expect their defeat will come soon. In Russia their troubles have multiplied. They are retreating along the entire front, particularly in the south. They have completely pulled back from the Donetsk region, the storehouse of coal. The Russians have retaken Mariupol,[173] and soon the Crimean Peninsula will be in danger. It is believed that they will retreat to the Dnieper,[174] where they will retrench. And in the north they will pull back to Lithuania, putting us in great danger as they will vent their fury on us.[175]

Hitler finally spoke yesterday,[176] though his speech was not like in times past[177]—much shorter, lasting only fifteen minutes instead of the usual two hours. His style was also unusual, lacking the normal hysterical screams and malicious tone, and he did not mention the Jews. Instead, there was sorrow and sighing[178] about the treasonous Italians, and his hope that God will intervene. May that indeed happen!

18 September

I have refrained from writing, anticipating decisive events after the capitulation in Italy. When they did not materialize I decided to wait until there was a significant change in the situation. Now there have been developments, sadly not decisive, but still important enough to merit recording.

First, Mussolini has been freed. The Germans showed exceptional initiative and daring. A platoon of heroes flew to Mussolini's jail in the Italian mountains. They frightened the cowardly, treasonous Italian guards who were under orders to kill Mussolini if there was any attempt to free him, and managed to get him to a safe place. This was a risky, complicated adventure, and the Germans now brag about it as a major victory. The Allies, who were planning to make a big propaganda show of moving him to America, were thwarted and badly let down. The English radio reportedly tried to offset this by saying that "the Germans have Mussolini, and we have the Italian fleet." Indeed the English have taken more than one hundred pieces of Italy's navy. And Mussolini is noisily issuing proclamations and orders, which will certainly be worth as much as Jonah's vine[179] because the Germans will not be able to hold Italy forever nor shelter a pretend ruler who has no subjects.

More important was the second development, which could have been disastrous for the American Fifth Army. This army did not properly assess the strength of the German units fortified in Salerno, and when they landed on the beach there, they fell into the fangs of lions,[180] an ambush that nearly wiped them out. The Germans bragged that the American Fifth Army was fighting for its life and would soon be annihilated; its only hope, the English Eighth Army was two hundred kilometers away. And then suddenly, a miracle happened: Montgomery's army found a pass through the mountains and rushed to the Americans' rescue. The Germans' defeat was total: attacked from both sea and land, they retreated to northern Italy, where their main forces are concentrated. That is where the decisive battle will certainly take place, determining the final outcome.

The Russian front is also putting hope in our hearts. The Russian attacks are astonishing, their energy outstanding. They are advancing and the Germans are pulling back in turmoil. The Russians are proving to be excellent students, learning from their enemy. Like Peter the Great[181] who learned strategy and maneuvers from the Swedish generals he captured, they too have absorbed their lessons and are using them against their German tutors. They are trying to achieve significant results before the coming autumn rains turn the battlefield into a swamp. These events are significant, and no one can predict their impact.

On the Jewish front, where the Germans have achieved their biggest victories, the last few days were relatively quiet until yesterday, when the ghetto was shaken to the core, leaving residents confused and fearful. Yesterday a German major[182] showed up and said he is now the ghetto commandant, in charge of all matters here from now on. He also said big changes are coming, which made us all very anxious since any changes will surely be to our disadvantage. And today the commandant returned and announced that the "higher-ups" demand the following:

First, groups of Jews may continue to work in only about five places in town. Individual employment in the city is terminated. This means my work in the polyclinic is over, a major disaster! I did not foresee this and cannot predict its consequences. My ability to obtain food and earn a little money will be lost, with no chance of returning. (Until redemption comes—but what strength do I have, that I should endure?[183] If we do not see help soon, I will not live to see redemption.) Worst of all is the "*kasernirung*," the decree putting us all into barracks. The new workplaces will be tent camps, surrounded by barbed wire, and workers will live there with their families, one hundred to a tent, with two- and three-tiered bunks. There was immense confusion in the ghetto about this order, similar to the time of deportations to the "synagogues" which proved to be way stations to the valleys of slaughter.

Imaginations ran wild: Most ghetto residents decided the commandant meant to divide us into groups and to kill all those who don't perish from exhaustion in the camps, although the commandant said there would be no shooting or killing for now. The order has left ghetto residents walking around like shadows, desperate and fearful. People's faces literally darkened, and a terrible desperation engulfed us all. Our miseries are still not enough for the villains, who are constantly devising new ways to embitter our lives. This new order is completely unnecessary as we have already become their slaves, doing all we are told without protest or resistance, even the hard and dangerous work that has already produced many casualties among us.

21 September

A bit of relief. The commandant issued temporary permits, allowing several of the city workplaces to remain open. These are for those who work directly with the German army, but we assume that it means he has some discretion about the details of this decree and that he may be persuaded to make some concessions. For now however, he reportedly demands that five hundred souls be sent to the aerodrome, where they will be housed in tents with thin walls and no heat. He wants this done by Thursday [September 23] even though the aerodrome's director says the tents are not yet ready. Regarding the physicians who work in the city as lab technicians, Dr. Jasaitis is making efforts on our behalf. He was supposed to receive an answer from the commandant today by 5:00 p.m. The prospects are doubtful; I have already given up hope. Dr. Wolpert and Dr. Feinberg have the heads of their institutions pleading for them, but I have no such "chief" to advocate for me. So I am giving up. I will probably stay in the ghetto and become director of the ambulatory service. Perhaps this will even help my health to improve, as the X-ray machine [in the city lab] poisoned my blood.

24 September

Yesterday 387 people were taken to the aerodrome. Their faces were white, their eyes tearful. There was loud moaning, quiet sighing, sadness, and desperate fear as they were forcibly taken away. Some fainted, some became hysterical, and some escaped and hid with farmers they knew. A platoon of armed Germans soldiers stood on the hill facing the ghetto, terrifying those waiting by the gate. The forced recruits left amid great confusion. Today's rumor mill says that their housing, food, and work conditions are all quite comfortable! Perhaps their situation will be as enviable as that of those sent to Latvia, who found a "delightful country"(!)[184] where the Germans treat workers with more kindness than do our brutal civilians.

For the doctors who work in the city as lab technicians, things are moving slowly. Dr. Jasaitis pressed the commandant to let us continue our work in the city, and at last he succeeded somewhat: our council met with him and told us the commandant agreed to give us temporary permits until the new camps need doctors. This was an enormous relief: It is essential these days to be able to spend a large part of the day in the city instead of the overcrowded ghetto, where anything can happen. The work itself is a barrier against deportation to the camps or joining the ranks of the unemployed, whose fate is uncertain. Finally the connection with the city provides food, either as gifts from patients or by purchase, and, importantly, a salary.

Suddenly the sun set on our joy![185] Some said the permits would extend only until the end of the month! Meaning that in just a few days we, too, will be barred from town. So all was in vain! When I tried to thank Jasaitis for his efforts, he pretended to be surprised and declined to shake my hand because the commandant had not given him a clear answer about the permits. When he learned that the council had given us good news, he was very pleased, but how disappointed will he be when he learns it is <u>only temporary</u>. It is possible that this announcement will hurt us if it discourages Jasaitis from further pleading on our behalf when he really needs to increase his efforts. Interestingly, some priests approached Jasaitis urging him to plead for the Jews, and wished him luck, even sprinkling him with "holy water" to bless his efforts.

Today the commandant was supposed to show up in my X-ray clinic, to have his stomach checked. They say he suffers from an ulcerated duodenum. Dr. Peisachowitz and I set aside an entire hour for him, but he did not appear. We were told later that he had traveled to Kuršėnai. He will surely come tomorrow.

Erev Rosh Hashana 5704[186]

The Days of Awe! But not the awe of heaven: Our fear and terror come from the commandant. Ghetto dwellers dash about madly like poisoned mice, void of sense.[187] The "camps" and the fate of those left in the ghetto drive us to despair. The commandant ordered people sent with their families to five camps: Linkaučiai, the aerodrome, Pavenčiai, Daugėliai, and Akmenė. They also increased the workforce at the Frenkel and Batas factories. We are being given some degree of choice: One can name a preferred camp. But then the obvious question arises: Which camp to choose? What kind of work is performed in this one or that one? What is the food like? What sort of supervision? Who faces more danger: those who stay in the ghetto or those who leave for the camps? Most ghetto residents tend to think the camps offer some protection against bigger troubles. Many invalids and children will be left in the ghetto and their fate is very much in doubt. They are more likely to be wiped out. On the other hand, the move into the barracks—what the Germans call "kasernirung"—our confinement to the ghetto with strict limits on going into town—all these happened because the front is getting closer. The commandant told Dr. Peisachowitz in circular terms that an order came from "above" to bar Jews from the city because "you are not our allies." What he meant was that the Jews are the Germans' enemy; they are likely to engage in espionage and incitement when the front is near, so "let us deal shrewdly with them."

The commandant promised that for now nothing bad will happen, but he must carry out his superiors' orders. The problem is that he is carrying out those orders to the letter, 100 percent. One may conclude that if he receives an order to exterminate us he will not hesitate to carry it out. And if the main motivation is the approaching front and the suspicions associated with it, it is possible that those in the villages and countryside will face trouble sooner than ghetto residents, who are under stricter supervision.

Notably, many of the more skittish people fled the ghetto for the villages to hide among the peasants they know. Refugees from Telšiai were particularly inclined to do so, having already had some experience with this. When they fled Telšiai they hid in peasants' homes and now want to do so again. The [Jewish] ghetto police are watching them carefully. An extensive escape might cause big problems, raising suspicion, reducing the number of workers, and causing disorder in the ghetto.

Yesterday the commandant himself appeared in my X-ray clinic at the invitation of Dr. Peisachowitz.[188] We both examined him, but my role was secondary because Dr. Peisachowitz is his primary physician. After talking to him for a while, I left them alone. Among other things, he talked about the front, as I mentioned. Before I left, he said "thank you," but did not offer his hand, because the foolish Dr. P. had not introduced us. The impression he left was completely unexceptional: a skinny German, slightly bent, with an ordinary face not particularly repulsive or coarse, suggesting he is not a fool. "We are not thieves," he said.

It appears that tomorrow will be my last day in town. The directors of the polyclinic were quite upset that I will no longer be able work there. For now there is no one to replace me, an experienced radiologist who can also examine a stomach. Moreover, my work is cheap: I slave like a Canaanite[189] for 4 marks and 40 pfennigs per day, providing an income for the German labor police. In short, stopping me from working will cause them a financial loss since they will have to pay a regular salary to my Lithuanian replacement if they can find one. Therefore, they decided to ask the commandant to let me continue my work. I am sure it will be in vain. The dental lab submitted a similar request and the commandant either never noticed or did not receive it.

Second Day Rosh Hashanah[190]

An ordinary day for our tormentors. A business day. And I am confined to the ghetto since the prohibition on going to town was published yesterday. All those who were not sent to the camps or do not work in the Frenkel or Batas factories are trapped like mice in the ghetto. What will happen to the elderly, the sick, and the children? The last brigades were sent yesterday to the lime quarries in Akmenė. Piles of belongings are accumulating in the streets: pillows, duvets, beddings, and clothes. Of course, furniture, kitchen utensils, and heavier items were left in the abandoned apartments, and those will be occupied by people from the Kaukazas ghetto, which will be eliminated soon. So much Jewish property wasted! All the fruits of our labor that we had managed to bring into the ghetto, and now most of it will be lost. And what troubles await us here? One "communal pot" for everyone, healthy and sick; no more traveling back and forth to the city and thus no chance to bring in extra food. Hunger and scarcity for all. And what will become of those unable to work, and of the children? Those leaving the ghetto know not what awaits them, and those left behind know even less.

It is hard to describe the mood: Dark faces reflect terrible inner turmoil. In the eyes you can actually see the fear of death, immeasurable confusion and desperation. This is not poetry and no exaggeration! My pen lacks the strength and talent to properly describe our feelings. My head spins and my strength is gone because of my old intestinal disease, which afflicts me terribly. I write as much as I am physically able because I want to leave behind some memory, even a vague one of our experience. Inside, a hope still flickers that we will live to see our redemption. If so our joy will be enhanced by the memory of our days of wretched poverty[191] because no nation on earth can match us for resilience and endurance. When these sad pages are read, hearts will swell in wonderment at a nation whose remnants carried on, quietly bearing the anguish and distress that came upon them.[192] But when will redemption arrive? The news suggests the war is nearly over: The Russians are advancing along the front, capturing important sites (Poltava, Chernigov, Smolensk, etc.).[193] The uprising in Yugoslavia[194] seems to be growing. Italy is in chaos: the English and Americans have concentrated their forces there and will certainly deal the Germans a decisive blow. All these signal the beginning of redemption. But when will it finally arrive? The Germans are retreating to spare their army, to concentrate on defending their own borders with all their might, possibly to achieve better terms at the time of their surrender, which may be delayed but will certainly come.[195]

In the city, the X-ray clinic has closed. This will be costly and disruptive to the polyclinic and shows how they must kowtow to the Germans in their supposedly independent country, particularly regarding the Jews. Jasaitis promised me he would go to the commandant in person to ask that I be escorted to the city under armed supervision at the polyclinic's expense. I am sure his pleading will be in vain, given the suspicions about espionage and sabotage by the Jews. I think Jasaitis sent his deputy Bazaras again. Interestingly, the commandant told Bazaras when they met the last time that he knew me "very well." Indeed since Peisachowitz and I examined him, maybe some good will come of it. We shall see how the matter turns out.[196] Although it was scandalous that P., the fool, did not introduce me to the commandant when he entered the X-ray clinic.

A definitive response: the commandant says no Jewish doctor will be permitted in the city. "Finita la commedia!"[197]

Simchat Torah 5704 [October 22, 1943]

Since the commandant banned me from working in town, I have been confined to the ghetto, working only as director of the ambulatory clinic. I felt better at first, thanks to the respite from work and from the X-ray device that was damaging my health, but then, possibly due to carelessness in my nutrition, the condition of my stomach and intestines worsened significantly, and in recent days, my condition turned critical. After eating some unminced chicken meat I was hit with actual cholera: endless diarrhea, vomiting, lack of appetite, pain in the legs, debilitating weakness. I spent several days in bed like a genuinely sick man, and therefore did not write anything—but events have occurred that move us to the core and demand to be recorded. So despite my wretched health due to living conditions in the ghetto, I cannot remain silent. These things need to be remembered:

(a.) The death of Žemaitiškis.[198] A young man of 28, upright[199] but lazy, whose speculator sisters nagged him constantly. At their insistence, he stood for hours by the barbed-wire fence, buying various things from the peasants for his sisters to resell. Looking for a way to get out of this "forced labor," he pretended to be sick. Once he complained about a stomach ailment, another time about his gallbladder, another about angina, and so on. He thus spent months without working, although the doctors considered him a hypochondriac. When the last brigade of workers went to the Akmenė lime quarries about two weeks ago, Žemaitiškis was registered among them. The day before their departure I was called and found him complaining of stomach pain. I prescribed some medications and reprimanded him for not working. The next day the ghetto police called me to see him again. When I arrived I found Dr. Peisachowitz there, who said he could find no reason to excuse him from the work at Akmenė. I concurred. The ghetto police, my son among them, got him dressed and dragged him to the truck, where the commandant saw him, and likely concluded that this young man was a slacker and a "simulant."[200] The commandant accompanied the convoy to Akmenė. There he approached the young man who was lying down and asked "Will you get up?" Žemaitiškis answered "I will not." After a while the commandant approached him again and asked "Do you intend to work?" The young man answered, "I will not." Without hesitating, the commandant pulled out his pistol, pressed it to the young man's temple and fired: one, two, three! What had been a young man full of hopes and emotions was now a lifeless corpse! And the commandant, behaving as if he had just killed a flea, turned away and continued giving orders to the camp. This is how Jewish life is valued now. No law and no judge!

Yes, the young man had been impertinent, but shot to death? What for? This death is even more of a shock than was Mazovetsky's hanging. There at least the decision supposedly followed some deliberation, and there were preparations and procedures. Here a man's soul just flew away like chaff whirled away from the threshing floor.[201] The commandant, who had already beaten many people including a young girl, for no reason at all, thus demonstrated his noble character: This crude, ignorant sergeant-major, a vicious Jew-hater who rose from secret-police clerk to prominence as a "bloodhound" and spy. Another version of this story claims that between his first and second questions, the commandant ordered that the young man be given twenty lashes, which does not increase or diminish his cruelty. The young man did not reply impertinently;[202] he just remained lying down and then our commandant and the "hangman from Dachau"[203] began beating him brutally, and then shot him.

(b.) The death of Kushelevsky.[204] A husband with his wife and two daughters chose to avoid the dangers of the ghetto and settled in Daugėliai, the camp where they labor at mortar and bricks.[205] An expert trader and smuggler, he continued practicing his trade in the camp and was going around the villages in his free time, bartering and "schnorring"—begging—for food. Last Sunday they conducted a hunt for [anti-German] partisans in the forests and prohibited those in the camp from leaving. Kushelevsky, either deliberately or by mistake, got out through a hole in the barbed wire that surrounds the camp and was heading for a nearby village when a Ukrainian guard shot him in the leg, seriously wounding him. His screaming attracted the attention of the camp commandant[206] who came and ended his suffering with a bullet. So died a husband and father who had never been content with his lot in life. In an earlier time he might have become an immensely rich miser; here he was reduced to petty wheeling and dealing, and he finally fell victim to his need to accumulate wealth. In fact he died not because he committed a trivial sin, which merited a trivial punishment, but because he was a Jew.

(c.) I could tell a long story about the adventures of all those who fled the ghetto based on rumors of what might happen to those who stay; how they left dwellings where they were settled, abandoning furniture and other belongings; the terrible torments they suffered in the camps; cold dirt floors, drafty tents, etc. Even now there are rumors of new camps, and the closing of the one at Bačiūnai. The new camp they are now planning will drain the ghetto of those who can still work, leaving behind only the elderly, sick, and young children. Their fate is worrisome and frightening.

(d.) The Allies' ministers are meeting right now in Moscow, aiming to speed the war's end and planning for the second front. But England and America are dragging their feet. They have been slogging through Italy for three months, and their preparations are taking forever. Maybe now they will move faster. The German leaders also held a conference, reportedly because of their army's worsening situation on the eastern front. The Russians broke through between Kremenchuk and Dnipropetrovsk,[207] opening a wide section in the front and surrounding an entire German army. If they do not escape, their defeat at Stalingrad will look like a pale shadow of this catastrophe. It is possible that soon, very soon, there will be decisive news. Our endurance is waning; there is no strength left to wait!

8 November

Vengeance like this, for the blood of a child, Satan has yet to devise....[208]

A deathly silence has descended on the ghetto. Not a person can be heard in the street, only mourning and moaning[209] from every direction. Terror and desperation, bereavement and loss spread their black wings over the entire population, like dreadful birds of prey, piercing our chests and tearing out our hearts. Rachel is weeping for her children; mothers cry for their babies, torn away from them and now gone. Has such a thing ever been heard of? Has anything like this ever happened?[210] They snatched children up to age thirteen from their parents' arms and loaded them like freight onto waiting trucks; when these were filled, they carried their cargo to the station. The heart is torn to pieces; we have no tears left to shed. Muffled wails carry through the air, and there is no more strength to live and suffer; life has become meaningless.

That our persecutors would do such a terrible thing must mean that we, too, are doomed. It is unimaginable that living people could be treated like this; only if we are about to die could they no longer care how this affects us. If they intended to keep us alive, they would not embitter our lives so terribly and indelibly. They took our bright, shining children and sent them away—to where? The blood freezes, the hair stands on end. Alas, what has happened to us! What has happened to us![211] Our eyes are swollen from crying and our nerves are paralyzed. It must be that in their eyes we are already dead; thus, they can torture us at will. Indeed, the hour of doom approaches,[212] the last chapter! The mouth of oblivion[213] is open and ready to swallow us. My memoirs, my notes, on which I have labored all the days of my confinement in the ghetto—they too will be lost, never to realize their purpose. Soon, very soon, even our own place will no longer know us![214] They will have no more need of us; for our labor only are they keeping us alive a little longer. As the front comes nearer and they have to retreat, they will certainly eliminate us.

We should have all died on that bitter and terrible day, November 5! How many horrors came upon us that day!

(a.) Pogroms. The Ukrainians, who are experienced at pogroms, broke into houses, shattered glasses and mirrors, dishes and bottles, tore suitcases, trampled boxes, and caused unimaginable destruction. The reasons: to create terror because they enjoy hurting Jews, and to find gold, jewels, watches, chains, coins, etc.

(b.) Robbery and violence.[215] They destroyed, terrorized, and battered us; lied that they would spare us; then took all the jewelry, silver, and other valuables with threats and beatings. Some gave up their goods willingly, hoping to save themselves and their children. But these murderers were merely doing the Germans' bidding, not acting on their own. They only pretended to be able to save those about to die.

(c.) Horror and bitter death.[216] We were thrown out of our houses and from the ambulatory and sent outside the gate. We were certain we were about to be taken away to our demise. Twice we were sent out of the ambulatory, and twice we returned. The third time they sent us to the hill outside the gate, where the entire ghetto population was waiting. We stood and waited, not knowing what was coming. We hoped it was to separate those capable of work from the handicapped, the active ones from the idle, but we were wrong. After a while they said they would send us back home within an hour. We waited! And suddenly a large company of soldiers arrived, all Ukrainians, and surrounded the crowd on the slope. We thought a mass shooting was about to start, but again we were wrong; they sent us home. We returned to find our homes emptied of what had remained of our valuables. We had nothing! And there are no words to describe the destruction: Fragments of dishes, shards of glass, pieces of mirrors, tables and chairs overturned, scraps of food—total chaos. And the young children—we could not find them. They were taken along with our souls and hearts, leaving us behind, trampled corpses.[217]

(d.) How Dr. Rozovsky,[218] the eldest of our colleagues, was ensnared in their traps[219] is a story by itself. A short, slender man, he was weak from illness and his face was drawn thin, like that of an elderly invalid. When we were ejected from the ambulatory the second time (after the Ukrainians did it first, the Germans brought us back, supposedly because there was work to do) Germans stood by the door. One of them noticed Dr. Rozovsky's thin face and short stature and called him over. They took him, and also the father of Dr. Fein-Getz, to the truck. Members of the council pleaded with the commandant, saying Dr. Rozovsky was the ghetto's best-loved doctor. The commandant replied, maliciously and deceitfully: "If he is such a nice doctor, we need him for the children!" I also said he was a physician, but nobody paid attention to me.

Who was Dr. Rozovsky? An honest man, an angel. Someone who would never harm a fly, a moral giant, dear and rare with deep national feelings, a uniquely gentle character. He had not an enemy in the world and was beloved by all who met him. He read voraciously, devouring classic literature. Fluent in Russian, he knew its writers well. Blessed with talent, he wrote beautiful poems in Russian and Yiddish and successfully translated some of Krylov's[220] fables into Yiddish. He even read Hebrew, though he did not write in it. Because his interest in literature exceeded his interest in medical writing he was not a particularly outstanding doctor, but he was experienced, attentive to his patients and fully dedicated to his work if always fearful. (His shortcoming was that he lacked courage, was not confident in his own abilities, and was unfamiliar with modern medicine.)

His most notable gift was musical talent. He came from a musical family: his nephew served as cantor in Riga. He excelled in his emotional singing and had an amazing musical memory. We would often hear a tune on the radio and wonder who composed it. He usually knew the answer. Indeed, he was a loyal friend, honest, intelligent, musical—and he is gone. Dear friend, how long will it be before I follow you to the grave? You were always so hungry for knowledge, so eager to learn the latest news. Days of vengeance and retribution are coming that we will not be here to witness. Happy the one who lives to see better times, but we are doomed. The hangman from Dachau will unleash his viper-wrath on us. And my writings, what will become of them? My notebook's pages will be used to wrap herrings and peppers. The thread of my life will be cut before I can record even half my memories.

Our son is trying to escape. If he manages to get away and save himself, I will go to my grave with greater peace of mind.[221]

12 November

On the ninth of this month, our modern Haman gave a big speech at the famous Munich cellar[222] to mark the twentieth anniversary of the Nazi Party. Such courage! Such hope for the future! Such pride and faith in the strength of the German nation! Does he really expect victory after all his defeats? Was he only trying to bolster his people's spirits? Nevertheless, his proud and confident talk shook us to the heart, and his words are like sword thrusts. Not a trace of fear, desperation or hesitation. Everything is clear with no uncertainty and boundless confidence! He even allowed himself to joke!

Along with Dr. Rozovsky, they also deported Rabbi Rubinshtein,[223] a sage and scholar of early Jewish law. Aside from his wisdom and vast knowledge of talmudic and rabbinic literature shown in the books he authored, he was preeminent among ten thousand[224] in his gentle demeanor and excellent character. His face radiated nobility and his countenance projected wisdom and knowledge. Also our neighbor Luria, still a strong man despite his hunched back, was taken along with his sick wife. He was a man blessed with a good mind and extensive knowledge. And Huna Rudnick, who suffered from "Liddle" disease[225] but had managed to finish gymnasium—he was said to have composed beautiful poems in Hebrew. Some two hundred elderly, sick, and handicapped people were deported, more than six hundred children stolen.[226] Among them was Maikele, the son of our tenant, an outstanding boy blessed with wisdom and musical talent. So many tears have we shed for him! I can

still see him, three years old, coatless on a cold day, shivering to his bones in
the chill, astonishment and fear in his black eyes as he walked quietly with the
Ukrainian to the truck. My gullible wife, like many others, thought she could
save the child with a bribe and offered them all the precious things she had in
the days of old[227]—our entire fortune, which I had hoped would help get us to
the land of our ancestors after the war. All is lost, our hope has evaporated, and
our lives hang by a thread day to day.

The chaos and panic in the ghetto are indescribable. Every mind is preoccupied with finding a way to flee the ghetto. The entire population has concluded
that if the Germans could do such a thing to us they must consider us already
dead; and that the hatred we feel, the desire for revenge that fills the minds of
fathers whose children were stolen from them, will go with us to our graves.
Yet those who witnessed these horrors could fill an entire book with wailing
and bitter weeping.

21 November

There is no strength left to continue living and suffering. Our condition worsened terribly at the start of the commandant's rule. But since our children were
kidnapped, each day is more accursed than the last, and our lives hang by a
thread. Who can describe the mood in the ghetto, where the loss of children
and widowhood are ever present, and the fear of death hovers over us? Dr. W.T.'s
attempt to escape the ghetto with his homely wife became a tragicomedy: two
days they hid in a bed, two more days in a cellar, and one day in the attic of a
barn, and the people who promised to come take them did not show up. All
my Christian friends from the old days are now unreliable. And Dr. L[untz]'s
escape attempt ended in tragedy: he and his family are now in prison, and who
knows when they will be released? The commandant is enraged because he
was not told that a doctor was missing from the hospital. What this means is
unclear.[228]

And I have been given a sad and sorrowful job. As director of the ambulatory I have to decide when people may be excused from work. Everyone in the
ghetto is tired and weak, tortured and depressed: skin diseases, abscesses, and
disabling foot injuries are frighteningly common. Half the population does not
have the energy to work. But the oppressor demands workers, so we must be
strict about issuing sick passes, which causes complaints, anger, and heartache.

Unexpected changes! In the morning I complained about being in charge
of distributing "sick passes" to workers, and by noon there was a change. The
new head of the labor office—a German Jew, [Georg] Pariser,[229] whom the
commandant likes—and his advisor, [Shmuel] Burgin, decided to appoint

Dr. Burstein, from the Memel district, also a German Jew, as head of the ambulatory. So I am rid of a responsibility that had taken up a significant amount of my time—this too is for the best.[230] On the other hand, I was appointed a physician in the ghetto hospital. What will I do there, particularly since the number of patients is diminishing? It will be a miracle if the commandant approves this new appointment. On his first visit he will ask, "What is this old man doing in the hospital?" Yes, I have grown old! I face the danger of deportation myself. I don't yet look like poor Rozovsky, but my age is dangerous. My position was solid as long as I was director of the ambulatory, but now I will be a redundant old doctor. Moreover, my wife has a fictitious position as cleaning supervisor; since she is unable to scrub floors and so on, the nurses agreed to do her work for her. As head of the ambulatory I could cover for her, but now what will be her fate? She also is very ill: her heart is dangerously weak. Not only for working; even a simple walk is hard for her. We will see how things turn out! The mood is depressing, but our troubles are a bit less acute.

I should mention one detail, which shocks the soul to its foundations. On the day of wrath[231] when our children and elders were abducted, some of our representatives asked where they were being taken. The hangman from Dachau replied: "If you want to know, you are welcome to join them." In fact, willingly or not, they did go. Maybe they were forced. More than two weeks have passed and we have heard not a word about them. How upsetting this is! How terrible are the thoughts that cross our minds! The victims are Katz and Kartun.[232] The first, a young man of great talent, blessed with a good mind and an agile tongue; the second, an honest old man, socially conscious and inclined to public service. What a pity! Woe for those lost who are no more![233]

27 November

Three weeks have passed since that terrible day when our children were stolen and our elders and ill ones kidnapped. There are no words to describe our terrible mood. Terrible bereavement and loss! "Let the mother go and take only the young":[234] the Torah taught us thousands of years ago that it was wrong to take chicks from a nest in a mother bird's presence, and these are only birds. And yet here they snatched babies from the arms of a fainting mother, beating her for good measure and the next day sent her to hard labor. So much cruelty, meanness, audacity! Words cannot describe our grief. We have been on the precipice since the day we fell into the hands of the commandant and our lives have become worthless. Each day is worse than the last, and events add to our torment daily. Dr. Luntz, who almost lost his mind from all that befell him, tried to escape the ghetto with his wife and mother-in-law. But someone informed the authorities, and he is now in jail. He is badly missed in the hospital, where he worked as an obstetrician and surgeon.[235] How much has he endured, beginning with the seizure of his lovely home by the Bolsheviks. What an ordeal he went through for this house, "the strife and contention" ending in a court battle with Dr. Goldberg. The loss of his home and property,[236] his dismissal from the hospital during the Bolshevik days, all the horrors under the Germans and finally the loss of his beautiful daughter: it is no wonder that he almost lost his mind and tried to escape to save his soul. They say the peasant who had sheltered him informed to get the things he had brought along. And now he and his wife are in prison! Who knows what will become of them?

Then came the matter of Dr. Feinberg. The German "orderly" assigned to spy on the doctors told the commandant he saw him speak to a Christian woman on his walk to the hospital. They detained the woman, who told them Dr. Feinberg spoke to her about butter and eggs. In fact he had asked that lady if she could hide him in case of danger, and Feinberg thought she had revealed that to the secret police. So when he was summoned to the commandant, he behaved clownishly, like a foolish baby. In front of the commandant, he asked Leibovich[237] in Russian, "Should I tell the truth?" He then proceeded to recount his entire conversation with the woman, including asking her to hide him if there was danger. The commandant sentenced him to work as a common laborer and to be whipped. Feinberg tried to whip himself in the presence of the Jewish policemen, and it turned into a real tragicomedy. This served to further expose the doctors to scorn and derision,[238] and people in the ghetto amused themselves imitating Dr. Feinberg trying to flog himself. In the end, of course, he did receive a whipping.

1 December

Today some who had tried to escape the ghetto were brought back as prisoners in chains. Among them was the former policeman Rayz[239] and his wife. This looks bad. Rumors say that last night Jews from the Kaunas ghetto were transported through the [Šiauliai] train station. We are overcome by fear. There is no escape, no shelter. And silence further darkens the mood in the ghetto: absent is the joy[240] of our children. They are gone, the lovely, bright ones, taken never to be returned, while their bereft and desolate[241] mothers break their bodies at hard labor. A first group left yesterday for a new camp on the [Šiauliai] exhibition grounds.[242] And my wife, what will become of her? She is a total invalid, irreparably. Her heart has declared a sabbatical, and that's all! Worrying about her keeps me awake at night.

I too have suffered a defeat: Dr. Rosenthal received permission to go back and forth from the ghetto to the hospital without an escort, but I have not. The commandant does not want to issue many such permits, and Burgin decided to reserve one for the young Rosenthal, who when necessary can walk to the hospital faster than me.

10 December

Some aspects of our accursed lives will never be erased and can scarcely be believed: How civilized people with high moral principles descended so far that we have now become destroyers and murderers. The edict prohibiting births in the ghetto still stands. And despite the danger that such incidents pose for the entire ghetto, several deliveries did occur: normal, living babies were born, to women who refused to terminate their pregnancies in time.[243] We the physicians are required to put healthy, living children to death (!) to prevent the annihilation of the whole ghetto.[244]

We carry out this repulsive mission by injecting them with powerful toxins. The life it fell to me to end was a phenomenon without precedent in the medical literature. The child survived without food, without a drop of water or milk for seven days! Dr. Burstein and I administered injections of morphine and heroin, in quantities sufficient to kill several adults! How tenacious is life! How powerfully does it resist all attempts to cut it short in its first days! I would never have believed that an infant, barely arrived in this world, would cling to life so powerfully. Nothing in the medical literature describes or explains it. After all, who would starve a child for seven or eight days? After injecting morphine and scopolamine, on the seventh day they injected him with heroin, and he expired. Thus they forced us to act as angels of death, as murderers. We have generally hardened our hearts and turned cruel to an extent we never expected. We hardly even notice the suffering of animals. A few days ago my son bought a chicken and took it to the *shochet*[245] to be slaughtered. The shochet was not in the ghetto so we decided to decapitate the poor chicken ourselves. I put its neck on the doorstep, and my son took an ax, but he hit in such a slow and clumsy manner that the chicken remained alive and screamed in a horrifying voice. Shaken, we finished the cruel deed and ended the chicken's life. But it is awfully hard to forget the poor chicken's tremors and palpitations after the first unsuccessful blow. To what depths of cruelty have our terrible conditions brought us!

Then there are the "banging" or "magic" tables. These illusionists' tricks have captivated the whole ghetto, and everybody is holding "séances." Night after night people gather around tables and ask them various questions, attempt to communicate with the dead and even try to foretell the future. Many truly believe in this hoax and find solace in the answers the tables supposedly give—about the stolen children, the end of the war and so on. Such foolishness arises from the desire to find some solace in these bad times. As the Russians say, "Let the child play with whatever he wants as long as he does not cry."

Fall has arrived and the rainy days have begun, turning the battlefield into mud and sludge. Heavy snow is falling in some places. The battles and struggles continue on the Russian front. It looks like the Russians are successfully advancing, but slowly, slowly, and there have been no decisive victories. We hear different rumors of new actions, but these are not sufficiently substantiated; we shall see. There was a conference in Cairo and an unusual meeting in Tehran between Stalin, Roosevelt, and Churchill, but the outcome has not been published.[246] We shall wait! A lot of promises. To our disappointment the English and Americans maintain their turtle's pace, moving as if still asleep.

Last days of December '43
Bitter weeping is heard again from the north. At the lime quarries in Akmenė, Rachel is weeping for her children. Last Thursday our commandant visited Akmenė, and on Sunday (December 19) the commandant at the quarries[247] announced that he had been ordered to exterminate all the elderly and children there, more than fifty people. The word was that he was a pleasant man who treated the workers with leniency and tolerance. The dentist Berger was at Akmenė on Sunday, and she says she saw him crying and seeking advice about how to handle this. He obviously cannot defy the order without risking his own life, but he decided to limit the number as much as possible. So he ordered the Jews to prepare a pit, and the Ukrainians murdered eight children[248] and one old woman. No commentary is needed!

31 December
The last day of a year filled with endless torments of body and soul. Our situation became exponentially worse the day we were passed from the district commissioner into the hands of the commandants. We are no longer in a ghetto: our dwelling place is called a "labor camp." Most of the previous ghetto residents are "attached" to one of several other camps: Linkaičiai—manufacturing weapons; Daugėliai—a brick works; Pavenčiai—a sugar factory; Akmenė—lime quarries; or A.B.A.—military clothing. In addition, there are workers in the leather factory (previously owned by Frenkel), the Batas shoe factory, and a brush-making shop. Small groups work in other places. Doctors are prohibited

from working in the city. German soldiers stand at the gate and also accompany those who walk to workshops in town. All the hardships and troubles are nothing compared with the theft of our children, which overwhelmed the ghetto with sorrow. At the end of the year, the question eats at our souls and our flesh: What became of the children taken from us? The popular view is they were deported to Germany, but where? Why? The questions gnaw at our brain, giving us no rest. Thus the year ends with no rays of light. Even the Germans' defeats and the terrible destruction of their cities bring us no comfort. The end is not coming soon.

1 January, 1944

We are in a concentration camp under the control of the commandant and his minions from the SS. There is no room for the elderly and the sick who cannot produce—such people are being eliminated. I am old and my wife is sick. Although I am not idle, and my wife is registered as the supervisor of the cleaning staff, nevertheless, if a miracle does not happen, we can anticipate trouble and suffering this year. But we are expecting a miracle.

The English radio announced that von Papen,[249] the German ambassador to Turkey, offered peace terms: withdrawing from all the occupied countries other than Austria, reconstructing all the destroyed cities, and replacing the supreme source of evil with von Papen himself. This bit of news was announced last, as if it were the least important, but it was accompanied by an interpretation that he must have done it with the knowledge of Germany's leaders and not on his own, or he would have been severely punished. But if that is so, then the English and their allies are no longer dealing with the Nazi Party, which still runs the country. Conclusion: the Germans have begun to think about ending the war. No wonder: The air raids are getting worse and more destructive, and the defeats on the eastern front are also frightening. It is being reported again that the breach in the German line near Zhytomyr[250] is about three hundred kilometers wide, and that the Germans face a much bigger catastrophe there than the one at Stalingrad. May this indeed be so.

The ghetto hospital is near the cemetery in the former Kaukazas ghetto section, which no longer exists. For now, I walk every morning to work with the hospital's lower-ranking staff accompanied by an SS soldier, and there I work until 1:00 p.m. In two weeks, the hospital will move to a new building in the Trakų section, and if I continue to work I will stay there for more of the day. "If I continue," is doubtful: The commandant has already said he thinks there are too many doctors in the hospital.

Fortune has always smiled at me. In my youth I was a famous teacher; I did well on my exams in the gymnasium; I finished university despite various obstacles and made a good living. I obtained my medical degree, worked as a doctor in the south of France, settled as a doctor in Šiauliai, and became director of the internal medicine and infectious disease departments. During the Bolshevik period, I was the director of the polyclinic, and during the German period I managed to work in the city as a lab technician for more than two years, which was a great advantage; and in the ghetto I was the director of the ambulatory. And now, an upheaval! My luck turned the day the ghetto was turned over to the commandants, and I am in danger of becoming redundant. Although my face does not look like that of Dr. Rozovsky, who was caught in the German vise, and I look younger than my real age, still I am old and not well—and fortune has turned its back on me. As the Russian proverb says, "Old age is not a happy time." If the war does not end this year, my wife and I will face troubles. And Goebbels doubts the war will end this year. Let us hope! Let us wait!

Once again a live girl was born in the hospital. The mother came from Joniškis. Jews came there from two camps in Švenčionys and Ashmyany, near Vilnius, to work on a road (or railway) from Lithuania to Latvia. The girl was big and healthy, and the entire ghetto would be endangered had she remained alive, especially since the ambulatory has been overseen by a [German] "orderly," a young soldier who understands medicine the way a rooster understands a prayer book.[251] He signs the work release notes for sick workers, watches out for "simulants" among the patients, and signs death certificates. This young man is a real spy and informer, apparently seeking to please his master, the commandant. Whatever his motives he is dangerous, and his visits in the hospital are frequent. He was planning to inspect the fetus that this woman had ostensibly miscarried, and could have discovered a live child, healthy, fat, and more developed than usual.

So it became necessary. . . to kill the girl and to do this terrible thing soon, before the orderly's visit. The toxic drugs, which could kill an adult, had not produced quick results. The previous child who received several such injections remained alive for seven days without food or liquids. And here it was necessary to kill the child without delay. So we decided . . . to drown her!!! We took a bucket of cold water and put the girl's head in and held her there until there were death convulsions—a total of six minutes, twice the time required to kill an adult by strangling. We removed the girl, her little mouth open, her nostrils filled with foam, and covered her with a blanket. Miraculously, the orderly did not come that morning. So we decided to bury the girl, the officially miscarried fetus. To our astonishment, when the baby was about to be lowered into her grave, she was found to be still alive! It was beyond belief! Day-old infants defy medical theory wondrously, surviving procedures fatal to adults! Indeed, medical research cannot have learned about the efficacy of killing such children by injection, starvation or drowning, for who could study such cases dispassionately, scientifically—cases that "Satan himself has yet to devise" in Bialik's words?

13 January

There is news of the children and elderly who were sent away. A woman was sent to Tauragė to inquire about their fate. The train with the children reached Tauragė on Saturday at 10:00 a.m.[252] There were no men with them: they and the handicapped ones were shot at Požerūnai. The children reached Tauragė with fifty women caretakers. There the Germans shaved them and took them further into Germany,[253] to upper Silesia together with the women and German nurses. About twenty sick children were among them. They were taken with the other children, but the men as I said did not cross the border. If this is so then Rozovsky, Kartun, and Katz have perished! Victims of these times, respected and honorable people: Dr. Rozovsky was a lovely man, a civilized man with good taste, a good friend and honest like no other. How acutely do I feel his loss! We used to meet almost every day, and now suddenly he is gone! And Kartun—a public servant, old and frail, who worked tirelessly for others. And young Katz—one in a thousand, a talented, clear thinker, devoted to the Šiauliai Jewish community. He was a true victim of the ghetto. Indeed "it was our sickness that he was bearing, our suffering that he endured."[254] Alas for those lost who will never be forgotten!

Ghetto tunes. My wife lies on her sick bed, terrified that the German "orderly" will begin checking homes and find her sick without a work-release. She needs a permanent release permit but that is not possible in a concentration camp. Here he who does not work may not eat. My son is ill as well. We suspect it is his left lung again, the same place where he had a dry infection of the pleura last year. He needs to rest in a sanatorium to restore his health—but who in our accursed condition can even dream of such things?

Encouraging news from the southern front: The Russians are advancing and the German position in Crimea is becoming more precarious.

3 February, 44

I have not written anything for a long time. First, there has been no important news while our old troubles continue; and second, my mood is so depressed, my soul so troubled and tired that there is no strength to concentrate and think. We live as in a nightmare, responding mechanically, out of necessity and without motivation. The ghetto conditions have beaten us: The constant fear, anxiety, and malnutrition have brought us to the gates of death. My wife and I are seriously ill and cannot go on in these conditions. We need mental and physical rest in an excellent sanatorium! Will we live to see such a moment? Hard to believe: The enemy's power is vast[255] and the snail's pace of the Americans and the English fill the soul with desperation. The suspicion grows that they intend to wait until their enemy is exhausted, letting others do the job while sparing their own troops.

Today I picked up my pen, not to rehash our troubles which worsen day by day, but to tell of something that happened yesterday. The commandant summoned Dr. Peisachowitz and told him angrily that Dr. Goldberg, his wife and two sons had fled the camp at Daugéliai. He was furious at such a scandal(!). The doctor brought shame on the physicians, who therefore all deserve to be put in chains! Such audacity from our tormentors! Goldberg must have read the speech given by the supreme source of evil a few days ago, which was infused with hatred for the Jews.[256] This mania, this madness that he cannot let go of must have terrified the doctor, who has been on edge since they abducted the children. When he read the madman's insistence that Jews are pestilent germs that must be destroyed, he decided to flee with his family to a shelter he had arranged in advance. Who dares criticize him other than our enemies who always judge us guilty?[257] Is it not logical to fear these haters who have the power to destroy all Jews? In revenge the commandant revoked all permits to go to town without an escort from those who had them, confining Pariser, Leibovich, Peisachowitz, and the policemen to the ghetto.[258]

Today his fury abated,[259] and he restored the permits.

Meanwhile there was another event, not quite as simple. A young woman who works in the shoe factory stole ten pairs of shoe covers, which were found in her possession as she passed the factory gate. She is now in jail. An honest, modest young woman whose husband has a dangerous heart disease, could not resist the temptation, particularly since theft is now a widespread, daily occurrence. Generally everyone who can steals food items, including rice, sugar, cheese, etc.; woolen socks and shirts, leather, furs, and so on. Eventually someone will fall into the inspectors' hands and will pay for the sins of all.

6 February

An official announcement printed yesterday in the German newspaper was wondrous and excellent in every aspect. The military wishes to explain the German retreat on the eastern front. It wants to remove from people's minds any suspicion that the army's strength is failing. Nothing of the sort! The German army is still powerful, its vigor unabated,[260] only conditions have changed. Now there is a second front—the western front—which takes priority, because that is where the break into Europe is starting and where the war will end. The decisive victory will happen there. Therefore Germany must concentrate more of its forces in the west and reduce somewhat its efforts on the eastern front. Of course they can still stage vigorous resistance in the east, but they choose to use a "flexible defense" and are withdrawing from various unimportant locations. This is like a chess game, where one gives up pieces to protect the king and queen.

In short, the Germans acknowledge that because of the new front, they are at a disadvantage in the east. They also acknowledge that the Allies are likely to attack and that they assume the war will be resolved in the west—notions they have dismissed and denied until now. All this is positive and encouraging but it is still doubtful that the few remaining Jews of the Baltics will be fortunate enough to see the coming salvation. The eastern front is approaching so slowly, and when the Germans are forced to abandon the Baltics, they will certainly exterminate us all! On the other hand, this winter is unusual: here it is February 6, and there has been little cold and snow. This evening's chill dried out the soil a bit, but during the day, the thin layer of snow on the roofs melted and the dripping water left the streets covered in mud and slush. It could be that because of the mud and slush the front has not yet reached us, and so we are still alive. We will know more soon.

The same newspaper contained another interesting piece of news, about a dispute between Weizmann and Ben-Gurion.[261] The former thinks we should act patiently and slowly regarding the land of our ancestors. He believes that after the Allies win the war, the problem will resolve itself, while Ben-Gurion thinks everything possible must be done to defy the English decision to implement the White Paper[262] and halt all immigration to Eretz Israel on April 1 of this year. Ben-Gurion traveled to America with the aim of forcing Weizmann, with the help of the American Zionists, to step down from the presidency [of the World Zionist Organization], but his trip only aggravated disagreements and caused a crisis in the movement. Consequently, he resigned [from the Jewish Agency], and the dispute continues.

18 February

The camp at Akmenė keeps adding to our grief in unexpected ways. That is where Žemaitiškis was shot, and where nine children were shot because of a cruel local commandant who claimed his heinous actions were merely orders from above, done against his will. Now there is a new commandant, and the troubles continue. The latest event is no less cruel than the earlier ones and in some ways exceeds them. Women there were returning from work escorted by a drunk Ukrainian who slipped on the ice and fell. The women helped him stand up, and in gratitude he aimed his automatic rifle at them and started shooting. The women ran for their lives, but the bullets caught up with them, and two were seriously injured in their legs. If the murderers could casually put an end to the lives of ten Jews, injuring two women would certainly count for nothing. But that was not the outrageous part: The women were injured on Tuesday but they were not brought to the hospital until Friday, because the commandant refused to provide transportation for Jews outside the regular schedule, and no truck was scheduled to go from Akmenė to Šiauliai until Friday. So the injured women, who lost a lot of blood, lay there for four days, with bullets in their bodies and no proper medical help. For this criminal decision the entire responsibility falls on the new commandant! An outrageous atrocity that should be recorded and remembered!

The wounded women were taken to the municipal hospital. The results are still unknown. It would be terrible if they have to amputate the leg of the young Klugman[263] woman. Her wounds, untreated for four days, became infected and the bullets shattered bones in a few locations. We can therefore assume it might be necessary to amputate the injured legs.

One detail must be emphasized. One of the injured—Edelstein—was sent to Akmenė with her daughter and husband, after he violated ghetto rules.[264] Will our leaders regret having sent her there only to lose her leg? No! They will have no regrets; they don't even know what it means. Many human feelings were paralyzed in the ghetto, particularly among our so-called captains.

25 February

The Akmenė incident is very upsetting. After their enormous suffering, the two victims each had to have their left legs amputated. The woman Edelstein passed away, cut down in her youth. The Klugman girl will be crippled and still hovers between life and death. Even after surgery, her wound still emits puss, and her fever is quite high. She may survive if her infection does not spread.

Yet again a true miracle has occurred: the Akmenė camp is closed,[265] and all the workers have returned! The work there was truly hard and the workers' treatment was terrible. The commandant there who murdered nine children and one old woman acted entirely on his own, as we learned later, for entertainment! Play! It is rumored that after his dismissal, he was found in possession of a fortune in Jewish property, money, and precious items. They were planning to send him to the front as punishment, so he shot himself to death! May they all end up like that! And the new commandant was even more vicious than his predecessor. He and his deputy were particularly hard on the son of Dr. W-ski, who first became the head of the Jewish police and then camp manager. So when "a new king arose,"[266] they made up charges[267] that he was a Bolshevik, and his torments were terrible. Had the camp continued operating a few more weeks, they say he would have perished.

26 March

There was an unusual search of the A.B.A camp carried out by the "battlefield police," who are now in Šiauliai, checking for deserters among the German soldiers in the city. These police were informed that A.B.A workers sometimes steal clothing and tools from the camp that are intended for the army. The inspection lasted about four hours. All the workers were required to stand, naked and barefoot, in a cold corridor, on a cold concrete floor.[268] The outcome was not too bad, because the German supervisors themselves warned that the inspection was coming and helped "eliminate the *chametz*."[269] Thus the police found nothing major. They still arrested about twenty-five people who had items in their clothing, suggesting they had used camp property, but they were released quickly. In fact most of the A.B.A workers live by the rule that says "the one who steals from a thief is blameless"[270] and eagerly steal warm clothing, socks, etc., sometimes in large quantities. One worker managed to filch enough leather for a full fur coat and sold it in town for a respectable sum. In the end they will be caught and face trouble.

1 April

There have been extensive changes in the management of the ghetto work camp. First, the director of the ghetto is now the apostate Pariser, and his chief advisor is that rude and impudent man, Burgin. Because of them the commandant dismissed the council's former chairman, M. Leibovich. He was the only honest man among our captains and has been demoted to a simple office clerk. He bore the burdens of the ghetto community for almost three years and did everything he could to help us; now he has been moved out of the manager's chair to some nearby office space. A humiliation and a disgrace![271]

The second change is the dismissal of the chief of the ghetto police, Gens.[272] He is a somewhat crude man, not very polished, a bit loud, but he still performed his difficult job honestly and with dedication. He was disliked by Pariser, who covets respect. He probably did not flatter him sufficiently and therefore was removed, supposedly after asking to be replaced, which, of course, was because of his treatment and his desire not to be fired outright.

The third change was my appointment as sanitary physician for the labor camp. Transferring me from job to job was the idea of the director and his deputy, who want to appear active. From head of the ambulatory I became a hospital doctor, then a deputy to the hospital manager, and now, as I mentioned, I am in charge of sanitation. In fact it is a very minor job: The camp is divided into twelve sections, each with a supervisor who monitors the cleanliness of the yards and toilets. They also distribute work cards, which each worker must turn in when they show up at their job site. A missing card means the worker is absent. Recently the supervisors were given a new assignment: to visit all homes and check on the residents. They must notify the police when someone is missing and this is because of a recent event: a master blacksmith whose work was essential fled the camp.[273] He is the husband of a Christian woman who converted and they have two sons. She left the camp a long time ago; now it seems he learned where his family was hiding and joined them. I oversee the supervisors, and I must make sure they are performing their jobs properly.

In the evenings I also have a temporary job checking the residents for lice. Anyway I am busy no more than two hours per day and free the rest of the time. Previously I used my free time to put together a diary in Yiddish, something I would not have been able to do without this job.[274] Now it is finished, and I am relieved because it turned into a burden, and now I can dedicate myself to something more serious. But I doubt I will be allowed to remain idle for the better part of the day. By the way, hospital doctors have been ordered to be in the hospital from 7:00 a.m. to 8:00 p.m. with only one hour off for lunch—meaning twelve hours of work per day, not an easy job.

12 April

I have been waiting to receive clearer and more detailed news about the terrible events in the Kaunas ghetto. The details are only now emerging, but no matter! The fact is that what happened to us on November 5 was repeated in Kaunas.[275] There too they took the children, the elderly and sick, and deported them. The numbers there are much larger than in Šiauliai. Not only that but there they searched for the children using a prepared list; if they could not find the children they took the parents instead. It is also said that they determined in advance the number of children to be taken, and made up for any shortfall by taking grownups. Much is still unclear about this. In addition to the Kaunas commandant,[276] a special guest arrived to carry out this murder. (Was it our friend Förster?) There is also a rumor that Jewish policemen refused to participate in this atrocity and were punished for it severely: they were imprisoned and reportedly beaten in the "Ninth Fort," a place known for its harshness.[277] What can we say about this now when the end appears so near? We have no words.

For a few days we did not read newspapers because of their holiday,[278] and no new news arrived. Today we received many reports but it is impossible to know how much truth is in them. They say that Odessa, Kovel, and Iaşi[279] were captured! In addition, Budapest and Bucharest were attacked heavily. If Odessa was captured then the entire southern front was eliminated, and the Crimean peninsula is cut off, and they will make sure there is no sea passage. We will wait for detailed information.

24 April

We are done checking the heads and body hair of the entire ghetto for lice eggs and scabies. Men who were diagnosed with lice were ordered to shave their hair down to the roots. The women were ordered to cut their hair short and give it a treatment. The "orderly," the supervisor of medical matters, participated in these inspections. It is interesting to note that several women cried when they saw their short hair. They did not recall the Russian maxim: "When heads were removed, no one cried for their hair."

Our camp is now attached to the one at Joniškis, where there are people from the Vilnius region, Ashmyany, and Švenčionys. The family has grown! In a few weeks, Dr. Wolpert will travel there briefly as a dermatology specialist.

Our commandant went on leave for a few weeks, and his substitute has already arrived. What will this temporary boss be like? Hopefully not worse than his predecessor. We have already gotten used to his capriciousness and madness.

10 May

Changes and reorganizations, tumult and confusion![280] The commandant's replacement is a wild man, crude, and ignorant. From his mouth come nothing but expletives and threats. He threatens shooting for every minor infraction. His demands are mostly ridiculous. "Barking dogs don't bite," so perhaps he will not do too much damage. But he insists on rigorously observing several rules: (1) In the fifth year of the war, the entire population without exception must work ten hours a day. (2) No holidays or days off for Jews. (3) No one may stay home without a release from the ambulatory. (4) A sick person may stay home in bed no more than three days. If he is still sick, he must go to the hospital. No homebound invalids! (5) Everyone in camp was to till their garden on Sunday; those who did not would be shot! But the Creator spoiled his plan:

the skies opened up and a cold, drenching rain fell all day so he was forced to cancel his order.

The day before yesterday, the important guest we were all expecting finally appeared: A visiting physician from Kaunas who brought chaos with him. He ordered the number of camp doctors reduced to three. Thus I too became redundant, and can expect to be given hard labor. When Dr. B. asked what job I should be assigned, the "orderly" answered, "As far as I am concerned, he can drive a horse-cart." We will see how things go, but in any event, I expect it will be hard and unpleasant.

One detail aroused his anger in particular: Dr. Wolpert was providing first aid to workers in the Frenkel factory. The visitor was outraged to find a Jew treating Lithuanians and immediately had him fired from that job, leaving him there as a manual laborer. So now four or five doctors work as manual laborers. Soon most likely I will be among them. I am becoming quite a success[281] in my old age!

Our new ghetto leaders tried to undermine Dr. P[eisachowitz], the hospital director, but he had become known to the authorities in Kaunas, so his position remained secure. The guest made him responsible for all medical matters. One of the administrators prepared a list of doctors who he thinks should remain in the camp. Its contents are still unknown; the visitor received it but has not yet responded.

The visitor also inspected the A.B.A camp where eight hundred Jews work, and found one unclean room. He commented about it to the management. What did they do to fix the problem? Yesterday at 4:00 a.m. they woke all the workers and pulled them outside, all of them, even those sick with pneumonia, and kept them outside in the cold snow and cold rain for several hours. Everyone thought they were about to be deported, and the commotion was enormous. They hid children in attics and basements and some adults tried to hide as well. At 6:30 some workers arrived from the ghetto and went as they do every day to their workstations. The resident A.B.A. workers joined them, and all ended peacefully. Apparently while they were standing outside shivering, their rooms were cleaned.

29 May

Second day of Shavuot. Yesterday in the evening, the whole administration celebrated our "time of liberation"[282] as the deputy commandant left our camp. It is hard to describe all the trouble and suffering he caused us these last three weeks. With his foul language, yelling and swearing, and threats to have people shot, he forced us to work in our gardens, moving rocks, cleaning latrines, uprooting dead trees and would give us no rest.[283] The man is certainly insane. He even "honored" the doctors and camp managers with these jobs. When he ordered Dr. B. to organize a pile of rocks, the latter dared to ask: "Is this a proper job for a doctor?" He replied: "Shut up or your eyeglasses will fall to the ground." And to Dr. W. he said: "If your garden is not in shape by four o'clock your own shape will suffer." When he passed through the gate once while my son was standing guard, he growled, for no reason: "The Jews are swine." In short he followed the maxim: "Let them hate, as long as they fear." "Oderint dum metuant."[284]

I feared meeting him, so I stayed in my house for ten days, like a prisoner. Our neighbor and my son left for work every day, and my wife was in the hospital after catching a cold that grew into double pneumonia, a very dangerous disease for a heart patient like her. But she has developed strong resistance to these diseases and she recovered. Most likely she will return home tomorrow after eighteen days in the hospital. Her illness is a direct result of our living conditions in the ghetto. A sickly woman like her is forced to get up at 5:30 a.m. and go to work in the sewing shop. Fearing the deputy commandant, she put in several full workdays, and because of the early spring weather she worked outside in the yard and caught a cold. All of our immune systems have weakened—I too am always sick lately and my stomach ailment is worsening day by day. If conditions do not change soon, the thread of my life will be severed.[285]

30 May
The eastern front is quiet—a quiet before the storm, because a massive army is concentrated there and certainly a major attack is coming. In Italy, the Allies woke up and are properly pushing the German army north. Today it is rumored that Rome has fallen.[286] The Germans are putting up stiff resistance. They are courageous, well-armed and battle-hardened and they know if they surrender their fate will be bitter. Their boldness, discipline, and defensive strength makes them believe they will win. We hear them talk a lot recently about the "invasion." They are certain it will happen, but they act as if it does not frighten them.

7 June
It has finally happened, and the results will undoubtedly be decisive. Yesterday the English and American armies entered France! The invasion that was expected for days and years is finally here. The Allied army chose the place with the greatest fortifications—Le Havre[287]—but the nearest to Paris. The Germans bragged that they had built a wall along the Atlantic so strong that "no weapon formed against it could succeed"[288] and no force could break through,

and yet the Allies came and stripped to its very foundations[289] the wall that the famous engineer Todt[290] and his organization worked for several years to fortify. June 6 will be remembered by all the world's people!

There is no point in dwelling on the many decrees and restrictions that they impose just to demean us, which are trivial compared with the things we have lived through: Our transfer from the city to the ghetto after being robbed and harassed; the demand for fifty human sacrifices, which was replaced by a confiscatory tax; the deportations through the synagogues, which were passageways to the killing fields; and above all the abduction of our children! I have no wish to write about the daily scourges that are nothing compared to our past troubles. But as long as I am holding my pen, I will mention one edict that came from Kaunas: that all male ghetto dwellers without exception must shave their heads. The edict was carried out, and now we all look like real prisoners, with tonsured heads![291]

This was Aharon Pick's final diary entry.

NOTES

RETRIEVING A VOICE FROM THE GHETTO

1. As in other occupied cities, the Germans demanded that Šiauliai's Jews select community leaders to act as liaisons and administrators of the ghetto's internal affairs. To Yiddish-speaking ghetto dwellers this body was known as the *yidnrat*—literally, "Jewish council," or the *forshteyershaft* ("delegation"). In his manuscript, Pick uses a Hebrew term *netzigut* (נציגות) which translates literally as "representation." For clarity here we use "council."

2. Unless otherwise noted, all Aharon Pick quotations are from his journal, "Notes from the Valley of Slaughter."

3. A history of the town was published by the Keidaner Association of New York (Cassel 1930) in a volume marking the organization's thirtieth anniversary.

4. Sirutavičius, Staliūnas, and Šiaučiūnaitė-Verbickienė 2020, 261.

5. Friedländer 2007, 230.

6. Sužiedėlis and Liekis 2013, 125.

7. Sužiedėlis and Liekis 2013, 125.

8. Arad 2004, 176.

9. Eliezer Yerushalmi's Šiauliai diary, written in Yiddish, was seized by the Soviets after the war. Heavily redacted excerpts were published in 1944 by the USSR's Jewish Antifascist Committee, in what became known as *The Black Book*. Yerushalmi, who survived the war, was able to reconstruct a version for the 1951 anthology *Lita* and published a Hebrew translation (Yerushalmi 1958).

10. From a second-century *midrash* (or commentary) on the book of Exodus.

11. Golan 1997.

12. Laczó 2018, 695.

13. Cohen 2013, 400–413.

14. Ringelblum 1974.

15. Kruk and Harshav 2002.

16. Shalit 1949, 299.

17. Golan 1997, 13.

18. Interview via Zoom with Devorah Shatz (granddaughter of Aharon Pick), October 9, 2020.

19. Golan 1997.

20. In 1957, the Yiddish newspaper *Forward* carried a series of articles by journalist S. L. Shneiderman, based on interviews with a number of Šiauliai survivors who ended up in the United States.

21. Cassedy 2012.

22. Morgan 2008.

23. See in particular Lipschitz 2001 and Gafnovitz-Preiss 2002.

24. Jasaitis 2002.

25. Sužiedėlis 2013.

NOTES ON THE TEXT

1. Golan 1997.

1. BEFORE THE BOLSHEVIKS' ARRIVAL (A PREFACE)

1. Leviticus 19:33.

2. Song of Songs 2:11.

3. One of many names used here for Hitler, most rooted in traditional texts. Haman was the Persian minister whose failed plot to destroy the Israelites is described in the book of Esther.

4. Psalms 11:6.

5. Nazi Germany. The tribe of Amalek is portrayed in the book of Exodus and elsewhere as the Israelites' eternal enemy; thus the name has been applied to foes and oppressors of Jews throughout history.

6. Deuteronomy 28:50.

7. Jeremiah 33:6.

8. From a second century *midrash* on the Book of Exodus.

9. Leviticus 2:2.

10. From the title of an 1882 book by Nahum Sokolow, journalist and Zionist leader.

11. Lamentations 3:45.

12. Judah Halevi was a twelfth-century Iberian Jewish poet and physician. Vincas Kudirka (1858–1899), was a poet and physician who became a leader in the Lithuanian national revival movement. Some of his writing portrayed Jews as oppressors and parasites.

13. Isaiah 10:14.

14. Isaiah 1:18.

15. The parliament (Seimas) created this ministry when Lithuania became independent in 1919, legally recognizing the Jews as a national minority with civil and political rights. It was abolished in March 1924.

16. Pick's preferred term for what later became the state of Israel.

17. Leviticus 19:34.

18. A term used in early rabbinic texts for a coveted realm of knowledge.

19. Isaiah 29:14.

20. From a commentary on Genesis by the eleventh-century Torah interpreter Rashi.

21. A Talmudic description of divine justice.

22. Samuel Petuchauskas (1894–1941) moved to Vilnius after the Soviet takeover in 1940 and was later shot at the Nazis' mass-killing site Ponary.

23. Song of Songs 5:10.

24. World War I.

25. A Hebrew term denoting a formally organized Jewish community.

26. Throughout his manuscript, Pick refers to Germany as Ashkenaz (אשכנז), an archaic name found in ancient Hebrew texts for the lands of central Europe. Germans, accordingly, are referred to as Ashkenazim. Since in modern usage that term has evolved to refer specifically to Jews of European origin, we here use Germany and Germans to avoid confusion.

27. Psalms 16:6.

28. Ruler of the grand duchy of Lithuania in the early fifteenth century.

29. Pick received his medical training in Paris and practiced medicine in the south of France during World War I.

30. A seaside Baltic town, popular as a vacation spot.

31. From a commentary by the seventeenth-century rabbi Yom Tov Lipman Heller.

32. *Cheder* is a Jewish elementary school.

33. Called Memel by the Germans, this port city was claimed by Hitler and annexed on March 23, 1939.

34. Empress of Russia, 1741–1762.

35. Isaiah 10:1.

36. Deuteronomy 29:17.

37. Literally "pioneers," one of several Zionist youth groups active in interwar Lithuania.

38. Antanas Stankus, formerly a captain in the Lithuanian army, was appointed Šiauliai deputy mayor for Jewish affairs in 1941, serving until February 1, 1942 (Bubnys 2014).

39. A phrase found often in the Talmud.

40. Jeremiah 50:17.

41. A phrase traditionally used during the celebration of Hanukkah.

42. About forty kilometers north-northeast of Šiauliai.

43. Esther 4:14.

2. THE BOLSHEVIKS IN LITHUANIA

1. Psalms 55:5.

2. Psalms 142:4.

3. II Chronicles 19:7.

4. Ecclesiastes 7:25.

5. Isaiah 53:3.

6. Genesis 1:9.

7. A Talmudic phrase (e.g., Mishnah Berachot 2:2).

8. Zephaniah 2:15.

9. II Samuel 20:13.

10. Secondary or high school. Pick was among the founders of this institution.

11. An earlier name for the Soviet secret police, which by 1940 had become the NKVD.

12. Literally meaning "culture," the name of a network of secular, Hebrew-language educational institutions in interwar Poland and Lithuania.

13. Job 3:25.

14. Petras Linkevičius, a lawyer, served as mayor of Šiauliai during the Soviet period and again under the Germans from 1941 to 1944 (Yerushalmi 1951, 1771).

15. Proverbs 12:18.

16. Genesis 3:19.

17. Job 24:13.

18. Russian acronym for the Society for the Protection of the Health of the Jewish Population, founded in St. Petersburg in 1912. Branches existed in many towns with Jewish populations in what had been imperial Russia.

19. Poland's seizure of the Lithuanian capital Vilnius (Wilno in Polish) in 1920 remained a bitter issue between the two countries until the Soviets handed the city back to Lithuania in 1939.

20. Antanas Smetona, President of Lithuania (1919–20, 1926–40) appointed his brother-in-law, Juozas Tūbelis, as prime minister in 1929, a post in which he remained until 1938.

21. A state-supported paramilitary organization, founded in 1919, disbanded by the Soviets but revived in 1989.

22. Also called Red Aid, a social-service organization for political prisoners and their families, created by the Communist International in the 1920s.

23. Until the Holocaust, Jewish intellectuals divided sharply over which language should be promoted and taught: Hebrew, favored by Zionists, or Yiddish, favored by socialists and those advocating cultural autonomy within Europe.

24. Crossed out in the manuscript.

25. Domas Jasaitis (1898–1977), Lithuanian physician and hospital administrator. Like Pick, he had studied medicine in France and was a prominent community leader in Šiauliai, publishing both medical and nonmedical articles. He left Lithuania in 1944 for Germany, where he chaired the Lithuanian Red Cross and worked with groups attempting to free Lithuania from Soviet control. In 1945, he immigrated to the United States, where he worked as a physician in Connecticut and Florida and remained active in Lithuanian national affairs.

26. Leviticus 18:6.

27. Hosea 9:7.

28. Isaiah 54:8.

29. Exceptionally hard workers, after the example of the legendary Soviet miner Alexey Stakhanov.

30. Genesis 19:9.

31. Deuteronomy 28:65.

32. Exodus 21:29.

33. Isaiah 13:20.

34. II Samuel 1:19 and 1:25.

35. The Nazis established two ghetto areas for Šiauliai's Jews, one in the area of Trakų Street and the second in the Kaukazas (Caucasus) neighborhood, so named because of its steep hillside.

36. Isaiah 32:8.

37. The Jews' exile from Palestine.

38. Tadas Ivanauskas (1882–1970), a prominent Lithuanian zoologist and a founder of Vytautas Magnus University.

39. From a prayer said on Rosh Hashana.

40. Job 3:25.

41. Proverbs 27:1.

42. Proverbs 8:14.

43. Tsemach Pick (1882–1952). A Russian medical journal described him in 2007 as "one of the leading scientists in the field of occupational health" in the Soviet Union, and the author of more than fifty research papers in that field.

44. II Kings 5:1.

45. Genesis 24:1.

46. Ezra 9:1.

47. Psalms 70:4.

48. A quotation from Russian composer Nikolai Rimsky-Korsakov (1923).

49. I Chronicles 12:34.

50. Isaiah 28:7.

51. The location of a mental health institution, approximately 125 miles south of Šiauliai.

52. Psalms 41:4.

53. A reference to Esther 6:1.

54. Shortwave diathermy, developed in the 1920s, uses high-frequency electromagnetic energy to treat pain from kidney stones, pelvic inflammatory disease, and muscle spasms.

55. Psalms 139:11.

56. Habakkuk 1:4.

57. Acute degeneration of the spinal cord.

58. From the mourner's kaddish prayer.

59. Isaiah 41:12.

60. Psalms 34:19.

61. In the Talmud, a frequently used term for God.

62. A semi-official Lithuanian paramilitary organization, active in 1928–1930 and briefly revived under the Nazis.

3. MY SON'S ADMISSION TO THE LITHUANIAN UNIVERSITY

1. Isaiah 5:14.

2. A common Talmudic questioning phrase (e.g., Berachot 27b:13).

3. Exodus 20:5.

4. Ezekiel 28:24.

5. Literally, the "The Young Guard," a leading left-wing Zionist youth movement, very active in interwar Lithuania and later in Palestine/Israel.

6. After the Soviet takeover, non-Communist youth movements were suppressed in Lithuania.

7. Esther 8:14.

8. Literally, "ascending"; referring to the immigration of Jews to Palestine/Israel.

9. Malachi 1:13.

10. Psalms 16:3.

11. A Talmudic phrase (e.g. Bekhorot 45a:15).

12. I Kings 5:5.

13. Proverbs 17:1.

14. Mykolas Biržiška (1882–1962), historian and educator, served as rector of Vilnius university from 1940–43 and again in 1944 until the Soviet reoccupation of Lithuania. Emigrated to the US in 1949.

15. A town sixty-eight kilometers northwest of Šiauliai.

16. Rosh Hashana 1940 actually began the evening of Wednesday, October 2. Here and elsewhere, Pick's memory for dates appears fallible.

17. Amos 4:1.

18. Lamentations 1:22.

19. Isaiah 58:7.

20. Dovid Hirsh Pick was a *melamed*, a teacher in a traditional Jewish cheder. Such positions were famously ill paid. To supplement the family income, Chana Leah Pick sold baked goods, becoming known in Kėdainiai as "*di bekerke*" (the lady baker) according to Golan (1997, 10).

21. Traditionally Talmud Torah schools were communally sponsored institutions for children whose families were too poor to afford private cheder instruction. In Šiauliai, however, what had been the Talmud Torah was replaced before World War I by a modern elementary school, funded by leather factory owner Chaim Frenkel. After World War I the school received government support and became known simply as the Jewish School (Maynard 1997).

22. A village four kilometers north of Šiauliai.

23. University town in Estonia, now called Tartu.

24. Town in eastern Lithuania, now called Zarasai.

25. Antanas Venclova (1906–71), appointed Minister of Education for Soviet Lithuania in 1940.

26. Devorah Tatz Pick, born 1900 in Raseiniai. Although Pick describes her as very ill during this period, she outlived him by several months. When the ghetto was liquidated in July 1944 (only weeks after her husband's death), she was transported with hundreds of others to the death camp at Stutthof, near Danzig. Most there were killed by gassing, although German records say she died of lung disease on November 17, 1944.

27. Lamentations 3:45.

28. Pick uses the Hebrew word for "emptying" to denote deportation.

29. The Jewish section of the Communist Party's propaganda arm, which worked to "assimilate" Jews into the USSR by suppressing all vestiges of both religion and nationalism (i.e., Zionism). The Yevsektsiya even altered Yiddish orthography to obscure the language's Hebrew roots.

30. The Bund was the union of Jewish workers in Lithuania, Poland, and Russia, founded in Vilna in 1897.

31. Jeremiah 29:23.

32. Lamentations 4:10.

33. A Russian term, literally meaning "fists," *kulaks* denotes wealthy peasant farmers. Their elimination was part of the Bolshevik program.

34. About seventy-five acres.

35. Jeremiah 51:34.

36. II Kings 19:3.

4. ON THE EVE OF WAR

1. Exodus 1:10.

2. Jeremiah 7:11.

3. Job 21:30.

4. Lamentations 4:5.

5. A reference to the Latin phrase *quod licet Iovi, non licet bovi*—what is permissible for Jupiter may not be permissible for a bull.

6. From a prayer said on Yom Kippur.

7. Ecclesiastes 7:25.

8. Ezekiel 20:33.

9. "Partisans" in this context denotes the armed bands of Lithuanians who collaborated with the Nazis after the German invasion, known in Lithuanian as *baltaraiščiai* ("white armbands").

10. From the Talmud: "Who is wise? He who sees and anticipates the consequences of his behavior."

11. Isaiah 5:7.

12. Jeremiah 1:14.

13. Ezekiel 23:32.

14. Ezekiel 2:10.

15. Isaiah 59:7.

16. From the Passover Haggadah.

17. Leviticus 16:10.

18. Jeremiah 31:15.

19. Isaiah 40:29.

20. The Talmud tells of Ben Abuyah, a second-century rabbi considered a heretic because he embraced secular values. Some accounts say he lost his faith after seeing the severed tongue of Hutzpit the Interpreter, a martyred Jewish scholar, discarded on the ground and said, "How can a tongue that uttered pearls lick dust?"

21. Hitler was a corporal during World War I.

22. Houston Stewart Chamberlain, British-born German professor whose writings promoted the superiority of Aryan races and greatly influenced Nazi ideology.

23. Esther 8:14.

24. I Kings 14:10.
25. Job 30:3.
26. Psalms 116:3.

5. THE START OF THE WAR

1. Isaiah 55:4.
2. Isaiah 44:22.
3. In German Tauroggen, in Yiddish Tavrig, 103 km southwest of Šiauliai.
4. Forty-five kilometers southwest of Šiauliai.
5. Isaiah 47:15.
6. "Shoe" in Lithuanian.
7. The factory owned by Pick's brother-in-law Zilberman.
8. Exodus 26:33.
9. Lamentations 2:5.
10. Job 12:20.
11. Deuteronomy 28:66.
12. A Talmudic and liturgic phrase.
13. Psalms 107:39.
14. A town twenty-five kilometers northeast of Šiauliai.
15. Deuteronomy 32:35.

6. THE GERMANS ENTER ŠIAULIAI

1. From the daily morning liturgy.
2. Hitler.
3. Job 20:8.
4. Isaiah 41:24.
5. Isaiah 5:14.
6. Job 30:2. The French had entrusted their defense to the Maginot Line of fortifications along their border with Germany. The German army simply bypassed these when it attacked in 1940.
7. Pick evidently wrote this passage in spring 1942. (See part C.)
8. Proverbs 30:22.
9. Song of Songs 8:6.
10. Lithuanian nationalists declared independence on June 23, 1941, a day after the German invasion began. Their provisional government lasted six weeks, until Germany established its formal administration of the area under the Reichskommisariat Ostland.
11. Jeremiah 40:7.
12. Deuteronomy 28:66.

13. From Jeremiah 18:6, the start of a prayer said on the eve of Yom Kippur.

14. Isaiah 58:4

15. Job 33:23.

16. Lamentations 3:23.

17. From the blessing of the food in the Passover Haggadah.

18. Chaim Nachman Bialik, whose influential poem (variously translated as "The Burden of Nemirov," or "The Prophecy of Nemirov," and later changed to "In the City of Slaughter") responded to the 1903 pogrom in Kishniev, (now Chişinău) Moldova.

19. Isaiah 9:3.

20. Proverbs 12:8.

21. Reference to the twelfth of Maimonides's thirteen principles of faith: "I believe with perfect faith in the coming of the Messiah; and even though he may tarry, nonetheless, I wait every day for his coming."

22. Psalms 69:16.

23. Esther 4:14.

7. AFFLICTIONS

1. Psalms 116:3.

2. Jeremiah 25:16.

3. Psalms 97:11.

4. Hitler.

5. The actual value of eighteen rubles in purchasing power or labor time under the Soviet regime is unclear. Under German occupation it equaled a little more than one day's wage for a Jewish worker.

6. Isaiah 35:3.

7. A street named for two Lithuanian-American aviators, who died attempting to fly nonstop from the United States to Lithuania in 1933.

8. Joel 1:4.

9. Haggai 1:6.

10. Psalms 144:13.

11. From the Talmud (tractate *Berakhot* 57b).

12. A Talmudic expression, e.g., Bava Batra 8a:8.

13. Isaiah 58:4.

14. Joshua 9:23.

15. A military airport at Zokniai, six kilometers southeast of Šiauliai.

16. A reference to the standard for removing leavened bread during Passover.

17. In German, the *Gebietskommissar*, the civilian official in charge of Šiauliai and its surrounding area.

18. Stasys Lukauskis, 1869–1925.

19. Hosea 9:7.

20. According to Avraham Tory, who served as secretary to the Jewish council in the Kaunas (Kovno) ghetto, on October 4, 1941, Germans locked and boarded up the infectious-disease hospital there, with scores of patients and medical staff inside, and then set it afire.

21. Isaiah 13:9.

22. As he noted earlier in the journal, Pick had six siblings. His one brother was Tsemach (see chap. 2, note 43).

23. Eugene Botkin, court physician to Tsar Nicholas II and Tsarina Alexandra.

24. Psalms 123:4.

25. Isaiah 53:3.

26. The nickname of David Theodor Pick (spelled Pieck in some documents), b. 1922 in Šiauliai, d. 1975 in Kibbutz Netzer Sereni, Israel.

27. A town fifty-seven kilometers east-northeast of Šiauliai.

28. Job 20:5.

29. I Kings 18:29.

30. Numbers 24:20.

31. Micah 6:10.

32. The account in Yerushalmi (1958, 46) of this incident is slightly different, saying that sixty-three Jewish workers worked for twenty-one days on a railroad track to the town of Joniškis, which is west and slightly north of Joniškėlis.

33. Hebrew transliteration; company's Lithuanian name unknown.

34. Leviticus 13:51–52.

35. Rabbi Avraham Yitzkhak Nochumovsky (1887–1941).

36. Rabbi Aharon Baksht, last chief rabbi of Šiauliai (1867–1941). His son-in-law was Rabbi Isaac Rabinowitz, of Telšiai.

37. Isaiah 53:7.

38. Lamentations 4:20.

39. Psalms 137:3.

40. Proverbs 25:20.

41. A virulently antisemitic tabloid newspaper, published by the Nazis.

42. Baksht, Nochumovsky, and the others (visible in picture #8) were murdered on July 11, 1941, supposedly in reprisal for an alleged Jewish attack on German soldiers (Megargee and Dean 2012, 1119).

43. Historic town twenty-eight kilometers west of Vilnius.

44. A Talmudic phrase.

45. A Talmudic phrase, sometimes associated with the heretic Elisha ben Abuya.

46. Antanas Stankus, formerly a captain in the Lithuanian army, was appointed Šiauliai deputy mayor for Jewish affairs in 1941, serving until February 1, 1942 (Bubnys).

47. 1 Kings 22:27.

48. Most of the approximately 1,500 Jews of Kelmė were murdered in July and August 1941.

49. Psalms 88:3.

50. Psalms 44:26.

51. Isaiah 5:14.

52. An extensive set of legal, social, and economic restrictions on Jews, enacted by Germany's Nazi government in 1935.

53. Hosea 7:2.

54. Traditionally, one who lobbied on behalf of Jewish communities with Gentile authorities.

55. Formally called the Šiauliai Remand Prison. Better known as the "red prison" for the color of its brick, it was built in 1911 and stood next to one of the ghetto areas designated by the Germans. It still stood in 2020. (See map in fig. 9.)

56. Lamentations 2:19.

57. Isaiah 57:15.

58. Psalms 16:6.

59. A Jewish charity, active in interwar Lithuania, that took over many communal functions after the semi-autonomous kehilla was abolished in 1926.

60. Ezekiel 20:43.

61. From the hymn "Adon Olam" (Lord of the world).

62. Exodus 32:12.

63. Deuteronomy 32:28.

64. Psalms 107:39.

65. Psalms 41:4.

66. I Kings 19:12.

67. Esther 1:8.

68. Malachi 3:4.

69. The Talmud (Gittin 56b:13) attributes the death of Roman emperor Titus, who had destroyed the Temple in Jerusalem, to a gnat that entered through his nose and picked at his brain for seven years.

70. Dostoevsky's semi-autobiographical novel of life in a Siberian prison, published in the early 1860s, sometimes translated as "Notes from a Dead House."

71. A Talmudic term, e.g., Chagigah 4a:1.

72. A small pellet or flake shaped pasta.

73. Deuteronomy 32:36.

74. Job 40:16.

75. Genesis 27:22.

76. One of Lithuania's premier Talmudic academies, famous for its focus on ethical teaching and morality, located near Kaunas until World War II. Pick wrote a detailed account of this incident in a memoir that was published in 1935 in *HaOlam*, the official organ of the World Zionist Organization.

77. This reference to Hitler, used often by Pick, translates literally as "the father of the fathers of defilement." In rabbinic writing it is used to denote something beyond redemption.

78. Called *artel* in Russian, this was a form of collective enterprise that the Soviets suppressed.

79. Psalms 50:19.

80. Ruth 4:1.

81. Numbers 16:30.

82. A dentist named Verbolinsky worked in the ghetto (Shalit 1949).

83. The Germans collected Jews in several Šiauliai synagogue buildings and the Jewish home for the elderly (on Vilnius St.) before taking them out of the city to be killed (Megargee and Dean 2012, 1119).

84. Communist youth league, also called the *komsomol*.

85. A work that apparently has been lost.

86. Ecclesiastes 4:14.

87. Zechariah 11:8.

88. Lamentations 1:16.

89. Pick's term for *pogrom* translates literally as "riots against Jews."

90. In 1648, Ukrainian leader Bohdan Khmelnytsky began a rebellion against the Polish-Lithuanian Commonwealth that led to the deaths of tens of thousands of Jews.

91. Psalms 55:6.

92. Genesis 4:10.

93. Petras Požėla, former lawyer, who served as security chief for the Šiauliai region. He was later found to have worked for the NKVD during the Soviet occupation and was shot by the Germans. (Jasaitis 2002, 62). Romualdas Kolokša, a lieutenant in a Lithuanian "self-defense" unit, formerly a lawyer in Užventis. (Megargee and Dean 2012, 1119 and 1154).

94. The name, literally meaning "God's poison," of a demon archangel mentioned in the Talmud, associated with Satan and the angel of death; here referring to Hitler.

95. Hosea 13:14.

96. Joshua 8:22.

97. The first of several mass murders in Kelmė took place on July 29, 1941: 1,200 Jews were shot on that day. A second occurred on August 22, wiping out most of the community (Megargee and Dean 2012, 1071–72).

98. Tisha B'Av—the ninth day of the month of Av—is a traditional day of mourning, commemorating the destruction of the Temple in Jerusalem. In 1941, the holiday fell on August 3.

99. The *musar* movement stressed moral teaching in yeshiva studies. Kelmė was the site of a leading musar school, as was Slabodka, the yeshiva Pick attended as a youth.

100. "*Shechinah*": In Jewish theology, the term denoting God's manifestation in the world.

101. Genesis 5:24.

102. Exodus 21:3.

103. Town 17 km east of Kelmė, known as a vacation resort. Its Jewish community was slaughtered in mid-August, 1941.

104. Isaiah 10:14.

105. II Samuel 20:19. An honorific applied historically to some important Jewish diaspora cities.

106. Job 37:1.

107. Karl Jäger, head of the *Einsatzkommando* unit that oversaw killings throughout Lithuania in 1941, reported on December 1 that between August 28 and September 2, 1941, a total of 1,125 Jews (448 men, 476 women, and 201 children) were shot in Krakės (Megargee and Dean 2012, 1074).

108. Psalms 107:39.

109. A town fifty-three kilometers south of Šiauliai, called Shidlove in Yiddish. On August 15–16, 1941, 115 to 120 Jewish men from here were shot en masse; on August 21, the remaining Jews, around 300 people, were shot (Megargee and Dean 2012, 1122).

110. Malachi 3:19.

111. On July 29, 1941, 254 Jews and 3 Lithuanian communists were shot near Raseiniai, including Jews from Tytuvėnai (Megargee and Dean 2012, 1109).

112. About thirty-seven kilometers east of Šiauliai. On August 4, 1941, Lithuanian police shot some 265 Jews in a nearby forest (Megargee and Dean 2012, 1101).

113. In Yiddish Ponevezh, about eighty kilometers east of Šiauliai. On August 23, 1941, 7,523 Jews (1,312 men, 4,602 women, and 1,609 children) were executed here. The numbers may include Jews from nearby villages, including Raguva, Ramygala, and Krekenava (Megargee and Dean 2012, 1103).

114. A recurring Aramaic phrase in the Talmud.

115. About thirty-three kilometers southwest of Šiauliai.

116. From Deuteronomy 5:15.

117. Lamentations 4:14.

118. July 19, 1941.

119. A town sixty-four kilometers north of Šiauliai. On October 2, 1942, residents of the Žagarė ghetto were marched to the market square. The German commander, Manteuffel, told them they were to be taken for work. But panic broke out when the square was surrounded by Lithuanian partisans and police, and many Jews tried to flee. Some 150 people were shot during the mayhem. The rest were marched to Naryshkin Park and shot. In all, 2,236 Jews (633 men, 1,107 women, and 496 children) were murdered (Megargee and Dean 2012, 1153).

120. On July 29, 1941, Jews from Vaiguva were shot in a gravel quarry near Grusewskis (Megargee and Dean 2012, 1072).

121. Jeremiah 6:1.

122. Numbers 11:20.

123. On July 12, 1941, Lithuanian gunmen rounded up some three hundred Jewish men from Radviliškis and shot them in the Durpynas forest near the Jewish cemetery. The remaining Jews were transferred to the Žagarė ghetto between August 25 and 29. On October 2, they were shot with the other Jews of the Žagarė ghetto (Megargee and Dean 2012, 1108).

124. A small town thirty kilometers southeast of Šiauliai (Megargee and Dean 2012, 1120).

125. Jeremiah 30:21.

126. Megargee and Dean 2012, 1108.

127. Exodus 1:8.

128. Psalms 107:40.

129. A town seventy-two kilometers west of Šiauliai.

130. The Telz yeshiva was known for introducing organizational innovations to Talmud study such as yearly examinations and class levels. But its students rejected the teaching of *musar*—ethics and morality, possibly influencing Pick's opinion of it. The Telz yeshiva was reestablished after 1945 in Cleveland, Ohio (Stampfer 2014).

131. II Samuel 20:19.

132. The *Sturmabteilung* (Storm Detachment), also called the "Brown Shirts," had been a Nazi paramilitary organization in the early 1930s but was largely replaced by the S.S. before World War II began. It is unclear if Pick here means this or another German military organization.

133. I Kings 21:25.

134. Megargee and Dean 2012, 1111 and 1131.

135. Hans Gewecke, a Nazi politician and member of the Reichstag, served as *Gebietskommissar* (district commissioner) of the Šiauliai area from June 1941 to October 1, 1943. He oversaw the civil administration and the transfer to ghettos of Jews who survived the first waves of killing. After the war he was interned temporarily and had his property confiscated, but lived as a private citizen until

1970, when a German court convicted him in connection with the hanging of Bezalel Mazovetsky in the Šiauliai ghetto (described in Part D of this memoir). Gewecke was sentenced to four and a half years in prison. In the 1960s he was interviewed by French filmmaker Claude Lanzmann for the documentary film *Shoah*. He died in 1991 (Megargee and Dean 2012, 1121).

136. Megargee and Dean 2012, 1132.

137. A phrase from the memorial prayer *"El maleh rekhamim"* (O Power, full of mercy).

138. Zechariah 3:2.

139. Megargee and Dean 2012, 1131.

140. Ezekiel 12:23.

141. Isaiah 51:17.

142. A Talmudic phrase.

143. Proverbs 25:15.

144. Numbers 17:28.

145. In Yiddish, Raseyn, seventy-two kilometers south of Šiauliai (Megargee and Dean 2012, 1109).

146. II Samuel 1:23.

147. In Yiddish, Keidan, ninety kilometers south-southeast of Šiauliai.

148. Ezekiel Katzenellenbogen (1668–1749) founded a rabbinic dynasty in Kėdainiai and later served as chief rabbi in Hamburg, Germany. He was a prominent scholar and critic of the Sabbatean heresy then sweeping through Europe.

149. Lamentations 1:16.

150. Also known as Senior Sachs, 1816–1892, a prominent scholar and editor in Russia and France.

151. Moshe Leib Lilienblum, 1843–1910, influential author and early Zionist activist. Pick lived next door and as a boy knew Lilienblum's father, who was known there as "Reb Hirsch the barrel-maker" (Cassel 1930, 52).

152. On August 28, 1941, Lithuanians and Germans shot 2,076 Jews (710 men, 767 women, and 599 children) from Kėdainiai and nearby communities at a predug pit near the town (Megargee and Dean 2012, 1071).

153. Some 4,000 Jews were murdered in pogroms in Kaunas (Kovno) in the first days after the German invasion. Later the uncoordinated attacks on Jews were channeled into an organized mass killing that took place in military forts surrounding the city. Approximately fifty thousand people were murdered, including many transported from the West (Megargee and Dean 2012, 1066–1069).

154. Vilnius (Vilna in Yiddish, Wilno in Polish) had a prewar Jewish population of some sixty thousand. From July to December, 1941, some

thirty-three thousand Jews were murdered, most in the Paneriai (Ponary) woods a few kilometers from the city (Megargee and Dean 2012, 1148–52).

155. Numbers 35:6.

156. Isaiah 6:13.

157. Exodus 24:7.

158. In early August 1941, Keidan's synagogue courtyard on Smilga (Smilgos) Street and the surrounding alleys were converted into a ghetto and surrounded by barbed wire (Megargee and Dean 2012, 1070).

159. Tzadok Schlapobersky, a Jewish Lithuanian army veteran, grabbed a pistol from a Lithuanian guard, wounded the German commandant, and killed a Lithuanian. He fell into the pit while grappling with the German and was bayonetted by other Lithuanians. Two other Jews were shot attempting to flee (Megargee and Dean 2012, 1070).

160. Judges 16:30.

8. THE EDICTS

1. Isaiah 6:10.

2. Micah 6:10 (literally "an accursed short *ephah*").

3. Jeremiah 16:18.

4. A Talmudic expression.

5. Isaiah 5:14.

6. Proverbs 24:16.

7. Proverbs 11:22.

8. Yerushalmi (1958, 45) identifies this person as Dr. Hendin.

9. *"Se non è vero, è ben trovato"*: an expression attributed to the sixteenth-century Italian philosopher Giordano Bruno.

10. Also called Odin, the principal deity in pre-Christian Norse mythology, and a character in Richard Wagner's Ring cycle operas, which influenced Nazi culture.

11. Esther 4:5.

12. An analogy used in the Talmud tractate Bava Kama (92b:13).

13. Leviticus 22:25.

14. Ezekiel 2:6.

9. THE RULES OF THE GHETTO

1. Psalms 119:143.

2. Deuteronomy 32:24.

3. See chapter 1, note 38.

4. Psalms 78:49.

5. Mendel Leibovich ("a well educated young man, well to do and well connected with the Lithuanians" [Rosin 1996, 658–72]; Yerushalmi 1956), Ber Kartun, and Fayvel Rubinstein (Megargee and Dean 2012, 1190).

6. Genesis 19:20. Žagarė is fifty-five kilometers north of Šiauliai, near the Latvian border.

7. On the southeastern edge of Šiauliai.

8. From the Talmud tractate Ketubot 8a:10.

9. Germany invaded Poland in September 1939.

10. According to his obituary notice in the *New York Times* (June 10, 2000), Dr. Wulf Peisachowitz was born in Šiauliai in 1902 and practiced medicine in Prague before the war. After the Šiauliai ghetto was liquidated he was sent to Dachau, where he was credited with saving numerous lives. After liberation he helped the allies contain a typhoid epidemic in Dachau and directed the Jewish Hospital in Munich. He continued his practice in New York, where he changed his name to William Pace. Affiliated with Mount Sinai Hospital until his retirement, he died June 8, 2000.

11. See also (Yerushalmi 1958, 36).

12. Pick uses the word "rabbits," though Hebrew typically uses "birds."

13. II Kings 6:9.

14. The *Landkremer shul,* a synagogue in the center of Šiauliai, built to serve rural tradesmen, was used to temporarily hold Jews who were later murdered at Žagarė or the Bubiai woods (Rosin 1996, 658–672).

15. One of the 613 *mitzvot* (commandments) mentioned in the Talmud, here an apparent reference to ransom paid for Jews' release.

16. Literally "so-and-so," Ruth 4:1.

17. Genesis 7:11.

18. In September 1941, near the village of Bubiai, approximately fifteen kilometers from Šiauliai, some five hundred Jews were brought in trucks, forced to undress, beaten, and then driven into the pits, where they were shot (Megargee and Dean 2012, 1119).

19. Genesis 4:10.

20. I Samuel 3:11.

21. "Among [those taken on Sept. 11] was the longtime devoted teacher Eliezer Goldstein. Even in the ghetto he had planned to establish a school, and had prepared paper, notebooks and pens for the children. He and his wife were among the first victims. They were all taken out the Kurshaner Road, in the direction of Riga" (Yerushalmi 1951, 1776).

22. Genesis 3:19.

23. From Isaiah 58:7.

24. Job 2:4.

25. See chapter 2, note 54.

26. A common Talmudic term of respect.

27. Isaiah 30:20.

28. Lit., "shunned by men." From Isaiah 53:3.

29. From the Talmud (Bava Metzia 71a): "Between a poor person of your city and one of another city, the one of your city takes precedence."

30. Job 3:22.

31. One of the largest leather factories in Eastern Europe, founded by Chaim Frenkel (1851–1920) and operated by his family until it was nationalized by the Soviets in 1940.

32. Proverbs 31:27.

33. A phrase in the Talmud describing the sukkah, a temporary structure built for the annual celebration of Sukkot.

34. Eliyahu Mordil (Golan 1997, 114 and 179).

35. Isaiah 58:7.

36. Jacob Frenkel (dates unknown).

37. Psalms 19:8.

38. That is, Zionism.

39. The Palestine Foundation Fund, started in 1920 by the World Zionist Organization to finance Jewish settlement.

40. Numbers 16:14.

41. The New York World's Fair opened in April 1939 and ran until October 1940.

42. Dora Frenkel, 1859–1941 (https://www.geni.com/people /Dora-Dvora-Frenkel/6000000043744753026).

43. Theodor Adrian von Renteln (1897–1946) was the *Generalkommissar* of German-occupied Lithuania from 1941–1944. According to the Jewish Virtual Library, he was executed in the Soviet Union for war crimes.

44. Esther 4:14.

45. Numbers 11:23.

46. A frequent Talmudic warning, e.g.,Kitzur Shulchan Aruch 192:3.

47. Psalms 44:23.

48. Numbers 33:55.

49. Commerce in imperial Russia was officially regulated according to a class system, with merchants of the first guild granted the broadest scope to travel and trade. Those of the third guild were mainly local traders and artisans in smaller towns.

50. Daniel 12:2.

51. Psalms 48:3.

52. Psalms 139:11.

53. See "Retrieving a Voice from the Ghetto," note 1.

54. *Dayanim,* judges who hear cases in Jewish law.

55. The Jewish police (in Yiddish, *ordnungs-dienst,* literally "security service") unarmed, mostly young men assigned to keep order inside the ghetto. They played a complex role, sometimes physically punishing Jews with the intention of preventing worse from the Germans or Lithuanians.

56. Yerushalmi (1951, 1785) credits Danuta Venclauskaite, the daughter of a prominent Lithuanian lawyer, for setting up workshops for Jewish women. To justify the number of workers, she fabricated financial statements and paid salaries from her own pocket.

57. Joshua 9:21.

58. A Talmudic phrase.

59. From Genesis 42:19.

60. A phrase used by Rashi in a commentary on Deuteronomy.

61. Deuteronomy 28:48.

62. Haggai 1:6.

63. From the *Shehecheyanu,* a traditional blessing recited to mark celebrations and joyous life events.

64. Hosea 13:3.

65. From the Talmud (Ketubot 111a:19).

66. Exodus 21:11.

67. Job 23:13.

68. Ecclesiastes 4:9.

69. A cooperative for wholesale of most food items from grains to imports (Yerushalmi 1958, 111).

70. An ironic play on a phrase recited on Passover to introduce the song "*Dayenu*": "How many are the blessings we received from the Almighty?"

71. Proverbs 8:18.

72. Deuteronomy 24:14.

73. Psalms 121:1.

74. Job 10:21.

75. Isaiah 58:4.

76. From the Talmud (Berachot 64a).

77. "... what will become of the vines?" From a fifth-century Babylonian Talmud passage.

78. II Kings 15:10.

79. Esther 1:18.

80. Isaiah 29:6.

81. Deuteronomy 1:12.

82. "*Kahal Kadosh,*" a Hebrew term denoting a traditional Jewish community.

83. I Samuel 15:32.

84. Isaiah 47:9.

85. Psalms 107:40.

86. Chronicles 12:18.

87. The cabinet holding scrolls of the Torah, a standard feature of Jewish synagogues.

88. II Samuel 1:23.

89. The first mass murder of Šiauliai's Jews took place in the Kužiai forest, twelve kilometers (seven and a half miles) from Šiauliai, on June 29, 1941. Witnesses said Germans perpetrated the Kužiai killings (Megargee and Dean 2012, 1119).

90. Nikolai Nikolaevich was cousin of the tsar and commander of the imperial Russian army in the first years of World War I. As the German army advanced in 1915, he ordered Jews expelled from areas near the front, which included much of Lithuania.

91. Psalms 109:23.

92. Daniel 9:25.

93. Deuteronomy 28:15–69.

94. Deuteronomy 28:19.

95. Deuteronomy 28:29.

96. Deuteronomy 28:34.

97. Deuteronomy 28:66–67.

98. Judges 5:30.

99. Pick uses the phrase "no bears, no woods," from the Talmud (Sotah 47a), referring to a story in II Kings 2:24.

100. Esther 3:13.

101. Hermann Göring, Nazi military leader and political figure, Hitler's designated successor, later convicted of war crimes.

102. Proverbs 26:11.

103. Lena, née Feinberg, age thirty-eight (Yerushalmi 1958, 54) and (Yerushalmi 1956).

104. From Proverbs 31:10, a traditional term of praise for a woman.

105. Esther, age twelve and Shmuel, age four (Yerushalmi 1958, 54) and (Yerushalmi 1956).

106. Daniel 12:2.

107. Joel 2:6.

108. An ironic reference to Don Quixote's spavined, half-starved horse, which he imagines is his noble steed.

109. Ecclesiastes 4:9.

110. Judges 5:6.

111. I Samuel 14:27.

112. From the Talmud (tractate Berakhot 5b:15).

113. Psalms 10:10.

114. Jeremiah 22:10.

115. Joshua 8:22.

116. Proverbs 25:20.

117. Isaiah 51:13.

118. See chapter 2, note 22.

119. In winter the sun sets in Šiauliai as early as 4:00 p.m.

120. Proverbs 25:26.

121. The *Deutsche Zeitung im Ostland* was publicshed in Riga from 1941 to 1944.

122. Micah 2:11.

123. *Kauener Zeitung* (Kaunas news) published 1941–44.

124. *Į Laisvę* (To freedom) began publishing in Kaunas in July 1941.

125. First called *Tėvynė*, and later *Tėviškė* (both of which mean "homeland") published in Šiauliai during the years of German occupation (Yerushalmi 1958, 88).

126. Known as the "blood libel," this ancient antisemitic myth was revived and promoted extensively by the Nazis.

127. The pen name of Asher Ginsberg (1857–1927), who promoted the concept of "cultural Zionism."

128. From a collection of midrash dating from the second century AD and republished in 1915.

129. Deuteronomy 28:30.

130. From a third-century Talmudic work, the *Mishnah Megillah*.

131. Lice or gnats, Exodus 8:12.

132. See chapter 7, note 20.

133. From the Passover Haggadah.

134. A Talmudic phrase.

135. From the weekday prayer book.

136. The hospital was set up in February, 1942, in the Kaukazas ghetto (Shalit 1949).

137. Where bodies were ritually prepared for burial.

138. Esther 1:12.

139. "Strenge was a German from Memel— tall, thin, with a red face and a still redder nose. He was constantly drunk. He spent his entire life dealing with Jewish horse dealers and smugglers. He was familiar with Yiddish and Yiddish sayings and used his Yiddish knowledge to extract the Jews' last coins" (Yerushalmi 1951, 1783).

140. Numbers 6:26.

141. I Kings 18:21.

142. *Pirkei Avot* (Sayings of the Fathers) 1:3.

143. Dr. Wulf Peisachowitz (see note 10) became director of the ghetto hospital.

144. Aharon Zeigarnik (also Zeigarnikas). After the Šiauliai ghetto's liquidation he was transferred to Stutthof and later to Dachau, where he died from disease on the day of liberation (Yerushalmi 1958, 53) and (Yerushalmi 1956).

145. Numbers 24:5; also a verse commonly used in daily prayers.

146. Isaiah 53:2.

147. Judges 21:16.

148. Aaron Katz, previously the manager of the Jewish Popular Bank in Šiauliai and a leader in the Socialist Zionist Party (Rosin 1996, 658–72).

149. From *Pirkei Avot* 2:6.

150. Psalms 106:23.

151. Ezekiel 20:43.

152. A region, formerly part of the Austro-Hungarian Empire, encompassing parts of contemporary southern Poland and western Ukraine.

153. Habakkuk 1:3.

154. A tube inserted into bodily cavities to empty their contents.

155. A frequent Talmudic expression, e.g., Shabbat 88a.

156. Exodus 1:10. Pharaoh's call to enslave the Israelites.

157. Under Nazi occupation, the value of the Soviet ruble (which had replaced Lithuania's national currency in April 1941) became fixed at an exchange rate of 10 rubles to 1 reichsmark.

158. Psalms 90:3.

159. Other sources (Shalit 1949; Yerushalmi 1958, 189) identify Šiauliai's two Jewish obstetrician-gynecologists as Drs. Goldberg and Luntz.

160. I Samuel 26:19.

161. I Samuel 2:36.

162. A frequent Talmudic phrase, e.g., Pele Yoetz 238:4.

163. Hats made of wooly lambskin, also called Astrakhans.

164. From the Talmud (Yevamot 62a) referring to a people with no lineage (in this case, Lithuanians).

165. Pick uses a rare term for quarantine, found in II Kings 15:5 and II Chronicles 26:21.

166. From the "Ma'ariv Aravim" prayer traditionally recited each evening.

167. Proverbs 15:23.

168. Proverbs 14:34.

169. January 6 is traditionally the date of Epiphany, celebrated as the last day of Christmas by many Christians.

170. July and August, 1941.

171. A legal principle mentioned frequently in the Talmud, for example at Ketubot 22a:5.

172. Jews forced to convert in fifteenth-century Spain and Portugal who nonetheless retained their Jewish identity and practices in secret.

173. I Samuel 16:14.

174. Twenty-three kilometers east of Šiauliai.

175. "In mid-April 1942, Dr. Charney, chief of the security service, summoned the Jewish representatives and informed them, in a categorical tone, that no more births were to occur in the ghetto. He ordered them to write this in a published notice. He added that, if the order was not followed, 'violators,' i.e., the mothers, together with their entire families, would be killed" (Yerushalmi 1951, 1781). The ban on births was to take effect on August 15, 1942.

176. Yerushalmi (1958, 27) says the Nazi political chief for the Šiauliai district, Ewald Bub, had proposed castrating Jewish men.

177. That is, they had to walk alongside the cart (Yerushalmi 1958, 57).

178. See note 139.

179. From a prayer said between Rosh Hashanah and Yom Kippur.

180. Mendel Leibovitch.

181. During the Third Reich, Germany conducted an annual charity drive, known as *Winterhilfswerk*, to provide clothing and food to the needy.

182. Portable kerosene burners, often used outdoors.

183. Psalms 31:11.

184. Daniel 12:6.

185. 2 Sivan 5702.

10. FROM MY DIARY

1. Approximately twenty-three kilometers.

2. From Isaiah 57:2.

3. From the Unetaneh Tokef prayer, said on Rosh Hashanah and Yom Kippur.

4. A city on the eastern end of the Crimean Peninsula, near the strait that connects the Sea of Azov to the Black Sea. A series of battles ended with the Germans in control of this area by mid-May 1942.

5. Kharkiv, in eastern Ukraine, was seized by the Germans in late 1941. A Red Army counteroffensive during May 1942 failed to retake the city.

6. From the blessings said after meals.

7. Likely referring to the Axis powers of Germany, Italy, and Japan.

8. A Talmudic phrase describing life after the destruction of the Temple in Jerusalem.

9. Psalms 119:123.

10. From the Talmud (Rosh Hashanah 25b).

11. Dairy meals are traditionally eaten on the Shavuot holiday.

12. Ezekiel 36:30.

13. From the fifth-century Talmud (Sanhedrin 96b:4).

14. Ezekiel 2:10.

15. Approximately seven ounces.

16. For men and women, respectively, equal to 1.5 and 1.3 German reichsmarks.

17. Proverbs 17:5.

18. British and Allied forces pushed the Italian army out of East Africa, including Ethiopia (also called Abyssinia) by the end of 1941.

19. Psalms 71:13.

20. British forces defending the Libyan city of Tobruk surrendered to a German army in June 1942. The Germans pushed eastward into Egypt and might have reached Palestine had the British not stopped them at El-Alamein later in 1942.

21. Before the State of Israel's establishment in 1948, Jews referred to Palestine as Eretz (Land of) Israel.

22. From the Talmud (Mishnah Keritot 3:8).

23. A city 515 kilometers south of Moscow.

24. From *Pirkei Avot* 2:6.

25. A cumulative song traditionally sung after the Passover Seder in which each "conqueror" in turn becomes conquered, with God delivering the final blow.

26. Esther 1:10.

27. Theodor Adrian von Renteln. See chapter 9, note 43.

28. Judges 5:31.

29. From the Mishnah, the "oral law" (Sanhedrin 5:2).

30. In 1942, this Hebrew month coincided with June 16–July 14.

31. Psalms 107:39.

32. Job 17:1.

33. Psalms 118:15.

34. Numbers 23:9. In rabbinic writing the nation of Israel is often called "a people that dwells apart."

35. Ber Menashe Abramovich. He was among those named to the Jewish council when the ghetto was set up (Yerushalmi 1958, 18).

36. Daniel 9:25.

37. Joshua 6:1.

38. Mizrachi was a movement and political party of religious Zionists in interwar Eastern Europe, representing what is today called "modern Orthodox" Judaism.

39. From the *Midrash Tanchuma*, a collection of stories, legal discussions and homilies connected to the Torah.

40. Isaiah 16:7.

41. Lamentations 2:15.

42. A city in western Belarus, about five hundred kilometers south of Šiauliai.

43. A phrase found in rabbinic literature (*Midrash Tanchuma*), originally referring to the Israelites' pursuers during the Exodus from Egypt.

44. A detailed account of this incident appears in Shalit (1949, 99).

45. Deuteronomy 7:6.

46. Hosea 1:2.

47. Job 4:12.

48. Known as the "*hagomel*" prayer, offered in thanks for surviving an illness or life-threatening ordeal.

49. *Nigella sativa*, also called black cumin or fennel flower seed, used to treat gastric and intestinal ailments.

50. From a Hebrew prayer recited weekday mornings and afternoons.

51. Proverbs 21:14.

52. Allied forces (mostly Canadians) attacked the northern French port of Dieppe on August 19, 1942, but were repelled by the Germans and suffered massive casualties.

53. Paul Joseph Goebbels, Hitler's minister for propaganda. After the Dieppe raid he published articles disparaging the Allied effort.

54. Isaiah 37:3.

55. The Gebietskommissar, Hans Gewecke.

56. The Trakų ghetto area, Žilvičių Street was near the Frenkel leather factory.

57. Judges 3:20.

58. II Kings 13:7.

59. Numbers 17:11.

60. Esther 9:28.

61. Daniel 12:2.

62. Literally, "bore into the heavier side of the beam," a phrase used by Rashi in a commentary on Genesis.

63. Esther 8:16.

64. Job 2:4.

65. The October 13, 1941, demand was for 500,000 rubles (10 rubles = 1 mark). Therefore the new demand equaled 200,000 rubles.

66. Job 21:7.

67. 1 Tishrei 5703 on the Hebrew calendar.

68. From the Talmud (Tractate Shabbat, 13b).

69. Leviticus 18:21. Moloch was a Canaanite god associated with child sacrifice.

70. From the Mishnah (Rosh Hashanah 3:8).

71. From the 1833 poem "Autumn," by Alexander Pushkin.

72. From the 1864 poem "The Railway" by Nikolai Nekrasov. (Quoted in Russian by Pick.)

73. The ten-day period encompassing Rosh Hashana and Yom Kippur.

74. September 14, 1939. The manuscript erroneously cites the Hebrew calendar date as 1 Tishrei 5699, which would have been September 26, 1938. Subsequent Hebrew dates in this paragraph are also off by one year.

75. This date was September 22, or 1 Tishrei 5702, whereas the manuscript shows Tishrei 1 5701.

76. Psalms 69:2.

77. The third to seventh days of the eight-day Sukkot festival.

78. Jeremiah 2:12.

79. One of the longest and bloodiest battles of World War I, lasting from February to December 1916 and producing more than 700,000 casualties. By comparison, casualty estimates for the battle of Stalingrad exceed 1.5 million.

80. From Jeremiah 51:30.

81. Title used in Soviet propaganda for Josef Stalin.

82. Proverbs 28:21.

83. In 1942, the Germans began a campaign to "Germanize" parts of Lithuania, beginning with Kaunas. Lithuanians living there were forced to relocate. Herman Kruk's Vilna ghetto diary suggests Lithuanians resisted the directive.

84. The annual holiday marking a new cycle of weekly Torah readings, normally celebrated with joyous drinking and dancing (hence the likely intended irony of Pick's opening sentence).

85. Proverbs 16:26.

86. Jeremiah 6:4.

87. Joshua 2:19.

88. Hitler gave a speech in Berlin on September 30, 1942. The translated text appeared in the *New York Times* October 1.

89. Isaiah 9:16 and 5:25.

90. The day following the close of the Sukkot holidays.

91. The last day of Sukkot, preceding Simchat Torah.

92. Isaiah 24:11.

93. Other sources (Morgan 2008, 76) identify him as Josef Leibovich, brother of Jewish council chairman Mendel Leibovich.

94. A reference to the Passover song *"Dayenu,"* expressing thanks to the almighty for the liberation from Egypt, the Torah, and so on.

95. Yerushalmi (1958, 123) identifies him as Yeshayahu Reiss, and the German attacker as Corporal Schultz.

96. Deuteronomy 28:48.

97. A liturgic phrase preceding a blessing (e.g., over wine).

98. Isaiah 35:10.

99. Benito Mussolini, Fascist leader of Italy from 1922 to 1943.

100. Joshua 8:22.

101. From an eighteenth-century commentary on Genesis.

102. Isaiah 5:5.

103. In the second battle of El Alamein, from October 23 to November 11, 1942, Allied forces halted the Axis advance in North Africa and took some thirty thousand German and Italian prisoners.

104. Esther 8:14.

105. Hitler spoke in Munich on November 8, the anniversary of his abortive coup attempt in 1923, known as the putsch.

106. A measure of weight used in agriculture, here about 150 kilograms.

107. Alfred Ernst Rosenberg, Nazi propagandist named Reich Minister for the Occupied Eastern Territories in 1941. His own diary of the war years is held by the US Holocaust Memorial Museum.

108. According to Yerushalmi (1958, 131), Dubkin was the buyer for the Jewish council.

109. Under the Vichy government headed by Marshal Pétain, François Darlan was military chief. He switched to the Allies after the invasion of North Africa in 1942 but was assassinated two months later.

110. Henri Honoré Giraud, leader of Free French forces 1942–44.

111. Leviticus 26:37.

112. Daniel 12:12.

113. A village twenty-eight kilometers northwest of Šiauliai.

114. The full text is reproduced in (Yerushalmi 1958, 134).

115. Psalms 121:4.

116. I Chronicles 4:43.

117. Psalms 86:13.

118. 104°F.

119. Numbers 12:14.

120. As in most traditional Jewish communities, cemeteries and internment in pre-war Šiauliai were overseen by the Burial Society (*chevra kadisha*), which established and managed the necessary facilities.

121. I Chronicles 4:43.

122. II Kings 13:7.

123. Deuteronomy 34:7.

124. Hebrew month corresponding to January–February.

125. Proverbs 6:10.

126. Isaiah 38:10.

127. Isaiah 45:17.

128. The Hungarian Second Army also participated, fighting in the Voronezh region and suffering immense casualties.

129. How Pick came to understand the magnitude of Jewish death in early 1943 is unclear. Reports that the toll had reached six million emerged near the end of the war. Adolf Eichmann estimated that number in a report to Hitler in August 1944 (Hilberg 2003, 631) and it also appeared in Soviet reports later that year.

130. Psalms 84:8.

131. Psalms 119:50.

132. Genesis 27:40.

133. Psalms 31:11.

134. Exodus 15:16.

135. Chol HaMoed is the third to sixth days of Passover, which began on April 20, 1943. Hence, April 23.

136. Psalms 88:5.

137. Also called pleurisy, affecting the tissue surrounding the lungs.

138. Robert Koch, German researcher credited with showing the connection between bacteria and diseases such as tuberculosis.

139. Exodus 32:12.

140. American planes bombed the Antwerp suburb of Mortsel on April 5, 1943, aiming for a German aircraft factory but mainly hitting civilian areas nearby.

141. The industrial center of Essen, in the Ruhr valley, was a prime target during a British and American bombing campaign that lasted for five months in 1943.

142. Genesis 6:7.

143. The massacres of Polish officers in the Katyn forest, near Smolensk, Russia, took place in April and May 1940. German soldiers discovered the bodies in April 1943. The Soviet government continued to blame Germany for the murders until 1990, when it finally admitted that NKVD agents had carried them out.

144. The Warsaw ghetto uprising began on April 19, 1943, and lasted until May 16.

145. April 24, 1943.

146. Thirty-four kilometers east of Šiauliai.

147. Elsewhere referred to (in Hebrew) as the labor police.

148. Mordechai Lipshitz, chief accountant and director of production at the Frenkel shoe factory. After the Šiauliai ghetto was liquidated, he was transported to Stutthof and then to Dachau, where he died on June 10, 1945 (Lipshitz 2002).

149. Proverbs 27:24.

150. Genesis 24:1.

151. April 25, 1943.

152. Joel 2:6.

153. Deuteronomy 28:66.

154. Proverbs 27:1.

155. Betzalel Mazovetsky. Yerushalmi (1958, 229) says this hanging took place on June 6, a month later than Pick dates it. However, excerpts from Yerushalmi's diary that were published in *The Black Book of Russian Jewry* (quoted in Hilberg 2003, 302) date it as May 4. Levi Shalit (1949) gives no exact date but implies it took place in May. See also Yad Vashem Pages of Testimony, under the name Mazowiecki Becalelis: https://yvng.yadvashem.org/nameDetails.html?language =en&itemId=1667762&ind=1.

156. Other accounts say his contraband consisted of cigarettes and sausage (Yerushalmi 1958, 223). Shalit (1949, 201) says that Günter, head of the labor police, told ghetto officials the hanging was meant as a warning to others. For his role in the hanging, the Nazi Gebietskommisar Hans Gewecke was convicted at a 1971 trial and sentenced to four and a half years in prison.

157. Job 20:14.

158. Psalms 17:11.

159. On July 25, Italy's king and cabinet removed Mussolini from office and arrested him.

160. Jeremiah 48:28.

161. A Latin phrase deriving from Hannibal's campaign against Rome when the Carthaginian general was at the city's gates.

162. This entry appears on the first page of the third volume of the manuscript.

163. Micah 7:11.

164. Italian troops invaded and occupied portions of southeastern France in 1940 and 1942.

165. Esther 4:14.

166. Isaiah 48:6.

167. Isaiah 30:30.

168. Genesis 21:7.

169. According to the historian Gibbon, when the Roman emperor Augustus was told that one of his generals, Quinctillius Varus, had lost most of his army in a battle with German tribes, the emperor lost his famously stoic composure, beat his head on a wall, and cried, "*Quintili Vare, legiones redde!*" (Give me back my legions!).

170. In August 1943, the Germans began deporting thousands of Jews from the Vilnius ghetto to labor and death camps in Estonia. In early September, members of the ghetto's underground resistance movement began fleeing to join anti-German partisans fighting in the nearby forests.

171. Deuteronomy 32:35.

172. Deuteronomy 29:22.

173. Southern Ukraine city on the Sea of Azov.

174. The large river dividing Eastern and Western Ukraine.

175. A Talmudic expression, e.g., Eicha Rabba 4:14.

176. September 10, broadcast (*New York Times* archive).

177. Exodus 4:10.

178. Isaiah 29:2, Lamentations 2:5.

179. From Jonah 4:6, referring to the shade plant that grew up and quickly died.

180. Psalms 58:7.

181. Tsar Peter I, whose successful wars against Sweden in the early eighteenth century left Russia the dominant power in the Baltic region.

182. Bubnys (2014, 58) says the SS took control of the Šiauliai ghetto on October 1, 1943, from Gebietskomissar (district commissioner) Hans Gewecke. Yerushalmi (1958, 270) says the handover took place September 18. SS Hauptsturmfürer (Captain) Heinrich Förster was the first commandant, later replaced by Oberscharführer Hermann Schlöf.

183. Job 6:11.

184. From Psalms 16:6.

185. Isaiah 24:11.

186. September 29, 1943.

187. Deuteronomy 32:28.

188. According to Shneiderman (1957c, 2), Peisachowitz successfully diagnosed and treated Förster's ulcer. As a result, Peisachowitz was allowed access to the municipal hospital, where he was able to obtain drugs and medical supplies for the ghetto and where a clandestine radio allowed the doctors to learn news of the war from BBC broadcasts.

189. The Talmud uses the term "Canaanite slave" to refer to any enslaved non-Jew.

190. October 1, 1943.

191. Isaiah 58:7.

192. Psalms 119:143.

193. Poltava and Chernigov (today Chernihiv) are cities in Ukraine, southeast and northeast of Kyiv, respectively. Smolensk is approximately four hundred miles west of Moscow. All three cities were recaptured by the Red Army in late September 1943.

194. Yugoslav partisan forces under Josip Broz Tito were officially recognized by the Allies in September 1943.

195. See chapter 6, note 21.

196. Ruth 3:18.

197. Italian-origin phrase, found also in Russian literature, roughly meaning "the game is over."

198. Gershon Žemaitiškis. Yerushalmi (1958, 287) reports he was shot by Schlöf on October 17, 1943.

199. Psalms 97:11.

200. "Simulant" was a ghetto term for those pretending illness.

201. Hosea 13:3.

202. Proverbs 18:23.

203. The identity of the "hangman from Dachau" is somewhat unclear. Golan (1997, 191) indicates it was Förster, but Yerushalmi (1958, 237) suggests it was Schlöf, who appears to have been assigned to Šiauliai after serving at the Dachau concentration camp complex.

204. October 17, 1943 (Yerushalmi 1958, 288).

205. Exodus 1:14.

206. According to Yerushalmi (1958, 288), the shooter was the sergeant major mentioned earlier.

207. Ukrainian cities on the Dnieper River, south of Kyiv. Dnipropetrovsk was known as Ekaterinoslav until 1925 and since 2016 has been called Dnipro.

208. From Hayim Nachman Bialik's poem "On the Slaughter" (Al HaShechita), published after the April 1903 pogrom in the Bessarabian city of Kishiniev. This entry describes the aktion of November 5, 1943, when hundreds of children and elderly people were deported from the Šiauliai ghetto, most to their deaths at Auschwitz.

209. Lamentations 2:5.

210. Ecclesiastes 1:10.

211. From a dirge recited on Tisha B'Av, the traditional day of mourning for the lost Temple in Jerusalem.

212. Ezekiel 7:6.

213. Psalms 88:13.

214. From Psalms 103:16.

215. Habakkuk 1:3.

216. I Samuel 15:32.

217. Isaiah 14:19.

218. Uri Rozovsky, b. 1871. See also Yerushalmi (1958, 309) and Yerushalmi (1956).

219. Lamentations 4:20.

220. Ivan Andreyevich Krylov (1768–1844), Russian writer known for his allegorical stories.

221. Tedik Pick did escape the ghetto, just before it was liquidated in July 1944. According to Shalit (1949, 299), he walked through the gate carrying a pot, telling the guard he was bringing lunch from ghetto chief Pariser to the commandant in town. Sofija Jasaitienė (the wife of Dr. Domas Jasaitis) wrote in 1946 that Tedik had obtained the identity papers of a Lithuanian student. German records indicate he went to Lodz, Poland, after it was liberated and later made his way to a displaced-persons camp near Munich, where he stayed until leaving for Israel via Marseilles in 1948.

222. Hitler spoke at the site of the 1923 "beer-hall *putsch*," an abortive coup against the government of Bavaria that left several of his supporters dead and landed him in the jail cell where he wrote *Mein Kampf*.

223. Samuel Rubinshtein. See Yerushalmi (1958, 308).

224. See chapter 1, note 23.

225. A form of chronic hypertension.

226. Bubnys (2014, 63) says 570 children and 260 elderly people were deported from Šiauliai in the November 5 aktion. Leiba Lipshitz (2001) adds those taken from the surrounding work camps to get a total of 725 children. Yerushalmi (1958, 309) says the total was 796, including 509 children under ten, 68 ages ten to thirteen, and 4 women who joined them voluntarily.

227. Lamentations 1:7. Yerushalmi (1958, 307) recounts that the boy, Maikele Movshovitz, not yet three years old, had lost his father before the ghetto was established. His mother "made superhuman efforts to keep the child well-fed and clean." During the November 5 aktion, Devorah Pick tried unsuccessfully to conceal the boy among some pillows. "When the Ukrainian found him, he stepped out quietly, hurrying to put on his coat. But the murderer would not let him, and pushed him quickly towards the door. Mrs. P[ick] offered the murderer all her precious jewelry in return for the child. He took them from her—and then took the child too."

228. The Luntz family's escape, recapture and release from prison was described in a series of articles by the Yiddish journalist S. L. Shneiderman (1957b and 1957d).

229. Pariser, who eventually became the de facto head of the Jewish ghetto administration, was married to a gentile woman who joined him voluntarily in the ghetto. Yerushalmi (1951, 1808) reports he used his position to live lavishly and was personally close to Förster, the SS commandant, but also that he was attentive to the remaining ghetto residents, bending rules and doing favors. According to Lipschitz (2001), the Germans freed him when the ghetto was liquidated, but after the war he was arrested by the Soviets and imprisoned for ten years. He later emigrated to West Germany.

230. Sanhedrin 108b:22.

231. Zephania 1:15.

232. Aaron Katz and Ber Kartun, both members of the Šiauliai ghetto Jewish council.

233. From the Talmud (Sanhedrin 111a).

234. Deuteronomy 22:7.

235. Yerushalmi (1958, 323) says Luntz was freed because he was the ghetto's only gynecologist-obstetrician. Shneiderman (1957d) reports that the German commandant, Schlöf, ordered Luntz and his wife, a nurse, freed so they could

perform an abortion on Schlöf's mistress before her husband, a Wehrmacht officer, returned on leave from the front.

236. Jasaitis (2002, 61) says Luntz's home and maternity hospital became the local headquarters for the Gestapo and SD police.

237. Mendel Leibovich, the Jewish council chairman.

238. Psalms 44:14.

239. Henich Rayz (Yerushalmi 1958, 321).

240. Lamentations 5:15.

241. From a dirge recited on Tisha B'Av, the traditional day of mourning for the lost Temple in Jerusalem.

242. This camp was known as the A.B.A., as it was under the supervision of the German *Armeebekleidungsamt*, or Army Clothing Office.

243. Minutes from a March 24, 1943, meeting of the Jewish council (Yerushalmi 1958, 188), describe the debate about what to do about some twenty Jewish women who were pregnant despite the ban on births. Dr. Luntz reported that three live births had taken place since the ban took effect on August 15. Two women were refusing to undergo abortions. Various proposals were discussed to persuade or force the women to abort while keeping the pregnancies secret from the Germans. Luntz noted that one woman was in her eighth month. "It will surely be impossible to convince her [to abort]. And what will happen to the infant if we cause a premature birth? We cannot carry out an operation like that in a private home, and it is forbidden to leave the child at the [ghetto] hospital. And what will happen if, despite everything, the child is born alive? Shall we kill it? I cannot accept such a responsibility on my conscience." The council decided to force early delivery of the child and then to administer a lethal injection.

244. From the testimony of nurse Chana Gafnovitz: "One woman was in her eighth month of pregnancy. It was necessary to abort her pregnancy. But it turned instead into an early delivery. I worked in the clinic and it was decided to perform it in the evening to make sure that neither the Germans nor the ghetto residents noticed. We covered the clinic's windows and Dr. Luntz did the abortion. But a live baby was born. He had to die. We had to inject him with high doses of morphine or scopolamine. There was a collapsed building in the ghetto, and I was ordered to take the baby there. We put him between pillows and took him there, me and a representative of the Jüdenrat. I went there a few times to see if he was still alive. I saw he was alive and returned to tell Dr. Pick that I don't want to inject him anymore. Dr. Pick replied: 'It's not your hands injecting him. These are Hitler's hands.' I could not look at the baby. He was shrinking from moment to moment. I injected him and looked the other way. The baby died after a week" (Chana Gafnovitz, 2002).

245. A Jewish ritual slaughterer.

246. From November 22 to November 26, 1943, Roosevelt and Churchill met in Cairo with Chinese leader Chiang Kai-Shek, regarding the Allies' war plans for Asia. FDR and Churchill then flew to Tehran to meet with Stalin. The American and British leaders returned to Cairo for a second meeting from December 2 to December 7 with the president of Turkey.

247. Feldwebel (sergeant) Graubel (Lipshitz 2002) and (Bubnys 2014) or Gaudel (Yerushalmi 1958, 329).

248. Yerushalmi (1958, 329) provides a partial list of the victims.

249. Franz von Papen, Nazi diplomat, was rumored in late 1943 to be floating peace proposals from his ambassadorial post in Turkey.

250. A Ukrainian city 140 kilometers west of Kyiv.

251. The image comes from the *kapores* ceremony performed before Yom Kippur, when devout Jews traditionally hold a live chicken while reciting prayers. On the orderly's role, see Yerushalmi (1958, 314).

252. November 6, 1943, the day after they were taken from Šiauliai.

253. Other sources, including Jasaitis (2002) and Bubnys (2014), say the train's final destination was Auschwitz.

254. Isaiah 53:4.

255. Isaiah 40:26.

256. From a broadcast speech on January 30, 1944.

257. A frequent Talmudic phrase, e.g., Jerusalem Talmud Sanhedrin 1:1.

258. The commandant initially intended to shoot two doctors in retaliation. He was persuaded to commute that sentence after being told that Dr. Goldberg worked as a common laborer (Yerushalmi 1958, 349).

259. Esther 7:10.

260. Deuteronomy 34:7.

261. Chaim Weizmann, president of the World Zionist Organization (and later the first president of the state of Israel) spent the war years in London, where he negotiated with the British on behalf of the Jews in Palestine, then under British control. David Ben-Gurion chaired the Jewish Agency, the de facto government of the Palestine settlement. He resigned that position in October 1943 to protest Weizmann's position regarding British policy.

262. A 1939 British policy paper that limited Jewish immigration to Palestine and proposed to end it entirely after five years.

263. Miriam Klugman, Yerushalmi (1958, 352) and Golan (1997, 207) identify her as the daughter of the former head of the Šiauliai Zionist Association and say she was killed at Stutthof because of the disability caused by her injury.

264. According to Yerushalmi (1958, 352), Alter Edelstein quarreled with a neighbor while drunk, and the following day verbally attacked Pariser, calling him a "provocateur."

265. Yerushalmi (1958, 360) reports that this occurred on March 7.

266. Exodus 1:8.

267. Deuteronomy 22:17.

268. Including women (Yerushalmi 1958, 362).

269. Literally leavened bread, which is prohibited during Passover and therefore removed during a preholiday ritual cleaning. Here it is a metaphor for getting rid of the evidence.

270. From the Mishna (Bava Kama 7:1).

271. Esther 1:18.

272. Ephraim Gens was head of the Ežero-Trakų ghetto police from September 1941 until March 25, 1944 (Megargee and Dean 2012, 1120). He was the brother of Jacob Gens, head of the Vilnius ghetto Jüdenrat. Ephraim Gens survived the war but was later arrested and tried by the Soviets in 1949. He was sentenced to twenty-five years in the gulag but was freed in 1956. He died in 1971 at age sixty (Cassedy 2015, 217).

273. According to Yerushalmi (1958, 368), he was an electrician working in a factory.

274. The original manuscript of Pick's Yiddish diary, which has never been published or translated, is held by the Vilna Gaon State Museum of Jewish History in Vilnius.

275. On March 27 and 28, some one thousand children and three hundred old people were taken from the Kaunas ghetto and sent to the German death camps (Megargee and Dean 2012, 850).

276. SS Obersturmbannführer (lieutenant colonel) Wilhelm Göcke.

277. A tsarist-era military emplacement built in 1913 outside Kaunas, converted by the Germans into a prison and mass-murder site. Some fifty thousand Jews from as far as France were killed there. In March 1944, members of the Kaunas ghetto Jewish police were brought there and brutally interrogated regarding ghetto hideouts and resistance movements (Megargee and Dean 2012, 850).

278. In 1944 Easter Sunday fell on April 9.

279. The Red Army recaptured Odessa, on the Black Sea, on April 10. Kovel, in northwestern Ukraine, and Iași, in eastern Romania, were retaken in July and August of that year, respectively. Budapest fell on February 13, 1945.

280. Isaiah 22:5.

281. From Rashi's commentary on Exodus.

282. From the Passover Haggadah, referring to the Exodus from Egypt.

283. Isaiah 62:7.

284. Said to have been a favorite saying of the Roman emperor Caligula.

285. Pick died sometime between June 7, when his last diary entry is dated, and July 15, when the Germans began liquidating the ghetto. Golan (1997, 14) reports

that Pick was among the last to be buried in the Šiauliai Jewish cemetery (near the Kaukazas ghetto area). The cemetery was destroyed after the war.

286. Allied forces entered Rome on June 4, 1944.

287. Le Havre was bombed on D-Day, but the invasion actually began on the Normandy beaches, 80 to 120 kilometers west of LeHavre.

288. Isaiah 54:17.

289. Psalms 137:7.

290. Fritz Todt, who built the German military construction organization and ran it until his death in 1942. He was succeeded by Albert Speer.

291. Amos 8:10.

REFERENCES

Alter, Robert. 1988. "Inventing Hebrew Prose." *Commentary* 85 (3): 35. ProQuest. Document number 1290134760.

Arad, Yitzhak. 2004. "The Murder of the Jews in German-Occupied Lithuania (1941–1944)." In *The Vanished World of Lithuanian Jews*, edited by Alvydas Nikžentaitis, Stefan Schreiner, and Darius Staliūnas, 175–99. Amsterdam: Rodopi.

Berg, Mary. 1945. *Warsaw Ghetto: A Diary*. Edited by S. L. Shneiderman. New York: L. B. Fischer.

Bohlman, Philip V. 2010. *Focus: Music, Nationalism, and the Making of the New Europe*. New York: Routledge. ProQuest Ebook Central. Document number 574527.

Bubnys, Arūnas. 2014. *The Šiauliai Ghetto*. Vilnius: Lithuanian Genocide and Resistance Research Center.

———. 2020. "The Holocaust in Lithuania, 1941–1944." In *The History of Jews in Lithuania, from the Middle Ages to the 1990s*, edited by Vladas Sirutavicius. Darius Staliūnas, and Jurgita Siaučiūnaitė. Leiden, Netherlands: Ferdinand Schoning, 2020.

Cassedy, Ellen. 2012. *We Are Here: Memories of the Lithuanian Holocaust*. Lincoln: University of Nebraska Press.

Cassel, Boruch Chaim. 1930. "Di shtot Keidan" [*The City of Keidan*]. In *Keidan: A zamel bukh* [*Keidan: An Anthology*]. New York: Keidaner Association of NY. A translation along with numerous memoirs and essays about the community are available online: https://keidaner.com/013the-city-of-keidan/.

Cohen, Boaz. 2013. "Jews, Jewish Studies and Holocaust Historiography." *Kwartalnik Historii Żydów* 246 (2): 400–413.

Dieckmann, Christoph. 2000. "The War and the Killing of Lithuanian Jews."
Chapter 9 in *National Socialist Extermination Policies: Contemporary German Perspectives and Controversies*, edited by Herbert Ulrich and Aly Götz. English-language ed. New York: Berghahn Books.

Eherenberg, Ilya, and Vassily Grossman. 2002. *The Complete Black Book of Russian Jewry*. Translated and edited by David Patterson. New Brunswick, NJ: Transaction Publishers.

Foer, Joshua, and Brett Lockspeiser. n.d. *Sefaria: A Living Library of Jewish Texts*. www.sefaria.org.

Friedländer, Saul. 2007. *Nazi Germany and the Jews: The Years of Extermination, 1939–1945*. New York: HarperCollins.

Gafnovitz-Preiss, Chana. 2002. *Testimony*. Catalog No. 14508. Ghetto Fighters' Kibbutz, Israel: Ghetto Fighters House Archives.

Garbarini, Alexandra. 2008. *Numbered Days: Diaries and the Holocaust*. New Haven, CT: Yale University Press.

Gidron, Noa. 2020. "Jewish Women Medical Practitioners Who Rescued Fellow Jews during the Holocaust." *Nashim: A Journal of Jewish Women's Studies and Gender Issues*, no. 36, 39–59. ProQuest. Document number 2421439435.

Ginzburg, Saul M., and P. S. Marek. 1991. *Yidishe folkslider in rusland* [Yiddish folksongs in Russia]. Photo reproduction of the 1901 St. Petersburg ed., edited by Dov Noy. Ramat Gan, Israel: Bar-Ilan University Press.

Golan, David. 1997. Introduction and commentary to *Reshimot mi-ge ha-haregah: Zikhronot ketuvim be-geto ha-Shavla'I (Liṭa) bi-shenot 5702, 5703, 5704* [Notes from the valley of slaughter: A memoir written in the Šiauliai Ghetto, 1942–44], by Dr. Aharon Pick. Tel Aviv, Israel: Association of the Lithuanian Jews in Israel.

Halkin, Hillel. 1983. "On Translating the Living and the Dead: Some Thoughts of a Hebrew-English Translator." *Prooftexts* 3 (1): 73–90. https://www.jstor.org/stable/20689058.

Hilberg, Raul. 2001. *Sources of Holocaust Research: An Analysis*. Chicago: I. R. Dee.
———. 2003. *The Destruction of the European Jews*. 3rd ed. New Haven, CT: Yale University Press.

Jasaitis, Domas. 2002. "The Rescuers Tell Their Tale." In *Whoever Saves One Life: The Efforts to Save Jews in Lithuania between 1941 and 1944*, edited by Alexander Fortescue, Rimantas Stankevičius, and D. Kuodytė, 43–69. Vilnius, Lithuania: Genocide and Resistance Research Centre of Lithuania. https://www.lituanistika.lt/content/84123.

Kaplan, Chaim Aron, and Abraham Isaac Katsh. 1999. *Scroll of Agony: The Warsaw Diary of Chaim A. Kaplan*. Bloomington: Indiana University Press.

Karnes, Kevin, and Emilis Melngailis. 2015. *Jewish Folk Songs from the Baltics: Selections from the Melngailis Collection*. Middleton, WI: A-R Editions.

Kassow, Samuel. 1999. "Vilna and Warsaw, Two Ghetto Diaries." In *Holocaust Chronicles: Individualizing the Holocaust through Diaries and Other Contemporaneous Personal Accounts*, edited by Robert Moses Shapiro, 171–215. Hoboken, NJ: Ktav.

Kruk, Herman, and Benjamin Harshav. 2002. *The Last Days of the Jerusalem of Lithuania: Chronicles from the Vilna Ghetto and the Camps, 1939–1944*. New Haven, CT: YIVO Institute for Jewish Research.

Laczó, Ferenc. 2018. "Beyond Helpless Victims and Survivor Trauma: New Historiography on Jews in the Age of the Holocaust." In *Contemporary European History* 27 (4): 693–707.

Lipshitz, Leiba. 2001. "The Šiauliai Ghetto, July 18, 1941–July 24, 1944." In *The Šiauliai Ghetto: Lists of Prisoners*, edited by Jevgenija Sedova and Irina Guzenberg. Vilnius, Lithuania: Vilna Gaon Jewish Museum. http://www .jmuseum.lt/old/media.search.lt/2faa3.doc?OID=270188&FID=788952.

Matthäus, Jürgen, and Emil Kerenji. 2017. *Jewish Responses to Persecution, 1933– 1946: A Source Reader*. Lanham, MD: Rowman and Littlefield in association with the United States Holocaust Memorial Museum.

Maynard, Jeffrey. 1997. "The Jewish Community of Siauliai." JewishGen Kehilla Links. Accessed July 20, 2022. https://kehilalinks.jewishgen.org/shavli /maynardHistory.html.

Megargee, Geoffrey P., and Martin Dean, 2012. *The United States Holocaust Memorial Museum Encyclopedia of Camps and Ghettos, 1933–1945*. Vol. 2, *Ghettos in German-Occupied Eastern Europe*. Bloomington: Indiana University Press.

Mendelsohn, Ezra. 2004. "Jewish Condition in Interwar East Central Europe." In *The Vanished World of Lithuanian Jews*, edited by Alvydas Nikžentaitis, Stefan Schreiner, and Darius Staliūnas. Amsterdam, Netherlands: Rodopi.

Morgan, Keith, with Ruth Kron Sigal. 2008. *Ruta's Closet*. London: Unicorn Press.

Offer, Miriam, 2014. "Medicine in the Shavli Ghetto: In Light of the Diary of Dr. Aaron Pik." In *Jewish Medical Resistance in the Holocaust*, edited by Michael A. Grodin and Myron Winick, 164–72. Oxford: Berghahn Books. ProQuest Ebook Central. Document number 1644358.

Patterson, David. 1999. *Along the Edge of Annihilation: The Collapse and Recovery of Life in the Holocaust Diary*. Seattle: University of Washington Press.

Pick, Aharon. 1930. "Reb Tsvi Hachavtan" [Reb Zvi the Cooper]. In *Keidan: A zamel bukh* [*Keidan: An Anthology*], edited by B. Cassel and H. Epstein, 52–55. New York: Keidaner Association of New York. English translation available at https://keidaner.com/203reb-zvi-the-cooper/.

Preiss, Leah. 1999. "Women's Health in the Ghettos of Eastern Europe." *Shalvi/ Hyman Encyclopedia of Jewish Women*, December 31, 1999. Jewish Women's Archive. Last modified February 27, 2009. https://jwa.org/encyclopedia/article /womens-health-in-ghettos-of-eastern-europe.

Rimsky-Korsakov, Nikolay. 1923. *My Musical Life*. 2nd ed. New York: A. A. Knopf.

Ringelblum, Emanuel. 1974. *Notes from the Warsaw Ghetto: The Journal of Emmanuel Ringelblum*. New York: Schocken Books.

Rosin, Joseph. 1996. *Pinkas Hakehilot Lita*. Jerusalem: Yad Vashem. Translation available at https://www.jewishgen.org/yizkor/pinkas_lita/lit_00658c.html.

Roskies, David G. 1999. *Against the Apocalypse: Responses to Catastrophe in Modern Jewish Culture*. Syracuse, NY: Syracuse University Press.

Shalit, Levi. 1949. *Azoy zaynen mir geshtorbn* [This is how we died. A Yizkor Book for Shavl, Lithuania]. Munich, Germany: Union of Lithuanian Jews in Germany. https://kehilalinks.jewishgen.org/shavli/leviShalit1.htm.

Shneiderman, S. L. 1957a. "Doktoyrim fun Shavler geto dertseylen vegn zeyere shtoynende iberlebungen" [Doctors of the Šiauliai ghetto recount their astonishing experiences]. *Forward*, June 23, 1957.

———. 1957b. "Dr. lunts hot geratevet dem leben fun hunderter yidishe froyen in shavler geto" [Dr. Luntz saved the lives of hundreds of Jewish women in the Shavel ghetto]. *Forward*, July 7, 1957.

———. 1957c. "Der merder fun litvishe yidn, ferster, ruft dr. peysakhovitsn tsu linderen zayne yesurim" [The murderer of Lithuanian Jews, Förster, summons Dr. Peisachowitz to relieve his suffering]. *Forward*, June 30, 1957.

———. 1957d. "Vi azoy der natzisher geto-komendant shleef iz gekumen nokh hilf tsu dr. yoysef lunts" [How the Nazi commandant Schlöf sought help from Dr. Josef Luntz]. *Forward*, July 14, 1957.

———. 1957e. "Yidish yingl fun kovne kumt keyn nyu york tsu zayne elteren, vos er hot keynmol in zayn leben nit gezen" [Jewish boy from Kaunas comes to New York to the parents he has never seen]. *Forward*, April 20, 1957.

Simon, Amy. 2020. "Imperfect Humans and Perfect Beasts: Changing Perceptions of German and Jewish Persecutors in Holocaust Ghetto Diaries." *Journal of Jewish Identities* 13 (1): 85–106. doi:10.1353/jji.2020.0011.

Sirutavičius, Vladas, Darius Staliūnas, and Jurgita Šiaučiūnaitė-Verbickienė. 2020. *The History of Jews in Lithuania, from the Middle Ages to the 1990s*. Leiden, Netherlands: Ferdinand Schonin.

Stampfer, Shaul. 2010. "Slobodka, Yeshiva of." *YIVO Encyclopedia of Jews in Eastern Europe*. New Haven, CT: YIVO Institute for Jewish Research. https://yivoencyclopedia.org/article.aspx/Slobodka_Yeshiva_of.

———. 2014. "Telz, Yeshiva of." *YIVO Encyclopedia of Jews in Eastern Europe*. New Haven, CT: YIVO Institute for Jewish Research. https://yivoencyclopedia.org/article.aspx/Telz_Yeshiva_of.

Sužiedėlis, Saulius. 2004. "Historical Sources for Antisemitism in Lithuania." In *The Vanished World of Lithuanian Jews*, edited by Alvydas Nikžentaitis, Stefan Schreiner, and Darius Staliūnas, 119–54. Amsterdam, Netherlands: Rodopi.

———. 2013. "'Listen, the Jews Are Ruling Us Now': Antisemitism and National Conflict during the First Soviet Occupation of Lithuania, 1940–1941." In *Jews in the Former Grand Duchy of Lithuania since 1772*, edited by Šarūnas Liekis, Antony Polonsky, and ChaeRan Freeze, 305–30. Oxford: Littman Library of Jewish Civilization. Ebook. https://quod.lib.umich.edu/cgi/t/text/text-idx?c=acls;cc=a cls;view=toc;idno=heb31386.0001.001.

Sužiedėlis, Saulius, and Šarūnas Liekis. 2013. "Conflicting Memories: The Reception of the Holocaust in Lithuania." In *Bringing the Dark Past to Light: The Reception of the Holocaust in Postcommunist Europe*, edited by John-Paul Himka, and Joanna Beata Michlic, 352–76. Lincoln: University of Nebraska Press.

Tory, Avraham, Martin Gilbert, and Dina Porat. 1990. *Surviving the Holocaust: The Kovno Ghetto Diary*. Cambridge, MA: Harvard University Press.

Yerushalmi, Eliezer. 1951. "Umkum fun yidn in shavler geto un in arumike shtetlekh" [The destruction of the Jews in the Šiauliai ghetto and surrounding towns]. In *Lita* [*Lithuania*], vol. 1, 1767–1832, edited by Mendel Sudarsky, Uriah Katzenelenbogen, and Yankel Kisin. New York: Kultur-gezelshaft fun litvishn yidn [Culture Society of Lithuanian Jews]. https://kehilalinks.jewishgen.org /shavli/YerushalmiUmkum.pdf.

———. 1956. Yad Vashem Pages of Testimony. Jerusalem, Israel: Yad Vashem. https://yvng.yadvashem.org/index.html?language=en&advancedSearch=tr ue&sln_value=Ierushalmi&sln_type=synonyms&sfn_value=Eliezer&sfn_ type=synonyms.

———. 1958. *Pinḵas shavli: Yoman mi-geṭo liṭa'i, 1941–1944* [Siauliai journal: A diary of a Lithuanian ghetto, 1941–1944]. Jerusalem, Israel: Mosad Byalik and Yad Vashem.

Young, James Edward. 1998. *Writing and Rewriting the Holocaust: Narrative and the Consequences of Interpretation*. Bloomington: Indiana University Press.

INDEX

Page numbers in italics refer to figures.

GABRIEL LAUFER, the son of two Holocaust survivors, was born in Budapest, grew up in Israel, and currently lives in Charlottesville, Virginia. He earned a PhD in mechanical and aerospace engineering from Princeton University and served as a professor at the Technion in Israel and at the University of Virginia until his retirement. He is the author of *A Survivor's Duty*, which describes the survival of his father in the Holocaust and his own participation in Israeli wars.

ANDREW CASSEL, born in 1950 and raised near New York City, spent thirty-five years writing and editing for US newspapers, covering business, politics, and culture. A graduate of Dartmouth College, in retirement he earned a Master of Liberal Arts degree at the University of Pennsylvania, also studying Yiddish in the United States and Europe. He has translated a range of historical and biographical essays and has curated a website devoted to Jewish history in Lithuania and elsewhere.